The King's Chamberlain

The King's Chamberlain

William Sandys of The Vyne, Chamberlain to Henry VIII

JOHN JENKINS

AMBERLEY

First published 2021

Amberley Publishing
The Hill, Stroud
Gloucestershire, GL5 4EP

www.amberley-books.com

British Library Cataloguing in Publication Data.
A catalogue record for this book is available from the British Library.

ISBN 978 1 3981 0281 1 (hardback)
ISBN 978 1 3981 0282 8 (ebook)

1 2 3 4 5 6 7 8 9 10

Typeset in 10pt on 12.5pt Sabon.
Typesetting by SJmagic DESIGN SERVICES, India.
Printed in the UK.

Contents

Family Trees (simplified)

The descendants of Sir John Sandys.

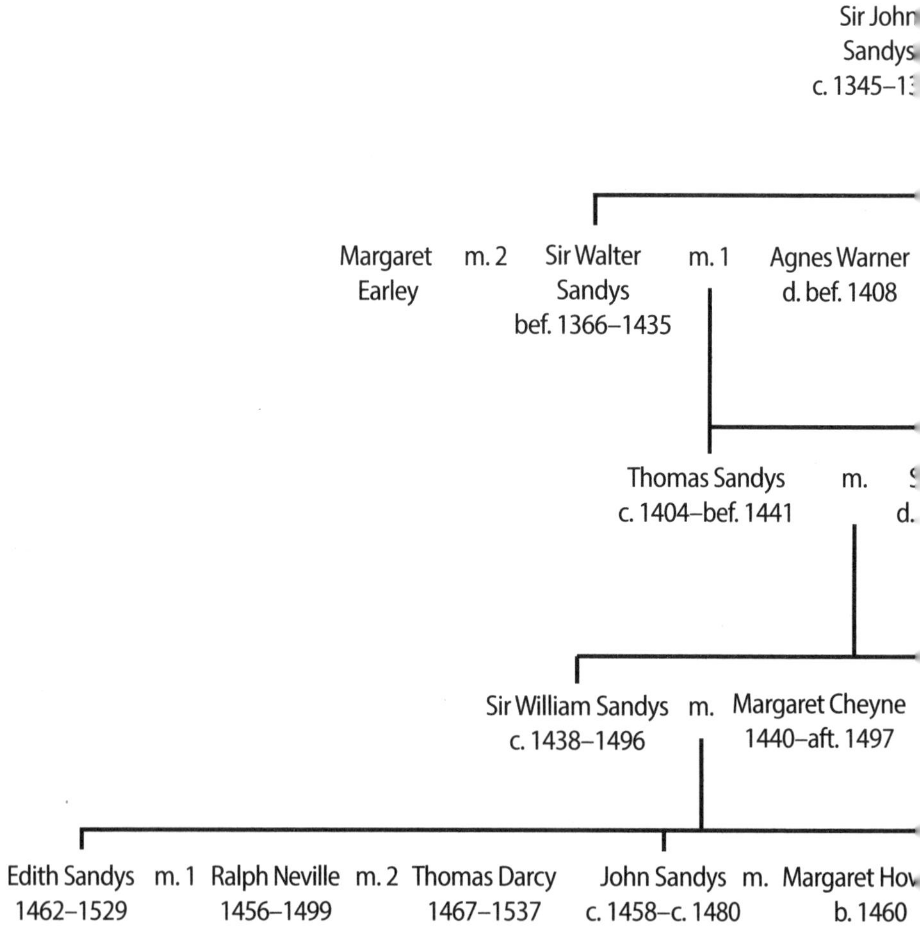

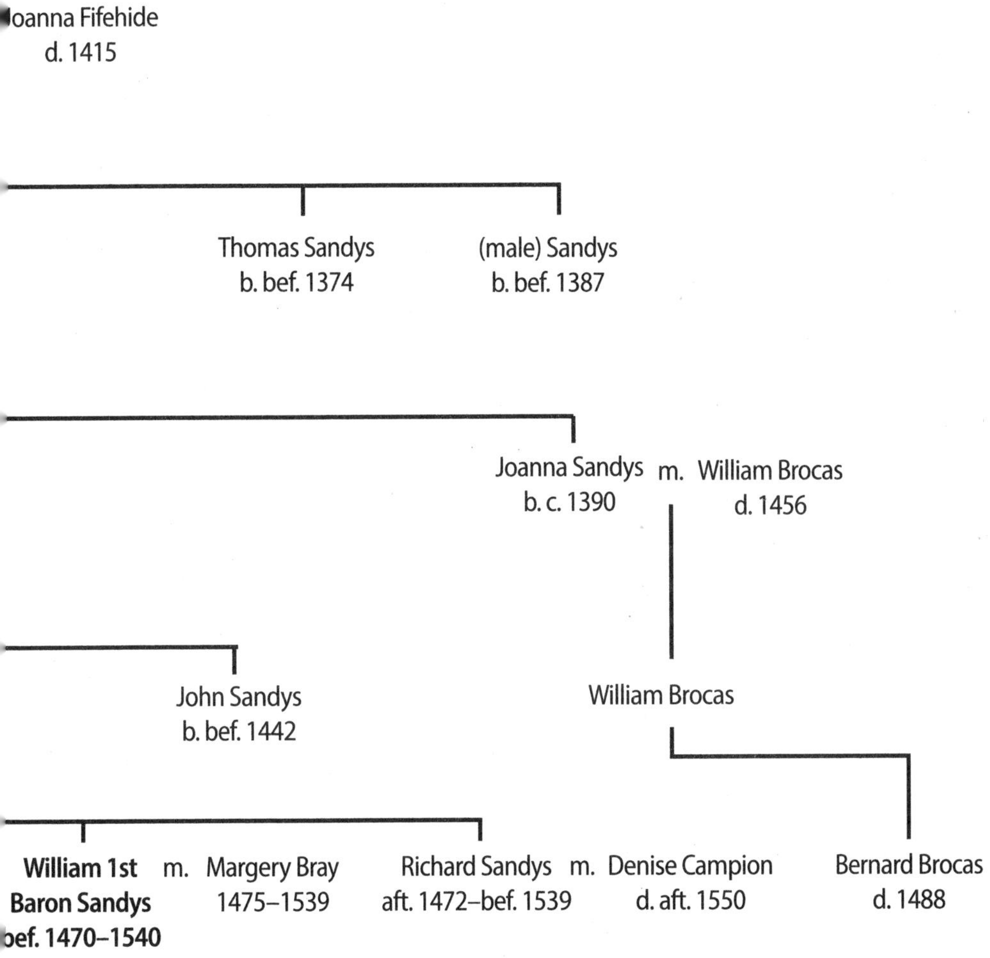

Joanna Fifehide
d. 1415
Thomas Sandys
b. bef. 1374
(male) Sandys
b. bef. 1387
Joanna Sandys m. William Brocas
b. c. 1390
d. 1456
John Sandys
b. bef. 1442
William Brocas
William 1st Baron Sandys
bef. 1470–1540
m. Margery Bray
1475–1539
Richard Sandys m. Denise Campion
aft. 1472–bef. 1539
d. aft. 1550
Bernard Brocas
d. 1488

The descendants of William 1st Baron Sandys.

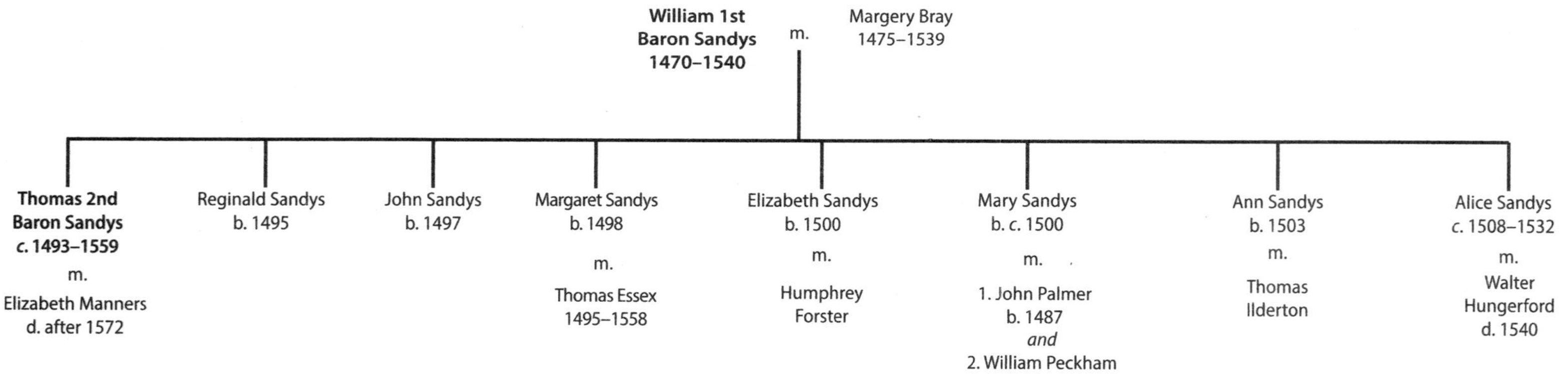

The descendants of Thomas 2nd Baron Sandys.

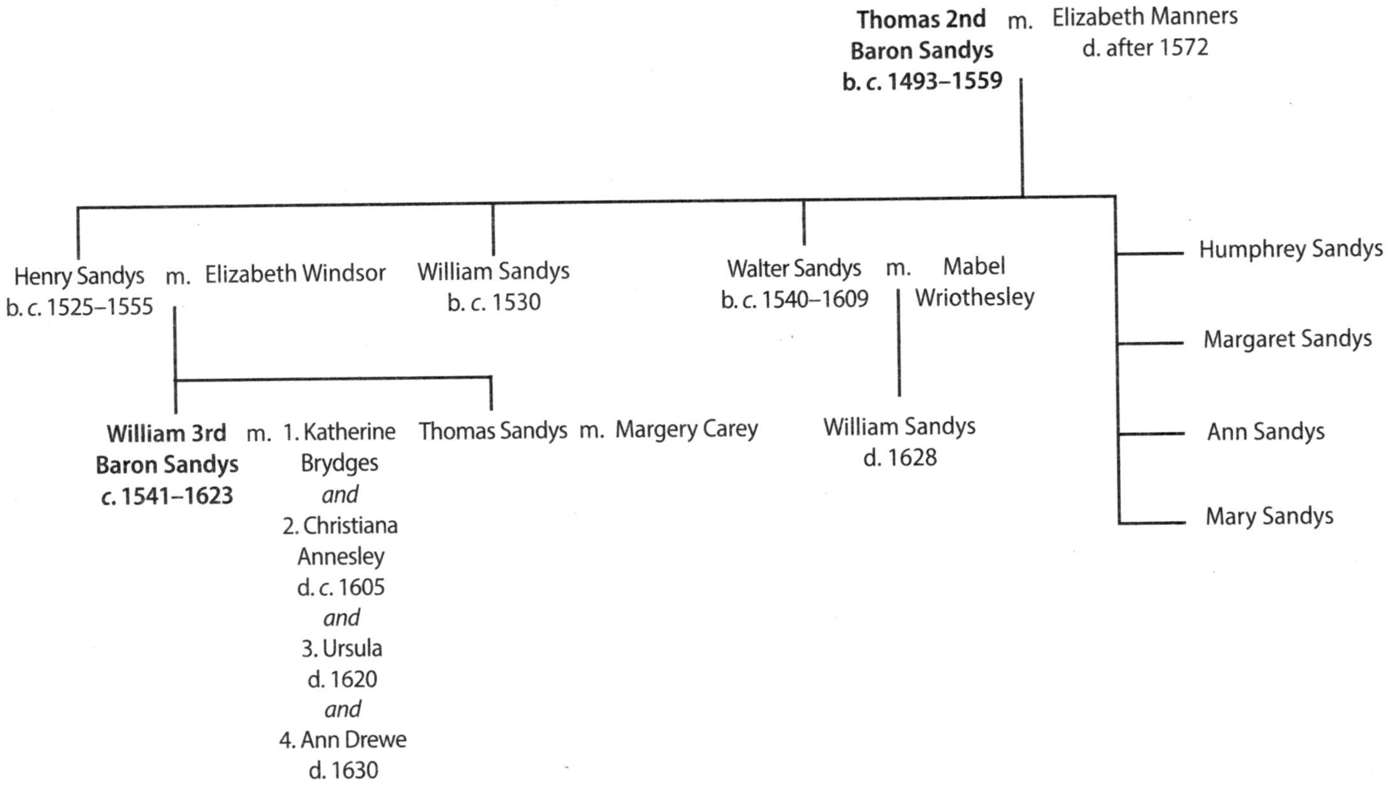

The descendants of William 3rd Baron Sandys.

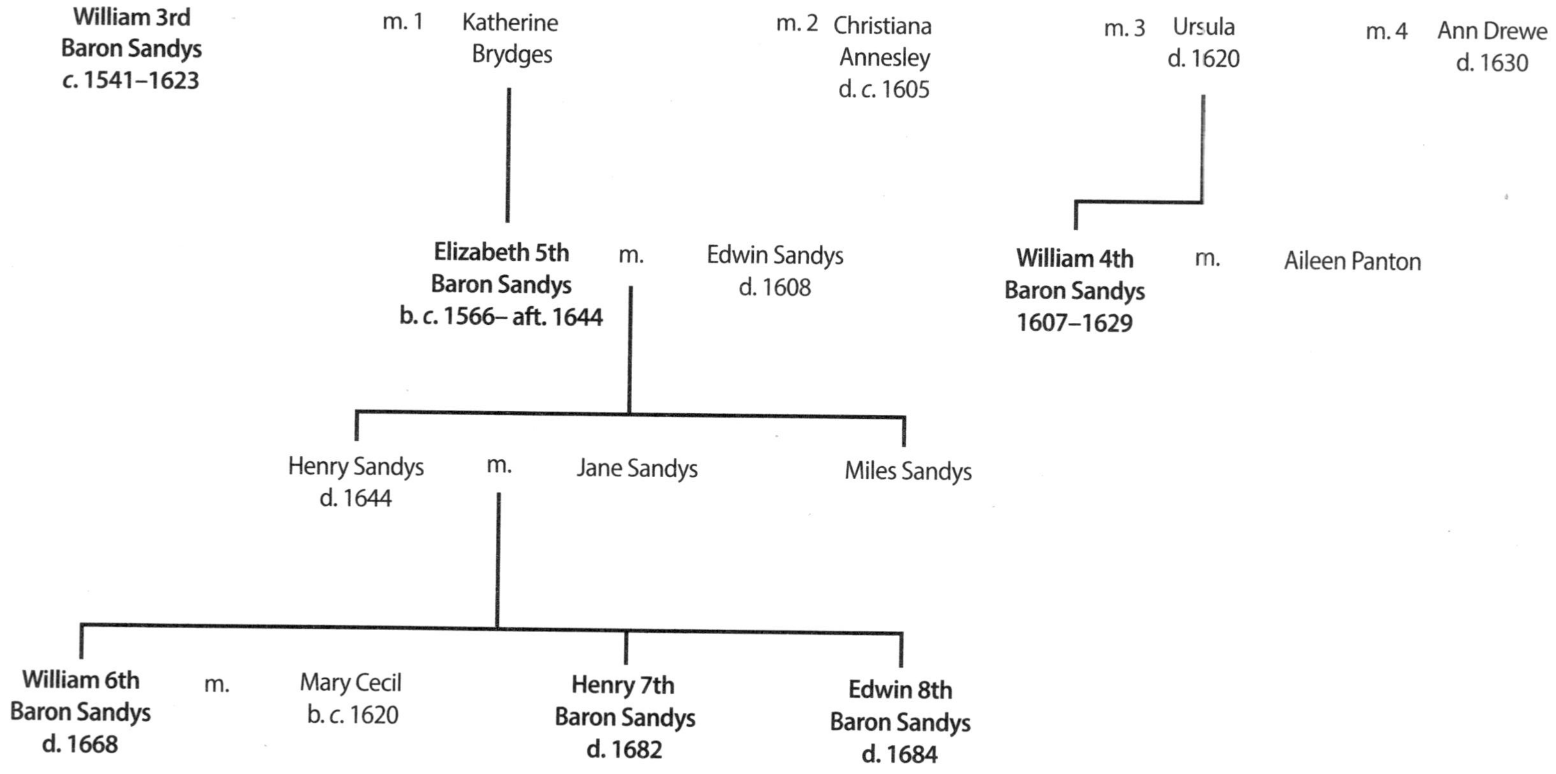

Introduction

'Sink a shaft as it were, in some chosen spot in the annals of England and you will come upon much that is never found in the books of general history.'[1] The life of Lord William Sandys of The Vyne in Hampshire (1470–1540) is a good example of this experience. Although it has been outlined in standard biographical works, such as *The Complete Peerage* and the *Dictionary of National Biography*, and fuller versions are available in Chaloner Chute's *The History of the Vyne* (1889), E. S. Sandys' *The History of the Sandys Family* (1930), and more recently in M. Woodward and E. Wilson's *The Vyne: A Tudor House Revealed* (1999), many gaps have remained. The aim of this work is to provide a more complete picture of Sandys' long and eventful life and, where possible, to 'flesh out the bones' of the current biographies.

Like the earlier works, the sources for this study include Henry VIII's *Letters and Papers, Foreign and Domestic*,[2] supplemented by more recent publications, which include *The Lisle Letters* by Muriel St Clare Byrne (1981, 1983),[3] but it also draws on Elis Gruffudd's *Chronicle of Six Ages of the World* at the National Library of Wales,[4] and unpublished theses and primary records at the Hampshire Record Office, The National Archives at Kew and the British Library.

As all experienced researchers will recognise, the evidence that emerges is not balanced, because much of the information comes from State Papers, which are orientated in favour of the monarchy; chronicles, which reflect the author's purpose; or from the letters of high-ranking courtiers such as Thomas Cromwell and Lord Lisle, whose papers were sequestrated by the State. There are many letters from and to Sandys, but nearly all are to the king or fellow courtiers such as Lord Lisle. They are essentially business letters, and their tone reflects the status of the recipient in relation to the author. This is most clearly illustrated by differences in the exchanges between Sandys and Cromwell, which change in the early 1530s when Cromwell rose rapidly through the ranks. Understanding of Lord Sandys' own nature is thus limited by the nature and context of the sources available.

Although Sandys was close to or at the centre of power throughout most of his life and inevitably involved in the political and religious issues of the day, this study does not dwell on these from a national or international perspective. Where possible, the focus is on the man, his family and colleagues, and placing them in the relevant contexts. His story is set out in five chapters: namely, his youth; the Knight of the Body; soldier; courtier; and patron of decorative arts, including his work on The Vyne property, which is now in the hands of the National Trust. While some repetition is inevitable, it also serves to highlight the man's main activities.

Sandys has attracted little attention in works on Tudor history, and what is said tends to focus on a particular aspect of his character. For example, Eric Ives mentions Sandys only once in his book on Anne Boleyn, in the phrase 'Sandes, the Lord Chamberlain and an archetypical sycophant'.[5] Alison Weir describes him as a 'popular and loyal courtier' and 'one of the King's favourite companions of the chase'.[6] Steven Gunn describes him as 'the dashing Lord Sandys – a widely respected veteran',[7] while John Guy, when discussing Cromwell, wrote, 'Yet Cromwell did not control Henry's policy before 1532. The most powerful group after Wolsey's fall comprised the Dukes of Norfolk and Suffolk, the Earls of Wiltshire and Sussex, the Bishop of Winchester, Lord Darcy and Lord Sandys.'[8] Derek Wilson wrote that 'Sandys had been a great court favourite, a soldier of panache and distinction', but also describes the Duke of Norfolk's inner circle in the 1530s, which included Sandys, as 'men of mediocre political talent'.[9] Similarly, the *Dictionary of National Biography* (1981–85) states that 'Sandes was not a good politician, and the Pilgrimage of Grace against which he took an active part may have frightened him'. Perhaps Suzannah Lipscomb offers the most colourful description of Sandys as a regular Tudor 'Flashman', constantly popping up for a front-row seat at an improbably large number of key events during Henry VIII's reign.[10] Finally, Muriel St Clare Byrne is somewhat contradictory about Sandys in her *Lisle Letters*, stating: 'Lisle did not have the vigour, the particular kind of address or push that fixed Lord Sandys and Sir William Fitzwilliam as great officers of the Household; nor did he have the knack of acquiring and husbanding the wealth that enabled Weston, Sandys and Fitzwilliam to build Sutton Place, The Vyne and Cowdray and figure as outstanding pioneer patrons of the new renaissance architecture in England.' She also says, 'His [Lord Sandys'] impact as a personality is slight compared with Sir Edward Ryngley or Sir Thomas Palmer or Lord Howard, and there is nothing in his manner to suggest the raffish gadabout into which he has been transformed in Shakespeare's *King Henry VIII*', and that 'like every successful official at the Court of Henry VIII, Sandys put his own interests first and would shift his position whenever expedient'.[11]

Revisiting contemporary evidence in detail has resulted in a fuller and better substantiated picture of William, Lord Sandys. This is preceded by a short history of his ancestors to assist in understanding his background, starting with John Sandys, the first member of the family to hold the manor of The Vyne.

The work concludes with brief accounts of the lives of the Lord William's direct descendants, followed by the summary and conclusions.

Throughout this work 'Sandys' is used as the family name, although the spelling did not become standard or generally accepted until late Tudor times. During the fourteenth century 'Sondes' or 'de Sonde' are the most common forms, although a pardon to 'John Sondes' in 1376 gives 'John Sandes' as his alias.[12] 'Sandrys' was also sometimes used,[13] but 'Sandes' becomes more common in the fifteenth century, followed by 'Sandys' or occasionally 'Sandis', 'Sandye' or 'Sannes'. French documents sometimes use 'Sans' or 'Sens'. 'Santhes' also occurs in a 1521 receipt.[14]

The current spelling is used for 'The Vyne', except in direct quotations, but variants over time include 'Vynnes', 'ler Vynde', 'Vine' and 'le Vine'.

The English part of Gascony in France was referred to as Aquitaine.[15]

1

William, Lord Sandys: His Ancestors and the Medieval Vyne, Hampshire

Sir John Sandys

Sir John, who died in 1395, was the first member of the Sandys family who owned the manor of The Vyne, or Sherborn Coudray as it was also known at that time, but it is worth noting that the property was known as 'The Vyne' from at least 1268.[1]

During the fourteenth century the Sandys family were based in and around Andover, Hampshire, and the earliest known reference to a member of the family being in Hampshire dates from 1316, which mentions a Johannes de Sands of Anne de Port (Amport) near Andover.[2] The 1327 tax returns for Hampshire do not mention a Sandys, but a 'John Sandre' is recorded in Abbots Ann, which is close to Amport,[3] while in November 1339 a 'Sir John Sonde' of Hampshire is mentioned in connection with lands in Sussex.[4] These two men may have been the grandfather and father of the John Sandys who acquired The Vyne and appears in the historical literature as a soldier in the retinue of Edward, Prince of Wales – the Black Prince.

His military career can be traced back to January 1367, when he was granted an annuity of £50 by the Black Prince, no doubt for prior service in France. Sandys was a well-established soldier by this date, so he may have served the prince at the Battle of Poitiers in 1356 or Rheims in 1359, assuming he was born before 1340. During the winter of 1366/67 the Black Prince, who was also Prince of Aquitaine, was in Aquitaine preparing for war in Castile. In 1362 Edward III had made a treaty with King Peter the Cruel of Castile, who was deposed by his half-brother Henry of Trastamara in 1366, but after his downfall Peter called upon Edward to honour the treaty and assist him in recovering the throne of Castile. Edward responded by dispatching an army to Castile, led by the Black Prince and John of Gaunt and including John Sandys, who was under the command of Sir John Chandos, one of the prince's most able, experienced and tough soldiers.[5]

When the English/Gascon army marched south to Castile, John Sandys was in the vanguard with John Chandos under the Duke of Lancaster. They crossed the Pyrenees in early February, encountering dreadful conditions in the cold and snow. It was so tough that the chronicler says, 'No one stopped for his companion, not even father for son. Everyone was afraid.' The rest of the army joined them later, and after several skirmishes they eventually engaged the full Castilian/French army at Nájera on 3 April 1367.[6]

Although this period is often described as 'the age of chivalry', the battles were fierce and bloody. A contemporary account of the Battle of Poitiers some twelve years earlier gives a first-hand impression of the ferocity: 'Then banners and their bearers began to fall; here men trampled on their own guts, others spat out their teeth; many were hewn to the ground, lost limbs while still standing. Dying men rolled in the blood of others, groaned under the weight of the fallen, and with proud hearts, groaned as they left their unworthy bodies.'[7]

At the Battle of Nájera the vanquished Castilians experienced an added horror from the proximity of a river, as one of the heralds (Sir John Chandos) described in his account:

> The site of the battle was a pleasant plain, without a tree or bush for a league around, beside a fine river, very swift and strong; and this river caused much harm to the Castilians that day, for the pursuit continued as far as the river. More than two thousand drowned there. On the bridge in front of Nájera the pursuit was very fierce; you could see knights leaping into the water for fear and dying one on top of each other. And the river ran crimson, to everyone's amazement, with the blood of dead men and horses. There was such slaughter there that I do not think that anyone ever saw anything like it; the dead were so many that the total came to seven thousand seven hundred.

Sir John Chandos was struck down by a Castilian who stabbed him through his visor, but he 'boldly took a dagger from his belt and struck the Castilian, burying the sharp weapon in his body. The Castilian stretched himself out dead, and Chandos got to his feet. He took his sword in hand and plunged into the melee again, which was very fierce and fearful and amazing to watch. Whoever he struck was sure to be killed.' The slaughter did not finish after the battle, however, as the herald writes:

> The Prince's men entered the town, and more than a thousand were killed there. The Grand Master of Calatrava was captured in a cellar; the Prior of the Hospitallers and the Master of Santiago were also taken. They had retreated behind a high wall, but this did not protect them, for men at arms climbed over it and were preparing to attack them when they humbly yielded rather than face them. So the Spaniards were killed and taken, much to the joy of the Prince, who waited on the battlefield, his standard raised, to rally his men.[8]

Evidently, John Sandys was not injured in this battle, and he no doubt benefited from the pillage of the town. The booty was particularly good, as 'they went to the lodgings of King Henry and other lords, where the first comers found quantities of plate and jewels; for King Henry and his army had come thither with much splendour'.

Such reports of courage and brutality reveal the type of person who became a successful man-at-arms in the Middle Ages. Gerald of Wales, in his *History of Ireland and Wales*, tells us what was expected of a knight in battle: 'In the midst of martial conflict it is a soldier's duty, clad in his helmet, to lust for blood, to concentrate on killing, and to plead his case with his sword alone, to show himself in all his actions an unyielding warrior, displaying ferocity more than ordinarily brutal. But by the same token, when the battle is over and he has laid aside his arms, ferocity too should be laid aside; a humane code of behaviour should be adopted.'[9]

Close-quarters combat and the behaviour described would have been much the same in the time of William, Lord Sandys 150 years later. Today, the fact that most of the men-at-arms, including the Black Prince, were devout Christians might seem contradictory.[10] Prior to the Battle of Poitiers, the Black Prince conducted a campaign from Bordeaux to Toulouse during which his army caused havoc and devastation, killing non-fighting men, women and children, setting fire to towns and seizing everything they could. However, they found time to stay in a monastery. They believed that God was on their side, as they were essentially unhindered by the French army, taking and successfully exploiting high-risk military moves.[11]

In 1368, John Sandys and John Alayn were both granted the rents and profits from the town of Middlewich by the Black Prince. It is possible that this gift was a reward for conduct at Nájera, and the benefits continued until John Alayn died in 1382.[12] Assuming that John Sandys remained in the service of the Black Prince, he would have returned to England in 1371 when the prince returned after further minor campaigns in France, already suffering from a disease contracted in Castile, which eventually led to his death at Westminster in 1376.

In December 1374, John and several others were given Letters of Protection by John de Montfort, Duke of Brittany and Earl of Richmond.[13] Such letters were normally granted to men who held property but were intent on serving in the royal army, to ensure that their properties were not acquired by others while they were on duty overseas. This suggests that John was out of the country early in 1375, serving the duke in Brittany.

In 1375–76, John married Joanna de Brugge, a widow and heiress born before 1351 and daughter of Agnes Fifehide.[14] Joan had previously married Giles Norman of Andover, Hampshire, who held properties in the area, but was widowed in 1361. This suggests that she was born sometime before 1349 – or widowed before the age of twelve, which does not seem credible. Children were certainly betrothed as young as seven, or earlier if of noble birth, but marriage was not formalised until consummated, which usually occurred at about fourteen for men and twelve for women.[15] She later married Peter de Brugge, whose properties in and around Andover she inherited on his death late in 1374.[16]

The circumstances of her marriage to John Sandys were dramatic. Following Peter's death, she and her household were at the Benedictine convent at

Romsey, Hampshire. Details of events there in October 1375 are unclear, but on 2 November a commission was issued to investigate the circumstances of Joanna's alleged rape by John Sandys. By 6 November, John, together with Thomas Leycestre of Fisherton, near Salisbury, and ten other men, was being hunted for 'ravishing Joanna, killing some of her men, abducting her to Cheshire and stealing gold rings, gold brooches with precious stones, clothes of linen and wool, and furs'. He was accused of 'homicide, rape of women, and other felonies'. Another commission was issued to arrest John, and his goods were sequestered. Two men, namely John Charnels, squire to the Black Prince, and Hugh Heryard, sergeant and deputy of the prince, were sent to Cheshire to return Joanna to London for questioning by the king and council.[17] On 16 November, Sir Robert Bealknap, Chief Justice of Common Pleas, Bernard Brocas and others were commissioned to examine the case of the 'evildoers who ravished Joanna and those who harboured the evildoers'. Things became even more serious for John on 25 November 1375, when the king witnessed a document tasking Richard Henbrygge, sergeant-at-arms, to seize John's goods and chattels, which were then in the possession of William de Upton. The gravity of the situation can be judged from information given to Richard: 'Authority is also given to each and every sheriff, mayor, bailiff, minister and other faithful subjects to assist him in this business.' The goods were to be taken to London to be disposed of by the king on the advice of his council. The sergeant-at-arms did his duty, and the goods were dispersed as follows:

- 100 marks to Isabelle, the king's daughter, as previously assigned by Peter de Brugge. Why Peter assigned this money to Isabelle is not known, but it was clearly a mistake by John Sandys to take money intended for the king's daughter.
- Most of the goods went to a Robert Ashton, with two items to Nicholas de Carren. Robert Ashton was well connected at court as he had been the king's treasurer, so stealing from him was not a good choice.

The goods listed were mainly silver items, with a total value of £122. For this task Sir Richard was paid 100*s* on 25 January 1376.[18] Surprisingly, the original white leather pouch for carrying the document still exists, with the commission inside it.[19]

Sometime during this episode John and Joanna were married in Cheshire by December 1375.[20] Shortly after, in 1376, they produced a son and heir, Walter, followed by two others sons, one of whom was named Thomas, and possibly a daughter, Margaret.[21] Although indicted, John was pardoned on 8 April 1376,[22] but on the same day was fined the large sum of £1,000 by the king,[23] which suggests that some form of deal was struck.

This episode raises interesting questions. Firstly, as suggested in the *History of the House of Commons*, did John Sandys have family origins in Cheshire?[24] If so, this would explain why he went there following the raid on Romsey. Perhaps not, however, because of the references to the Sandys family in Hampshire from 1316. But he may have taken his bride-to-be to Cheshire because some of his former comrades in arms came from that area and he derived some of his wealth from Middlewich, as already noted. At least three of the others arrested with John had Cheshire connections.[25] Cheshire was also a 'County Palatine' with substantial autonomy from the king, including its own administration and courts, but it owed allegiance to the king. The men of Cheshire were also reputed to be excellent soldiers with experience in fighting the Welsh, and the Black Prince, who was also Earl of Cheshire, recognised their qualities. He drew many of his men and their leaders from that area, and their toughness and skills were feared by the French. On the negative side, Cheshire was recognised as a haven for outlaws and escaped convicts where English law was not recognised.[26] So, it is not surprising that John fled there with Joanna and his band of men.

Secondly, was Joanna de Brugge perhaps a willing participant in this instead? Although some members of her household were killed in the raid in Romsey, John received a royal pardon, the marriage was not annulled, and they stayed married for the rest of his life, so perhaps this episode was more of an elopement than abduction. Joanna and John had been living in the same area of Hampshire before the death of Peter de Brugge, so they probably knew each other then. Perhaps she was in a convent after Peter's death because her family hoped that she would forget John, a theory that may be supported by the fact that two of her male relatives, John and William Fifehide, were among those involved in arresting John and his men. Moreover, the records of Romsey Abbey indicate that she was a lodger at the abbey and that her chaplain, John Stonly, aided and abetted the crime.[27]

Thirdly, was John Sandys close to the Black Prince? The answer is certainly yes. Before his death in 1376 the prince made it known that he wanted John Sandys to continue to receive the annuity granted to him in 1367, and the £1,000 fine imposed on John was cancelled on the prince's wishes. When young Richard II ascended the throne in 1377, he (or more probably his advisors) concurred with the wishes of the Black Prince.[28] After this hiatus, John and Joanna prospered, and eventually the de Brugge properties came to her in 1376, while John was appointed a Commissioner of Array for Hampshire in July 1377.[29]

This muster of troops was necessary because of the threat of raids by a combined Franco-Castilian fleet when the Anglo-French Treaty ended on 24 June 1377, and the perceived weakness of the English after the death of its two outstanding military leaders, the Black Prince and Edward III. In late June and July, the combined force wreaked destruction in several English Channel ports, before moving westwards and attacking coastal towns as far west as Dartmouth and Plymouth. Rye was particularly badly hit, as the allies 'put to death the inhabitants without sparing man or woman'. In Lewes they defeated an English scratch force led by the Abbot of Lewes and two knights, killing 200 Englishmen and taking the knights and abbot as prisoners. The French and Castilians then returned to Harfleur in France, but came back in August to attack Poole, Portsmouth, Southampton and the Isle of Wight. The Commissioners of Array gathered enough men to protect Southampton, and the allied army was repelled. On 20 August the Isle of Wight was attacked and several towns burned, but it was not overrun and many Frenchmen were killed, yet they exacted a 'ransom of 1000 silver marks to save the residue of their houses and goods' as they left.[30]

Following the Commission of Array and battle at Southampton, John Sandys, who was by then an esquire, was engaged for three months as a soldier in the navy by an indenture dated 20 September 1377. He was tasked with leading a retinue of thirty-nine men-at-arms and forty archers under Thomas, Duke of Gloucester and Edward III's youngest son. John eventually mustered his company at Bristol on 23 October and sailed on 1 November in pursuit of the Franco-Castilian fleet. The English fleet of nearly 100 vessels was not successful in its main objective, which was to destroy the enemy fleet, but it routed a fleet of Spanish merchantmen and captured the French castle at Brest.

John and his company, and others on board, were there to fight similar forces on the enemy ships. Before guns and gunpowder were sufficiently developed, sea battles were largely conducted by ships getting alongside each other and archers and men-at-arms fighting at close quarters; the enemy ship would be defeated by boarding rather than sinking. Not until the late Tudor period did naval gunnery take precedence over close-quarters hand-to-hand combat. John and his company survived the campaign, landing at Southampton on 1 January 1378 after ninety-four days of service. John duly submitted his claim for £406 to cover his own and his retinue's service and received interim payments in money and gold bullion. The final account was not settled until April 1383, five years after he was discharged, but he did receive £13 over the bill he had submitted. Sometime around 1378 he started to use the cross raguly as his coat of arms, with a winged goat as crest,[31] both of which would be used by the family through William, Lord Sandys and his descendants.[32]

In May 1379, John was appointed an Assessor of Taxes for Hampshire,[33] and was a verderer of Chute Forest in the same year.[34] However, his fighting days were not over, as on 24 August he was indented, along with Richard Craddock of Nantwich, Cheshire, to muster at Plymouth on 26 September 1379 a force of 100 men-at-arms and the same number of mounted archers to serve under Lord Neville, Lord of Bordeaux, in the defence of Aquitaine. All members of this force were to be paid double the normal rate. John and Richard were to provide arms and supplies for their men for the half-year, and to fund their force they used loans made to the Crown by four wealthy London merchants, totalling £4,185. As security, the Crown offered the merchants some of the Crown Jewels, including a large crown set with balas rubies, emeralds and pearls, and a coronet set with rubies, balas rubies, emeralds and pearls.[35] In the event, the muster was delayed until 22 October and happened at Dartmouth – a long march from Hampshire. They arrived in Bordeaux on 1 November.[36]

John was in Aquitaine in the spring of 1381, and it was during this, his last foreign campaign, that he was knighted. The English army in France was fighting the French to hold on to Aquitaine, which was effectively a colony administered by soldiers. When not fighting, some soldiers were given offices such as mayors and justices in Aquitaine.[37] There is no direct evidence that Sir John Sandys held a senior administrative post there, but it is very likely that he was involved as he was a member of the Black Prince's retinue and a leader of men in battle.[38] This prepared him for civilian administrative roles, and when he returned from Aquitaine he became a Member of Parliament for Hampshire and held a variety of administrative posts, including High Sheriff of Hampshire in 1382 and 1394.[39]

In order to pay for the French campaigns, the government instigated a high tax regime in England, causing increasing resentment throughout the population, especially as the campaigns did not prevent the loss of territories in France. The final straw was the imposition of a flat-rate poll tax in November 1380, which hit the poor particularly hard. Poll taxes were not new, but this one not only taxed everybody but was also high, and not graduated according to means. So, the poorest in society suffered most, as they were taxed at the same rate as the wealthy. May 1381 saw the first uprising of what would become known as 'the Peasants' Revolt' and spread rapidly across the south of England, through the ranks of functionaries such as bailiffs and constables to the middle classes. By mid-June the rebels had occupied large areas of London and killed some of the residents, including the Archbishop of Canterbury, the Prior of the Hospital of St John, and the Chief Justice, and destroyed the Savoy Palace of John of Gaunt, the king's uncle.[40]

Control of the rebellion followed a meeting between Richard II, aged fourteen, and the rebel leader, Wat Tyler. Accounts are confused, but after seeming to reach agreement one of the king's men killed Tyler, which broke the spirit of the rebels. Order was restored in London, and commissions were set up to enforce the peace around the country. On 23 June, peers, sheriffs and other worthies, including Sir John Sandys for Hampshire, were instructed to issue proclamations forbidding unlawful assemblies and 'empowered to resist and punish the insurgents' in the counties. This was followed by a commission dated 14 December to 'preserve the peace with power to arrest those who congregate in unlawful assemblies or incite insurrections, put down the rebels and with armed force, if necessary, suppress the said assemblies'. John was included in this and a similar commission in December 1382.

Although the riotous behaviour peaked in 1381 with the Peasants' Revolt, general disaffection and disorder in the south included Hampshire, where the city of Winchester had a bad reputation for prostitution, intolerance towards foreigners and drunkenness.[41] In the midst of the turmoil John was elected to the 1381–82 Parliament, and in February 1382, together with a fellow member and the Steward of the Household, raised a schedule of those rebels deemed to be beyond pardon. Of the twenty-five named, fourteen came from Winchester, including William Wigge and Henry Clerk, both of whom demonstrate that not only the poor rebelled, as Wigge was wealthy and became mayor of Winchester, while Clerk later became a Member of Parliament.[42]

John advanced to become a junior member of the court, holding office as Esquire of the Chamber and working for the Chamberlain of the Household, which brought him into close contact with the king. The Esquires of the Chamber were in the royal presence and privy to the intrigues of the court, thus generating influence.[43]

This was followed by an increasing number of administrative roles in Hampshire. He served as a Commissioner of Oyer and Terminer, who was a judge at the Assize Courts tasked with 'hearing and determining' all treasons, felonies and misdemeanours committed in the county, [44] and as a Commissioner of the Peace, the equivalent of a Justice of the Peace today but with power to arrest, imprison, judge, fine and hang people. By November 1382 he was Sheriff of Hampshire and Governor of Winchester Castle. The sheriff was the most powerful officer in each county, appointed by the king and carrying out the king's orders, such as summoning juries, making arrests, holding elections for Parliament, conducting inquiries and operating the county courts. Some sheriffs, but by no means all, were corrupt, misusing their power to extort money or applying pressure if it was to their advantage. Given John's background, perhaps he was no better than others.[45]

In response to a threat of invasion by the French in June 1386, Thomas Holland, the Earl of Kent and the king's half-brother, appointed John as his deputy in charge of Southampton Castle. By August the threat had continued, so he was also tasked with surveying Southampton to improve its defences by repairing and fortifying walls and dykes, along with arming and arraying the local men.[46]

On 24 January 1387, Sir William Fifehide died, leaving his estates in Hampshire and Sussex, including Sherborn Cowdray (The Vyne), to his cousin Joanna, wife of Sir John Sandys.[47] Sir William Fifehide's father, another Sir William, had died in 1361, when an Inquisition Post Mortem described The Vyne as consisting of a manor house of no value, apart from 326 acres of arable land, 14 acres of meadow, 24 acres of pasture, an enclosed park, rents from twenty-two tenants and the advowson of the chapel of the manor of Sherborne St John.[48] This probably reflects the well-known disastrous effect of the Black Death in 1349 on many manors in England, reducing the population by more than 50 per cent in some places. Hampshire and the neighbouring counties were no exception, and the loss in Winchester is estimated at 66 per cent.[49]

The serious decline of landed estates was not unusual. The history of Sutton Place in Surrey notes the decline of the earlier manor house by 1352, describing it as a 'ruinous messuage' with the 'the dovecote entirely ruined' and a value of nothing.[50] An Inquisition Post Mortem relating to Padworth Manor in Berkshire on 30 June 1349 records that 'the pleas etc. of the court are worth nothing this year because almost all the people are dead'.[51] Some Hampshire manor houses disappeared completely and others fell into disrepair: the decline and eventual disappearance of the manor of Faccombe Netherton has been studied in detail by Fairbrother.[52] Like The Vyne and Sutton Place, its manor house was valued at nothing at this time, but this site was particularly suitable for study as it was largely undisturbed since it was abandoned in the fifteenth century. Archaeology revealed that the manor house complex prior to the Black Death comprised a large house with hall and chamber (solar), separate kitchen and bakery buildings, a dovecote and a church. There was also a walled enclosure with gatehouse in front of the house. After the Black Death the manor buildings, apart from the church, fell into decay through disuse some 600 years ago.

On 24 March 1370, Sir William Fifehide had leased to William Gregory The Vyne manor, which included a hall with chambers, a grange (probably a home farm), a granary and a chantry chapel in the manor park at the house.[53] It can be assumed that the manor house had at least been partially restored by then. The new translation of the lease implies that the chapel was not part of the medieval manor house, as has been suggested, and thus not in the location of the present chapel. The medieval manor house was most probably in the same location as the existing house. Underneath the sixteenth-century east and west walls of the space now called the Dining Parlour are two large flint foundations, which are probably medieval. Much of the cellar beneath the staircase hall also predates the sixteenth-century construction period, confirming that the Tudor house and the earlier house were co-located.[54] In his *Itinerary*, Leland says of the medieval manor house: 'There was no great or sumptuous maner place, and was contenid within the mote.'[55] Traces of the deep defensive moat were found by Wilson in his 1996–98 archaeological studies,[56] while the major subsidence seen today in the west wall of the east wing of The Vyne house is an indication of the line of the medieval moat, which ran beneath the east and west wings.

Another source at The National Archives reveals that the chapel was situated a mile from St Andrew's Parish Church.[57] This is not inconsistent with the location being in The Vyne Park, but the changes from the thirteenth to early sixteenth centuries make it difficult to decipher from surface studies alone the configuration and development of the underlying structures that predated the Tudor palace of Lord William Sandys.

Sir John continued to carry out his civic duties for county and State from 1386. In June 1387, he and three others were required to act on behalf of the king regarding the behaviour of 'evildoers' in Berkshire, Hampshire, Surrey and Wiltshire, which had been drawn to the king's attention. They were apparently wandering around in great numbers, watching and 'lying in wait for travellers, beating them, killing some and robbing them of their goods and chattels'. Sandys was commissioned to arrest all those suspected and commit them to justice.[58]

He was again summoned to Parliament at Winchester for twenty-two days in February 1393 at 4*s* per day.[59] He also was Seneschal (Steward) of Andover for many years, dealing with very local matters, and again served as Sheriff of Hampshire in 1394/95. He became one of the wealthiest men in Hampshire and could, for example, raise a bond for £1,000 in 1389 to contest a dispute over some of the Fifehide lands that he and Joanna won.[60]

One of his most notable contacts, who became beneficial to the family, was the powerful and wealthy William Wykeham, who rose from humble beginnings to become Bishop of Winchester and Chancellor of England, serving both Edward III and Richard II, and was a close associate of both. He founded Winchester College and New College Oxford. Sandys knew William sufficiently well to dine with him on occasion.[61]

Sir John died in the summer of 1395, naming his wife and two of his sons as executors of his will.[62] As one of Hampshire's wealthiest residents,[63] he had established the Sandys family as a leading county family and was also recognised nationally and at court, which laid wider foundations for his descendants, including William, Lord Sandys of The Vyne. The Sandys family would not have such a powerful and influential head for another three generations.

Joanna died in April 1415 after marrying her fourth husband, Sir Thomas Skelton, Chief Steward of the Duchy of Lancaster. The estates accumulated in Hampshire and Wiltshire through her marriages remained with her, and it was not until her death that The Vyne once again became part of the Sandys' estates.[64]

Sir Walter Sandys

John's son and heir, Walter, was born around 1376. By January 1403, he had married well to Agnes Warner, daughter of Thomas and Joan Warner and cousin of William Wykeham, Bishop of Winchester, from whom she inherited £100. The family association with Wykeham had arisen through Sir John Sandys.[65] William was also a close associate of Edward III and Richard II, serving both as Chancellor of England. Sometime around September 1404 Walter's son and heir, Thomas, was born and christened in Andover.[66]

Thomas and Joan Warner held the manors of North Ashley and Preston Candover from William Wykeham for the nominal rent of 'a rose'. On Thomas Warner's death in September 1408, both these manors were inherited by the infant Thomas Sandys, as his mother Agnes had already died. Walter and Agnes also had a daughter, Joanna, in around 1405, who will feature later in this story. Walter later married Margaret Earley (de Erleigh) who was about twenty years his junior.[67]

Like his father, Walter was an active soldier, serving in Gascony and being knighted before 1402.[68] In 1404, he was called to naval service under Lord Berkley,[69] and in 1407 served in the garrison at Guînes Castle on the outskirts of the English land around Calais.[70] In 1415, on 29 April, Walter was among the knights and lords summoned to the Palace of Westminster to sign and seal their indentures to provide and provision themselves, men-at-arms and archers for the forthcoming campaign to France.[71] He agreed to take a small team of three men-at-arms and nine archers for one year, which was a marked reduction in numbers compared to his father's commitments in earlier campaigns. There is some doubt that Walter fought at Agincourt, as earlier biographers of the Sandys family have cited his indenture to fight as evidence of his involvement,[72] but they ignored the fact that his name does not appear on the so-called Agincourt Roll, or on any payment lists after the battle. Perhaps he was not present because:

a) He missed the muster at Southampton, as did others.
b) He fell sick with dysentery at Harfleur and was sent home. It is estimated that about 15,000 men left Southampton and approximately 2,000 were sent home because of sickness, but Walter's absence from the extant list makes it unlikely that he succumbed to sickness.[73]
c) He was assigned to the garrison of around 1,200 that Henry V required to man Harfleur.

Recent thorough research into the battle, notably by Anne Curry, Ian Mortimer and Juliet Barker,[74] and doubt over Walter's participation justifies no further discussion of the battle.

Three months after Agincourt, an indenture required him to take three men-at-arms and six archers to fight in Henry V's second campaign in France.[75] The Normandy campaign did not take place until 1417, resulting in the English conquest of Normandy. Walter was in France at least until summer 1418.[76]

This was the last of his military activities abroad, although he was commissioned to muster men-at-arms at Hampton Heath for another campaign in France, which did not happen.[77] Yet, his martial activities were not entirely abandoned, as he was called upon as a Commissioner of Array to muster troops against the threat of naval action and seaborne invasion by the kings of Castile and Aragon in 1421.[78]

During this period he fulfilled several significant roles, serving his country as a Member of Parliament in 1411, and his county as sheriff in 1410–11 and 1423–24, and Justice of the Peace.[79] Like his father, he was appointed at various times to be a Commissioner of the Peace and of Oyer and Terminer,[80] while in May 1434 Walter and other knights of the shires, including William Brocas for Hampshire, were instructed to swear not to shelter peace-breakers mentioned in the Act of Parliament.[81]

Following the death of his mother on 8 April 1415, Walter took possession of her dower properties, including the manor of Sherborn Cowdray (The Vyne). At about this time, Walter's daughter married William Brocas, grandson of Sir Bernard Brocas and son of another Sir Bernard. The elder Sir Bernard, a favourite of Edward the Black Prince, had fought at the prince's famous victories at Crécy, Poitiers and Nájera, and in 1356 inherited the title of Lord of Beaurepaire, the estate adjacent to The Vyne, and later became Master of the Royal Buckhounds. He also prospered under Richard II, becoming Captain of Calais and chamberlain to Ann, Richard's queen. Sir Bernard Brocas was contemporary with Sir John Sandys, and not only did both serve the Black Prince, but they were Members of Parliament at the same time and held several simultaneous appointments, such as Commissioners of Array for Hampshire. Sir Bernard was also a colleague of William Wykeham, like Sir John.

By the time of his death in 1395, Sir Bernard the Elder had accumulated considerable wealth and influence and was buried in St Edmund's Chapel at Windsor by order of the king. Indeed, the Brocas family was more important than the Sandys at this time.[82] After his death, Beaurepaire was inherited by his son, Sir Bernard Jr, then his grandson, Sir William. The marriage of Joanna, daughter of Sir Walter Sandys, to Sir William must have enhanced the prestige of the Sandys family, so it is not surprising that Sir Walter supported the marriage by leasing The Vyne to the couple for £10 p.a., to be paid to Sir Walter out of the income of The Vyne during his life. The lease also stated that if Joanna died childless the manor would revert to Sir Walter or his heirs.[83]

William Brocas moved to The Vyne from Beaurepaire, which he handed over to his son by an earlier marriage, also called William. With his background and undoubted aspirations, it is probable that he and Joanna improved the property where they would live for many years.[84] In June 1449, William arranged for the chapel of The Vyne to be licensed for marriage, possibly for that of his son by

Joanna, Bernard. After William's death in 1456, Bernard and his wife Philippa took over The Vyne, remaining until Bernard's death in 1488, when it defaulted to Sir William Sandys as the couple were childless.[85]

Walter remained in the Andover area and was steward in 1424. In many respects he followed in his father's footsteps, but did not significantly enhance the estate, had little contact with the court, and his military and civic achievements were modest compared with those of his father.[86] Walter died in October 1435, and his wife, Margaret Earley, subsequently married Chief Justice Sir William Cheyne,[87] thus creating another, albeit indirect, family link between the Cheyne and Sandys families. An existing link is revealed in the will of William Cheyne, a knight of London, buried in St Benedict's Church in 1443, when William requests to be buried near to the body of his wife Margaret, and makes bequests of £10 to his cousin William Sandys and a ring to Sandys' wife.[88] This William Sandys may have been the third son of Sir John Sandys.

Thomas Sandys

In 1435, Walter's estate passed to his son Thomas, born in 1404 to Agnes Warner and named after her father. Shortly after Thomas inherited the estate, he married Sybille. Little is known about Thomas, except that he was a bailiff in Andover in 1433,[89] or his wife, other than that they had a son, William, by 23 October 1439, who was born and baptised in Upper Clatford, a village about a mile and a half from the centre of Andover.[90]

The long-accepted location of the main home of the Sandys family was East Cholderton, a village some 4 miles from Andover. This is based on John Leland's statement in *c.* 1535 that 'the auncient house, as far as I can lerne, that the Sannes hath possessid is Choldretoun, a mile and a half from Andover'.[91] However, the location of William's birth and baptism, and the error in the distance from Andover, suggest that Upper Clatford was where they lived in the fifteenth century. From the end of the previous century the Sandys family were associated with Clatford, where they held a property called 'Normans',[92] but there is no doubt that they held East Cholderton manor as well as other properties in the area, and that it was important to them because William's first son and heir, John, died there in around 1479.

Thomas died when he was about thirty-eight years old, shortly before 10 August 1442, without achieving a knighthood or other recognition,[93] apart from being a bailiff in Andover.[94] His wife died in 1445, leaving William an orphan at the age of six, so it may be no coincidence that Sir William Brocas described himself as 'Lord of the Vyne' in that year. Before William's mother died he became a ward of Henry VI, but we do not know who raised him. The estate and William's custody were granted to a king's sergeant, William Ludlow, Yeoman of the Cellar (keeper of the king's wine cellar, responsible for the purchase and storage of wines/ales), in December 1443 until William reached twenty-one in 1460. Ludlow's home was in Wiltshire and he was Member of Parliament for Salisbury, which is close to Andover, but although he was William

Sandys' guardian and had control and use of the lands of the deceased Thomas, this does not mean that William necessarily lived in the Ludlow household. He may have moved in with his aunt, Joan Brocas, who was living at The Vyne, or with a member of the Cheyne family who were related to the Sandys.[95]

Sir William Sandys, 1439–96

There is little information about William until he reached his majority in 1460, apart from occasional references in deeds in the late 1450s, but he was born in Clatford, near Andover, as already noted. The 'proof of age' document issued on 10 November 1460 reveals some details about his christening, which would have applied to other infants of similar social status. The principal witness was George Lisle, but his statement is missing; other witnesses merely agreed with his evidence, but some added to it. The baptism took place on the Feast of the Holy Trinity 1439 and there were three godparents: Lady Margery Lisle, Sir John Green, the rector of the nearby parish of Ludgershall, and William Barrel from Andover. Baby William, wrapped in a red silk cloth, was carried to the church in Clatford by Johanna Foresbury, baptised by Sir John and lifted from the font by Lady Lisle. The ceremony was followed by a feast that included six capons, which were brought by Sir John's servant.[96] By 1464, William was married and father to his first child, John, born at around that time,[97] and by 1469 was definitely married to Margaret Cheyne and living an active life in the Andover area.[98] He and his wife headed a donor list for the 'Sawndersweurd' society in Andover Church, which was a trust for maintaining a chantry chapel in the southern part of the church.[99] At Michaelmas 1473, Sandys, who was given the title '*miles*' (knight), paid for torches for Andover Church, perhaps to celebrate a special occasion such as the birth of a child.[100]

At this point it is relevant to mention the possibility of a wife other than Margaret Cheyne. There is no doubt that Margaret Cheyne was William's wife from 1469, and she was buried with her husband in the Chapel of the Holy Ghost, Basingstoke. The fact that she was a member of the Cheyne family is confirmed by the account of the visitation of the heralds to Hampshire in 1686, which describes a black marble monument on which there are three lozenges, one of which is the Sandys/Cheyne coat of arms.[101] In the Hampshire Record Office a letter from the College of Arms dated 1840 confirms this evidence, as it is illustrated by a drawing of a shield bearing the arms of 'Sir William Sandys the Elder of the Vine and Andover of the County of Hampshire impaled with that of his wife Margaret Cheney daughter of Sir John Cheney'.[102] Also, William, Lord Sandys recognised Margaret as his mother in building The Vyne, by displaying many heraldic badges of the Cheyne family in the Oak Gallery and chapel.[103] Yet, a document commissioned by William, 3rd Baron Sandys, in 1613 lists the family deeds and documents and states that William married a widow who was the daughter of Lord Stourton and mother of William, Lord Sandys. In other respects, the summary of the family history is correct, but this element warranted further investigation.[104] Some support for a Stourton lady being William's first wife is given by a manuscript note citing work by Revd William Bingley in the early part of the nineteenth century that depicts the ancestry of William, Lord Sandys.[105] Although generally correct, it names Edith Stourton, widow, as wife of Sir William Sandys and mother of William, Lord Sandys, and further undermines credibility by stating that her first two husbands were Sir John Beauchamp and Sir Robert Shottesbrook. Those two men were actually husbands of Edith Stourton, grandmother of Margaret Beaufort, the mother of Henry VII, and grandmother of Margaret Cheyne, William, Lord Sandys' mother.[106] This Edith could not have been the wife of Sir William Sandys, but this does not preclude the possibility that Sir William was first married to an unrecorded daughter of Lord John Stourton (1403–62).[107] However, as Edith Stourton was Margaret Cheyne's grandmother, Edith was obviously a family name, so it is no surprise that Sir William's first daughter was named after her.

Given that Thomas Sandys died in 1442 without any notable status or achievements, it is surprising how well connected were the first three children of his son William. In 1478, John married Margaret Howard, daughter of Thomas, and granddaughter of Lord John, who in 1483 were made Earl of Surrey and Duke of Norfolk respectively by Richard III. In 1466, Lord John Howard married Lady Margaret Wydville, widow of Nicholas, the deceased Lord Mayor of London. Within her retinue was a William Sandye, who received 4¼ yards of cloth for clothing for her wedding – much more than any other member of her retinue. Sir William Sandys' will, dated 1492, spells his surname as 'Sandye',[108] so if the Sandye in the retinue of Lady Margaret Wydville was William Sandys, a prior connection for the marriage of his son John to a granddaughter of John Howard is established.[109]

John Sandys' marriage to Margaret Howard did not last long, as he died when he was about twenty-one years old, around 1485, leaving Margaret pregnant. She then struggled with her father-in-law, William Sandys, described as 'the Elder', and after his death she also struggled with his son, William 'the Younger', for the full income of 60 marks a year from her dower lands. She petitioned John Morton, Archbishop of Canterbury and later Chancellor of England, and finally the king. Unfortunately, only one response from the Sandys family exists, and that is by the elder Sandys, stating that Margaret was receiving 50 marks a year and that the extra 10 marks were not forthcoming because that provision depended on John reaching his majority or having an heir. As far as William was concerned, neither condition had been met, contradicting Margaret's statements. Sandys also stated that John had incurred large debts that had to be paid off. The five petitions illustrate that the Sandys family did not give up money easily. They also reveal that the trustees for the marriage agreement made in 1478 were high ranking and included Lord John Howard, later Duke of Norfolk under Richard III in 1483, and Thomas Bourchier, Archbishop of Canterbury 1454–86. They imply that John was around fourteen years old when he married Margaret and that the child, if there was one, died very young. One also states that John Sandys died at East Cholderton.[110]

Edith Sandys, eldest daughter of Sir William, did equally well by marrying Lord Ralph Neville, son and heir of the 3rd Earl of Westmorland, and the marriage ceremony was attended by Henry VII.[111] Ralph died before his father on 10 September 1497, so did not succeed him, but the couple had a son, Ralph, who became the 4th Earl of Westmorland. This connection meant that William Sandys the Younger was uncle to the earl and is described as such by William following Ralph's visit to The Vyne in January 1537.[112] Edith retained her title of Lady Neville for the rest of her life, although she remarried, this time to Sir Thomas Darcy, later Lord Darcy. She died at Stepney in August 1529 and was buried in Greenwich.[113]

The Cheyne family, as noted, were kinsfolk of the Sandys, and branches of the family were in the Andover area from at least 1374, when a William Cheyne was steward of the town. In 1376, he was party to the administration of the de Brugges' estate, which eventually came to Sir John Sandys in 1386. A John Cheyne was in Henry V's 1415 campaign, in which Sir Walter served and which culminated in the English victory at Agincourt. This relationship resulted in the marriage of William Sandys the Elder to Margaret Cheyne when William became brother-in-law to John Cheyne. John was born *c.* 1445, and by 1471 was Esquire of the Body and later Master of Horse to Edward IV, for whom he fought in the battles of Barnet and Tewkesbury. At the funeral of Edward IV, John had the honour of being a coffin bearer. Under Richard III he lost his position as Master of Horse and after the imprisonment of the boy Edward V and his brother in the Tower of London he, along with Margaret Beaufort and Sir Reynold Bray, was one of the leaders of the plot to release them.[114]

Following the alleged murder of the royal brothers by order of Richard III in October 1483, John joined the Duke of Buckingham's rebellion against the king. On 23 November, he was attainted with many others, after which he moved to Brittany and joined forces with the exiled Henry Tudor. When Henry landed at Milford Haven on 7 August 1485, John was knighted,[115] and at the Battle of Bosworth on 22 August he was one of Henry's inner defensive circle.

Following Henry's victory at Bosworth, John was awarded the Faulston estate, near Salisbury in Wiltshire, which became his main residence for the rest of his life. In September 1487, he distinguished himself again, fighting for the king at the Battle of Stoke against the army of the pretender Lambert Simnel. He was a close advisor to Henry VII as privy counsellor, and participated in the christening ceremony of Prince Arthur, the heir apparent, at Winchester Cathedral in 1496. In April that year he was elected Knight of the Garter.

He died on 30 May 1499 and was interred at Salisbury Cathedral, where his monument still lies.[116] When his tomb was investigated in 1973, it was confirmed that he was buried there and was nearly 7 feet tall.[117] His brother Edward was Dean of Salisbury from 1486 to 1502, and was probably instrumental in securing John's burial there.[118]

These excellent family connections were less important to the Sandys family than the link between Margaret Cheyne and Margaret Beaufort, the mother of Henry VII.[119] They were first cousins and Margaret Beaufort, who was a remarkable woman, not least for her role in placing her son on the throne and maintaining her influence over him throughout his reign, is known to have used the connection.

The marriage between Edith Sandys and Lord Ralph Neville almost certainly came about through the connection between the Cheyne family and the king's mother. When Henry Tudor took the throne in 1485, he attainted the 3rd Earl of Westmorland for supporting Richard III and placed him and his son, Lord Ralph, in Margaret's custody. She, in turn, transferred Lord Ralph's maintenance to the Cheyne family.

William and Margaret had more children after William's birth, but only one other who rose to prominence: Richard, who was knighted in 1523 and served in France.[120]

William Sandys the Elder held senior positions in Hampshire from 1460 until around 1481, including Commissioner of Array (1468, 1469, 1472), Commissioner of the Peace (1474–76) and (1477–81), and Commissioner of Oyer and Terminer (1462). Like John Cheyne, he fought for Edward IV at the Battle of Tewksbury in May 1471, earning a knighthood, and in 1483 participated in the coronation of Richard III.[121] Unlike John Cheyne, William remained loyal to Richard during the Buckingham Rebellion, and in November was commissioned with others to seize the lands and goods of the rebels in Wiltshire and Hampshire.[122] As John Cheyne and his brothers, Humphrey and Robert, were rebel leaders in Wiltshire, they would have been affected by this commission.[123]

It seems that Margaret Cheyne was placed in the unenviable position of having a Yorkist husband sequestering the property of her brothers, who had become supporters of the House of Lancaster. After 1483 William Sandys the Elder kept a low profile, and there were no more royal commissions and barely a mention in the national records; for example, there is no record of him fighting for Richard at the Battle of Bosworth. He was not attainted when Henry Tudor took the throne, as he was probably not seen as a threat.

The later years of the elder William Sandys appear to have been uneventful, except for the death of his eldest son in around 1485 and subsequent prolonged dispute with his daughter-in-law. He took The Vyne back into his own estate after being leased to the Brocas family for about seventy years, as previously mentioned. William the Elder made his will in October 1493 but did not die until October 1496. His widow and son William were executors of the will, by which William took possession of the Sandys' properties,[124] which included two manors in Sussex and eleven in Hampshire, together with several other Hampshire properties.[125] In addition to this material legacy, William the Elder's son inherited a network of connections with influential people (including the court), military training as a man-at-arms and a background in administration.

2

The Young William Sandys

William Sandys was born in around 1470 to Sir William Sandys and Margaret Cheyne, probably in Upper Clatford, near Andover, Hampshire.[1] He had at least one elder brother, John, so he was not Sir William's heir, and he had an older sister, Edith. As already noted, the Sandys family was connected through the Cheyne family to the Beaufort family and later, as William grew up, to the Howard and Neville families through the marriages of John and Edith. The family owned several estates, mainly in and around Andover, and the income from these and the county offices held by young William's father meant that he was born into a relatively wealthy family with county influence. Given that he was not Sir William's heir, he would have expected to enter a military, administrative or ecclesiastical career.

No details have emerged about his youth, but his military career suggests that he was trained to become a man-at-arms from an early age, because he fought for Henry VII as a young man. This training would have started when he was seven years old, but even before that he would have been encouraged to 'play soldiers' with toys such as jousting knights on horseback.[2] The next step was to learn the arts of warfare by using wooden swords and lances and being mounted on a wooden horse pulled along on wheels.[3] At seven he would have left home to be mentored in the arts of chivalry and warfare through training as squire to a knight. The usual tradition was to go to a maternal uncle,[4] so it is reasonable to assume that William went to Sir John Cheyne. If he was indeed a squire to Sir John Cheyne and stayed with him, he would have spent time in Brittany and France as a young teenager. When Richard III became king, John Cheyne and his brothers were among those who rebelled against him in October 1483 under the leadership of the Duke of Buckingham, and when the rebellion failed the Cheyne brothers were forced into exile to join Henry Tudor, the pretender to the English throne. It was there that John formed a close liaison with Henry and became one of his close advisors. These various circumstances would explain why William was obviously quite at home in Calais and familiar with France later in life.

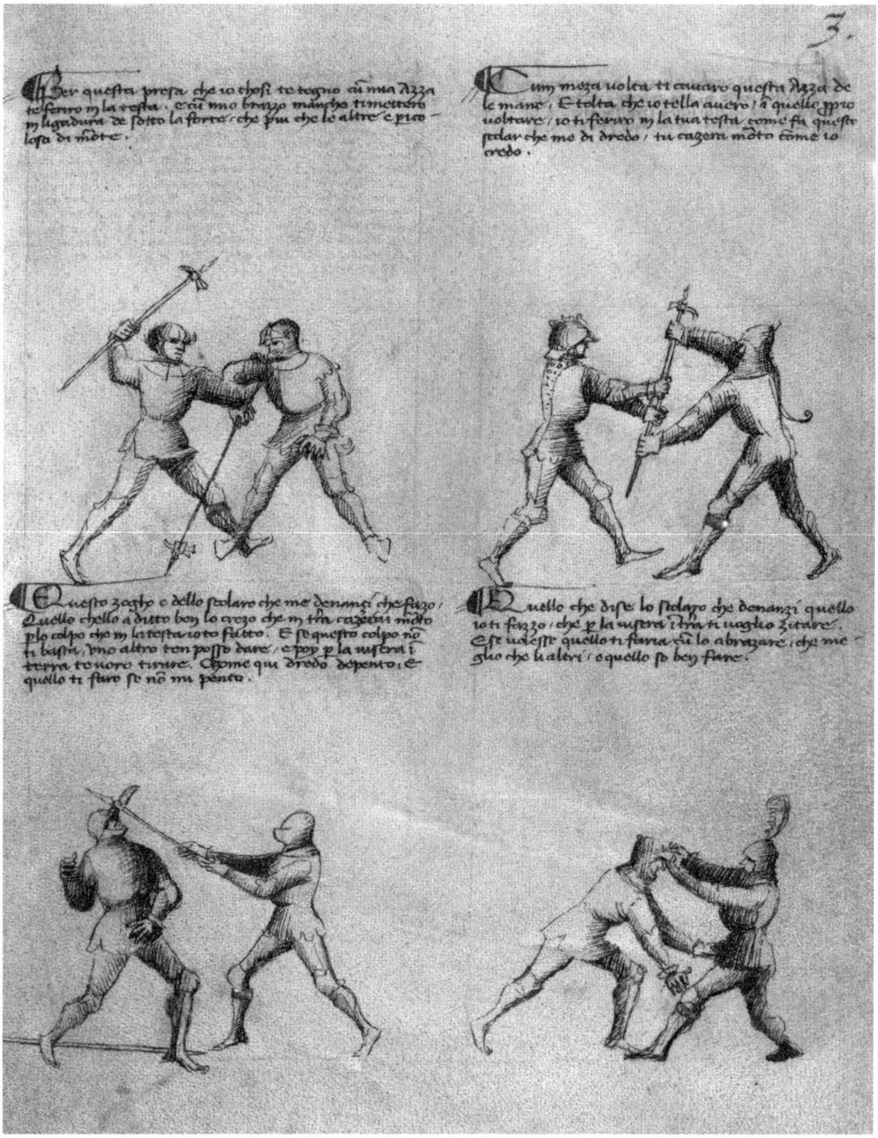

Training in the use of the poleaxe. (Author's collection, Il Fior di Battaglia: MS Ludwig XV 13, p.9)

Training for knighthood was rigorous because the aspiring knight needed to be physically strong and agile, with rapid reactions and great stamina. Learning the necessary moves for attack and defence was assisted by manuals, which detailed wrestling and combat and exercises with staves, but controlling a large frightened war horse in the heat of battle would be a different challenge which required practical experience. In addition, the young trainee would become familiar with his knight's armour and enduring the heat stress of wearing armour with internal padding. Contrary to popular belief, a fully clad knight could move with relative ease, even performing a cartwheel, because mobility was not as much of a problem as internal temperature. As the trainee knight grew stronger and fitter, he would learn to fight with a range of weapons, including the lance, poleaxe, mace, sword and dagger. Fighting skills would be honed by robust combat with other squires and knights, using blunted weapons, which could still cause injury and bruises, while tournaments for horse and foot combat further developed and maintained the fighting skills. In addition to this practical training, a squire would perform duties for his master, the knight, one of the most dangerous being providing him with fresh horses in battle. The one thing that could not be taught was the ruthless dedication required for success as a soldier.[5] Success in his development and skills would enable the young man to graduate as a qualified man-at-arms at the age of fifteen.

William Sandys would have been about fifteen at the time of the Battle of Bosworth Field on 22 August 1485 between the forces of Richard III and Henry Tudor. On that occasion Sir John Cheyne was a leading man-at-arms for Henry Tudor, so William was probably in the thick of the battle supporting Sir John, either as his squire or as an attendant knight. We know that Sir John was close to Henry Tudor during the battle, and that when Richard made his desperate charge to kill Henry Sir John was unhorsed, despite his formidable size and strength (he was nearly 7 feet tall). However, he recovered quickly and rescued the red dragon banner, which he carried to the end of the battle. Such an event would leave a lasting impression on a young man and demonstrate that determination was essential to victory.

Although there is no evidence that William received a formal education, surviving correspondence and other documents reveal that he was literate and at least familiar with Latin. It can also be assumed that he was fluent in French, which was still an important language at court and would have been essential during his years in Calais and France. His appointments as treasurer for the expedition in Spain (1512) and Treasurer of Calais (1517–26), coupled with his attention to his personal financial transactions, indicate that he was certainly numerate and probably had some experience of accounting practice in his youth. Where and when he acquired such knowledge is unknown, but the inventory of The Vyne indicates that there was a schoolmaster there,[6] so he must have been familiar with private tuition from childhood and may also have been supported by well-educated clergy, which was not uncommon at that time.

On 2 November 1486, Prince Arthur, the first child of Henry VII and his wife, Lady Elizabeth, daughter of Edward IV, was christened at Winchester

Cathedral. Sir John Cheyne played an important role as train-bearer for Lady Cecil, who carried the infant Arthur. According to a contemporary source, many knights and squires were also at the ceremony, so it is likely that William Sandys, the young Hampshire man, was there as squire to John Cheyne.[7] The next year – 1487 – was important for William. The fact that Henry Tudor had taken the throne was not universally popular, especially with followers of the deposed Richard III, so it is not surprising that several pretenders emerged. The first of consequence was the young Lambert Simnel, who had been trained to impersonate the Earl of Warwick, who had a legitimate claim to the throne through his uncle, the late Edward IV. The fact that the earl was a prisoner in the Tower and was displayed to the people in Westminster Abbey did not deter the conspirators, who were led by the Earl of Lincoln and Lord Lovell. During April 1487, the king became seriously concerned about the challenge to the throne, and by 8 May had begun to gather an army in the Midlands, with the Duke of Bedford and Earl of Oxford as leaders. He moved to Nottingham, where he was joined by other nobles and 'experts of war', including Sir John Cheyne, with their retinues. On 4 June, the Earl of Lincoln and the rebels landed at Furness, in Lancashire, having sailed from Ireland after Lambert Simnel had been crowned as Edward VI in Dublin. They were supported by 2,000 German mercenaries funded by Margaret of Burgundy, sister of Edward IV and a staunch Yorkist, and some Irish soldiers.

King Henry gathered an army and marched to confront the pretender's forces. They clashed at Stoke on 16 June, but before that battle Henry had elevated Sir John Cheyne and a few other knights to the rank of knight bannerette, which was above knight bachelor and entitled Sir John to have his men, including knights bachelor, serving under his banner on the battlefield. He was also subsequently known as Lord Cheyne. The battle on 16 June was fierce, because the Germans fought hard and were expertly led by Martin Swart to great effect. The Irish also fought valiantly but were slain like 'dull and brute beasts' because they wore no armour, and their slaughter demoralised the rest of the pretender's army. The final outcome was doubtful for some time, but the king's army gradually prevailed after the death of Swart and many other Germans. The leader of the Irish contingent was killed, as were Lord Lovell and the Earl of Lincoln, but Lambert Simnel escaped alive, only to be captured later. It is said that the pretender's army lost some 4,000 men, while the king lost about half that number.[8]

After this battle William Sandys was knighted by the king, together with fifty-three others who fought with distinction. He was around seventeen at the time and it was unusual for a commoner to be given such rank at that age, so it is assumed that he fought with exceptional courage and vigour.[9] It has been suggested that the William Sandys who was knighted at Stoke was not a Hampshire Sandys but one of the Cumberland branch,[10] but the new knight's coat of arms was the cross raguly, which confirms that he was a Hampshire Sandys.[11] The arms also carry a 'label',[12] which indicates that his father was still alive.[13] Following the death of his father, the label was removed. A later variant of his arms has the arms of Bray in the centre (an inescutcheon as described by Gwillim[14]). This probably occurred

Sandys' coat of arms with label after the Battle of Stoke 1487. These arms were in use after the Battle of Stoke but before his father's death in 1496. (BL Cotton Claudius C III f. 60 © British Library Board. All Rights Reserved / Bridgeman Images)

when his wife, Margery Bray, inherited a large portion of the estate of her uncle Sir Reynold Bray, increasing their fortunes considerably. The arms on Sandys' stall plate in Windsor Castle are of this form. Several examples of Sandys carry his motto, '*Aides Dieu*' (Assistance God).[15] There is also a version of the arms that are quartered – Sandys/Bray/Bray/Sandys – but this is rarely seen.[16]

The date when William Sandys the Younger was made a knight thus falls between 1485, when his brother John, heir to Sir William Sandys the Elder, died, and 1493, the date of his father's will, which refers to Sir William Sandys. All these details are consistent with the knighthood being awarded to the Hampshire William Sandys at the Battle of Stoke in 1487.

It follows that from 1487 to the death of the elder Sir William in 1496, there were two Sir William Sandys: the Elder and the Younger. This obviously raises questions as to which is being mentioned in records dating from this period at The National Archives. There is no doubt regarding the pleas of Margaret Sandys, as previously discussed, because the relevant documents differentiate between the two men who are referred to as 'the Elder' and 'the Younger'. Other references suggest that as the influence of the elder Sir William waned that of the younger Sir William waxed, and this is supported by an almost uninterrupted flow of references to a William Sandys at court from 1487, which continues after the death of the elder Sir William. As already noted, the elder Sir William accepted a commission to arrest John Cheyne and his brothers who joined Henry Tudor in exile and fought for him at Bosworth. However, shortly after the younger William Sandys was knighted after the Battle of Stoke in 1487, a Sir William Sandys was present at the coronation of Henry's wife, Elizabeth of York, at Westminster Abbey. All but a handful of the fifty-four new knights created at Stoke were also at the ceremony, and William is listed among them, which adds weight to the evidence that it is the younger Sir William who is at court. Finally, the will of William Sandys' father, dated 17 October 1493, refers to the testator as Sir William Sandys 'the Elder', confirming that by that time his son and namesake was also a knight.

After the Battle of Stoke and the christening of Prince Arthur, the king charged the Duke of Bedford, the Earl of Oxford and others to arrange the coronation of his wife, the Lady Elizabeth, as queen. This important event was intended to both celebrate and demonstrate the king's stature to the populace, the arrival of the new dynasty and the bond between Yorkist and Lancastrian camps. Those recently knighted after the Battle of Stoke were invited, including Sir William Sandys. By contrast with the terror and excitement of battle, Sandys and the others must have been delighted and proud to attend this magnificent occasion as their first royal event as knights of the realm. The ceremonies lasted for three days, starting on 23 November, when the queen travelled from Greenwich to the Tower by barge with an entourage including her mother-in-law, Margaret Beaufort, many noble lords and ladies, the Lord Mayor of London with aldermen, sheriffs of the city, and men of the livery companies. All were splendidly dressed and accompanied by trumpeters and minstrels, while the barges were decorated with banners and streamers of richly coloured silk, one sporting a large red dragon that spouted flames. On arrival at the Tower, the queen was met by the king and they spent the night there. During an evening ceremony, the king created ten Knights of the Bath. The following day the queen, dressed in cloth of gold and ermine with a circlet of precious stones on her head, was carried through the city from the Tower to Westminster in a litter, with a canopy of cloth of gold supported by relays of high-ranking knights. The streets had been cleaned and decorated with tapestries and, in places, with hangings of gold, velvet and silk, while the route from the Tower to St Paul's was lined with men from the guilds in their splendid liveries, and children dressed as angels and virgins sang along the route. The procession was led by knights with their esquires, followed by the newly elevated Knights of the Bath in their blue gowns, the heralds, high-ranking nobility, the Lord Mayor of London and his entourage, and officers of State immediately preceding the queen's litter. Behind the litter came the queen's household, the queen's sister and high-ranking ladies of the court, followed by other ladies of the court, and a contemporary source remarks on the magnificence of the gold chains and necklaces worn by the ladies. This spectacular procession eventually reached Westminster Palace.

The coronation took place the following day at Westminster Abbey. The queen wore purple velvet trimmed with ermine and a circlet of gold embellished with pearls and precious stones. She was the focus of a procession from Westminster Hall to the abbey, where she was crowned by the Archbishop of Canterbury in an elaborate ceremony, followed by a great feast in the hall. It was attended by thirty-two high-ranking clergy; thirty-nine lords and ladies; thirty-one knights bannerette, including Sir John Cheyne; 150 knights, including Sir Reynold Bray and Sir William Sandys; and a further twenty-five ladies and gentlewomen. The first course comprised twenty-four dishes based on venison, pheasant, swan, capons, lamprey, crane, pike, carp, kid, perch, rabbit, mutton, custards and sweetmeats. The second course was equally magnificent, with perch, sturgeon, partridges, tarts and castles of jelly.

Through this splendid event, the king hoped to make it clear to all that he recognised the House of York, had nurtured the nascent dynasty, and that the nobility supported him. It would be surprising if the young Sir William was not impressed by this display of power and wealth and inspired to seek further advancement both at court and in Hampshire.[17]

In addition to his connection with the Cheyne family young Sir William developed an important link with the Bray family, which resulted in his marriage to Margery Bray, niece to Sir Reynold Bray, who is often described as Sir Reginald Bray, although his signature clearly indicates that the former was correct at the time. Bray had risen to be a national figure through service to Margaret Beaufort, mother of Henry VII, and two of her husbands, namely Henry Stafford and subsequently Thomas Lord Stanley. He was employed as their Receiver General from around 1465 to 1485. During the plot to depose Richard III and replace him with Margaret's son Henry Tudor, she used Bray to enlist support for the Tudor cause, but he was eventually forced to join Henry in exile on the Continent. It is unlikely that Bray fought at Bosworth, but like John Cheyne his contribution was enough to gain entry to the inner circle of courtiers and advisors to the new king.[18] After Bosworth he was made knight bannerette, Knight of the King's Body,[19] Knight of the Order of the Bath at Henry's coronation, and later Knight of the Garter. A Knight of the Body was one of a group of knights who were considered reliable, capable and closely bound to the king, and performed a range of administrative, military or diplomatic duties.[20]

Another highly responsible senior role that was granted to Bray for life was that of Chancellor of the Duchy of Lancaster. For a short while in 1486 he was Lord Treasurer of England, and although he lost that post he remained involved with the Exchequer almost until his death and was Treasurer of War in the 1490s. Throughout, he maintained a close link with Margaret Beaufort who exerted considerable influence on her son, the king, and his wife. In the early days of the new reign, Bray loaned large sums of money to the king and arranged for loans from the merchant community, and it is clear that he accumulated a large fortune, not so much from his public offices but through patronage, manipulation and opportunism.[21] His wealth was such that he paid for the decoration of St George's Chapel, Windsor, and made a substantial contribution to the Henry VII Chapel at Westminster Abbey. On his death he was described as 'Pater Patriae', 'a righteous man and one who was almost unique in his unswerving devotion to justice; when Henry fell into error he was bold enough moderately to admonish and reprove him'. Hall added that Bray was 'a sage and a grave person'.[22] He is buried in St George's Chapel, Windsor.

Bray's estates included properties in Bedfordshire, Berkshire, Buckinghamshire, Cambridgeshire, Essex, Gloucestershire, Hertfordshire, Middlesex, Northamptonshire, Oxfordshire, Somerset, Hampshire, Suffolk, Surrey and Sussex, Warwickshire and Worcestershire. It is reasonable to assume that Cheyne and Bray knew each other well and that it was through Cheyne that Sir William Sandys became associated with the Bray family. Bray's wife, Katherine, was lady-in-waiting to Queen Elizabeth, and is frequently referred to in the 'Expenses of the Queen' and her other accounts. Most entries refer to money paid by the queen through Lady Bray; for example, on 10 November 1502 she was paid £6 18*s* 8*d* for fifty-two barrels of beer delivered to the Friars Observantes at Canterbury for a year. On other occasions she was repaid loans she had made to the queen, as on 6 June 1502 when she received 26*s* for money loaned the queen.[23] So Sandys' connections with Bray and Cheyne led directly to the queen's court, which was dominated by the queen mother.

In the light of Sandys' later career, it is tempting to assume that he gained experience in the arts of war from Cheyne, and in financial administration from Bray. He may have been at court during the 1487 Christmas and 1488 Easter feasts, but he is not specifically mentioned in the sources. However, he was certainly present at the court's Whitsuntide celebrations at Windsor in 1488, with Sir Reynold Bray. The others who were knighted after the Battle of Stoke were not mentioned.[24] So, by the end of 1488 the young William Sandys had been knighted and was recognised at court, which was a promising start for an ambitious commoner.

3

Knight of the Body for Henry VII

In 1489 Henry VII's armies were fighting in Scotland, Brittany and Flanders. Lord John Cheyne was a leader of the campaign in Brittany, so it is probable that Sandys' first battle on the other side of the English Channel took place there under Lord John's banner, although he is not mentioned, probably because he was a minor member of the contingent at this time.

An event on 28 June 1491 would have a significant impact on Sandys' life, namely the birth of Prince Henry, second in line to the throne after Prince Arthur. While Arthur was raised in the king's household, Henry, the younger son, was raised in the queen's household. Evidence suggests that the queen mother made the important decisions regarding the royal children at this time, as she exerted considerable influence on the queen and her household. At the same time Sandys was associated with the queen mother's household through the Cheyne and Bray connections.

It is also clear that Sandys had a relationship with the queen through the Lady Bray contact, and other evidence supports this. Sandys was bound to the queen by an obligation to perform some task either for her or on her behalf, and if he failed he would forfeit a sum of money to her.[1] A tantalising entry in the queen's expenses in November 1502 states that William Sandys' servants had hurt Nicholas Mathewe, yeoman of the queen, and she paid compensation to Mathewe,[2] who was a banner carrier at her funeral.[3] While there is no documentary evidence that Sandys had a formal role in Henry's upbringing, it is a reasonable to suppose that he had direct contact with the young prince, which fostered a lasting friendship until Sandys' death.

In 1492, Henry VII found himself at odds with the King of France. Along with the Holy Roman Emperor, he had promised to support Brittany in its attempt to remain independent of France, but by December 1491 Maximilian, King of the Romans, had withdrawn his support for the agreement and Charles VIII of France had conquered Brittany and married Anne, the twelve-year-old heiress to Brittany, thus making himself Duke of Brittany. Henry then tried to honour his part of the bargain: after claiming the crown of France for himself he invaded the country with a large army. In October 1492, he besieged Boulogne, but peace broke out before the fighting became fierce. The French king was not prepared to fight the English at that time, so a treaty was agreed, by which he would not support any pretenders to the English throne and would give Henry a handsome sum of money.[4]

There is no doubt that Sir William Sandys was part of that army because his indenture, dated April 1492, and a subsequent record of payment survive. He was contracted to serve in the king's army anywhere and at any time for up to a year from the date of the first muster, and to equip himself, and presumably his horses, with armour and be supported by a 'custrell',[5] a page, and six fit and able foot archers. By contrast, Sir John Risley, one of the king's Knights of the Body, was required to provide, in addition to himself, a custrell, a page, three men-at-arms, eight light cavalry (demi-lancers), twenty-five mounted archers, forty foot archers and eighteen billmen. Sandys and his men were to muster at Winchester on 15 June before marching to Portsmouth. Each man was entitled to 6*d* for every 20 miles travelled from home, while Sandys would receive 18*d* a day for himself, his custrell and page, with each archer receiving 6*d* a day. In addition, each soldier was required to donate one-third of any ransom money and/or 'winnings' he obtained to Sandys as the captain, while Sandys was obliged to give the king one-third of the ransom monies he received directly, and one-third of the money given to him by his soldiers.[6]

To avoid any misunderstanding, Sandys would be given a set of 'rules' for his conduct and that of his men during the campaign. If these were disobeyed, he could expect to be punished, and if his men misbehaved, he was responsible for bringing them to justice.[7]

While Henry was gathering his army, he sent the Bishop of Exeter and Lord Daubney to negotiate the treaty. They entered France via Calais and were escorted by an armed guard of about fifty lords and knights, including Sandys.[8] Henry sailed for Calais with 25,000 foot soldiers and 1,600 mounted troops. On 6 October 1492, a siege of Boulogne began, with English guns attacking the town walls, but after only nine days and before the full commencement of battle a ceasefire was negotiated and the Peace of Étaples was signed. The English agreed to go home in return for a large payment to Henry and a substantial pension to follow. That treaty was honoured for more than two decades.

Sandys was paid for his efforts through the office of the Treasurer of War, Sir Reynold Bray, at the rate of 2*s* a day, more than he was contracted to receive, and for ten archers more than his original contract.[9] According to Hall, Henry's action upset many lords and men because they lost their opportunities for lucrative ransom money and booty. Many had borrowed money, or mortgaged property, to equip themselves and their retinue against the prospect, and this led to accusations that the king had concluded the peace treaty because he feared his enemies.[10] It is unlikely that Sandys complained, or if he did it was not heard by the king, because two years later, in 1494, he held a prestigious role in a ceremony involving young Prince Henry.

Henry VII was keen to ensure the stability of the Tudor dynasty by raising the status of Prince Henry, whom he made a Knight of the Bath and Duke of York when he was only three years old. The ceremony to create twenty-three knights, including young Henry, commenced after dinner on Thursday 30 October, and a bath and bed were set up for the young prince in the king's closet at Westminster, while the others had their baths and beds in Westminster Hall. Prince Henry was immersed, and the Earl of Oxford charged him with the duties and responsibilities of a knight before the king put water on his son's shoulder, made the sign of the Cross and kissed the sign. In Westminster Hall the other bathing knights were charged, followed by a visit from the king in turn. When the king had finished, they dried, donned hermit's robes and went to the chapel for an all-night vigil. In the morning they were shaved (except young Henry!) and heard Mass, which was followed by bed rest. Finally, after dressing, they proceeded to Westminster Hall, where Sir William Sandys carried Prince Henry to the king, who commanded the Earl of Oxford to put a spur on the boy's right foot and the Duke of Buckingham to do the same for the left foot. The king then girded the boy with his sword and dubbed him Knight of the Bath before Sir William carried him to St Stephen's Chapel, where the prince and the others offered their swords. The following day, an equally elaborate ceremony raised young Henry to Duke of York, which was celebrated by a tournament, followed by a great feast attended by the nobility, senior clergy, and many knights including Sandys.[11]

At about this time, but certainly before April 1494, William Sandys married Margery Bray[12], niece of Sir Reynold. Although the marriage was not of immediate financial benefit, it served to enhance William's status and consolidate his links at court. In October 1496, the elder Sir William Sandys died, and the younger Sir William, by now his heir, acquired his estate, which at this time consisted mainly of several Hampshire properties and a few in Wiltshire and Berkshire.[13]

William did not have much time to enjoy his inheritance because, shortly after the estate was settled, he was required to don his armour in 1497 to fight for the king. James IV of Scotland had been threatening to invade England and Henry levied heavy taxes to pay for the defence of the country, which caused a rebellion in Cornwall. The rebels managed to get as far as Blackheath in June 1497, where they were confronted by the king's army and heavily defeated. Sir William Sandys was in that army, led by Giles, Lord Daubney, and was paid £21 5*s* for himself and his retinue.[14] Sir Reynold Bray was also in the king's army[15] and made a will before the battle, naming Sandys as his heir in case of his death.[16] A few years later, on 3 August 1503, two days before he died, Bray changed his will to include the nephews and nieces of his brother John, including Marjorie Sandys, while the bulk was to go to Edmund Bray, the eldest son.[17] This will was contested by William and Marjorie Sandys, who took advantage of Edmund's minority and gained much of the Bray property, considerably enriching their fortune.[18]

From 1491, another pretender claimed to be Richard, Duke of York, the younger of the two princes who died in the Tower during the reign of

Richard III. He was Perkin Warbeck, who gathered support from Margaret of Burgundy (who acknowledged him as her nephew), the Holy Roman Emperor Maximilian, James IV of Scotland and Sir William Stanley, brother-in-law to the queen mother, and thus posed a real threat to the king. Henry uncovered the plot in July 1493 and the identity of the pretender, after which Warbeck's support gradually evaporated. With diminished forces, the pretender's army landed in Cornwall from Ireland on 7 September 1497, only three months after the Cornishmen had been defeated by Henry's forces at Blackheath, so they had no stomach for another fight with the king and the desired mass uprising never occurred. Nevertheless, the army grew to about 8,000 men and reached Exeter on 17 September, but the city was well defended under the leadership of the Earl of Devon. After several attempts to breach the walls the besieging army was driven back and resumed the march north-eastward, reaching Taunton on 19 September. The king was fully aware of the army's progress and had commissioned musters by Lord Daubney for Somerset, Gloucester, Wiltshire and South Wales, while Lord St Amand and Sir John Cheyne received similar commissions for Dorset and Hampshire. Sir William Sandys, Sir Edward Berkeley, and others from Hampshire were summoned by the king's messenger during 10 and 12 September.[19] Henry planned to trap Warbeck's army between the Earl of Devon to the west, Daubney to the north-east and St Amand/Cheyne to the south-east.[20]

At Taunton the pretender's army realised that there was little hope of winning a battle with the king's forces, which were rapidly approaching from three directions, in the unfortified town. Henry had also mustered a bigger army at Woodstock, which was marching towards Taunton. Warbeck's army melted away and he fled, abandoning his remaining troops rather than fight. Daubney reached Taunton on 22 September and the king on 4 October, and on the following day Henry received the captured pretender at Taunton. Warbeck was jailed at the Tower of London where he and the Earl of Warwick later plotted to escape and overthrow the king, but their plot was discovered, and both were executed in November 1499.

When the king left Taunton he returned to London via Salisbury, stopping at Andover on 15 November, at Sir Reynold Bray's manor, Freefolk, on 18 November, Basingstoke on the 19th and Windsor on the 21st.[21] There are no details of where he stayed in Andover and Basingstoke, but it may have been with Sir Richard Kingsmill, where Catherine of Aragon stayed in 1501, or with Sir William Sandys, who was associated with both towns. Andover was Sandys' hometown, but he held one of the most important manors in Basingstoke and probably lived there by that time because The Vyne had been repossessed by the Sandys family from the Brocas family in 1488. As the elder Sir William and his wife were long-time residents of Andover, and most of their property was in the vicinity, it is possible that they stayed there until Sir William the Elder died in 1496. Indeed, his will, dated 1493, states that the elder Sir William came from Andover. It is not therefore unreasonable to assume that they handed The Vyne over to their newly knighted up-and-coming son William in 1488. When John Leland was writing in the 1540s, his reference to The Vyne suggests that the younger William lived there: 'The Vine was given out in marriage to one of the Brocas family and so remained until the late Lord Sandys, afore he was made Baron, recovered it into his possession.'[22]

Perhaps it was after this royal visit to Basingstoke that the young Sir William realised that The Vyne should be developed into a regular staging post for royal visits to the region to increase his prestige, influence and royal favour. In September 1499 the king returned from a visit to Southampton via Winchester and broke his journey in Basingstoke on the 26th.[23] Although his departure is not recorded, he arrived at Windsor on 9 October. There is no mention of where the royal party stayed, but as Sandys was by that time a Knight of the Body[24] and a sergeant-at-law,[25] it is possible that the royal party visited The Vyne. As a Knight for the Body, Sandys would serve the king personally and have direct contact with him.

After fighting in 1497, Sandys was not required to deploy his military talents again during the remaining years of Henry VII's reign, as it was a time of peace. In 1499, his uncle Lord John Cheyne died,[26] and although this may have been a personal loss to Sandys and his mother he was by then well-established at court, so the loss did not hinder his further advancement. In the same year, Sandys was nominated for election as a Knight of the Garter by the Earl of Worcester, Sir Charles Somerset, cousin to the queen mother.[27] Although he did not receive enough votes to be accepted into the order, nomination by the queen mother's cousin is a measure of his increasing influence at court. Indeed, by the end of the fifteenth century he was well established as a soldier and courtier and had begun to receive Crown grants of land and offices, such as Constable of Christchurch Castle, and Steward of Christchurch and Ringwood in Hampshire.[28]

On 2 October 1501, Catherine, Princess of Aragon, landed at Plymouth after a stormy voyage from Spain to marry Prince Arthur. She and her retinue were escorted from Devon to London by a succession of nobles, noble ladies and knights under the charge of Lord Brook, Steward of the King's Household. On 17 October, the train arrived at Exeter, reaching Honiton on the 20th, where the nobility of Devon and Cornwall were replaced by local worthies who escorted her through Shaftesbury towards Amesbury. Shortly before reaching the town her escorts changed again and to a more senior rank, including the Lord Treasurer, the bishops of Bath and Hereford, the abbots of Abingdon and Reading abbeys, Lord Dacre of the South, Lord Zouche, Sir Robert Poyntz, Sir William Sandys and six other knights. On arrival at Amesbury Abbey, Catherine was received by the Duchess of Norfolk before the convoy trundled through Andover and Basingstoke to arrive in Dogmersfield, Hampshire, accompanied by the same escort. In the meantime, the king and Prince Arthur and their retinue made their way towards Catherine, meeting on 6 November at Dogmersfield, where bride and groom had their first sight of each other. The king's retinue, and Arthur and Catherine, returned to London by separate ways.

The wedding ceremony at St Paul's on 14 November was followed by several days of feasting, jousting and pageantry.[29]

The next major event at court was the proxy marriage of Henry VII's eldest daughter, Margaret, to James IV of Scotland at Richmond Palace on 25 January 1502,[30] but Margaret would stay in England for another eighteen months until she was thirteen years old. Any satisfaction that the king derived from this occasion was to be overshadowed by the death of Prince Arthur at Ludlow Castle on 2 April, and his burial twenty-five days later at Worcester Cathedral. Sandys' presence is not recorded at these two events, but it would be surprising if he was not there given his role as a Knight of the Body. There is no doubt that he was in close contact with the court, because on 28 November the pregnant Queen Elizabeth paid 26*s* 8*d* out of her privy purse to Nicholas Mathewe, yeoman of the queen's chamber, to compensate him for the 'hurt' he had suffered at the hands of Sir William's servants.[31]

The queen gave birth to a daughter on 2 February 1503, but the child died on 10 February, as did the queen the following day. Her corpse was embalmed and placed in both a lead and a wooden coffin, then covered in white and black velvet with a cross in white damask. The following day, the coffin was taken from her room at the Tower to the chapel, where Mass was celebrated, and then watched over by selected ladies and officers of arms. Mass was repeated at the Tower for the next ten days until, on 22 February, the coffin was taken by carriage and drawn by six horses to Westminster, accompanied by the nobility, high-ranking clergy, judges, knights and foreign dignitaries. The funeral took place the following day. Sir William Sandys was one of the knights selected to carry a banner in the ceremonies in the retinue of the Marquis of Exeter. His sister Edith, Lady Darcy – often referred to as 'Lady Neville', although her husband Lord Neville had died in 1498[32] – also participated.[33]

The following June, the king left London accompanied by his daughter Margaret and progressed to Collyweston where his mother was staying, arriving on 8 July. This was the start of the long trek to Scotland where Margaret was to be married to James IV. After bidding goodbye to her father and grandmother she left, escorted by a large train of English and Scots dignitaries that included Sir William Sandys and his sister Edith. Their numbers were augmented by local worthies at the various stopping places. Margaret's personal transport was either a richly decorated horse or a litter with two horses; the rest, including the ladies, were on horseback. The route went via Grantham, Newark, Doncaster, York, Durham, Newcastle, Berwick, Lamberton Kirk, Scotland and then on to Edinburgh where Margaret was married. The town was richly decorated in preparation for the ceremony, which took place with due pomp and magnificence on 8 August, a month after Margaret had left her father. Edith Sandys was one of the ladies who accompanied her to the church where the marriage was conducted by the archbishops of Glasgow and York. It was followed by a feast and days of jousting. Eventually, the English escort left Scotland with gifts from King James.[34]

Following the queen's death in February 1503 and Margaret's marriage in August, it seems that the king withdrew from court and his health began to deteriorate. His loyal supporter Sir Reynold Bray died on 5 August that year, creating another loss that directly impacted on Sir William Sandys. He had lost an important connection at court, but his wife Margery eventually inherited a large part of Sir Reynold's fortune.[35]

Between 1498 and 1504 Sandys served as Commissioner of Peace for Hampshire for many years,[36] and Wiltshire.[37] However, from 1504 to 1509 the sources and historical literature are almost silent about him, although he must have maintained a court presence as the king appointed him Keeper of Stratfield Mortimer, Berkshire, and Keeper of the Park of Easthampstede in 1508.[38] Sometime before that he was accused of trespass in the king's forest, possibly for selling timber and hunting deer, but pardoned for these offences in February 1505,[39] just after he had forfeited the office of King's Ranger of Chute Forest (January 1505),[40] a post he had been granted in 1501.[41] In January 1506, Sandys was probably involved with the accidental visit of the King of Castile to England, when King Philip and his queen attempted to sail from the Spanish Netherlands to Spain but encountered a violent storm, which caused the fleet to seek shelter in harbours on the south-west coast of England. When news of the enforced landing reached Henry VII, he sent courtiers to escort Philip to Windsor with instructions to take their time so that he could prepare for the visit. At the end of January, the procession arrived at Winchester where Bishop Richard Fox entertained the king and his escort. On 30 January, Prince Henry also arrived, 'escorted by a great and noble company',[42] and on the following day accompanied Philip to Windsor. As Sandys was a Knight of the Body and friend of Bishop Fox, his involvement is very likely, either as part of Prince Henry's escort or in Winchester.

When Prince Arthur died on 2 April 1502, Prince Henry became the heir apparent and was transferred from the queen's care to that of the king. It seems that he was firmly controlled by his father, largely confined to rooms close by and only allowed out when supervised by the king's trusted servants. Sandys was apparently one those who was in contact with Prince Henry during this period because he began to receive royal grants immediately after the prince took the throne. Henry VIII also visited The Vyne in 1510, only fifteen months after his succession.[43]

Henry VII died on 21 April 1509 at Richmond Palace and was buried in Westminster Abbey. Sir William Sandys and his younger brother Richard were both in attendance at the funeral, but that marked the end of William's service to Henry VII as a Knight of the Body and the beginning of a new phase, which would prove more lucrative and influential.[44]

4

High Marshal of the Army

In 1523, Henry VIII appointed William Sandys as High Marshal of the Army under Charles Brandon, Duke of Suffolk, for the expedition to northern France. This made Sandys the senior field commander,[1] a rank not earned overnight but resulting from his military service for Henry VII and Henry VIII both in England and mainland Europe, in what is now France and Belgium, from at least 1487. After being knighted as early as 1497 at the age of seventeen at the Battle of Stoke,[2] he was involved in several of Henry VII's campaigns, including France in 1489 (possibly) and 1492, and Blackheath and Taunton in 1497. There are no contemporary accounts of his deeds during that period, but he clearly fought with distinction as is reflected in his rise to senior military rank under Henry VIII.

Increasing Duties under Henry VIII and Responsibility in Calais

The young Prince Henry and future Henry VIII matured into a formidable young man with health, strength, stamina and athletic ability, although his physical activity was restrained by his father, including jousting, which he loved, because it was considered too dangerous. His lively mind responded well to education, and he was fluent in French and Latin,[3] could read Italian and Greek,[4] and no doubt picked up some Spanish from Spaniards in the household of Queen Catherine. His talents extended to writing poetry and songs, but he also had a quick temper.

The year 1509 brought major changes in young Henry's life. When his father, Henry VII, died on 21 April, he left a country that was stable, at peace and financially sound, but the death of his grandmother Margaret Beaufort in June removed another important influence and a constraint. It is not surprising that the strong, handsome and intelligent seventeen-year-old Henry VIII, the new king, was keen to raise his own status and that of his court and country in the eyes of the European rulers. He soon began a major building programme of royal residences and embellishment of the court, but also wanted England to be recognised as a military power by the Holy Roman Emperor, Maximilian I, and King Ferdinand II of Aragon. He was determined to recapture the lands in France that had belonged to England, and in 1509 declared that he was the great enemy of the French.[5]

His first step towards international recognition was to marry Catherine of Aragon, daughter of Ferdinand II of Aragon and widow of Henry's elder brother, Arthur. Ferdinand responded by promising Henry a powerful army, ships and engines of war in the event of any opposition to his succession to the throne, and added that, if necessary, he would lead the army himself.[6]

A combination of ambition and naivety led Henry to send an English army to northern Spain in 1511 and 1512. In 1511, 1,500 archers under Lord Darcy went to assist Ferdinand against the Moors, but by the time they arrived Ferdinand had changed his mind and kept his troops at home, leaving the English to find their own way home without spoils.[7] Later that year, Ferdinand again suggested a joint campaign and agreed to support an English army to reconquer the former English parts of Guienne (south-western Aquitaine). By February 1512, he agreed to provide large ordnance pieces, horse soldiers and transport for an English force to attack south-west France via northern Castile. Parliament was convened and granted Henry the taxes he required for the expedition. In early May, Thomas Grey, Marquis of Dorset, was appointed to lead the army with Thomas, Lord Howard, as his deputy, Sir Maurice Berkely as marshal and Sir Henry Willoughby as Master of Ordnance. William Sandys was made Treasurer of War[8] and allocated over £80,000 by the Treasury as his war chest,[9] and was also charged with leading a retinue of 500 men and officers.

The total force would consist of around 7,000 Englishmen and 400 German mercenaries, and by the end of May the English army mustered at Southampton, where the scene is described by Hall:

> To see the lords and gentlemen, so well-armed and so richly apparelled in clothes of gold, and of silver and velvets of sundry colours pounced and embroidered and all petty captains in satin and damask of white and green, and yeomen in cloth of the same colours. The Banners, Standards and Gittons (a small flag bearing a heraldic badge of the owner)[10] fresh and newly painted, with sundry beasts and devise it was a pleasure to behold.[11]

After Sandys was appointed Treasurer of War and had paid the men their wages they boarded a fleet of Spanish ships, which left Southampton on 26 May, landing on the coast of northern Spain on 7 June after a good voyage. They set up camp close to the Spanish border with Navarre and the French border at Fuenterrabia, but, much to their consternation, the locals told them they were not expected and the promised provisions and military supplies were not there, so the army was forced to spend nights 'under the bushes'. To make matters worse, the weather was foul with heavy rain, and the locals were distraught because they expected, with some justification, that the English would take revenge on them for their unhappy plight. Meanwhile, the French seized an opportunity to cross the border and attack the camp. Although the English had no horsemen, their archers managed to drive off the French, but they were struck down by dysentery and many died. The English chroniclers attributed the outbreak to garlic in the food they had to eat, the lack of beer, and that they were not used to drinking wine.[12] The Welsh soldier chronicler Elis Gruffudd, who claimed he was there, blamed the rotten fruit that the English were forced to eat.[13]

Early in July, messengers from Ferdinand reported that an army was on its way to provide relief and start the campaign against the French, and Sandys was sent to persuade Ferdinand to act, but nothing happened.[14] Lord Howard wrote to Wolsey that they were in great peril and that Sandys and Willoughby were safeguarding the ordnance. Eventually the English heard that a great army under the Duke of Alva was on its way to provide the promised support, but when Alva's army was about a day's journey from the English camp it suddenly changed direction and attacked Navarre. The surprise attack worked, the city of Pamplona surrendered, and Alva conquered the country. However, the English discipline collapsed, and the men went into France and attacked the coastal town of St Jean de Luz and nearby villages, which they burned and looted, killing many inhabitants. They also attacked some of the locals. The marquis became ill, so Howard took command and divided the army into four to regain control: he commanded one part, the marquis the second part, Willoughby a third part and Sandys the fourth part. By the end of August, Dorset's War Council decided to return home and to send Knight, one of the king's secretaries, to break the news to Henry. Knight protested that Ferdinand would deliver his promise. At the same time Sandys, and unnamed others, opposed sending Knight because he was a favourite of Wolsey, who was 'the cause of all this mischief', and they feared that the message that would reach the king was that the army should stay in Spain. Knight set off for England, but soon returned because of violent storms at sea. Ships were hired in September and by December they were home in England. Meanwhile, Ferdinand wrote to the Holy Roman Emperor, criticising the English and saying that it had been agreed that the joint forces should first conquer Navarre, then move to conquer Guienne, and that victory would have been easy. According to Elis Gruffudd, the attack on Navarre was not for Ferdinand's self-interest: it was to break the alliance between the King of Navarre and the French king, and make it easier for the English to reclaim Guienne. Elis's view probably reflects what he was told by Sir Robert Wingfield, English ambassador to the Holy Roman Emperor, who was often accused of being too close to the emperor. Elis would later become Sir Robert's servant.

Not surprisingly, Henry was angry about the failure of the expedition, and on 19 November examined the chief captains of the army, including William Sandys, in the presence of Ferdinand's ambassador, forcing them to kneel throughout the interrogation. They gave three reasons for failure, namely the lack of provisions, mutiny of the soldiers, and incompetence of the marquis, and eventually begged to be allowed to stand up, even if they had erred and merited punishment. It seems that the king was trying to impress Ferdinand's ambassador, as he later told the Venetian ambassador that he was very angry with the Spaniards.[15] Henry's first major expedition into Continental Europe therefore failed, while Ferdinand got what he wanted – namely the kingdom of Navarre. He also signed a peace treaty with France, leaving Henry isolated.

When Sandys returned to England, he completed his accounts, which covered the wages of soldiers and spies, ship hire, provisions and the return of the men to their home towns from Southampton. The records reveal that he was paid 6*s* 8*d* a day, had two clerks at 1*s* a day, and eight servants at 6*d* a day. His younger brother, Richard, travelled from Southampton to The Vyne with eighty-nine soldiers, taking two days for the journey. Sandys went to London rather than The Vyne, taking five days and being accompanied by two clerks and an escort of forty-four men with their captain, probably to return the remnants of the War Treasury. The escort then marched to The Vyne in three days, prior to the soldiers returning to their own homes.[16] This return to The Vyne suggests that it was a mustering point and probably an armoury for the men from north Hampshire.

At the end of December Sandys submitted his accounts to the Treasury, revealing that he had paid out £46,631 of the £80,858 given to him before the campaign and returned £34,395 to the Treasury.[17] It was also noted that £895 'remaineth in the said Sir William Sandys' hands'. There is no record of that money being returned to the Treasury, so it seems that he profited from the expedition, although there was little plunder and no ransom money.[18]

In January 1513, Sir William Sandys and Sir John Lisle were appointed chief captains of the military forces for the counties of Wiltshire, Hampshire and Dorset in response to the perceived threat of a French invasion.[19]

Despite the failure of the two Spanish expeditions, Henry continued to prepare for a large campaign to northern France in 1513 with support from Maximilian, the Holy Roman Emperor. This time Henry would lead the army himself, believing that the English and Welsh soldiers would be more disciplined and resolute in his presence and that he could achieve military glory like Edward III and Henry V. Around 35,000 native soldiers, supplemented by 700 German mercenaries, were mustered in London in May 1513,[20] and in order to avoid saturation of Calais and the English Pale in France, the army comprised three 'wards' or divisions. George Talbot, Earl of Shrewsbury, led the foreward (12,000 men); Charles Brandon, Viscount Lisle, the middleward (16,000 men) and Sir Charles Somerset, Lord Herbert, the rearward (7,000 men). Brandon was the senior officer under the king.

On this occasion Sandys was attached to the middleward, which was divided into the avouantguarde and the king's ward, both of which were subdivided into three. The centre of the avouantguarde consisted of 3,000 men under Charles Brandon, flanked by a right wing under Thomas, Lord Darcy (Sandys' brother-in law) with 1,500 men, and a left wing under Sir William Sandys with 1,500 men. Sandys mustered a retinue from his lands in Hampshire and Northamptonshire, comprising a captain, a petty captain, and eighty-eight men,[21] while his contingent included 600 spears (mounted soldiers in full armour), 700 German mercenaries and light artillery.[22] The German mercenaries were a mixed blessing because although they had a reputation for discipline and ferocity in battle they were also known for ignoring camp discipline, pillaging and fighting with allies as it suited them, all of which were displayed in this campaign. In mid-August 1513, they started fighting with their English allies, even taking English guns and firing upon their owners. Many men were killed, but a much bigger fight was prevented by the swift intervention of officers on both sides, which was praised by the emperor. Later in the campaign and without warning the Germans deserted the left wing of the king's battle, leaving it exposed.[23] The structure of the Middleward as given in the State Papers differs from that described in the Talbot Papers,[24] which divides the middleward into vanguard, middleward and rearward, but the participants are much the same as in the State Papers. No doubt the structure of the wards varied according to circumstances. The king's ward consisted of a central force of 600 men led by Henry, a left wing of 1,500 men under Sir Henry Marney, and a right wing of about the same size under Sir George Neville, Lord Abergavenny.[25]

The foreward and rearward were ferried to Calais between 6 and 10 June, and by the 16th had set out for the first major objective: the town of Thérouanne, which was reached on 22 June. The siege began on 25 June. Sandys and his men reached Calais on 17 June, followed by Darcy and his troops on 22 June.[26] The king, Brandon, and the main body of the middleward arrived on 1 July. Unlike the foreward and rearward, this ward stayed in Calais until 16 July when the avouantguarde, including Sandys, marched to 'clear the way' for the king, who left on 21 July. This delayed the fighting season by three weeks but, on the positive side, the king's ward had been augmented by 4,000 additional German pikemen and a troop of Burgundian horse soldiers as part of Emperor Maximilian's agreement to provide support and advice to the expedition on a strictly commercial basis. The king travelled with numerous staff and extensive baggage to ensure his comfort, so in addition to many grand tents he had a portable wooden house, minstrels and a full entourage of servants, which caused the royal entourage to move slowly, not reaching Thérouanne until 4 August. The French did not rest during this invasion, but a major confrontation with the emperor's troops in Italy had reduced their strength for engagement in direct battle with the allied army, so they relied on hit-and-run tactics.

The largest skirmish began on 28 July 1513, when the English master carpenter and his men, without informing senior officers, set out to rescue a large siege gun that had slid into a pond in transit to Thérouanne.[27] They managed to drag the gun onto a cart, but a French force of 800 men attacked and killed most of them. The king responded by sending a party of 700 horse soldiers, led by Henry Bourchier, Lord Essex, from the middleward, who rescued the gun despite it being protected by 2,000 mounted French men-at-arms. The French later claimed that they were obeying royal instructions to avoid any large-scale battle with the allies.

While Henry slowly made his way to Thérouanne, the siege was not progressing well because the town's defences were strong. As Hall explains, 'The city was strongly fortified with walls, ramparts with diverse fortresses in the ditches which were so broad and so plumb steep that it was a wonder to behold.'[28] A Welsh soldier wrote to the Earl of Devon that the ditches outside the walls were so deep that a man walking and looking into them feared falling into them, that the banks were wooded, backed by wide walls with great bulwarks, and that the inner sides of the walls were fortified with great trenches, bulwarks of timber and earth and, in certain places, trenches with deep pits full of the town's stinking waste.[29]

It was only after the middleward arrived that the English miners could move the great siege guns close enough to attack the town walls effectively. At this point Sir George Talbot, Earl of Shrewsbury, and his men were on the west of the city; Sir Charles Somerset, Lord Herbert, was to the north; and the king, with Lord Lisle and Sandys, was on the west, closest to Aire-sur-la-Lys, where the emperor was camped. When the emperor eventually appeared, real progress with the siege began. The English forces had wrongly assumed that the River Lys, to the south, was an adequate natural barrier to prevent French operations to supply the town. The emperor recognised this error and recommended to Henry, whom he met on 14 August, that the middleward should be repositioned on the south side of the river to seal off the town, and Henry agreed. Sometime before 15 August the allies learned from their spies that the French intended to send a force with a large escort from the south to provision the city, while launching a diversionary attack on the north-west. It was time for swift action.

During the night of 15/16 August, the English carpenters were tasked with constructing five bridges to enable the middleward, with its soldiers in full armour, to cross the river by daybreak, ready to set up the southern blockade. Sandys and the other men-at-arms must have had little sleep that night while preparing for battle. Mass would be heard before being armed, which could not be done by a warrior alone. Linen underpants and shirt were donned first, followed by an arming doublet, which was a padded suit with waxed thongs to attach parts of the plate armour. This was followed by the chain mail doublet, which had inserts under the armpits to cover gaps in the plate, and then it was necessary for a servant or squire to fit the outer plate armour, working from the feet upwards, the helmet being the last item. In the meantime, each destrier (war horse) was prepared for battle, as it would be just as much a target as the rider. First, a padded coat was fitted, followed by the massive war saddle and armoured plates for the head and sides, all covered with a cloth. Finally, each rider mounted his horse and took his weapons, usually a lance, sword and/or poleaxe, and a stout narrow dagger for plunging into the gaps in the enemy's armour. A painting by Graham Turner in Christopher Gravett's book *Tudor Knight* depicts two men-at-arms beginning the charge,[30] and the same book shows a set of horse armour of this period.[31]

Soon after the crossing, the English light horse reported a large French supply train approaching from the south, escorted by a significant armed force. The events that followed led to the so-called Battle of the Spurs, which was Henry's moment of glory in this campaign. Acting on the emperor's advice he deployed the troops, positioning the light artillery on a hill overlooking the path of the oncoming French force, and the mounted archers behind hedgerows. The rest of the middleward was split into two – around 1,000 English men-at-arms and 10,000 infantry – with Henry following around a mile behind. The emperor's cavalry from Burgundy and Hainault were somewhere at a distance from the English front rank. As the English men-at-arms moved forward, they were seen by the French, whose men-at-arms assembled to challenge them and protect the supply convoy. The allied chroniclers tell us that there were three times more French than English, although it was probably more like two to one, but the English had the element of surprise on their side. The French rode into the trap and were met by a barrage of arrows from the archers and the guns on their flanks. The English men-at-arms, led by Henry Bourchier, Earl of Essex,[32] then charged and clashed with the French and fierce fighting ensued. Hall tells us that 'the dust was great and the cries more', while Elis Gruffudd adds that 'many men on both sides had been struck to the ground from the horses back'. Men were killed and wounded on both sides. During this melee, the French saw the large allied infantry coming toward them, which resulted in chaos as the French front ranks turned tail and ran into their advancing rear ranks. The English waded in, followed by the cavalry from Burgundy and Hainault, and the French fled, discarding their horses' armour to shed weight.

After the initial clash there was relatively little bloodshed on either side, but the allies gave chase for 6 miles and 300 French were captured, some of high rank. A few French tried to turn the tide. The French knight Bayart describes his experience of this encounter as he retreated from the initial rout with around fifteen men-at-arms until they reached a bridge over a canal, which they could hold for a while, and sent a messenger to the French camp to prepare to defend themselves. Eventually his pursuers, men from Burgundy and Hainault who had joined the allied chase, crossed the canal behind Bayart and his men. Realising that he was surrounded, he said that they should surrender because their horses were exhausted and the enemy ten to one against them, and if they waited longer the English bowmen could arrive and cut them to pieces. Bayart saw one of his exhausted adversaries resting under a tree and tried to surrender to him, but the resting knight thought he was being captured so he tried to surrender. Bayart made it clear that he wanted to surrender and asked the knight to escort his men and offer them protection from Englishmen who would kill them. The knight kept his promise and protected the prisoners from the English, which illustrates the enmity between the English and French at this time. While this was going on, Sir Rhys ap Thomas and his men defeated the diversionary attack.[33]

Henry declared the Battle of the Spurs a glorious victory over the French. It was so named because the English said that spurs were all they could see of the fleeing French. It is celebrated in a painting in the Royal Collection at Hampton Court, which shows the English men-at-arms riding in full armour and attacking the retreating French with lances, swords, battleaxes and maces. Incorrectly, the painting shows Henry receiving the surrender of one of the senior Frenchmen, but Henry was in fact with the infantry behind the men-at-arms. To commemorate this victory Henry commissioned a painted glass window, depicting himself, for the church of St Nicholas in Calais.[34] The same battle is the subject of a drawing by the German artist Hans Burgkmair, which is also inaccurate because it shows the Holy Roman Emperor's troops in the first charge, which they were not, but it does depict the guns and English longbowmen.[35]

Thérouanne held out for six days after the battle, but the French finally agreed to surrender, and the French garrison and their German mercenaries left the city. On 24 August, Henry and the emperor and their men entered the town in triumph. After they had been to St Mary's Church, they inspected the defences and instructed that they should be destroyed, except for the cathedral and the religious houses, but the destruction went further and much of the town was burned down.

From Thérouanne, the allied army marched south-east towards Lille, which was then in Flanders – the emperor's domain. By 10 September, the army was close to the French/Flanders border at a narrow bridge called Pont-a-Vendin, a stone causeway that was only about a quarter of a mile long and wide enough for one carriage, but the only route between two marshes for crossing the border from France.[36] The French, having partly recovered from the Battle of the Spurs, decided to pursue the allied army to this pinch point.

When the foreward and heavy artillery had crossed the bridge, and Henry's ward was in the process of doing so, the French appeared, so Sandys and 700 men and guns were selected to act as a rearguard to protect the rest of the allied army, especially Henry's entourage.[37] They succeeded in defending the bridge for long enough to allow the main army to proceed to Lille, where Henry and the emperor were entertained for three days by Maximilian's niece, Margaret of Austria, who was ruling Flanders for the emperor. During these 'jollities', as Herbert wrote,[38] both rulers had to decide what they would do during the rest of the fighting season: they could either return west and attack Boulogne, which could enlarge the English territory in France, or move further east to take the important city of Tournai and make Maximilian's borders with France more secure at that point. The emperor had his way, and the attack on Tournai began on 16 September; the city surrendered on 21 September after lengthy negotiations and Henry entered in triumph on 24 September.

Henry and the bulk of the English army started to withdraw on 13 October 1513, but on the way home a treaty was signed at Lille that committed Henry, Maximilian and Ferdinand to invade France by June 1514.[39] They reached Calais on 19 October and England shortly after. Henry returned in triumph, although the actual result of this exercise was that he garrisoned Tournai for four years at great cost and encumbered England with a large debt and ongoing expenses for maintaining an isolated garrison in eastern Picardy. In effect,

Maximilian and his army had been paid to protect the interests of the Holy Roman Empire rather than England.

While Henry had been away, Queen Catherine served as regent in charge of England, with power to 'wage war against any of our enemies in our absence'.[40] She responded to Scottish raids in northern England by raising a counter-attack army, led by the Earl of Surrey, which achieved a major victory at the Battle of Flodden: the Scottish army was heavily defeated and James IV killed with many of his nobles.[41] This decisive English victory is recognised as such, but it was not allowed to overshadow Henry's victory at the Battle of the Spurs.

Henry's army was paid off in November 1513, including Sir William Sandys and his retinue who had landed at Dover on 27 October and marched the 109 miles home; most went to The Vyne, taking nine days, but a few made their way to Sandys' manors in Northamptonshire. The captain received 4*s* a day for the homeward march and the same rate when fighting abroad, the petty captain 2*s* a day, and the rest of the men 6*d* a day.[42]

Sandys was not home long, because in May 1514 the king raised an army for the pledged attack on France. The muster took place and the Channel crossing proceeded, but no fighting ensued because a peace treaty was negotiated between the French and English and sealed by the marriage of Henry's younger sister, Princess Mary, who was eighteen years old, to Louis XII, the King of France, who was thirty years her senior. [43] Sandys was a member of her escort from England to Montreuil and present at the marriage, but when the ceremonies were over, the escort, led by the Duke of Norfolk, returned to England.[44] King Louis was in poor health and died eighty-two days after the marriage, and the French chronicler Monstrelet wrote that 'the King and Queen lay the night (the wedding night) at the Royal Palace, which served to shorten his days'. Mary then returned to England with her dowry and the peace held for eight years, until 1522.[45]

Sandys had a relatively calm period from 1514 until the Southampton riots in 1517, but his response to those riots and his key role in the ensuing settlement led to major changes in his lifestyle and wealth. In March 1517, the mayor and burgesses of Southampton issued an ordinance that the inhabitants of the salt marshes to the east of the town should pay for the completed works to prevent the marshlands from flooding. In addition, the area that had been common land for sheep grazing was to be enclosed. The inhabitants responded by rioting and demolishing the flood-prevention banks and ditches, before marching into the town armed with picks, shovels and pikes. Sir William Sandys was Constable of Southampton Castle, and in that capacity was instructed by the king's council to quell the riots, round up the rioters and arrest them. He managed to negotiate a settlement, but those regarded as ringleaders had escaped, so six others were arrested and taken for trial at the Star Chamber in London while the townspeople petitioned on their behalf and undertook to repair the damage. Although the six were found guilty, they received a light sentence that required them to spend time in the town stocks, but the ringleaders were banished from the town.[46] Richard Fox, Bishop of Winchester, wrote to Cardinal Wolsey about this matter on 10 May 1517, revealing that Sandys was instrumental in devising a peaceful solution:

> A more meet person than is Mr Sandys for the ordering of the matter could not have been found. For being among them he is their Mayor, Bailiff, and all the ruler of the town; and with the authority that he has under the King's grace, the love and credit that he has among the people, when he is present, he may do more with them than do the Mayor and all officers that belong both to the town and to the port ... And with his indifference between the two parties he has left the whole town in sure quietness, rest and peace ... Also my Lord, though I assuredly know Mr Sandys steadfastness, kindness and love of the King's grace and his readiness always to spend his life and land in his service as any gentleman in this realm ... And yet it is to my great comfort that your Lordship by your said letters written with your own hand affirms the same.[47]

These good opinions from Fox and Wolsey resulted in Sandys being granted an annuity for his services in Spain, Guienne, Flanders and Picardy.[48] More significantly, he was appointed to the important and lucrative position of Treasurer of Calais, after being considered for appointment as Master of the King's Horse and Master of the King's Henchmen.[49] From this point onwards, he would remain involved in the government of Calais for the rest of his life, first as Treasurer, then as Deputy (Governor) of Guînes Castle.

Sandys was actually in Calais on 9 July 1517 when Wolsey summoned him back to England,[50] where he learned on 28 July that he was to become treasurer from 6 October that year.[51] Unlike the Deputy of Calais, the treasurer was not expected to be in full-time residence there, so he would not be forgotten at court as tended to happen to the deputy. During the next seven years, Sandys spent about eight months of the year in Calais, sometimes making several journeys back to England for short stays. The Channel crossing was not easy in Tudor ships, and there are several accounts of shipwrecks, narrow escapes, unplanned detours and piracy. Elis Gruffudd had a particularly memorable journey from England to Calais in 1530 when the weather was windy and cloudy. Soon after reaching open sea the ship was at the mercy of the waves, there was panic on board, and everybody called on their patron saint to save them from drowning, including Elis: 'At which time I proved to be as weak in faith as anyone else and so I vowed that I would go on foot with a penny for St Dwynwen whensoever God and the Saints would allow me to tread a foot on English soil.' It was also necessary to throw some of the cargo overboard, including salted fish, leather, cheeses, butter, nails and clothes, and Elis lost all the valuable clothes which London gentlemen had given him as gifts. Fortunately, the ship was saved and everyone on board reached Calais 'feeling greatly relieved that they had escaped the cruelty of the sea and the fury of the storm'.[52] Less fortunate was the fate of those who were on the ship *Lubeck* in 1514, which was carrying soldiers and marines to escort Princess Mary to her wedding to the French king but foundered west of Calais. Only a hundred of the 500 men on board survived, and they may have included William Sandys as he was in Mary's escort party.[53] Sometimes there were long delays waiting for better weather. When Catherine of Aragon left Spain to marry Prince Arthur in 1501, the first crossing from Corunna was abandoned and the second started in September from Laredo, but terrible storms off Brittany caused great anxiety to those on board. She eventually landed safely in Plymouth on 2 October.

Calais and Its Hinterland, and the Treasurer's Role

As William Sandys held two key positions in Calais and the surrounding area from 1517 onwards, it is necessary to describe how this area of English sovereignty in mainland Europe operated, and to outline Sandys' highly responsible roles. The standard work on Calais and its Pale under English control was written by Viscount Dillon in 1893, so the information that follows draws on that, but also on subsequent work by Colvin, Grummitt, Sandeman and St Claire Byrne.[54]

The town of Calais and the Pale was captured from the French by Edward III in 1347 and remained under English control until 1558. By early Tudor times it extended around 18 miles along the coast and was roughly 10 miles deep. It was enclosed by sea to the north, France to the west and south, and Flanders on the east, allowing direct access to potentially important trading partners or powerful enemies. The border of the Pale was defended by four main fortresses: Rysbank, with a garrison of around twenty men, was situated at the entrance to the harbour; Newhambridge to the west; Hammes to the south-west; and Guînes to the south. These castles were supplemented by a series of small forts and bulwarks along the borders. Another essential defence element was the low-lying marshland that stretched from the estuary of the River Hammes at the harbour into the area south and west of the town. Close to the estuary was the small but vital fort of Newhambridge, which controlled the bridge over the river and, equally important, the sluice gates across the river. When closed, these gates caused a large area to the west and south of the town to be flooded; when open, the area was arable land drained by ditches and dykes. To the east of the town the land was higher and drier.

Guînes Castle and its town were both encircled by a common moat. The castle was the largest in the Pale with eleven towers and a garrison of around a hundred men. It played a prominent role in the meeting between Henry VIII and Francis I, King of France, in 1520, and features prominently in the painting at Hampton Court that celebrates that occasion. To the east of Guînes and across the border with France, was Ardres Castle, from which the French launched frequent attacks on the Pale, and Guînes bore the brunt of the onslaughts. Near to the town was the Forest of Guînes, the only source of timber for the Pale but adequate for the demands of the English community.[55] Hammes was a small castle with a garrison of about twenty-five men, approximately a mile and a half north-west of Guînes. Scattered across the Pale between the castles and Calais town were several small hamlets.

The town of Calais was rectangular, around three-quarters of a mile long and one-third of a mile deep, with the long axis parallel to the harbour. It was protected by its own moat and walls with towers and had gates and a castle at the north-west end. The population was over 4,000 – about the size of Tudor Colchester or half of a large town such as York or Norwich. In most respects it was what would be expected for a seaport, including harbour facilities, churches, taverns, brewhouses, a market, almshouses, a prison, warehouses, a hospital, town hall, convent and mills. Many of the properties had 'wool houses', presumably wool warehouses, reflecting the principal trade. Another commercial activity was herring fishing and smoking, carried out at 'herring hangings'. The town was divided into seven wards that were sub-divided into quadrants containing four-sided blocks, and each quadrant usually contained several properties. Three long streets ran east to west, crossed by a dozen streets at right angles. The administration and commercial centre lay to the west of the town centre, around the market square. The skyline was dominated by four buildings, namely the Church of Our Lady (St Mary's), the Church of St Nicholas, the Town Hall and the Staple Hall. A plan of part of the town shows that some buildings had stepped gables, which gave them a Flemish appearance,[56] but no visitor would have doubted its English heritage with street names such as Cow Lane, Farthing Lane, Penny Lane, Hemp Street and Castle Street, and taverns called The Plough and Kinges Armes.

Many properties were well endowed with gardens, which were considered a feature of the town, and some houses were large. In 1536, Lord Lisle, the deputy, moved into a property called The Staple Inn, which was one of the largest and described by one of the town's inhabitants as a 'vast palace'.[57] It comprised a 100-foot-square court surrounded on four sides by buildings, one of which was three storeys high. At the external corners were towers, and on one side a tall gateway adorned with the coats of arms of the king and the Staple. A smaller courtyard, containing the stable block and smaller dwellings, was attached to a side at right angles to the gateway, and there were gardens and grounds outside the courtyard building.[58] In William Sandys' time the deputy lived in a more modest building in the far south-east corner of the town. By 1556, the whole block had been pulled down and a monument erected there, next to the Dublin bulwark.[59]

Calais differed from English mainland ports in that it was a military stronghold that housed the great trading centre of the Staple. The town needed to be able to defend itself in the event of an attack by sea or land from France or the Holy Roman Empire, and for long enough to allow reinforcements to arrive from England. It also acted as a safe haven for English shipping and a relatively safe gateway, warehouse and administration centre for English armies on their way to France and Burgundy. It was constantly ready for war, to the extent that a royal proclamation in 1527 described Calais as 'a town of war'.[60] The town's defences, when properly maintained, were formidable, including an encircling wall with many towers along its length and four fortified gates. Outside the wall was a moat, in which there were six massive towers and bulwarks to the south and east of the town, while the west side was protected by the castle. The town gates were normally locked, except for the Lantern Gate on the harbour front, opposite the fort of Rysbank, which was locked at lunchtime and then at four o'clock in the afternoon for the night, the keys being returned to the deputy's residence. These defences were manned by a permanent garrison, which fluctuated in size but was between 350 and 400 men in early Tudor times – around one person in ten of the population. This garrison was the nearest thing that England had to a professional army, so it provided a valuable core of seasoned soldiers for campaigns outside the Pale. As a further defensive measure, the council ran a network of spies who operated in the adjacent territory.

The Welsh chronicler Elis Gruffudd was a professional soldier based in Calais, and he is a fascinating example. Born in North Wales around 1490, he was a soldier in the king's army by 1512, serving in Spain, while the following year he was in the allied army under Henry VIII that conquered Thérouanne and Tournai. One year later Elis Gruffudd was in the service of the English courtier Sir Robert Wingfield, and he was part of Wingfield's entourage at the Field of the Cloth of Gold in 1520 and the reception of the Holy Roman Emperor at Dover in the same year. In 1523, Wingfield became lieutenant of the castle of Calais and was in the army led by Charles Brandon, Duke of Suffolk, which campaigned in northern France in that year. Elis Gruffudd was not only with him but wrote an account of the experience, before returning to England as keeper of Sir Robert's palace from 1524 until January 1530. He then moved to Calais to join the permanent garrison force called the Vyntene, a body of some 180 men who reported to the deputy through a senior captain. Wingfield was the deputy at that time but left that post in 1531 to be replaced by Lord Berners. Elis Gruffudd remained in the Calais militia until at least 1556 – which may have been the date of his death – during which time he married and had two children. By 1556 he lived in a tenement in the south-west of the town in an area called the Haven. The fact that he wrote his chronicle makes him exceptional, but writing it in Welsh, his native language, makes him more unusual, as does his level of literacy. In other ways he was typical of the soldiers in the Pale and concludes his chronicle, completed in 1552, by describing himself as 'a soldier of Calais'.

Throughout Sandys' roles at Calais there were periodic campaigns to tackle maintenance and defence upgrades, both at Calais and the outlying castles, usually prompted by perceived threats from the French. This important work had been neglected through lack of funding and consistent support. As with timber, the Pale was not self-sufficient in food, other commodities or tools, so it relied on imports from England and was vulnerable to naval blockade. The only industry was brewing beer and, in season, smoking herrings, but by far the main source of income was the Staple. To ensure that the Crown received the tax levied on the export of wool, a monopoly called the Merchants of the Staple had been established in the thirteenth century, through which the whole business of exporting wool from England to the great weaving centres in Flanders was managed. Following the English acquisition of Calais, the wool monopoly was moved from England to Calais and administered by the Staple at Calais. At its peak, the Staple generated sufficient income to both pay for the garrison and provide a handsome profit for the merchants and the Crown, an arrangement that generally worked well. However, Henry VII and Henry VIII gave priority to extracting cash from the Staple over maintaining the defences and town. When combined with a decline in the English wool trade in the early 1500s, this resulted in a situation in 1523–24 where the income extracted exceeded the value of the tax collected. Inevitably, the town and defences showed obvious neglect as insufficient funds were allocated by the Crown to cover the shortfall.

Calais and the Pale were governed through the Deputy of Calais, who, like the other senior officers, was appointed by the king. He represented the king's authority and had wide-ranging delegated powers, including making appointments to subsidiary posts. He was also responsible for ensuring that the town was safe, and the defences and garrison fit for purpose, but this was not easy without adequate funding. The deputy was also expected to be in Calais full time, thus losing direct contact with the king and court. He was supported by the Council of Calais, which was, in effect, a permanent council of war, comprising the treasurer, high marshal, comptroller, high porter and the lieutenants of the castles.

The treasurer – the position held by Sir William Sandys from 1517 until 1526 – was the most important member after the deputy, and the only one apart from the deputy who had authority to make appointments. His main duties were threefold: namely, supervising the Crown finances in Calais, sharing responsibility for defence of the Pale as a member of the Council of Calais, and presiding over the Calais Court of the Exchequer.

Supervising the Crown finances included raising revenue from the Company of the Staple, supplying victuals to and paying the garrison and spies, and letting lands. Copies of the treasurer's accounts were at one time located at The Vyne, including receipts and payments from the town and marches of Calais and the same from the Staple of Calais, but these are now lost. Fortunately, summaries of some of these records have survived in a document at the Hampshire Record Office, which reveals that the accumulated sums were substantial: one note reveals that Sandys collected over £10,000 a year from the Staple alone, and another that he paid £5,000 to Lord Ferrers.[61] A group of fourteen warrants at The National Archives, spanning the first eighteen months of Sandys' time as treasurer, are also useful in this context, some bearing the king's signature, stamped on his behalf, while others are from Thomas Wolsey, and they all provide insight into the wide range of business dealt with by Sandys and his office.[62] Wolsey's usual tone is friendly, as in greetings such as, 'Master Sandys, I commend me unto you in my hearty manor,' and endings such as, 'And fare you heartily well. At our palace before Westminster 13th day of March, your loving friend, Thos. Card' Ebor,' but Sandys did not always act sufficiently quickly for Wolsey. For example, in February, probably 1519, the warrant starts with a curt 'Master Sandys whereas by mine other letters I have signified the

King's pleasure afore' and ends with 'at Westminster the 5th day of February'. Warrants from the king's office start with standard greetings for loyal trusted servants, such as, 'Trusty and right wellbeloved counsellor and Knight for our body Sir William Sandys.'

As might be expected, these warrants relate to diverse financial transactions, as in the examples below, but they all indicate the importance of Calais to English business at that time, and that Sandys was involved in many court activities, albeit indirectly. They also show that bills were not paid quickly.

On 1 November 1517, the king issued a warrant to Sandys about a new suit of armour for himself, and sent John Crochet, Clerk of the Stable at the Greenwich Armoury, to Calais to complete the purchase of a suit made 'over the seas', possibly in Germany, from Boulogne. Henry had already agreed a minimum cost of 100 marks (£66), and if the armourer was content with the suit, he was to negotiate the final price, which Sandys would pay on behalf of the king. On 27 January 1518, a lengthy royal warrant included several payments to cover transportation, the first being £10 for shipping 200 men home from the English garrison at Tournai. Another warrant from Henry required £16 to be paid for the five ships used by Cardinal Campeius and his entourage to travel to England in April 1518, on his mission to persuade Henry to support a crusade. The mission failed. Yet another related to Henry's sister Mary and her return from France after her brief marriage to Louis XII, requiring £10 to be paid for shipping Mary home in 1515. She was presumably travelling with Charles Brandon, the Duke of Suffolk, who had been dispatched to bring her home. They married during the journey, although he was already married, and they did not have Henry's permission.

A warrant from Wolsey related to events on the 13 March 1518, five months after Sandys was tasked with the role of treasurer, when the Master of Posts and his men who operated between Calais and Flanders ceased working because they had not been paid since Sandys had become treasurer, because he lacked a warrant to do so. Wolsey tells him to make up the arrears and pay the wages with immediate effect to restart the service. On 17 July 1518, Wolsey instructs Sandys to pay William Brisewood, the king's Surveyor of Works at Calais, £339 for work already completed, to be taken from the revenues of the town and marches, and to improve the defences. He was also required, with other members of the Council of Calais, to carry out repairs as they saw fit but 'at as little charge as conveniently may be done'.

As a senior member of the Council of Calais, treasurer Sandys shared responsibility for the defences of the Pale with the deputy. The town was divided into segments, and the treasurer was responsible for the south-western part. This included the Boulogne Gate with its protective bulwark outside the walls, and the walls and towers to the west and north-west of that gate up to the castle. The treasurer and other senior council members took turns on watch duty, especially at such times as the herring harvest and smoking period and at Christmas, when an influx of foreigners arrived. The Ordinances for the Watches required that every night during the Banner Watch at herring time, the herring boats and people in them should be counted. The information was passed to the treasurer, who appointed the spears, mounted archers and soldiers for duty. The watch on the first night of the cycle was led by the comptroller, the second by the deputy, the third by the high marshal, the fourth by the treasurer, the fifth by the master porter and the sixth by the under marshal. The councillor on duty was accompanied by the troop of spears, mounted archers and soldiers, and trumpeters, fifers and drummers.[63] The treasurer had his personal retinue of four spears and around fifty soldiers, presumably to accompany him and protect the Treasury and Mint.

The treasurer and the Comptroller of Calais presided over the Calais Court of the Exchequer, which sat in Calais and Guînes and was a powerful force in the Pale, responsible for hearing cases concerning the king's revenues and treasures and dealing with levying taxes and inheritance issues. Commercial agreements required the court's permission and family affairs fell under its jurisdiction, including the guardianship of minors (males under seventeen, females under fourteen) and matters relating to 'lunatics and incapable persons'. Intermarriage between English people and foreigners who wished to reside in the Pale also required the court's permission, and the offspring of mixed marriages needed English names. It was also expected that foreigners who wished to stay should speak English.

For all these duties and the maintenance of his retinue, Sandys as treasurer was paid £1,912 per year, but this varied according to the size of his retinue.[64] His expenses were greater, exceeding £10,000 in 1530. His offices and residence were situated in a complex called the Treasury, which occupied one whole block to the west of St Nicholas's Church, between (appropriately) Penny Lane and Farthing Street. The Treasury was described in the 1556 survey as a great palace, with the Calais Mint and Exchequer. The Mint issued its own coinage and had its own gardens and grounds.[65] The domestic apartments were sufficiently palatial to accommodate royalty, and when Henry VII met with Emperor Maximilian and his daughter Margaret, the Archduchess of Austria, in 1508 she was accommodated at the Exchequer. Her apartment comprised three chambers, decorated with rich tapestries on the walls and a bed draped in cloth of gold. The same fabric covered other furnishings, while crimson velvet was used for the curtains, and woollen carpets covered the floors. There was a separate room for her chamberlain, and space for nine truckle beds for her attendants.[66] In 1520, the Exchequer was occupied by Henry VIII and Catherine of Aragon, prior to moving to their castle at Guînes for the Field of the Cloth of Gold meeting with Francis I. Henry VIII used it again when he took Anne Boleyn to Calais on the way to meet the French king at Boulogne, but on their return from Boulogne to Calais the French king stayed at the Exchequer. A plan of the Exchequer prepared for Henry and Anne Boleyn's visit in 1532 shows a building with multiple courtyards and a tennis court. The king and Anne had separate suites, each with its own garden.[67]

The treasurer's office also occupied the cellars below the county courts in the Town Hall to store the 'King's stuff and Treasure' and held tenements and grounds in the block to the west of the Treasury, as well as land outside the town.[68] All in all, he could be described as a 'large fish in the small but important pond'.

New Roles at Court, New Responsibilities, and Work at The Vyne

Sir William Sandys ceased to be Treasurer of Calais in 1526 when he became King's Chamberlain (see chapter 6), frequently called the Lord Chamberlain of the Household, but retained his Calais connection as he was appointed Lieutenant or Deputy (Governor) of Guînes Castle in the same year, a position held until his death in 1540, and he continued to be a member of the Council of Calais. His position at court as Lord Chamberlain of the Household also meant that he ranked above the Treasurer of Calais and was second only to its deputy.

In order to maintain control over the day-to-day operation of the castle, he appointed a deputy – his son John, who occupied that position for many years. The massive castle was in a dilapidated state, largely due to neglect during the reign of Henry VII. Some reconstruction took place in the 1520s, but it was not until 1532 when Charles Brandon, Duke of Suffolk, was appointed to investigate the state of the castle, aided by Sandys and others, that a major refurbishment programme was carried out.[69]

As Lieutenant of Guînes, William Sandys was paid 2*s* a day plus £27 per year, the same as the Calais deputy, Viscount Lisle, but these relatively modest amounts were supplemented by whatever they managed to retain for themselves out of necessary expenditure on wages and victuals that passed through their hands and from the sale of positions in their patronage. Indeed, it was not unknown for commanders to maintain the number of soldiers below the complement for which they were paid.[70] Sandys also supplemented his income as lieutenant through a licence to sell livestock and grain to Guînes and Hammes.[71]

Several years earlier William Sandys had also joined the oldest British order of chivalry, founded by Edward III in 1348. On 24 April 1518, after four attempts since 1499, his nomination as a Knight of the Order of the Garter was successful, and he was formally installed in St George's Chapel, Windsor, on 16 May, at the same time as Lord Dacre.[72] Membership was reserved for those who had served the sovereign personally or made an outstanding contribution to the country, and the number of knights was restricted to twenty-five and the sovereign. The patron saint was, and is, St George.

Lord Sandys would be a Knight Companion of the Order of the Garter for more than twenty years, so it is appropriate to note the ceremonies that this honour entailed in the reign of Henry VIII, based on Ashmole's *Book of the Garter* and Anstis' *Register of the Order of the Garter*. The editors' appendices to these books include the statutes of the Order of the Garter at that time and Sandys' duties as King's Chamberlain, such as waiting on the king and overseeing his meeting arrangements.

When one of the knights died, a replacement would be elected by the existing knights, each voting for three candidates. Any existing Knight Companion could nominate a candidate. The name of the selected candidate(s) was put to the king, whose decision was final. The knight elect was informed of his honour and was ceremonially invested, usually in the chapter house of St George's Chapel, Windsor. This required him to put his left leg on a stool, and a garter embroidered with the phrase '*Honi soit qui mal y pense*' and decorated with gold and diamonds would be strapped around the leg by a Knight Companion. The king then placed a narrow blue ribbon bearing the 'Lesser George' medallion, which was made of pure gold, weighing around 30 grams and showing an image of St George, around the neck of the knight elect.[73] During the reign of Henry VIII it was decreed that every Garter knight would wear the Lesser George medallion to distinguish him from members of lower orders of knighthood. This essentially completed the investiture, but the knight was not yet a member of the order because that required the installation ceremony, which was usually held in St George's Chapel at Windsor. Before the installation, and at his own expense, the knight elect had to acquire his mantle, collar, cap of velvet, a helm with crest and mantlings (pieces of cloth that hung on either side of the helm), a sword, a banner carrying his arms, a stall plate carrying his full achievement of arms (arms, crest, motto, supporters), a cushion to carry his robes and collar, and plates to put on his allocated lodgings. The helm in Henry VIII's time was steel, burnished with gold, and specifically intended for display as it was larger than a normal helm.[74] On the day before his installation, the knight elect and the other knights would arrive at Windsor Castle early in the afternoon and proceed to the chapel, where they made an offering followed by vespers and a supper to close the day. The next day was the heart of ceremony. It began with a procession of the knights and officers of the order to the chapter house of St George's Chapel. The knight elect was presented formally to the king, speeches were exchanged, and he received his sword and robe. He was then conducted by two Knight Companions to the high altar in St George's Chapel. 'The Black Book of the Garter' in the Windsor Chapel archives includes an illustration of the early part of the installation of a new knight, dated around 1534. Although it depicts an event that did not occur, because it shows all the royal knights from other countries, it clearly shows the arrangement for the ceremony in which the Garter knights proceeded two by two, followed by the officers of the order and then Henry VIII on his own at the rear. Each knight is identified by the coat of arms on his cloak, and all are shown in profile. In a separate image, three knights are abreast at the front of the procession, facing the chapel altar and about to bow before the altar. They have their backs to the viewer and their faces are not visible, but they are identifiable by the coats of arms on the back of their cloaks: these knights are William, Lord Sandys and Sir William Fitzwilliam on either side of a new knight elect, the Grand Admiral of France, Philippe Chabot. In a separate picture King Henry is shown with all his Knights of the Garter – thirteen to the king's right and twelve to his left. All except the king are three-quarter face; the king is full face. These knights are not identifiable except for the royal knights, who are identified by the crowns they wear and are at the front. Because of Sandys' ranking in the order of precedence, and his stall position at the time, it is probable that he is either in the back or middle rows furthest from the king. Following obeisance before the altar, the three knights did the same and the knight elect was conducted to the front of his allocated stall where he took the Oath of the Order. In Henry VIII's time he would be required to swear to defend the honour and dominions of the king and obey the rules of the order. He was then presented with the Garter Collar with its 'Great George' and took his place in his allocated stall. The installation day concluded with an elaborate dinner paid for by the new knight.

In Lord Sandys' time, the Garter Collar was made up of twenty-six enamelled gold medallions, each depicting a white and red double rose encircled by the Garter and linked with gold knots to form the collar. From one medallion hung the Great George, an image of St George slaying a dragon, which was made in gold, usually encrusted with diamonds, and weighing around a kilogram.[75] The Statutes of the Order, issued in 1522, required a Knight Companion to wear the collar with its Great George on many holy days in the Christian

The Collar and Star of a Knight of the Order of the Garter. (Burke, B., *The General Armory of England, Scotland, Ireland and Wales*, London, 1884, p. lxvii)

calendar, including the Feast of St George, and a few secular occasions such as the sovereign's birthday.[76]

Sandys was obviously proud of his membership and regalia, as his depiction in the painted-glass windows of the Holy Ghost Chapel, Basingstoke, shows his surcoat with the Garter Collar and Great George upon it (see chapter 7). He also decorated the Oak Gallery at The Vyne with the coat of arms of the order and a roundel carved with a gilded image of the Great George, while an enlarged replica of a Great George appears over the mantelpiece in the Oak Gallery.

As a member of the order he was expected to attend the main function, which was the Grand Feast of St George celebrated on 23 April. This was normally held in St George's Chapel at Windsor Castle, except for the Grand Dinner, which was held in St George's Hall. These functions extended over three days, 22–24 April. On the first day the king and other knights travelled from the king's lodgings in formal procession to Windsor to attend vespers and a supper. St George's Day began with matins in the chapel, followed by a chapter meeting in the chapter house, after which they returned to the chapel for Mass, during which the Grand Procession was held. This involved the king, knights and officers, all in full ceremonial regalia, leaving the chapel and processing in the grounds of Windsor Castle to return to the chapel. For the Grand Dinner, the hall was decorated with expensive tapestries and cloth of gold, and the salts and plate for the king were of gold while the knights were served on silver gilt plate.[77] The king dined alone at a table on a raised dais, facing the body of the hall, while the Knight Companions were seated at a series of small tables against one long wall and in descending order of rank from the king's table. As a junior knight in 1519, Sandys is on record as being at the last table, which he shared with Sir Henry Marney.[78] Along the other long wall was a sideboard laden with pots, basins and other ware to serve the Knights of the Garter. The body of the hall was filled with officers of the order, courtiers and servers. The amount and variety of food was prodigious, the king being served with fifteen dishes of meat for the first course, while Sandys and the junior knights had only nine. The second course was similar.

On the final day of the feast, a Requiem Mass was held in the morning. If a knight had died since the last meeting his achievements (banner, sword, helm and mantel) were removed from his stall and placed on the altar by Companion Knights, a task undertaken by Sandys on at least two occasions.[79] The day then closed with evensong and supper.

The sovereign could delay (prorogue) the St George's Day feast if circumstances made that desirable, but he would still require his Knight Companions to 'wait on him' on St George's Day. The revised date would be announced in advance, and in Henry VIII's time the prorogued feast was often held around mid-May. Sandys is on record as attending nineteen meetings of the Order of the Garter (see Appendix 1). In some years he attended twice, usually if the celebration of the feast was prorogued, in which case he would wait upon the king on St George's Day and attend the prorogued feast day in May. Occasionally there was a special meeting, such as when the King of France was invested in November 1527.[80] There were some years when Sandys

Interior of St George's Chapel, Windsor. It shows stalls in the chapel, with the king's side on the left to the viewer and the princes' side on the right. William, 1st Baron Sandys' stall position always was close to the viewer because of his relatively low rank in the peerage. (Author's collection, Ashmole, E., *The Institution, Laws and Ceremonies of the Most Noble Order of the Garter*, London, 1672 (facsimile published by Muller, 1971))

failed to attend because of foreign service or sickness, and his last meeting was the Grand Dinner on 17 May 1540.

Each knight was allocated a stall in St George's Chapel, either on the south side, known as the king's side, or the north, called the prince's side. Sandys was allocated the thirteenth stall on the prince's side – the lowest in order of precedence.[81] Throughout the 1520s and 1530s his position fluctuated between twelve and thirteen, but his final position was twelfth on the king's side.[82] Within the chapel each knight's banner of arms, helmet, crest and sword were displayed while he was alive, and his stall plate showed his coat of arms. When the knight died the heraldic symbols were removed, except for the stall plate, so Sandys' plate is still visible.

Henry VIII's arms are displayed on the ceiling of St George's Chapel above the organ loft, surrounded by the coats of arms of the Knights of the Garter of his time, so Sandys' coat of arms is included.[83] His coat of arms is also depicted on the ceiling of St George's Hall, Windsor. When Sandys commissioned painted-glass windows for the Holy Ghost Chapel in Basingstoke, Hampshire, they included an image of him in full armour, wearing a surcoat bearing his coat of arms (a black cross raguly on a silver background) and the collar of the Order of the Garter. A fragment of this glass, showing the collar and surcoat, is now in one of the north windows at St Michael's Church, Basingstoke.[84]

Although Sandys spent most of his time in Calais and northern France from the end of May 1518 until 1526, he succeeded in instigating a major rebuild of The Vyne in that period, converting it from a large mansion house to a Tudor palace, and he also commissioned the refurbishment and expansion of the Holy Ghost Chapel at Basingstoke. He was very conscious of his extended absences, as indicated in a letter to Wolsey on 26 March 1522, which says he is 'here [The Vyne] in his little house, seeing to business which he has not looked on for three or four years, but is hourly at Wolsey's command'.[85] It is also possible that his absence is reflected in a formal complaint against him in the court leet at Basingstoke in November 1518 'that he keeps many more sheep upon the common of the town than he should do, and moreover that his servants misorder their cattle, whereby the many poor men of the town take great damage'.[86]

In summer 1518, soon after Sandys had become a Knight of the Garter, Henry VIII and Francis I reached an outline agreement on the return of Tournai, which had been occupied by the English since 1513. The French sent a team of eighty noblemen and support staff to London to conduct detailed negotiations, and Sandys was tasked by Wolsey with providing shipping to convey 500 horses for the French from Calais to Dover.[87] Although the actual number of horses exceeded 500, the arrangements worked well, and the formal treaty, which included a proposal for Henry's daughter Mary to marry the dauphin, was agreed in October. Tournai would be returned to France in return for a large sum of money, and six high-ranking French hostages would be handed over to the English to ensure that the agreed sum was paid in timely manner. Sandys was Treasurer of Calais at this time, and in November 1518 he and Sir Richard Wingfield, the Deputy of Calais, were authorised to receive the money from the French, and no doubt be responsible for it until it could be forwarded to England. Similar arrangements had been made in May that year for payment of a French instalment relating to the 1514 treaty,[88] and further payments were made in subsequent years.[89] It was also agreed that the two kings would meet on neutral ground to enhance the 'friendship' between them, and later in 1519 both kings gave Wolsey authority to arrange the meeting, which occurred in 1520 and is known as the Field of the Cloth of Gold.

Before Sandys' appointment as Treasurer of Calais, Wolsey had entrusted him with several tasks there. In April 1517, Wolsey issued a commission to 'view the sad ruins and decays and thereupon to advise his Grace (the king) what reformations, reparations and fortifications be necessary—and to examine the ancient ordinances and insufficiencies of the soldiers be necessary'.[90] Sandys was included in that commission, along with Sir Thomas Docwra and Sir Edward Poynings. By May, Sandys and Poynings were in Calais to 'determine disputes and establish the garrison',[91] and in June Wolsey instructed Sandys and others to provide information on ordinances and retinues in Calais.[92] While this work was in progress, Sandys authorised small sums of money for urgent repairs to the Calais moat and its backing wall,[93] but larger sums were subsequently authorised by the original commission for repairs to the fortifications.[94] Almost ten years later, in 1526, another inquiry again reported the dilapidated state of the Calais defences, and when Wolsey visited in 1527 he found that the town 'was in no little disorder, clearly unfurnished in timber, stone and board'. The harbour was also in disrepair, and a large section of the jetty was broken.

Shortly after taking up his appointment as Treasurer of Calais, Sandys and Sir John Peachey, who was later to become deputy for a short period, wrote to Wolsey expressing concern about the governance of the town and dilapidation of its defences. The governance issues arose from the existence of two mayors, one for the town and the other for the Staple, as their duties were poorly defined and both disputed who had pre-eminence, which created confusion in roles and responsibilities. They sought Wolsey's permission to clarify the lines of demarcation between the mayors, but also reported that the town and Pale were falling into disrepair because absentee landlords, including the Duke of Buckingham and Sandys' brother-in-law, Lord Darcy, failed to maintain their properties. They were concerned that the rents, and hence the taxes for the Crown, fell below those that could be realised if properties were in good condition, and asked Wolsey to put pressure on the delinquent landlords to improve their properties.[95] This demonstrates that efforts to restore the town were made while Sandys was treasurer, and that the basic problem was a lack of funding for maintenance and defences to compensate for neglect under Henry VII and in the early part of Henry VIII's reign. This financial struggle to maintain the strength of the town and the Pale would continue until it was lost to the French in 1558.

Two years after he was appointed treasurer, Sandys was rewarded with the lordship of Mark and Oye in the Pale, with its rents and privileges for a period of seven years. Mark and Oye were adjacent villages, which formed a distinct community with a separate identity from Calais and Guînes. Sandys responded in December 1519 by sending Wolsey a New Year gift of a bowl with cover.[96] The area of the lordship was originally very marshy, but English occupation had created effective drainage channels and good arable land, so when it was granted to Sandys its rental value was high.[97] Yet, he needed to be watchful to achieve his due return, because his tenants embezzled him and were not caught until 1521.[98]

In a letter from Calais to his sister, Lady Darcy, dated 4 October 1518, we see a rare glimpse of Sandys' domestic affairs at this time. It concerns the marriage of their sister Ann, who was part of Lady Darcy's household, to Sir Thomas Ilderton. Lady Darcy's husband, Lord Thomas Darcy, had apparently negotiated a deal with Sir Thomas that he would receive 200 marks (£133), 100 each from Lord Darcy and Sir William Sandys, and that the latter would also provide the bride's wedding outfit. Sandys agrees to the arrangement but said he could not provide his share of the money at that time. He asked that Lord Darcy should pay the total sum, but promised to pay his share in two instalments, the first on 1 November along with her wedding outfit, and the second the following Easter.[99] He also explained the reasons for his financial difficulty as 'my charges in the King's wars, suit of my lands, marriage of my children and £400 lent to soldiers of this town until Christmas'. Darcy obviously agreed with the arrangement, as Ilderton acknowledged receipt of his final payment from Darcy in October 1520.[100] In spite of his difficulty regarding the payments to Anne, Darcy found Sandys useful as a supplier of wine, as he obviously had good sources in France through his trade dealings and booty received on pillaging raids.[101]

At court, Sandys used his long-standing position to lobby the king, often through Wolsey, as in November 1519 when he asked Wolsey to persuade Henry to pardon a prisoner in Calais. A month later, he asked a courtier to present the Secretary of Calais, who was visiting London, to Wolsey so that he might 'further his suit'. Whether Sandys sought financial reward is not recorded, but it would be surprising if he did not.[102]

Despite the declarations of peace between Henry and Francis, during their lifetimes local confrontations between the soldiers of the two countries continued on the border of the Pale. Sandys and Sir John Peachey reported to Wolsey on 7 January 1520 that an English soldier was taken prisoner in a skirmish near Guînes, but such incidents did not interrupt preparation for the forthcoming meeting of the two monarchs.[103] Francis had a strong reason to maintain peace with England following the death of Emperor Maximilian in 1519. Maximilian was succeeded by Charles V, nephew of Catherine of Aragon and the Archduchess Margaret, regent of Flanders. Charles had succeeded Ferdinand as King of Castile and Aragon before he inherited Maximilian's empire, which included what is now Belgium, Luxemburg, Holland, Germany, Austria, Switzerland and parts of Italy. This meant that France was effectively surrounded by the empire on land, apart from Calais, which was in English hands. Henry, for his part, sought to enhance his status through meeting with a king of a much richer and larger country.

Setting up the meeting was not a trivial task, because neither monarch wanted to be outshone by the other. The main difficulty was a lack of trust between the two participants. The English lords were suspicious that the French would use this gathering as a precursor to the return of Calais to the French, and the French did little to contradict the notion. There was also concern that the French might use the occasion to kidnap some lords as hostages or start a war on their own territory. The distrust was such that it was agreed that neither king would visit the other's camp when the other king was present; each would visit the other's camp to see the other's queen, effectively acting as a hostage for the other. The English reinforced their network of spies and 'counter spies', and nobles were exhorted to deploy men to keep watch on potential ambush locations and scour the countryside for military activity by the French. To ensure that the nobles carried out this duty, a force of 100 mounted soldiers under Sir Griffith Rhys was employed and tasked with reporting to the king's council daily on the state of security in the Pale.[104]

The location of the royal meeting place was contentious. Ideally, it should have been on neutral territory but neither wanted it to be in Flanders, so it was eventually agreed to meet close to the border of the English Pale between English Guînes and French Ardres. Undaunted by the diplomatic niceties and distrust, the organisers on both sides wanted to demonstrate the magnificence of their lord and his court and overcome the serious problems of accommodation for the kings. Guînes Castle was not considered fit for Henry, and Ardres was in no fit state for Francis, so the solution was to erect temporary accommodation. In March 1520, Wolsey appointed the Lord Chamberlain, the Earl of Worcester, to oversee the works with Sir Nicolas Vaux, Sir William Sandys and Sir Edward Belknap, and execute the king's wishes and Wolsey's plans. The overriding priority was that the king's magnificence should be fully displayed. The commissioners were therefore charged with:

a) Selecting a place close to Guînes for the temporary residence, and, with all diligence and according to a prepared drawing, ensuring that the palace was constructed on time.
b) Selecting, in consultation with their French counterparts, a venue equidistant between Guînes and Ardres where a meeting between the kings would be possible and constructing temporary accommodation and a tournament field where jousting and other military feats of arms on foot or horseback could be performed. The place had to be secure and supported by the necessary tents and pavilions for ladies, nobility and servants.
c) Finding and making lodgings for the army of nobles, gentry, their ladies and servants at Guînes, and arranging a 'solemn, honourable and triumphant' banquet for the French king and his court in the Guînes sector.[105]

Others were commissioned to supply provisions, transport, and lodgings at Calais, clothing for the household, religious services and to keep order.

Although preliminary work had started when these commissions were issued, only ten weeks remained for meeting the deadline of 4 June. The size of the contingent was daunting, given the limitations of the transport facilities at sea and on land, because the king's retinue consisted of 4,544 persons, which was larger than the population of Calais and the Pale. It included high-ranking clerics and courtiers such as Cardinal Wolsey, the Archbishop of Canterbury, two dukes, one marquis, ten earls, twenty-one barons, three Knights of the Garter (including William Sandys) and ninety-seven other knights, all with their servants. In addition, there were armourers, musicians, cooks, tent makers and kitchen staff. The queen's retinue was smaller at 1,260, with a similar mix of people. There were also 3,223 horses to be fed, transported, groomed and accommodated. William Sandys and the two other Garter knights were each allowed two chaplains, two gentlemen, eighteen servants and twelve horses.[106] To add to the logistical problems, Henry required that everyone, including horses, should be in their finest livery throughout the event. To complicate matters further, Henry and the Holy Roman Emperor had agreed to meet in Dover on 30 May, and immediately after the meeting with Francis in Gravelines on the Flemish side of the border, between the Pale and Flanders.

The facilities constructed for the Field of the Cloth of Gold are described by Sidney Anglo in his paper in *The Antiquaries Journal* and summarised here.[107] The temporary palace, located by the bridge over the moat at Guînes Castle, was approximately 300 feet square and two storeys, the configuration of which is not known, but it consisted of four ranges around a central courtyard. The ground floor contained a large entrance hall opposite the entrance gateway, the service and storage areas and a corridor connecting the king's and queen's apartments. The upper floor comprised a range to the left of the entrance gate, containing suites for the king and Wolsey, and one to the right containing apartments for the queen and Mary, Henry's younger sister and former Queen of France. The king's suite consisted of a great chamber, 60 by 42 feet, a dining room 40 by 34 feet, and a withdrawing chamber, 60 by 34 feet. The queen's suite was similar, while the apartments for Mary and Wolsey each comprised three smaller rooms. Between the suites for the king and queen was a room connected by a corridor to a chapel, which included a closet for the king and one for the queen.

Hall's description of the chapel indicates the lavish decoration:

> Also to the same Palace was rered a Chapell with two closettes, the quire of the said Chapell filed with clothe of golde, and thereon frete ingrailed bent clothes of silke, all then was silke and golde. The aultars of this Chapell were hanged with rich revesture of cloth of golde of tissue, embroudered with pearles. Over the High aultar was hanged a rich canaby of merveilous greatness, the aultar was appareled with five paire of candelsticks of golde, and on the aultar an halpas [a high step] and thereon stode a Corpus Domini, all of fine golde, and on the same halpas stoode twelve images of the bigness of a childe of foure yeres of age all gold: And all the Coopes and Vestements so riche as might be

prepared or bought in the city of Florens, for all the copes and vestements were of one piece, so woven for the purpose cloth of tissue and poudered with red roses purled with fine golde: the Orfrys sette with pearles and precious stones. And all the walles and deskes of his chapell was hanged with right Clothe of golde, and three ryche greate Crosses were there ready to be borne at festival times. And basyns and senseres, Gospellers, Paxes, Crewettes, holy water vessels and other ornamentes all of golde. Also in the first closet was a traverse for the Kynges person of cloth of gold: and within that the Kynges place and Chaire, with Cusshins of clothe of golde: before the travers was an aultar of presence, whiche aultar was adourned with clothe of broderie, and rich pearles and precious stones, set in goldsmiths woorke of fine golde. On the aultar was a deske or halpas, whereon stoode a patible [a cross/the horizontal bar of a cross] of the Crucifix of fine golde, with an Image of the Trinitee, an image of oure Lady, and twelve other images all of fine golde, with basens, crewettes. Paxes, and other ornaments, the saied Closet was hanged with Tappettes, embroaudered with rich worke fret with perles and stones, the roffe of the same closet was siled with woorke of Inmoulded gylt with fine Golde and Senepar and Bice. The seconde closet was for the quenes person, in whiche was a traverse of riche clothe of golde, the aultare so richly appareled, that there lacked neither pearle nor stones of riches: on the aultar were twelve great images of golde, the closet hanged with clothe of golde all othe jewelles Missall. I suppose never such like were seen, and the rooffe of the same closet was filed with like work that the kynges closet was as before rehearsed.[108]

Other rooms in the temporary castle and facilities were equally sumptuous, including a large banqueting room on the upper floor. The whole was built on a stone foundation, which supported 8-foot-high brick walls, then a wooden section containing windows glazed with the finest French glass. The exterior wooden walls were painted to resemble bricks and the roof was sealed by oilcloth painted to look like slate tiles. From the queen's apartments there was a corridor leading to Guînes Castle. The temporary castle was sumptuously decorated both inside and out.[109]

The construction of the field for jousting and tournaments was a joint Anglo-French project. It was rectangular, 900 feet long by 220 feet wide, bounded by an outer ditch that was breached by gateways on the two shorter sides. Inside was a stepped gallery for royalty and nobility, stands for spectators, the tilt fence, and arming tents for the two kings. Outside, close to one of the gates, were the arming tents for other combatants.

In addition to these works, the commissioners were required to oversee construction of the pavilions, including the Cloth of Gold pavilion, where the kings would meet and banquet together. Others were for dining, support facilities such as an armoury, a large bakehouse and stables. Vaux, Sandys and Belknap were responsible for organising the accommodation at Guînes,[110] and Sandys had lead responsibility for allocating the sites of the king's hall, tents and pavilions.[111]

Not long after the start of the project the commissioners sought additional manpower and materials from Cardinal Wolsey. Sandys returned to Calais on 16 March, and ten days later wrote to Wolsey urging him to provide more men and timber.[112] On his arrival, he found 140 carpenters and sawyers in action, but they were demanding more money as they had to work longer days and holidays. To keep the project moving, he advanced money to the workmen from his own pocket until Wolsey decided the way forward. Timber was running out, because the 450 tons they had for repairing the town and castle of Guînes would be exhausted by the end of the week.[113] A letter from the commissioners and Sir John Peachey, Deputy of Calais, was sent to Wolsey soon after Sandys' letter, urgently requesting 250 carpenters, 100 joiners, thirty pairs of sawyers, forty plasterers and forty bricklayers. They reported that there were insufficient timber boards in the whole of England, so they had to procure them from Flanders and float them down to Calais.[114] Other similar letters to Wolsey were dated 10 and 18 April, while another from the same group, dated 18 April, responded to a command from the king to provide victuals and horses for him and his nobles, explaining that not enough beef, mutton or fuel was available and provisions would have to come from England. On 21 May the commissioners again wrote to Wolsey to say that if they worked to the king's plans the cost would be great and they doubted they could finish in time. Yet, with great effort and expense, they succeeded. The king arrived at Guînes on 5 June and the ceremonies started on that day as required by the monarchs.

Of the three commissioners, Sir William Sandys was probably the busiest. In late May he returned to England to join the king's retinue during the brief meeting between Henry and Charles V, Emperor Maximilian's successor, at Dover on 26 May, followed by a Whitsun celebration at Canterbury. On 30 May, he was present at the Garter ceremonies at Windsor before taking up duties in France at the meeting between Henry and Francis where he, among others, was commanded to be in attendance on the king. During the jousts and tourneys from 10 to 22 June, Sandys, with three other assistant marshals and a troop of soldiers, policed the jousting field.[115] On 23 June, the festivities were suspended when the kings and queens attended Mass, which was led by Wolsey in a chapel erected overnight on the tournament field. The proceedings concluded on 24 June with visits by Henry to the Queen of France and Francis to Catherine of Aragon, followed by a formal leave taking by the two kings, including the exchange of gifts. Much had been expected from the meeting, but in the end it was considered a 'fruitless and heartless display'.[116]

The English royal party did not immediately return home but stayed in Calais to meet again with Charles and the Lady Margaret, Charles's aunt and his regent in Flanders. On 4 July, Charles's ambassadors arrived in Calais to finalise details. Sandys, as Treasurer of Calais, and Sir Edward Ponyngs, Treasurer of the King's Household, were tasked with organising the meeting place for Henry and Charles at a location equidistant between Calais and Gravelines. Another one of the commissioners at the Field of the Cloth of Gold, Sir Edward Belknap, was responsible for the necessary organisation at the Staple Inn in

Calais, where the emperor and Lady Margaret were accommodated, and where Henry entertained Charles and his party. The rest of the emperor's party were in lodgings appointed by the Deputy of Calais, Sandys, and other members of the Council of Calais. The first meeting took place in the afternoon of 10 July. The following day Henry, escorted by 200 nobles and guards, visited Charles for a day and a half at Gravelines, before the whole party returned to Calais to be entertained by the English. The next day was Sunday, so everybody attended Mass, followed by supper, a banquet, dancing and entertainment. After a farewell dinner on Monday, the royals returned to their home countries. This meeting was much friendlier than the meeting with Francis and cemented relations between the two royal families and their countries for several years, much to the annoyance of Francis. The English royal party arrived back in England on 18 July, and those responsible for organising both meetings, including Sandys, must have felt relieved when the events concluded without any recorded mishaps.

It was not long before the French reacted by starting to rebuild the derelict fortress of Ardres, to the consternation of the English in Calais and at home. Sandys kept watch on developments and wrote separately to Henry and Wolsey on 6 October from Calais to say that work at Ardres had ceased but he would keep an eye on the situation. No reason was suggested for the cessation of work on the fortress at Ardres, but the French king may have realised that he should focus on the emperor rather than Henry. Sandys also suggested to the king that the proposed work to reinforce Guînes Castle need not proceed because he thought it could be defended as was, but he requested that repairs to Calais town and its fortifications should begin that year.[117] He remained in Calais until mid-March 1521.[118]

Sandys clearly had no concern about writing directly to the king, a practice that continued when he worked for Wolsey and later Cromwell, but although the king recognised Sandys as a trusted colleague he does not appear to have confided in him on State matters until the middle of 1521. At this point there is evidence of a change, when Henry instructed Wolsey to give both Sandys and Sir Thomas More information on negotiations being conducted at Calais, presumably with the King of France and the Holy Roman Emperor.[119]

A little earlier, in spring 1521, Sandys was involved in a less pleasant matter following the king's decision that the Duke of Buckingham had overreached himself to the point of committing treason. Buckingham was tried and convicted at Westminster and sentenced by the Duke of Norfolk to be 'hanged, cut down alive, your members to be cut off and cast in the fire, your bowels burned before you, your head smitten off and your body quartered and divided'. It was Sandys and his erstwhile fellow commissioner in preparations for the Field of the Cloth of Gold, Sir Nicholas Vaux, who escorted the condemned duke through the city to the Tower: 'Sir William Sandys having him by the right arm and Sir Nicholas Vaux by the left arm'. Henry subsequently reduced the duke's sentence to beheading, carried out on 17 May at Tower Hill, and his head and body were buried in the church of the Augustinian friars.[120]

During the summer of 1521, Sandys was the subject of debate between Wolsey and Henry about the leadership of a force of 6,000 archers to go to France to defend Calais against the French. Henry wrote to Wolsey on 28 July, agreeing that it was necessary to raise such a force and that he favoured the Lord Marquis, or the Earl of Shrewsbury, or the Earl of Worcester as leader.[121] Wolsey's response, dated 31 July, suggested that Sandys should lead, because 'a captain of lower degree might suffice for this time and amongst others in my opinion a more valiant, apt and convenient person could not be devised than Sir William Sandys, Treasurer of Calais [a few illegible words] and well determined mind to do unto you acceptable service is well known'.[122] Henry replied at the beginning of August that 'the King will have more need of him at home, and cannot with his honour send an army out of his realm under any captain lower than an Earl ... and as many good knights of experience must go with it, they would distain to be under Sandys'. Wolsey responded that he did not accept the case that Sandys should not be the leader because of his low rank, then praised the leaders favoured by the king before adding that 'some of the best knights ... were better minded to go because Sandys was named as their chieftain'.[123] He wrote again on the 7 August, reiterating his belief that Sandys should lead, but Henry replied that he had made up his mind and the Earl of Essex was his choice, thus ending the debate.[124]

It is surprising that Wolsey chose to pursue the matter after the king had made his view clear. Perhaps he thought it was time that Sandys was elevated to the peerage, and it is worth considering why that had not happened. He was around fifty-one years old and both the king and Wolsey obviously thought highly of him as a soldier and administrator, but he had not been entrusted with diplomatic missions of any consequence nor was he a policymaker. They recognised him as a trusted servant of the king, almost to the point of sycophancy. Henry was not against promoting commoners, as shown by his elevation of Wolsey and later Cromwell to high office, and he made that point in 1536 when one of the challenges against him by the Pilgrimage of Grace rebels was that so many of his councillors were noblemen. He replied that only two were worth calling noble by birth – the Treasurer of England, Thomas Howard, and the High Steward, George Earl of Shrewsbury – while the rest were 'scant well born gentlemen' before their elevation. Sandys was included in that category, and his correspondence suggests that he was courteous and rather ponderous.[125] Although he shared an excessive spending habit with other courtiers, he does not appear to have jousted in royal tournaments or participated in the elaborate court masques, unlike Charles Brandon, Duke of Suffolk, who enjoyed both and became and one of Henry's favourites from an early age. It seems that Sandys was content to assist with the organisation and administration of events, like the Field of the Cloth of Gold and the celebrated banquet given by Wolsey in 1527, and did not resemble the character with his name in Shakespeare's play about Henry VIII, which depicts him as lightweight, flirtatious and garrulous when seated next to Anne Boleyn, who called him a 'merry gamester' after he kissed her.[126] It is also unlikely that he behaved like the Lord Sands described in *The Household of Sir Thomas More*, who sings a ballad called 'The King's Hunt Is Up' and is portrayed sitting down, stamping his feet and raising his arm.[127] The historical evidence suggests that he was neither a statesman nor an intimate in Henry's social life, so it is not surprising that promotion came later in life.

In the meantime, Wolsey was commissioned to 'settle the differences between Francis and Charles' and travelled to Calais,[128] arriving on 2 August, to lead a conference to arrange a peace treaty between the three powers.[129] He was accompanied by a large escort of lords and esquires, including Sir William Sandys in his retinue, but the conference failed and by September the emperor and King of France were effectively at war with each other.[130] Wolsey returned to England on 27 November, preceded by Sandys, who soon returned to Calais – probably in the early New Year.[131]

It was not long before England was involved in confrontation because several incidents occurred between the French and English before hostilities were declared. On 6 March 1522, the French arrested all Englishmen in Bordeaux, and the Earl of Surrey was preparing the royal navy for war. The threat of conflict was probably the reason why Sandys brought his wife and children home from Calais to The Vyne in spring 1522,[132] and she did not return with him to Calais that year.[133] It was not unusual for the wives of senior courtiers to accompany their husbands to Calais, just as Lady Lisle accompanied her husband, Lord Lisle, when he was Deputy of Calais in 1533–40.[134] Sandys clearly missed his family, as he wrote to Lady Lisle from Guînes in 1536 describing himself as 'in my lonely wise'.[135]

When Sir William Sandys brought his family home in 1522 he was certainly in England and at The Vyne by March,[136] but before the end of April he was on his way to Calais, where Charles V wrote to him asking for the release of two Englishmen in the service of the empire who had been taken prisoner by officers in Calais for 'doing their duty against my enemies'.[137] On 2 May, Sandys wrote to Wolsey from Calais, seeking instructions concerning the emperor's forthcoming visit there and warning that French troops were gathering in Picardy. Another note, dated 6 May, warned Wolsey that the French were mustering large numbers of troops in the area, and that they had commandeered 1,500 tuns of wine owned by English merchants from Bordeaux.[138]

Although the situation was rapidly deteriorating, the emperor's visit to England went ahead. The Lord Marquis of Dorset, the Earl of Essex and the Bishop of Exeter, accompanied by Sandys and other members of the Council of Calais, except for the deputy and the porter, escorted the emperor's party from Gravelines in Flanders to Calais, where they were welcomed on 25 May by the deputy and the porter, and the mayors of the Staple and Calais itself. The council was responsible for providing lodgings, victuals and entertainment for the emperor and his party, who then sailed from Calais to England to be met by Henry and Wolsey.[139] The visit included the drafting of a treaty, which required the English to support the Holy Roman Emperor's forces by invading France, so war with France was inevitable. The English would attack from Calais in the north, the emperor from the south through Spain, and the Duke of Bourbon from the south-east.

Conflict between the English and French over the next eighteen months again demonstrated Sandys' talents as a fighting soldier and led to his elevation to the peerage. In a letter to Wolsey, he made it clear that his wife and brother, presumably Richard, were not with him in Calais at this time, so it seems he was expecting trouble, but as Marjorie was in England, she would have time to supervise the remodelling work at The Vyne.[140]

Sandys' military activities from 1522 are described more fully than previously by the contemporary chroniclers, who recognised his new status in the king's eyes. Action started in earnest in the first days of June when around 1,000 French attacked Calais, but they were not successful.[141] This was followed by a mocking letter from the Captain of Boulogne who challenged the Marshal of Calais, Sir Edward Guildford, to battle. Guildford and Sandys accepted and left Calais with 1,200 men, but the Captain of Boulogne failed to appear. Guildford, Sandys and their men then set fire to Marguison and villages nearby, and 'all the crew came home with good pillage'.[142] It is worth noting that Hall and others do not mention Sandys' involvement in this raid, but a letter from Sandys to the king dated 22 June says, 'Since he was at Marguison, the French have kept at home and not meddled with the Pale.' He also wrote to Wolsey that he was trying to get support from the emperor's men but without success, and that he had reinforced Guînes Castle with bows, arrows, pikes, powder and shot. The shortage of fuel and food in Calais was becoming desperate, because English merchant ships would not operate without naval protection after a ship carrying large quantities of wheat was sunk by the French outside Calais harbour. Sandys concludes a letter to Henry on 27 June with: 'To keep this town secure the seas must be made safe.'[143]

On 21 June, the Earl of Surrey, Thomas Howard, who was on board the *Mary Rose* off the Isle of Wight, reported that he had embarked 5,000 men and the fleet was ready to sail to France but was short of beer, meat and fish.[144] Nevertheless, they sailed, arriving in Brittany on 1 July, and attacked and sacked the town of Morlaix before sailing into and attacking Brest. The English fleet then returned to Cowes on the Isle of Wight with their booty.

Meanwhile, on 3 July the French attacked Guînes and killed the few English and Welshmen who left the castle to oppose them. Then, on 25 July, Sandys and Guildford decided to attack Boulogne, and especially its captain whom they deemed to be a 'great mocker and coward', so they left Calais with a force of 1,300 men. When the captain again failed to respond, they attacked the town of Wissant and set fire to it. The townspeople fled to the church, which was fortified, so the English attacked and took it. Some people were trapped in the steeple, which caught fire; those who jumped were killed, and any who survived were taken prisoner. A marginal note in Holinshed's chronicle for July reads, 'Sir William Sandys and Sir Edward Guildford; two whips to the Frenchmen.'

Back in London it was decided that all French and Scots resident in England were to be imprisoned and their goods seized. The war was escalating. Henry and the council decided to send a major expedition to France under the leadership of Thomas Howard, the Lord Admiral, later Duke of Norfolk. In the meantime, Sandys dispatched Sir Rhys ap Thomas and 100 horsemen to Guînes from Calais and moved himself to Newnham Bridge.[145] On 4 July, he wrote to Wolsey to warn him that the French forces were increasing and seemed to be preparing a two-pronged attack on the Pale.[146] They needed to be alert. On 22 July, 400 French soldiers passed Calais town and attacked the lodgings of some Welsh soldiers quartered in a nearby village; they destroyed the lodgings and took the horses, but the Welshmen survived by running naked into the surrounding marshes. In Hall's words, this happened because of a lack of 'good watch'.[147] By 16 August, Sandys had made a short visit to England, possibly to plead for more supplies, but it may have been in response to charges against him that he had illegally commandeered a cargo that belonged to London-based Spanish subjects. No more was heard on this matter, so it is assumed that it was settled, but it indicates that Sandys was able to confiscate shiploads if he thought they were French. Back in Calais there were shortages, particularly of beer, and there was no point in sending a large force from England unless the logistics were improved.

Thomas Howard went to Calais around that time, with his force in Spanish ships provided by the emperor. After that, the supply of goods began to improve, but it remained inadequate throughout. Howard assembled his army into three wards or divisions, the first led by Sir Robert Radcliffe, Lord Walter, the middle by himself, and the rear by Sir William Sandys and Sir Richard Wingfield.[148] On 19 August, Howard wrote to the king about the shortage of provisions, informing him that there was no beer, and bread would only be available if the wind was favourable to operate the mills. He also said that if Sandys had not taken great pains to grind wheat with horse mills and hand mills day and night, they would already be without bread, and that the rest of the army should not be sent over until more provisions were available.

It seems that additional supplies arrived, because on 30 August the army left Calais to arrive in Guînes on Monday 1 September, and the following day they joined up with Burgundian troops supplied by the emperor at Ardres on the English–French border. Sandys described this campaign in three letters, one to the king and two to Wolsey.[149] They are generally in line with the reports of the chroniclers, but their tone indicates that Sandys was in his element carrying out these devastating raids. He reported that they could not move quickly because of the scarcity of supplies and that, while at Ardres, Howard sent out raiding parties that destroyed some villages and took prisoners. On Saturday 6 September the main army moved to a place they called Lodingham:

> Burning everything in our way for the space of five miles in length and eight in breadth. As the church was fortified more like a house of war than the house of God the council ordered it to be burnt. On Monday the 8th, we moved to Daverne, where we threw down the town and castle, and burned down another town called Samere de Boyse [Samer] which was fortified like

> a castle with all the castles and country round about eight miles in diameter. Thursday the 9th we removed to Burthes [Bourthes], destroying the country as before. By the way, 400 Frenchmen made a show to us, but vanished without any meddling. We shall remove to Fauxe in the Emperor's dominions and there consult about our further course. As for the Boulonnais, from Harlow [Hardelot?] to within six miles of Guînes we have swept them clean, both of corn, cattle and housing. Cannot hear of any assembling of the French yet. Victual is becoming scarce and always brings us to a standstill; yet the Lieutenant is marvellously well disposed and so are all here. from Burthes [Bourthes] 10th September.

It seems that after ten days of destruction of French lands and towns, the French were not prepared to rise to the challenge. Furthermore, the allied army did not know what it was going to do next. Two days later, Sandys wrote to Wolsey:

> On Tuesday the 9th we camped at Burthes. Next morning we set the town on fire and proceeded to Fauxe in Artois where we shall consult about further proceedings. On our progress we burned Hughclere, a goodly castle of the Duke of Vendome, with the village it stood in. That day the French appeared again but soon avoided. On Tuesday two of my archers were taken and bought to Montrell. I wrote to the Duke of Vendome for their redemption, on which he wrote to my lord lieutenant that if he would put in writing the ransoms of all prisoners according to their degrees, the Duke would do likewise. No answer has been made to this. The Duke complained about our burning, saying it was a foul war and that he had knowledge of the burning of his castle and would revenge it upon Beaurayn [one of the emperor's men] who lay in it the night before. Today again the French showed themselves and departed in the same fashion as before ... are to leave for Frigies where we shall destroy the town and castle; thence to Dorlans [Doulens]. All this day we still lay at Fauxe waiting for the arrival of victuals, which are very scanty. If we were not obliged so frequently to wait for victuals we might have done better service.
>
> Fauxe 12 September

The last letter from Sandys was sent on 22 September: '... advanced to Hedyn [Hesdin], reached there on the 16th ... Were advised it could be taken in 6 hours; attacked it without success ... The Lord Lieutenant has sent for more powder and Sir Edward Guildford at St Omers.'

On 22 September, the allies agreed that the castle could not be taken without mining, which would take a long time. They moved on to Doulens, which they burned and destroyed. The emperor's contingent began to depart, and disease broke out among them and the English, so the campaign was called off. The English then turned northwards to Calais, where they arrived on 16 October. Finally, Thomas Howard sent Sandys, Sir Morice Berkeley and Sir William Fitzwillam to burn Marquison again along with the neighbouring villages, which

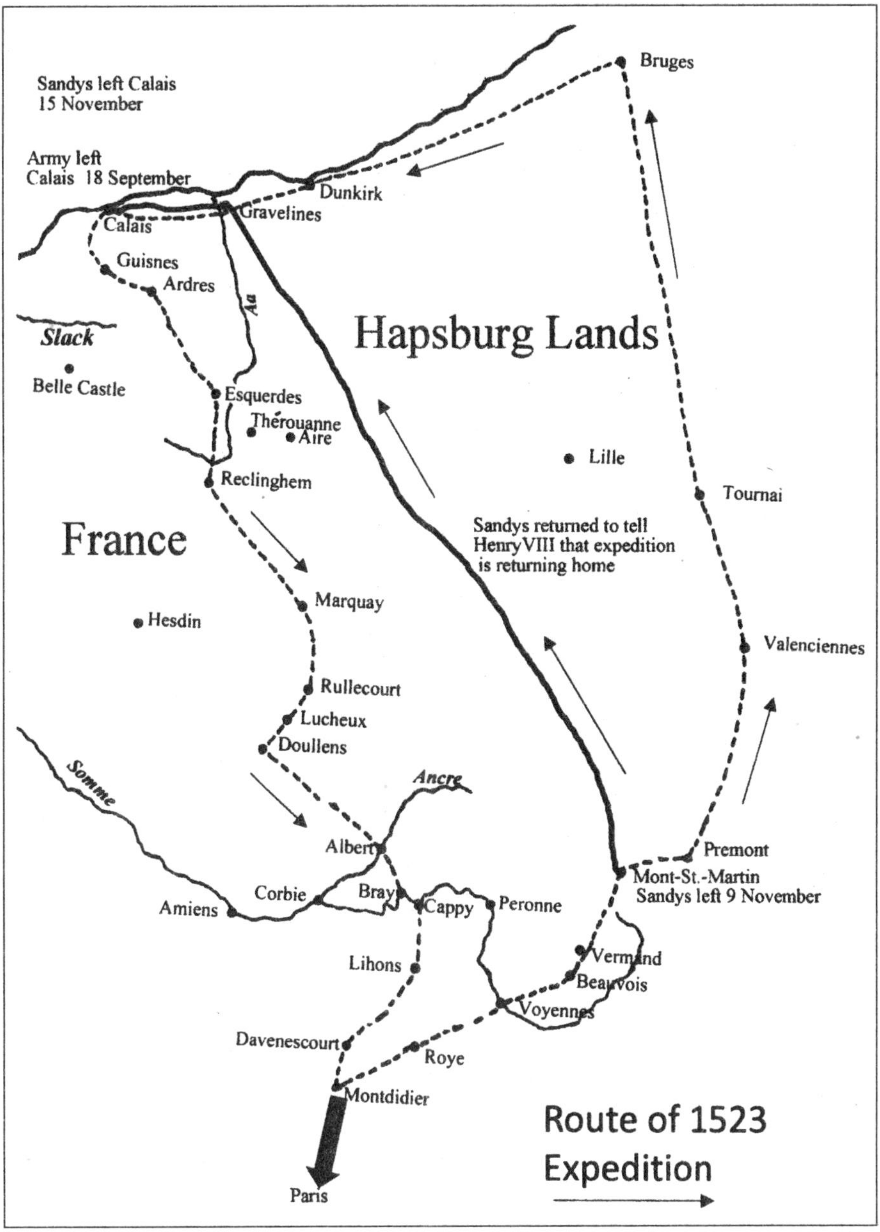

William, 1st Baron Sandys, High Marshal of the Army, was deputed by the War Council to leave the main body of the army to inform Henry VIII that the expedition had failed. The head of the expedition, the Duke of Suffolk, stayed in Calais for several months fearful of the king's wrath. (Author's collection)

they did, returning with '1,200 sheep, 1,400 cattle, 800 hogs and 1,100 horses'. Howard returned to England with his men, where he was welcomed by the king, but this was another expensive expedition for little gain. Sandys stayed in Calais at least until 2 December, when Margaret of Austria wrote, asking for troops to help her forces, but there is no evidence that he responded.[150]

The year 1523 was to be another busy one for Sandys. In February he was in Calais, then back in England in April when his efforts as soldier and administrator were formally recognised by the king.[151] On 27 April, he was made baron with the title William, Lord Sandys of The Vyne. On the same day Sir Arthur Plantagenet was made Viscount Lisle, and Sir Thomas Boleyn, Sir Morris Berkley and Sir Nicholas Vaux were made barons.[152] They took their seats in the House of Lords on the first day of the 1523 Parliament, which had been called to grant funding for the king's battles in France.

However, Sandys had no time to sit in the House of Lords for the rest of the 1523 session, because he soon returned to Calais and was back in action against the French. As he was now Lord Sandys, his actions are reported by the chroniclers in more detail than before, particularly by Hall, but we can assume that his approach to fighting did not change because a dramatic change of style after April 1523 is most unlikely. For this reason, and because evidence is available, more space can be devoted to his martial activities.

Lord Sandys and Martial Duties

On the war front there were minor skirmishes around Calais, but there is no record of Sandys' involvement. This situation changed on 24 May 1523, when activity escalated and Sandys was very much to the fore. The French decided to attack Calais and it was necessary to create a blockade to prevent goods and men entering the harbour, so they loaded an old ship with 400 tons of stone and removed her main mast, which gave the impression that she was in trouble. The ship was sailed from Dieppe towards Calais harbour, and at ten o'clock on the night of 24 May the skeleton French crew abandoned it in the harbour entry and set the hull on fire, expecting it to sink and block the channel. Fortunately for the inhabitants of the town, the ship drifted off course and did not sink in the shipping lane. The following day, after the fire had died out, the Council of Calais, including Sir William Sandys, wrote to the Captain of Boulogne thanking him for the gift of the stone, which would be used in the town fortifications. The deputy, treasurer and the lieutenant of the town also decided to mount an expedition of 100 men against the French, which set off and succeeded in removing 'great booti'. The French garrison retaliated with 500 men, resulting in forty-six French and twenty-two Englishmen being killed and the French taking twenty prisoners. Hall reports the English response as follows: 'The Lord Sandys, Treasurer of Calais, intending to be revenged on the Frenchmen, called the council together and declared to them that the Frenchmen and especially the Captain of Boulogne daily imagined to destroy the English Pale and that on the English part they had done nothing yet against them.'[153] It was time for action, and Sandys would lead it. Early in the morning of 9 July the town was closed by 200 horsemen to prevent people leaving, while Sandys and his men with light ordnance left Calais and reached the River Slack around 9 kilometres north of Boulogne, arriving on the morning of 10 July. When the Captain of Boulogne saw the English force, he met them with seventy men-at-arms and 400 men on foot. Hard fighting began at four o'clock in the morning and did not end until nine o'clock, when the French were overcome. Hall attributes this success to Sandys: 'Before the skirmish was ended, came the Lord Sandys with his footmen, with his spear on his thigh and his helm on his head and greatly encouraged his campaign.' Some of the French retreated to the fortified church of Odirsell (possibly Audresselles), but when Sandys found out he marched to the church, which the French were defending vigorously with handguns, crossbows and pikes, and ordered that the church be attacked with cannon. The shot went through the church, causing the French to surrender; seventy-two Frenchmen then left the church and were taken prisoner. Other French soldiers had retreated to the church of Odyngham (perhaps Audinghen), which was also fortified, and defended it until the steeple caught fire. They were forced to surrender at midnight on 10 July and forty were taken prisoner. Only then did Sandys set up camp for the night. Early next morning he summoned the priests of the two churches and told them that they should not be men of war, but that he would not keep them as prisoners on this occasion. He also gave a clear message that if they repeated this action, he would hang them on the next gallows. When the English broke camp at eight o'clock in the morning they marched to Hedyngham Castle, which they destroyed and burned. Sandys returned to Calais on 11 July, having gained 'great store of bestiall and pillage'. He lost twelve of the 700 men with whom he had set out, but he must have felt that he had taught the Captain of Boulogne a lesson.[154]

Meanwhile, in England, Henry was preparing for yet another large-scale invasion of France. He and the Holy Roman Emperor had agreed at the end of 1521 to wage war on France in the summer of 1523. Early that year the plan seemed to be going nowhere, but the two rulers then received word that the powerful Duke of Bourbon would change his allegiance from the French king to the emperor. This would form a powerful coalition, including Henry, the emperor, and the Duke of Bourbon. It was agreed that Charles Brandon, Duke of Suffolk, would lead an allied army, and Sir William Sandys was named as High Marshal of the Army in recognition of his military and administrative expertise. A grand three-pronged assault on France was devised, by which the emperor would attack France from northern Spain, Henry from the north through Calais, and Bourbon from the east. It was anticipated that Paris would be taken, and France divided up among the allies. This seemed a good strategy, but it apparently ignored the fact that France had persuaded the Scots to attack northern England, and that France and the emperor were fighting in Italy and Flanders, so most of western Europe was at war, which would diminish the resources available for any one front. There was also disagreement between the emperor and Margaret of Austria, his regent in

Flanders, over resources she could provide, as she was already committed to conflict with the Duke of Gelders, and the degree of commitment by Duke of Bourbon was unknown. Other divisions emerged over the objective. Henry's ambition to enlarge the Pale by taking Boulogne and its hinterland was realistic and probably viable, and Henry would end up with another French port, but Wolsey was more ambitious and persuaded Henry to cooperate in the grand plan to divide France between them.

The campaign is described in detail by Hall, Sir John Daunce and Elis Gruffudd, who reflected more of the battlefield experience.[155] Steven Gunn published his detailed account in the *English Historical Review* in 1986, providing an excellent retrospective view of the war.[156] This account will therefore focus on Lord Sandys' activities as described by the chroniclers and mentioned in the *Letters and Papers* of Henry VIII.

After Brandon's appointment as leader at 100*s* a day, Sandys was appointed High Marshal of the Army Royal at a wage of 20*s* a day. There were over 12,000 soldiers in the English/Welsh contingent, made up of 600 demi-lances, 200 mounted archers, 3,000 archers, 5,000 bill men and 2,600 pioneers and labourers. They were joined by another 1,700 men from the garrisons at Calais and the Pale, who were significant as seasoned campaigners who knew northern France, unlike many of the others. Sandys was put in charge of the vanguard, Charles Brandon the middleward and Sir Richard Wingfield, the rearward. The right wing was the responsibility of Sir William Kingston, while Sir Everard Digby was in charge of the left wing, and Sir Edward Guildford was captain of the horsemen.[157] Unlike the army raised the previous year, this one was well equipped and supported by Dutch gunners and professional miners, but it was short of heavy cavalry and the wagons that were essential for maintaining a supply train, which were to be provided by Margaret of Austria.[158]

Sandys was ferried to Calais on 12 August 1523 with the Master of Ordnance and others, followed by the main body of the army with the Duke of Suffolk, and reached Calais on 24 August.[159] This coincided with an outbreak of smallpox in the town, and after losing some to the pox Brandon moved the men out of Calais on 9 September.[160] The campaign proper did not start until 18 September, because of a lack of baggage and food wagons, but the fighting season was already ebbing away. The English/Welsh soldiers were joined a few days later at Ardres by the Captain General of the Netherlands, Florys van Egmont, Graaf van Buren,[161] one of the few Continental commanders respected by Sandys. This admiration seems to have been reciprocated, because Van Buren signs himself 'Florys' in letters to Sandys.[162] Buren suggested a diversionary attack on Belle Castle, which was close to Boulogne and west of their position,[163] and known to be relatively weak with only around sixty men defending it, as this would serve to 'settle in' the army, exercise a siege attack, boost morale and perhaps confuse the French over the direction of the campaign. This was agreed, and Brandon sent Sandys with Lord Ferrers and 500 Burgundian horsemen and 500 foot soldiers, while Sir William Skevington was in charge of the guns and gunners.[164] On the night of 26 September, Sandys moved out of camp and arrived at Belle Castle before 4 a.m. Skevington and his gunners pounded it from four until six o'clock, and Skevington had a lucky escape when a bullet went through his sleeve without hurting him.[165] The walls were breached, and Sandys with his men stormed through the opening and took the castle.[166] Skevington was given the honour of formally receiving the surrender of the castle, and the allied army soon took it and left with pride and lots of booty, arriving back at the main camp on the evening of 28 September. Suffolk then proceeded south to meet the 3,000 footmen from Spain, Germany and Cleves and 500 heavy cavalrymen provided by the emperor at Esquerdes.[167]

At this stage the logistics train was working well, as the cargo ships were getting into Calais from England thanks to the English navy, and there was sufficient cartage to supply the front line. The agreed strategy, proposed by Buren, was to rapidly move towards the east of Paris,[168] where they would meet the Duke of Bourbon who had finally decided to join the allies. Paris would then be attacked and this, combined with the emperor's incursion from Spain, would split France. Apart from the weather, which was worsening, things looked good for Henry, Margaret and the emperor.

On 28 September, the allied army moved south and, according to plan, bypassed the strongly fortified towns of Thérouanne, Hesdin and Doullens, as the first target was the walled town of Ancre. On 17 October, Suffolk again called on Sandys, and he and 3,000 men marched towards Ancre expecting a battle, which did not happen as the French had departed. When they had taken their booty, a garrison was left in the town.[169] The rest marched on to Bray on Somme where they arrived on 20 October. The town was heavily fortified, protected by ditches that were 35 feet deep and garrisoned by 2,000 fighting men.[170] It was not an easy target, but it was necessary to take it as it guarded the easiest crossing of the River Somme in that part of France, so the allied army attacked the fortress with heavy guns, starting at four o'clock in the morning. Unlike at Belle Castle, they met heavy return fire, but after five hours of bombardment they had opened a gap 'as broad as a cart in the walls beside a tower at the corner of the town'. Inspired by Sandys' example, the English, Burgundian and Flemish troops crossed the deep ditches before being confronted at the walls by defenders armed with pikes, halberds, guns and crossbows, but the French eventually gave way and the English followed the fleeing defenders and 'killed and slew in every part'.[171] The retreating French foot soldiers fled across the bridge and narrow causeway that crossed the river and marshes to the south. Some protection was given by French horsemen, who waited to keep the escape route open. The French also tried to destroy the bridge but were not quick enough, and many French were driven into the marsh where they drowned. The southern end of the causeway was defended by two large earthen bulwarks, which the allies took after a fierce exchange, and the remaining defenders were captured. At the northern end of the town, Suffolk, with the rest of the allied army and baggage train, found the gate blocked by a great mound of earth and dung, which had to be removed to allow the bulk of the army and its carts to pass. Before they left, the defenders had strewn the town with gunpowder, which they lit on their departure, so when the English returned it was ablaze and there was little plunder, except for some wine. The bridges were quickly repaired, and on the following day, 21 October, the vanguard led by Lord Sandys prepared to cross the river, but some refused because they believed they would not be able to have victuals brought to them. Sandys heard the shouting and said, 'Sirs behold what I do, and with that he took a banner of Saint George and said as many as love the king of England and be true to him and to the crown, follow me. Then he and Sir William Kingston set forward and passed the water which ran in three streams and then all other persons courageously followed, and the ordinance and victuals.'[172] Sandys and the vanguard set up camp on the south side of the river by the bulwark and were relatively comfortable.

More trouble was brewing in the rearguard led by Lord Ferrers. The men were kept on a marshy slope, so their feet were sodden, and the weather was very wet. Being cold and wet made them unhappy to the point that some of the Welshmen turned and re-entered the remains of the town to seek shelter and warmth.[173] Unfortunately, this was portrayed to Suffolk as a mutiny among the Welshmen, as he was told that they had started to march back to England. The War Council met, and some wanted to 'hang all the Welshmen, others to kill them', but Suffolk decided not to follow this advice, no doubt partly because his numbers had been reduced through disease. The next morning he sent men to get bread, which they did and paid for it, while Elis Gruffudd records that they found plenty of wine, corn for making bread, sheep, fat pigs, and cattle.[174] Suffolk also recalled the men he had left at Ancres, and the whole force crossed the river and the bridge and boats were destroyed. He had mustered all the men, including wagoners, and found that no more than 10,000 were left out of the total of 15,000 after Van Buren's men had joined them.[175] Although many had been lost and signs of discontent were growing, the War Council decided to continue towards Montdidier. They found the town of Cappy abandoned by the French, so there was no fighting. Perhaps the reputation of Suffolk's army had preceded it.

On 27 October, the army arrived at Montdidier, to be confronted by a heavily fortified town garrisoned by 2,000 foot soldiers and 1,000 horse soldiers. The allies immediately sent their heralds to demand surrender, but to no avail. The French sent out a large company of men-at-arms, but after losing forty they returned. Suffolk then encamped and prepared for a siege. In the meantime, a French commander, Lord Pontdormy, heard about the siege and mustered a force of 150 men-at-arms and many footmen to try to supply the town with gunpowder and other supplies. They approached by night but were intercepted by English scouts under Thomas Palmer and a fierce skirmish followed, providing the English with many prisoners.[176] While this was going on, the allies were digging trenches and setting up the big siege guns. At four o'clock in the morning the great guns started to batter the walls and continued for five hours, by which time the walls were ready for assault and the French ready to parley. It was agreed that the soldiers and inhabitants could leave the town, but without their goods. Lord Sandys led the team to receive the town, and the allies entered and raised their standards. This was followed by a dispute, because it had been agreed that the French soldiers should leave their arms, but they started to march out with them. Sandys said that they could not do so, which led to an altercation, but he insisted, and the French soldiers departed empty handed, leaving much equipment behind. Initially, the allied soldiers found that valuable goods had been taken,[177] but Elis Gruffudd tells us that he knew that the town was built on limestone containing a network of caves and describes his discovery:

> [We] went through the ashes that were smouldering in the courtyard of one of the houses which had caught fire the night before ... they found an upper cellar which contained only a few vessels of wine. From there they took a wide stair going down which they followed till they found the floor of a cave which was very spacious. Through this cave and others they went until they came underground to the other end of the town where they found a great deal of worldly wealth, had there been means of carrying it from there: honey, wine, leather, pieces of pewter and salt of which some of the lower cases were full.[178]

He goes on to say that around the town there was plenty of fodder and wine and the fattest pigs he had ever seen. Others found feather beds and linen. A French account says that the town was pillaged for six days and partly destroyed by fire, and the same author was justified when he wrote that the English and the Burgundians were held in equal dread.[179] Sussex summoned the War Council to decide on the next move. The options were:

1) To stay in Montdidier and wait for the Duke of Bourbon then continue to Paris, around 55 miles away.
2) To attack Paris without the support of the Duke of Bourbon.
3) To make a tactical retreat and move north-east towards Artois to shorten the supply train, and overwinter close to or in Burgundian territory. This would also provide a place where they could meet the Duke of Bourbon.

They chose the third option without knowing that the Bourbon invasion had failed and the duke had fled to Italy, but they knew that they lacked enough men to defend Montdidier and their extended supply line, or to take Paris, and that they were short of munitions, especially gunpowder. This option would serve to bring them closer to Burgundy, the emperor's territory, thus reducing the length and fragility of the supply chain. The decision did not please the soldiers, who fancied staying in Montdidier over the winter where they would be comfortable in deteriorating weather, but Suffolk wasted no time: he razed the town and moved north-east to Roy, arriving there on 31 October where they rested. In the meantime, the men were tired and suffering from wet and cold. On 1 November, in Roy, Suffolk knighted sixteen men, including Richard Sandys, Lord Sandys' younger brother.[180] The next day the army marched on to Nesle, but problems with the men began in earnest because the rain did not stop, it was getting colder and men were dying every day. Another factor was the threat of defection by the Burgundians who, like the British, had not been paid for months but could go home relatively easily. This threat was particularly upsetting for the English and Welsh, because the Burgundians provided most of the transport and could cart away the plunder while the others could not.[181] Suffolk insisted that they move on towards Burgundy, which was by now the only viable option. On 6 November, Sandys led the vanguard in a fight to capture the small town of Voyennes, enabling the army to cross the Somme. Again, the allies were successful, so the way to Burgundy was easier and they continued to move north-east through Beauvois and Mount Saint Martin.

On 8 November, Suffolk recognised that he needed further instructions from the king: should they overwinter in France or the Burgundian land, or come home? Would they receive reinforcements? It was decided that Sandys should go to the king for instructions and he moved quickly; on 15 November he was aboard *The Peter Baylye* from Calais to Dover.[182] Suffolk could not go himself because he was leader of the expedition, and he probably thought that Sandys would receive attention from the king and Wolsey. Elis Gruffudd says that Suffolk believed that a relief army was coming, but would it be soon enough? This may have been a story to boost the men's morale as their anger increased and they wanted to be at home looking after their farms and enjoying home comforts. The final straw was a change in the weather from very wet to extremely cold, which happened between 8 and 13 November.

Elis Gruffudd describes the conditions endured by the fighting men in one of the most graphic accounts of its kind and merits quotation:

> During this time grey bearded winter began to show his face in black cold frost wind and short days and long nights which caused the decrepit shivering soldiers to complain and groan to each other. Some said it was too much for them lying on the earth under hedges and bushes dying of cold, another said 'that he wished to be at home with his nose in his wife's arse of whom he said that her arse was much warmer than his head at this time'.[183] This complaint many of the English and Welsh made with great weeping and wailing. And yet they had no reason to complain except of their own sluggishness and slovenliness. For there was no lack of food or drink or wood for fire or making huts, and plenty of straw to roof them and lie on if only they had fetched it. But there was many a man weak in body who preferred from sheer laziness to lie under the hedge rather than take the trouble to make a snug warm hut to keep him from the frost, wind and snow. They preferred to shiver with cold rather than take the trouble to light a fire. ... On the second day of the frost these (men) were divided into two parts. Some went with the cart to fetch wood and the others stayed at home to make a turf bank and earth to keep off the wind which was blowing from the East. Inside the bank, after the wood had come, they made a big fire. But by the time the fire was hot enough for a man to warm himself by it, none of the men who had taken the trouble to

make it could get near enough to warm his paw, because the others would not move from it for words fair or foul. Many young men lay round it all through the night and I saw there one young man who had turned his backside to the fire and turned his stockings down over his knees and taken off his wrappings to warm his feet and legs, and in this way he lay with his back to the fire until the heat had blistered his legs and the soles of his feet, which was an extraordinary sight that a man could be so sluggish as to sleep so soundly that he could not feel his own flesh burning. But however great the cold they (the War Council) did not intend to leave there until getting letters from the King, though there was much murmuring among the common soldiers.

At last on Wednesday night there rose a noise and shouting amongst the host and especially around the tents of the Duke and some soldiers said that they would tarry there no longer and that they would go home willy nilly the next day. This talk spread from there among the men from Suffolk and Norfolk who began to swear mightily in the hall (?tent) of a knight called Sir Thomas Wainford that they would take their leave as soon as they saw the light of day. Against this some of their comrades said that it was well to ask leave of their captains before quitting the camp, for fear of their lives, and what they were discussing was no less than treason, namely to leave the king's captain in the field with the ordnance and to go off without knowing their captains, which could not go without punishment. To this these obstinate senseless men answered that it was no worse being hanged in England than dying of cold in France. My master Sir Robert Wingfield heard all the noise and talking and made me get out of my bed where I was snug as a small pig to listen to the talk and make a note of those men who were making this noise. After a long argument they put their heads down and shut up and I came to my master's tent and told him all about it, after which I laid my head on the straw again. But before I had warmed my bed one of the people next to me got up to make water in the door of the tent and shouted 'Ah sirs, if I had known at the beginning of the night that there was much frost and snow as this I would not have taken so much trouble to search my shirt for lice, but I should have hung it out in the wind and let them die of cold, as we shall do if we stay here any longer.' To listen to what he was saying I had to get up from my pallet the second time when the man was in the door of the tent and said 'If any of you were of the same idea as myself I should shout "Let us go home".' But because it was near the dead of night his neighbours told him to lie down till day came which he did. And as soon as the day came they began to talk about the journey to England all through the host and then shouted out loud 'Home, Home' especially the men of Essex and Suffolk among whom there were many wealthy farmers who used this confusion to urge the poor men to go home. It is certain that the Duke and all the captains who had any sense were amazed at this shouting, not only from shame that the foreigners from Burgundy should see the shiftlessness, the weakness and unruliness of the English soldiers but also for fear lest the enemy should get to know of this tumult and fall suddenly upon them. So sensible men got up and went

> each to his company to pacify the unruly ones with fair words and promises that they should take their journey back to England next morning. This made them shut their jaws and silenced their clamour and after the people had been quieted the Duke and his captains went into Council to decide which way they should next take with their goods in safety. Next morning the whole host struck its tents and booths and set fire to the huts.
>
> And so the host marched against the freezing wind throughout that day which was Friday towards a town called le chateau [?] Cambresis which was one of the worst and hardest days for frost that the oldest man in the host had ever seen and there were many men who were over sixty years of age. This day if people can be believed many men on horse and on foot died from sheer cold. Others said some had lost the use of their limbs from the force of the frost wind. And others said that they had lost the use of their water pipes and could not pass water that way until they had got fire and warm water to thaw them. Indeed this was a greater misfortune to some men than others for in truth I was on a horse riding among men who had little enough round them to keep the cold wind from the body, as myself. In this company there were old men and young who were on horseback from six o'clock in the morning till nine o'clock at night, but I saw none of the afflictions aforesaid happen or fall upon any of them. Still, this matter may be true and might have happened to those stubborn men who had long been sick in the same members of a disease and a hurt that it was not easy for doctors to cure, in which places the cold wind struck so severely that the nature of the flesh was unable to strengthen the blood to give natural warmth to the members which had been overcome by the cold, where they were lost, as it is treated of before in this work.[184]

It had obviously been decided that overwintering in France was no longer an option, as the army moved towards Hainault, part of the emperor's domain, and although it was getting weaker it was still a fighting force and managed to fend off French attacks. The remnants of the allied army left French territory around 14 November. At Valenciennes the Burgundians departed to go home, and Suffolk put the guns in safe custody prior to shipping them home. The campaign was finished. The English/Welsh contingents went home via Tournai, Bruges and Dunkirk, disgruntled after being away for two months, and soaked and frozen for nothing. All the booty was left behind in France or Burgundy.

When Suffolk left Bruges he was aware that the king was very unhappy with him, so he decided it was safer to move to Calais for a while to let Henry's anger subside. He stayed until mid-January 1524, but he was not allowed access to the king until 24 June.[185] Eventually, their cordial relationship resumed.

To return to how Sandys fared on his mission to the king for further instruction, he left the army on 8 November 1523 and 'came over to the Kinge by post, the cause why is not yet knowne',[186] but probably did not reach London until about 15 November. What he said to the king is not known, but Henry was displeased. He had heard about the difficulties and commissioned Lord Mountjoy to muster 6,000 men to provide relief to Suffolk's army, presumably on the assumption that they would overwinter in France or Burgundy ready for a spring campaign. But it was too little and too late. He was either not aware of, or had disregarded, the diminished size of the army, the disease, Bourbon's failure, the supply problems and the disgruntled Burgundians, but nevertheless dispatched Sir Robert Jerningham to tell Suffolk of his wishes and plans. The two men met on 2 December in Bruges, where Suffolk had to declare that he had no army left and the campaign was over. Henry was clearly unhappy when he heard the news, but Lord Mountjoy and the men he had already mustered were stood down.

Sandys left London on the return journey to Calais and arrived there before 2 December, when he wrote to Wolsey concerning payment for 1,000 men retained by Thomas Howard in Flanders, but concluded by asking for his recall.[187] He had endured enough, which was not surprising after being on war footing since May 1522, and he was around fifty-three years of age, which was 'old' by the standards of the day.

The war between Charles V and Francis I continued, mainly in Italy, reaching a climax on 25 February 1525 at the Battle of Pavia, where the French were heavily defeated and Francis was taken prisoner by the emperor's men. In January 1526, the emperor agreed to release Francis on condition that the French would:

1) Surrender all claims to Flanders, Artois, Tournai, Hesdin and Arras.
2) Never help the King of Navarre against the empire.
3) Pay the emperor sufficient money to fund 500 men-at-arms and 10,000 footmen for six months to support the emperor's campaign against Rome.
4) Settle the emperor's debts to Henry VIII.

To ensure compliance with these conditions, Francis was required to hand over his two eldest sons to the emperor as hostages. He agreed to the terms and was released, but issues between the two parties were not settled until 1529 by the Treaty of Cambrai.

While Francis was in captivity Wolsey negotiated a treaty with France, which effectively led to a declaration of war between England and the empire. In May 1527, after Francis was released, Wolsey headed a delegation, which included William Sandys, to France. From the end of 1526 to spring 1528, Wolsey and Henry contemplated taking up arms to support Francis against Charles, and they planned that Sandys would take a force of 1,000 men to Guînes to be joined by an army of 10,000 men led by Suffolk. But this did not happen, probably because of lobbying by English merchants who would not support a cause that harmed lucrative trade with Flanders and Spain.[188] Other factors included a mutiny at Guînes over lack of food early in 1528 and Sandys' illness at the same time. He does not seem to have recovered until April 1528.[189]

After his return to England, Sandys did not exercise his battlefield skills again until 1536, when he accompanied the Duke of Norfolk in his army to quell the northern rebellion known as 'the Pilgrimage of Grace', but the anticipated battle did not materialise.[190] However, he maintained an interest in martial matters as Captain of Guînes Castle until his death, and in 1539/40 advised the king on reinforcing the castle's defences because the French were strengthening defences at Ardes, the castle on the borders of the Pale. When he arrived at Guînes in March 1539 he was 'received with salvoes of artillery and preparations were made just as in a time of war'.[191] Interestingly, he sought advice from Italian military architects, and in May 1540 the French ambassador to Henry VIII wrote: 'Lord Sandys having informed himself about various fortresses in Italy, has left to reside in and fortify Guînes.'[192] Italian military architects were in England at that time, and one of them, Giovanni Portinari, masterminded the demolition of the dissolved priory at Lewes in 1538 and was a member of the royal household. After a short break when he worked for the French, Portinari served in England designing fortifications until his death in the reign of Queen Elizabeth.[193] A plan of the new design for the Guînes Castle shows a large complex facility, but Henry was not ready for modern Italian designs, unlike King Francis who had Italian engineers in his service for many years.[194] So, the design that Sandys had influenced was not implemented in the upgrade of Guînes Castle.[195] Instead, a simpler, smaller and, no doubt less expensive, design was built.[196] In late August 1540, just a few months before his death, Sandys and the then Deputy of Calais and others wrote to the king that the bridge at Cowbridge should be destroyed. It had been built by the French when they were rebuilding Ardres Castle and afforded easy passage across the river, which was the boundary between the castle and the English Pale.[197] The bridge was duly destroyed, which upset the French, who rebuilt it in October 1540.

In summary and conclusion, it is clear that Sandys was involved with military activities throughout his life. When not fighting on campaign he held positions such as Constable of Southampton Castle, Treasurer of Calais, Captain of Guînes, Commissioner of Array and Commissioner of Peace, all of which had military responsibilities. His military roles and experience steadily increased from his knighthood, gained at the Battle of Stoke in 1487 where he fought for Henry VII, through campaigns in England, Spain, Flanders and, most of all, France. The chroniclers mentioned his presence in campaigns and battles from the start, but it was only after he was made a Knight of the Garter in 1518 that some of his feats were recorded. Sandys' military skills were also recognised by the king and senior courtiers, as reflected in the grant of an annuity in July 1517 for his service in Spain, Guienne, Picardy and Flanders.

By contrast, there is no evidence that he participated in royal jousts or tournaments, which were vehicles for demonstrating military skill and courage and becoming close to the king. In 1521, Cardinal Wolsey tried to persuade the king that Sandys should lead the next campaign in France as chief captain of the army,[198] but Henry did not agree because he thought other senior soldiers would not follow Sandys as a mere knight. When Wolsey responded that some of the best knights had already indicated to him that they would follow Sandys, Henry refused to discuss the matter further, and Thomas Howard, the Earl of

Surrey, was appointed chief captain for the 1522 expedition. Whether Sandys could have led an expedition is questionable, as there is no evidence that he was a strategist like his colleague Van Buren, the Flemish general who provided Charles Brandon with direction in the 1523 campaign. Yet, on 13 January 1535, Eustace Chapuys, the Holy Roman Emperor's ambassador to the English court, wrote to the emperor that Lord Sandys was 'the King's chamberlain, Captain of Guînes, and one of the best men of war in the kingdom'.[199] Two weeks later he wrote again, stating that Sandys was the best captain.[200]

In 1540, Sandys was at Guînes, overseeing reinforcements to the defences. Elis Gruffudd reported on the French at that time, saying, 'For they greatly feared the Lord Chamberlain and his men, he being the Captain at Guînes.'[201] On hearing of Sandys' death some months later, the French ambassador wrote that Sandys was much esteemed and was one of the few ancient captains left.[202]

All the historical evidence therefore indicates that William Sandys was military leader with notable courage, ruthlessness, stamina, determination and ability.

5

The King's Chamberlain

William, Lord Sandys was appointed the King's Chamberlain in 1526,[1] and confirmation of this title was later recorded in the 1539 House of Lords Precedence Act.[2] He first knew about this appointment sometime before 23 August 1525, when Wolsey informed him that he was to be appointed chamberlain and also Captain of Guînes Castle.[3] Although he was officially the King's Chamberlain he was more often described as the Lord Chamberlain of the Household, while the king sometimes referred to him as 'our Chamberlain'.[4]

Immediately before he became chamberlain, Sandys was involved in a range of activities at home and in Calais between the 1523 campaign and early 1526. On 9 July 1524, he had returned to Calais to deal with Treasury business, and things must have seemed relatively quiet after the previous events, which was fortunate because he had two major projects in progress back in Hampshire, namely the rebuilding of The Vyne mansion and the extension of the Chapel of the Holy Ghost in Basingstoke. Work on the chapel was almost certainly completed that year because Sandys and his friend Richard Fox, Bishop of Winchester, petitioned Henry VIII that the voluntary Guild of the Holy Ghost should be formally established, and the licence was granted in November 1524.[5]

In February 1524, Sandys had been appointed Keeper of Chute Forest, and in November he became Commissioner of the Peace, also in April 1525. However, 1525 began with a complaint to Wolsey against Sandys, once again for not paying the postmen. The Master of Posts said that they had served well but Sandys had not paid them, although Wolsey had ordered him to do so, and that they had been paid for only two months out of twenty-two months' service. Nothing further is known about this matter,[6] probably because Sandys made the required payments or because he was called home at the end of February.[7]

Early in June 1525, he played host to the 2nd Earl of Devon, Henry Courtenay, who was travelling with his wife from Exeter to London to receive the title of Marquis of Exeter. The party arrived at The Vyne on 10 June and left with Sandys on the 12th, but during their stay he showed the earl the Chapel of the Holy Ghost where he made a modest offering, which indicates that The Vyne was in a fit state to entertain senior courtiers and that work on the Chapel of the Holy Ghost was indeed complete. Sandys and Courtenay were joined by the Lords Roos and Mountjoy at Blackwater, where they stopped for drinks before making their way to Bridewell Palace, London.[8] There, on 18 June, the king bestowed the earldom of Nottingham on his illegitimate son Henry Fitzroy and made him a Knight of the Garter, and later that day made Courtney Marquis of Exeter.[9]

Mid-July 1525 saw Sandys back in Calais and dealing with a dispute over wool cargoes.[10] In late August he undertook one of his last tasks as Treasurer of Calais, when he and Sir William Fitzwilliam, Baron of the Exchequer and Solicitor General, drafted a new set of ordinances relating to land tenure in Guînes.[11] As peace had been agreed between the French and English, he had formally declared the cessation of war in Calais.[12] A week later, Sandys and Fitzwilliam reported to Wolsey that they had discharged the garrisons in the Pale, and Sandys asked to be transferred home as peace had been declared.[13]

Income and Costs

When Sandys first heard that he would become Lord Chamberlain of the Household and Captain of Guînes Castle, sometime before 23 August 1525,[14] his reply to Wolsey suggests an appetite for money:

> [He is] thankful to Wolsey for having procured to him the reversion of the lord Chamberlainship, and that he shall have the castle of Guînes in the same manner as Sir William Fitzwilliam held it. Hopes he will not be deprived of the advantage he derives from the Treasureship, considering his great poverty, without some equivalent to keep him out of debt. The Treasureship which was held by the late Lord Vaux included the farm of Mark and Oye, which the King now proposes to keep in his hands. Begs he may have the little grange held by Wyndebank before Vaux with all its appurtenances and rights ... His income does not exceed 300 or 400 marks [£200–336] a year.

Although the king took the lordship of Mark and Oye in the Pale, it appears that Sandys rented it and made a profit. In August 1526, he wrote to Wolsey, requesting that the rent, which was about to be increased, should be minimal, otherwise 'it would greatly injure him',[15] and wrote again on 24 August to say that he needed a great deal of money because he was owed a lot by foreign merchants.[16] Two years later, in July 1528, in a letter to Wolsey from The Vyne he asked to have some of the offices held by the late Sir William Compton, and that some should also be given to his brother, and even sent Wolsey a list of the positions made vacant by Compton's death.[17] In October that same year he sought payment from Wolsey for debts he had incurred as Captain of Guînes.[18]

The figures for Sandys' income and poverty do not square with his tax assessment for 1524, which estimated his income at 2,000 marks (£1,333) and would not have impressed Wolsey, who signed the return for peers. The table below sets the £1,333 in perspective by showing shows that Sandys' assessment was near the top for senior courtiers.

Income of Senior Courtiers, 1524

Name	Title	Income (£) p.a.	Refs
Thomas Wolsey	Cardinal, Lord Chancellor	Estimated income 30,000	1
William Warham	Archbishop of Canterbury	3,500	2
Henry Percy	Earl of Northumberland	2,920	3
Edward Stanley	Earl of Derby	2,903	4
Thomas Howard	Duke of Norfolk	2,800	4
William FitzAlan	Earl of Arundel	2,207	6
Charles Worcester	Earl of Worcester	2,000	3
George Talbot	Earl of Shrewsbury	1,400	3
Mary Hungerford	Lady Hastings	1,333	5
William Sandys	**Baron Sandys of The Vyne**	**1,333**	3
Margaret	Countess of Salisbury	1,220	3
Henry Clifford	Baron de Clifford	1,198	5
William Compton	Knight	1,100	6
Thomas Boleyn	Knight, Treasurer of the Household	1,100	6
Thomas Darcy	Lord Darcy	1,065	5
William	Lord Mountjoy	1,000	5
Charles Brandon	Duke of Suffolk	1,000	3
Thomas Hoard	Earl of Surrey	1,000	3
N.B.	Peers median Knights median Esquires median Gentleman median	800 200 80 17	4
1) Gunn & Lindley, *Cardinal Wolsey*, 1991, p.6 2) Cornwall, *Wealth and Society in Early Sixteenth Century England*, 1988, p.131 3) TNA E179/69/5 4) Cornwall, *Wealth and Society in Early Sixteenth Century England*, 1988, pp.143–45			

A similar comparative table created for the 1534 assessment shows that Sandys' taxed income was less, at £1,000, and that his ranking had fallen, yet he was the highest-paid lord.[19]

It is difficult to understand his financial affairs. He and his wife certainly held many manors in Hampshire and Berkshire, and also in Gloucestershire, Hertfordshire, Middlesex, Northamptonshire, Surrey, Sussex, Somerset and Wiltshire, and these were supplemented by properties and advowsons in some of the same counties.[20] The portfolio originated in properties inherited from Sandys' father in 1496 and from Sir Reynold Bray in 1503, and others acquired or given. In 1536, Sandys would exchange property he owned at Chelsea and Paddington with the king for Mottisfont Priory and its estate. He also received the profits of the lordship of Mark and Oye in the Calais Pale, which he rented from the Crown at £1,320 per year,[21] and various annuities from the Crown and others, including the French.[22]

It is clear that by the early 1520s Sandys had sufficient credit to convert The Vyne manor house into a palatial mansion and refurbish the Chapel of the Holy Ghost at Basingstoke, both of which were furnished to high standards, and he also had a London house, close to St Paul's Cathedral.[23] Yet, despite his large income he was in debt (see chapter 5 for debts in 1521). When he mentioned his need for money to Wolsey in August 1526, he blamed the fact that foreign merchants owed him money.[24] His position did not improve, and in May 1528 he negotiated an agreement with Wolsey and the Treasurer, Sir Henry Wyatt, to restructure his debts to the Crown,[25] at which time he owed more than £6,000 (£6,121),[26] more than £5,000 of which arose from his time as Treasurer of Calais, which coincided with construction at The Vyne. Other items included unpaid rent for a tenement in Windsor (nineteen years), unpaid taxes and other obligations. The king generously dismissed half the debt, reducing it to £3,600 'in consideration of the acceptable service unto his grace [Wolsey]', while Sandys agreed to pay 200 marks (£133) a year in return, which the Crown would receive from the profits of five of his manors, namely Broadwater, Jevington and Lampham in Sussex, and Steane and Hinton in Northamptonshire. Sandys would retain any profits above the sum due to the Crown, and as the net profits of five of these manors were more than 200 marks a year, his claim to Wolsey that his annual income in 1526 was 300–400 marks seems a gross understatement (see Appendix 1).[27] In addition to his debt to the Crown, he was also indebted to the abbots of Reading and Glastonbury, Bishop Richard Fox and Cardinal Wolsey.[28]

Although Sandys fulfilled the terms of the 1528 agreement, his debts were not cleared before his death and he was not pressed to do so. He also found the resources to rebuild Mottisfont Priory as a large mansion, no doubt because of his position and access to the king, but the situation changed when his son Thomas inherited the estate, because he was subject to considerable pressure and forced to sell and mortgage properties. Not until May 1548 did the Court of Augmentations declare that Thomas had cleared his father's debts.

Lord William Sandys was often criticised for not meeting his financial obligations, and on at least two occasions his family expressed disappointment at his lack generosity. A letter to Cromwell in 1539 from Henry Lacy, a

Probable location of William, 1st Baron Sandys' house in St Paul's district of London. It was close to the river and downstream of Baynard's Castle.

long-time resident of Calais, reported a meeting between Sandys and the soldiers at Guînes where he asked whether they had any complaints. After a long silence, one said that the men were suffering because they had not received wages for the last six months. Sandys replied that he would pay them when he was paid by the king in October, and they accepted this because they dared not complain. The letter also said that Sandys was paid £1,000 a year by the king for 100 soldiers, but apart from the deputy (his son), the Constable of the Keep and the Porter of the Gate, who received full pay, the soldiers received less than half pay. It seems that Sandys also took the profit from the brewhouse in the castle, which was over £500 a year.[29] The same Henry Lacy had previously complained in 1521 that Sandys had taken some of the lands and kept the last two years' profits, and it is not surprising that he was instructed to return the land and the profits.[30] As already noted, Sandys' sister Lady Darcy (formerly Lady Neville) had chided him in 1518 for his reluctance to pay his share of the wedding outfit of their sister Ann,[31] while in 1521 his brother-in-law Lord Thomas Darcy expressed regret that Sandys could not settle his financial differences with a cousin.[32]

The Chamberlain's Role

Sandys was formally appointed to the office of King's Chamberlain on 26 February 1526, but was already acting as substitute before that date.[33]

The Earl of Worcester had evidently become too elderly to undertake these duties, so the king instructed that Sandys should 'bear a white staff within the court' in Worcester's absence, and receive the same allowances as the earl would have received if present.[34] The appointment almost certainly resulted from intervention by Wolsey, to whom Sandys was close in such a way that his wife Margery was able to approach Wolsey to secure a position for their son Reynolde, which would bring him into closer contact with the king and court.[35]

Sandys was close to the court from an early age, probably through the relationship he and his mother had with Margaret Beaufort, her son Henry VII and grandson Henry VIII, so the details are worth noting. In 1494, Sandys was present at the coronation of Elizabeth, Henry VII's wife, and had the honour of carrying the young Prince Henry at the ceremony in which the prince was made Duke of York. By 1499 he had been made Knight of the Body by Henry VII, a position continued by Henry VIII, and the same year saw his first nomination for the Order of the Garter. Two years later he was part of the escort for Princess Catherine of Aragon when she travelled from the south coast to meet Prince Arthur in London, and he had similar escort duties when Princess Margaret travelled to Edinburgh to marry King James IV. Sandys was also in attendance at Henry VII's funeral and Henry VIII's coronation. Although his position as Treasurer of Calais often involved geographical separation, it also kept him in touch with the king, Wolsey and other senior members of the court.

The duties of the King's Chamberlain of the Household, who is frequently described as Lord Chamberlain of the Household, were not clearly defined. Essentially, he was responsible for 'ordering', i.e. managing, the operation of the household. The nature of the role can be gleaned from the Eltham Ordinances, drafted in 1526 and issued by Wolsey to reform the rather bloated and expensive court, but they were never fully applied.[36] Support below stairs was managed by the Comptroller of the Household, Sir Henry Guildford.

The chamberlain was allocated lodgings at court and allowed a page, seven servants and stabling for eighteen horses. He was a member of the king's council, which dealt with complaints, and responsible for ensuring that the king's rooms were kept in good order and properly staffed, but he also had authority to allow people to be absent from the king's service and to control who saw the king. He attended the king when he was dining, but could not dine with him except at the king's request. An example of the position of the King's Chamberlain at State functions, before Sandy's time in office, is shown in a sketch, showing the positions of participants at the reception of Cardinal Campeggio when he visited Henry VIII in August 1518. The king was seated on a dais at one end of the hall, and facing him on his right were cardinals Campeggio and Wolsey. The King's Chamberlain was immediately adjacent to the king by his left shoulder, and the Lords Temporal were seated along the left side of the hall with the Lords Spiritual along the right side.[37]

The chamberlain's normal dining place was the Watching Chamber or Great Chamber, usually the largest room in the building, in company with the vice-chamberlain, nobles, the Captain of the Guard, Master of the Horse, Lord Steward, comptroller, foreign ambassadors and members of the king's council. He also guarded the entrance to the presence chamber where the king dined in public. The privy chamber, the king's 'inner sanctum', was managed by the Groom of the Stool.

The proceedings of the Privy Council in 1526 indicate the order of precedence at court:

> It is ordered and appointed by his Royal Highness, that a good number of honourable, virtuous, sad, wise, expert and discreet persons of his council shall give their attendance upon his most royal person, whose names hereafter follow, that is to say, the:
>
> Cardinal (Wolsey), Chancellor of England
> Duke of Norfolk, Treasurer of England
> Bishop of London, the Keeper of the King's Privy Seal
> Duke of Suffolk, Marshall of England
> Marquis of Dorset
> Marquis of Exeter
> Earl of Shrewsbury, steward of the Royal Household
> The Lord Chamberlain, Etc.

It continues with:

> It is ordered that the persons hereafter mentioned shall give their continual attendance in the causes of his said council, unto what place whosoever his highness shall resort, that is to say, The Lord Chamberlain, The Bishop of Bath, The Treasurer and Comptroller of the King's household, the Secretary, the Chancellor of the Duchy of Lancaster, the Dean of the King's Chapel, the Vice Chamberlain, the Captain of the Guard and Dr Woolman.

The King's Chamberlain was also a member of the king's Privy Council and the Court of the Star Chamber, which was essentially a subsection of the Privy Council established to deal swiftly with cases.[38] It was not bound by common law and had no jury. The king was nominally its leader, but in practice the Lord Chancellor was the presiding judge. In addition to members of the Privy Council, there were men 'learned in the law'. This court dealt mainly with sedition, corruption, robbery, rebellion, murder, libel, slander and causing riots. Unlike other courts, it could summon people on suspicion without a formal complaint. It could not by itself pronounce the death sentence, but could inflict punishment by fines, imprisonment and mutilation, such as branding, cutting off ears and slitting noses. One benefit for members of the Star Chamber was the food provided.[39]

The structure of the King's Chamberlain's department varied from time to time but remained essentially the same throughout the Tudor period, as follows:

The king
|
King's Chamberlain / Lord Chamberlain
|
Vice-Chamberlain
|
Treasurer
|
Groom of the Stool
|
Privy Purse
|
Gentlemen / Women
|
Ushers / Grooms / Pages / Chamberers / Maids[40]

Before Sandys had time to settle into his new job, the king, Catherine of Aragon and the court made a short visit to The Vyne on 31 July 1526 on their way to Arundel.[41] It was Henry's first visit since 1510,[42] and probably planned to enable him to see the remodelled and expanded Vyne, although the work was not completed until a year later when the Oak Gallery was finished. As might be expected of the King's Chamberlain, Sandys accompanied the royal party to Arundel and Winchester.[43] More evidence for this royal visit in 1526 is contained in a letter from Sir Arthur Darcy to his father, which says that a visit to the Bishop of Winchester and the Lord Chamberlain was planned for that summer. The letter has no year date, as was common practice, but the *Letters and Papers of Henry VIII* give the date as 30 June 1527.[44] This is incorrect, because the court never repeated the same itinerary in successive years and while Henry visited the Bishop of Winchester's residence at Farnham Castle before The Vyne in 1526, he did not leave his palaces in 1527 as plague was prevalent.

Continuing Responsibilities in Calais and France

Although Sandys was expected to be close to the king as his chamberlain, it is obvious that he was absent for lengthy periods, such as when he accompanied Wolsey to France in 1527. As Lieutenant of Guînes, he was in charge of the castle and town and was paid for this role, also receiving money for the ninety-nine soldiers in the garrison and his spies. Yet, he was rarely there and delegated his duties to deputies, one of whom was his son John.[45] In 1533, he received over £1,060 to cover expenses and his pay – and it would be unusual if all his expenses reflected costs incurred.[46]

Sandys' increasing authority is indicated by the fact that the king delegated to him the appointment of Sir Robert Wingfield as Deputy of Calais and Sir William

Fitzwilliam as Governor of Calais Castle.[47] In October 1526, he travelled to Calais to formally hand over the keys to Wingfield.[48] He also wrote to Wolsey and the king that Guînes Castle was in need of repair, which seems surprising because he had been Treasurer of Calais a few months before and could not have been unaware of conditions at Guînes.[49] Perhaps his new responsibility for the well-being of the castle had changed his perspective; if so, it did not last, because it has been suggested that when he was absent from the castle no more than six men were stationed there and it was vulnerable to French attack.[50]

At the end of this landmark year in Sandys' career he returned to England late in 1526,[51] but his change of role from colonial administrator and soldier to home-based courtier was probably no less challenging and only a little less dangerous. If he thought his duties at Guînes would be trivial, that was not so, as they became more onerous and fraught.

Also, in summer 1527 he would be required in France for a different reason. Together with other senior courtiers, he was assigned to accompany Cardinal Wolsey on a visit to the newly released King of France. The original object was for Wolsey to ratify the peace treaty that he had drawn up between England and France with the French king's mother, but the mission gained an added dimension when some of the emperor's troops, under the Duke of Bourbon, ransacked Rome. The pope took refuge in Castel Sant'Angelo and was trapped there, as a prisoner under house arrest. Wolsey saw an opportunity for alliance with the French against the emperor, but foremost in his mind was the possibility of taking papal authority. Accordingly, he summoned the cardinals to France for a conclave that would, in effect, allow him to become pope.

The journey to France commenced in July and Sandys was in Calais on the 11th.[52] On 22 July, Wolsey left Calais, accompanied by the Bishop of London, Sandys, the Earl of Derby, Sir Henry Guildford, Sir Thomas More, 700 knights and squires, eighty carriages and 900 horses, all heading for Amiens via Abbeville. The French king and his entourage arrived at Amiens on 3 August in time to greet Wolsey, who arrived the following day and introduced the king to the Bishop of London, Sandys, Sir Henry Guildford and Sir Thomas More.[53] That evening Wolsey, together with the same four and the Earl of Derby, met the Queen Mother of France, with whom he had drafted the peace treaty the previous year.[54] The next day the cardinal and his escort met the king and the royal court, but spoke to the king in private, thus excluding the Bishop of London and Sandys from discussions. When they had finished, the peace treaty was formally ratified and Mass duly celebrated.[55]

Sandys and the other senior courtiers did little except to act as foils for Wolsey, but they went hunting with the French king and apparently disliked the way he hunted.[56] Wolsey's party was at Compiègne for the meeting of cardinals between 5 and 13 September, but it was a waste of time from his perspective because only four arrived.[57]

The party returned to England at the end of September 1527, having achieved little, and the pope was released by the emperor's troops in December. Yet, Wolsey's reception in France apparently encouraged him to exceed his authority, as he tried to declare war on the emperor without the authority of the Privy Council or the king. This was his first serious mistake. He managed to alienate the emperor, who by this time had effective control over the pope, and Henry VIII needed the pope's support in pursuing his separation from Catherine. There was no war because the emperor did not want one, and the English merchants refused to support actions that would interfere with their trade with Flanders. Also, the emperor was moving towards a peace treaty with France.[58] It therefore seems that Sandys' boss and champion at court was losing his touch.

Major Events at Court and Difficulties in England

Sandys' increased authority following his appointment as the King's Chamberlain is further revealed in a letter to Wolsey in March 1527, when he tells the cardinal that he had sent for the Archdeacon of Westminster and then advises Wolsey what to do.[59]

The year 1527 had begun with a notable function at Hampton Court on 3 January, which was so memorable that it is described by Cavendish,[60] Hall,[61] and Gasparo Spinelli, secretary to the Venetian ambassador at the English court.[62] It provides the basis for the scene in Shakespeare's play about the life of Henry VIII which portrays Sandys as light-hearted and flirtatious and brings Anne Boleyn to Henry's notice for the first time.[63] Although there is no specific evidence, it is likely that Anne was present, as were several other good-looking women. Eric Ives, in his thoroughly researched book on Anne Boleyn, suggests that Henry began courting her early in 1526, and that by autumn he had sent his first love letter – almost a year before this function.[64] However, according to the Venetian ambassador, Henry did not 'divorce the Queen from his bed' until October 1529.[65]

This event reveals another aspect of Sandys' character. According to George Cavendish, Sandys and Sir Henry Guildford were credited with organising this grand function, which began with a banquet given by Wolsey in the large presence chamber at Hampton Court. Wolsey was seated at his own table, opposite a long table at which the guests were seated, including the papal, French and Venetian ambassadors and senior nobility of the English court. According to Spinelli, each unescorted male was placed next to a 'beautiful damsel'. When the merriment was interrupted by gunfire outside the palace, Wolsey instructed Sandys and Guildford – who pretended that they were unaware of what was happening – to investigate the source. They did so by looking through a window overlooking the Thames and reported that a party of noblemen and a foreign prince were outside. Wolsey sent them to meet the party, as they spoke French, and to escort them to the presence chamber to join the banquet and entertainment. Each member of the party was apparently in disguise, and they assembled in front of Wolsey at his table. Sandys then announced that as they were strangers and could speak no English they had asked him to speak for them, and he recounted that they had heard about this magnificent banquet where there were 'such a number of excellent fair dames that they had to come to view their incomparable beauty, to play dice with them and after dance with them and so get to know them'. The cardinal duly welcomed the visitors and they played dice. Afterwards, Wolsey said he had been told that one of their number was worthier than himself to sit at his table, and Sandys repeated the message in French. The reply agreed that this was the case, and that the person would take Wolsey's place if Wolsey could identify him. Wolsey tried, and selected Sir Edward Neville, who had the same build and stature as the king, which caused the king to burst out laughing and unmask himself before leaving the room with his entourage to change clothing. In his absence the tables were cleared and the cloths replaced, and the whole assembly began a new banquet of over 200 dishes: 'Wonderous costly and devices subtly devised.'

After the meal the entertainment began with a play, which was the highlight for Spinelli. A girl dressed as Venus appeared on stage with six attractive girls dressed as nymphs at her feet. Cupid arrived in a cart drawn by three naked boys. At the rear of the cart were six men, posing as old men in country clothes made of silver and silk, and Venus commanded the six nymphs, the sweethearts of the men, to take the 'old men' by the hand and dance with them. The king and his entourage then commenced dancing with the ladies in the room and spent the whole night dancing and being entertained, which is remarkable because Henry had spent the whole day jousting. Spinelli concludes his report with 'and the night ended, for it was already daybreak. I went home sated with so much revelry.'

By contrast with the riches and revelry at court, ordinary people were enduring hardship caused by rain and floods, following heavy rain in the last quarter of the previous year. Then, on 26 January 1527, torrential rain destroyed wheat fields and pastures and drowned sheep and cattle. This was followed by two months of dry weather and six weeks of heavy rain, which caused extensive flooding and destroyed that year's wheat crop. Serious effects would follow, as England was hit by an epidemic and a cereal famine.

The epidemic severely restricted the king's movements and he stayed out of London for much of the time, spending most of July and August at his house at Beaulieu.[66] Sandys was lucky to be in France with Wolsey from July, but the famine affected him indirectly as it became increasingly serious through the autumn, winter, and early part of 1528. Attempts were made to buy wheat from abroad, and cereals were bought from Cyprus, Flanders, Denmark, Bremen, and Hamburg.[67] Ironically, France would not provide any, and the French were detaining ships carrying wheat imports, despite a high-level delegation from the King of France visiting London in late September and early October to present Henry with the French Order of St Michael. In return, Henry presented the Order of the Garter to the French king. Elaborate festivities greeted the delegation, expensive presents were exchanged, and mutual love was declared between the two sovereigns.[68]

On 11 November, the Venetian ambassador to England reported that the English were reduced to eating bean flour, and on 27 November that bread was scarce. To make matters worse for the common people it was very cold with heavy snow, but the king was sufficiently gracious to release some of his grain stores. In the same month Sandys, together with Wolsey, the Duke of Suffolk, the king and a few others, received payment of pensions from Francis I, the French king.[69]

For Sandys, this grain shortage led to a row with Sir Robert Wingfield, Deputy of Calais, who had written to Wolsey to complain that the English ports would not release any wheat for Calais, although it had been paid for by Calais merchants, and that Sandys' men at Guînes refused to allow any of the wheat collected in lieu of rent to be used in the Pale. Sandys was upset that Wingfield had gone above him to Wolsey, and wrote to Wingfield from The Vyne on 9 December, criticising him for usurping Sandys' authority in Guînes and disobeying Wolsey's command that the wheat was the king's only security for unpaid rents. He also said he had asked his men to find any spare wheat they could, but concluded by asking Wingfield not to interfere with his jurisdiction.[70] Wingfield's reply, dated 14 December, clearly reflects Sandys' new status as he undertakes to respond to every point made, 'hoping that Sandys will take it in good part, as from one who will honour and serve him as a poor gentleman should a great Lord', and assuring him that he had no reason to consider Wingfield unfriendly. He was unaware of Wolsey's edict and that Sandys' authority extended beyond the castle of Guînes to the county of Guînes. It seems that they resolved their differences, as no more was heard about these issues.[71]

Meanwhile, preparations were in progress for a possible war with the emperor. Sandys was employing spies in Flanders and one, Gyles Kevalle, was nearly caught. John Cheyne, Sandys' deputy at Guînes, wrote from there saying that Gyles met with a Spanish soldier in Gravelines in Flanders and they had a drink together. Unfortunately, the Spaniard had married Gyles's sister-in-law and turned him in to his captain. Gyles claimed he had been on a pilgrimage to a place just outside Dunkirk, but the captain did not believe him and said he should hang him, but instead told him to leave town.[72] This story reveals the closeness and diversity of people at the borders of the Pale and inside its boundaries, and how difficult it was to prevent spying. Many were there for legitimate trade reasons, others because of marriage.

On the personal front, Richard Fox appointed Sandys as an executor of his will, along with the Marquis of Exeter, Henry Courtenay. When Fox died on 5 October 1528 he bequeathed a set of tapestries, called the Vineyard, and a bed with furnishings to Sandys.[73] It is possible that this bed, which would have been carved, is connected with an altar at St Mary's Church at Hambleden, Buckinghamshire, which has carved wooden panels at the front and rear, bearing the coats of arms of Cardinal Wolsey and Bishop Fox. These panels may have been part of a bed that came from The Vyne because of the connection between the church and the Sandys family – Lord William's grandson Henry is entombed in this church and has a fine stone memorial. The altar panels bearing Fox's coat of arms may therefore have come from the bed that Fox bequeathed to Sandys. There is little record of the relationship between the two men, but they were certainly colleagues and probably friends who had known each other from Henry VII's time. Fox commended Sandys to Wolsey for his role in settling the Southampton riots in September 1517, and they jointly applied for the licence for the Guild of the Holy Ghost Chapel, Basingstoke. Several examples of Fox's coat of arms and badge, showing a pelican pecking its breast, can also be seen in the Oak Gallery at The Vyne.

Early in 1528, Sandys was told to prepare himself to lead an army to fight the emperor's troops, but no conflict happened and he was stood down. In any case, he could not have undertaken this role as he was taken ill in the spring,[74] but not with the sweating sickness that was endemic in England in summer 1528. In July, the Venetian ambassador reported: 'On account of the plague no business is transacted. The King and Cardinal have departed.'[75]

More Problems in Calais and Family Loss

At the end of 1528 there was increasing concern over the defences in the Calais Pale. Sandys and Wingfield, Deputy of Calais, were therefore in Calais and Guînes from November of that year until mid-1529,[76] trying to improve the defences and gather information from spies. Sandys was again unwell during January in Calais, and at the end of the month was reported to be bedridden and unable to walk.[77] One of his younger sons, John, was in France, but whether he was Sandys' deputy at Guînes at that time is not clear.[78]

Sandys left Calais on 30 August 1529, and Elis Gruffudd noted that he tipped the soldiers and servants of the Deputy of Calais 'to give them cheer'.[79] Despite recent ill health in Calais, he was lucky to be away from England because 'the disease' had returned in summer 1529. This time, the Venetian ambassador had 'the plague' in his London house, so he moved to a village outside the city,[80] and the court also stayed out of London. Sandys was affected in a different way: the disease killed his sister Edith, Lady Neville, who died on 22 August of 'the great sicknesses' in Stepney, east of London, where presumably Lord Darcy had a home. By that evening her body had been disembowelled and 'cerred' (waxed), and because she had died of the sickness Darcy ordered a more modest funeral than might be expected and discouraged people from attending. Early the following Wednesday her body was carried by her servants and Black Friars, with two banners at the front of the coffin and two behind. Alongside the coffin were a dozen poor men in black, hooded habits and the same number of yeomen carrying torches, while in front were four orders of friars, ministers of the church, gentlemen and Garter Principal of Arms, Richmond Herald, in his coat of arms. The coffin was followed by the chief mourner, Lady Strickland, Edith's daughter by Ralph Neville, Earl of Westmorland, who was followed by other lady mourners and Lord Darcy's servants dressed in black. The procession walked to the hamlet of Ratcliff on the north side of the Thames adjacent to Stepney;

from there, two barges decked in black cloth decorated with her arms took them to the King's Bridge, Greenwich. The body was then taken to a friary church where, after a service, she was buried. The mourners then returned via the barges to Stepney or London.[81]

Parliament, Religion and the King's Marriages

On 9 August 1529, Henry set the machinery in motion to call Parliament. Elections were held for the Commons, and the peers, including Sandys, were summoned. The original purpose is debatable, but it became known as the Reformation Parliament, comprising seven sessions from 1529 to April 1536 and enacting some of the most significant changes made by any parliament.[82] It was formally opened at Westminster on 3 November and, although no description survives, a drawing made at the 1512 Parliament shows that the opening procession went from the Palace of Westminster to Westminster Abbey for Mass and then returned to the palace. This was the normal procedure, although it was sometimes held elsewhere, such as Bridewell Palace.[83] The configuration of the procession in subsequent parliaments and sessions did not change much, but the personnel did. The 1512 procession was led by high-ranking clergy, beginning with abbots, followed by bishops, then the Archbishop of Canterbury. Then came the Duke of Buckingham holding the Cap of Maintenance, with his son, Lord Stafford, at his side bearing the Sword of State. The king came next, under a Canopy of State supported at each corner, probably by knights. The king's train is supported by an unidentified marquis, whose rank is denoted by four ermine stripes across the chest of his red gown, and he is followed by another of the same rank carrying a stick of office. At that time the two marquises were those of Dorset and Exeter. It has been claimed that the stick carrier was the Earl of Oxford, the Lord Great Chamberlain,[84] because sticks were usually carried by the High Chamberlain and King's Chamberlain, but neither of the two marquises bore that rank. They were followed by the rest of the peers in descending order of rank: earls, viscounts and then barons.

A painting now in the royal collection shows the arrangement of the 1523 Parliament, and it is almost certain that this configuration continued.[85] In the centre at the top of the painting, on a raised dais and facing the viewer, is the enthroned king. To his right and in front are Cardinal Wolsey, William Warham, Archbishop of Canterbury, and the Bishop of London. To his left are the Lord Chancellor, Lord Treasurer and Garter King of Arms, all facing the viewer. In front of the archbishops on the Cloth of State an earl holds the Cap of Maintenance. In front of the Lord Chancellor and Lord Treasurer another earl holds the Sword of State, and to his left is a Lord Chamberlain holding his stick of office. Professor Lehmberg identifies this person as the Lord Chamberlain of the Household, which was Sandys after 1526, but the official Royal Library catalogue describes him as an earl from his robes, which suggests the Earl of Oxford, the Lord Great Chamberlain. Clearly, there is confusion, and there may have been changes from session to session. In 1539, an Act established the order of precedence in Parliament, and the same applied to the Court of Star Chamber, as follows:

House of Lords Precedence Act 1539
Lords Temporal

Rank of Office	Title	Person 1539	Highest Rank of Person
1	Lord Chancellor	Baron, Thomas Audley	1
2	Lord Treasurer	Duke of Norfolk, Thomas Howard	2
3	Lord President of the Council	Duke of Suffolk, Charles Brandon	3
4	Lord Privy Seal	Thomas Cromwell, Baron Cromwell	4
5	Great Chamberlain	John de Vere 14th Earl of Oxford	5
6	Constable	Vacant 1521–47	6
7	Marshal	Duke of Norfolk, Thomas Howard	4
8,7	Admiral	William Fitzwilliam, Earl of Southampton	7
9,8	Grand Master/Steward	George Talbot, 4th Earl of Shrewsbury to 1538	8
10,9	King's Chamberlain	William Sandys, Baron Sandys	9
11,4	King's Chief Secretary	Thomas Cromwell	4
12–*c.* 50	Other nobility in the following order: Dukes Marquises Earls Viscounts King's Chief Secretary Barons		
		1–10 will sit on the left of the Parliament Chamber (assumed to be the king's left) above all dukes, unless they are an immediate relative of the king. 11 will sit above the barons.	

To return to the 1523 painting, the Lords Spiritual are on the viewer's left in the main body of the hall, nine bishops with seventeen abbots behind, facing inwards. On the right are the Lords Temporal in order of rank, except for the barons. Some barons face the king but at right angles to the other lords. Four wool sacks are in the centre, where two chief justices, eight judges, and four sergeants of law are seated. Behind these are two kneeling clerks, Sir Thomas More, as Speaker of the House of Commons, and thirteen other members of the Commons barely discernible at the bottom of the picture below the Bar of the House.

At that time the House of Lords had 107 members, fifty Spiritual and fifty-seven Temporal, and proxies were allowed. Sandys was one of two Lords Temporal who served as proxies for Lords Spiritual, but he was himself often represented by proxy. Longer absences required a licence ('passport') from the king, as held by Sandys when in Calais in 1540.[86]

The opening procession for the 1529 Parliament, in similar order to that shown in 1512, set out from Bridewell Palace and walked to the Blackfriars Monastery for Mass. The king and his nobles were dressed in appropriate regalia, with Sandys providing the king with direct support. After Mass the Members of Parliament processed to Bridewell for the formal opening, with Sandys supporting the royal train. As the King's Chamberlain, he was not seated with the rest of the lords but with the marquises of Dorset and Exeter, who preceded the king carrying the royal symbols of office. Sandys was to their left, carrying his stick of office.[87] Unfortunately, the records represented by the House of Lords' Journal are sparse for the first part of the sixteenth century, and during Sandys' time there between 1523 and 1540 they exist only for 1534 (first session only), 1536 (June–July), and the 1539 and 1540 sessions.[88] In 1534, he attended twenty-three days (about half of those possible); in 1536, three days during June and July; and only one day in 1539. The following session, 1540, was unusual as his attendance was recorded for forty-one days, but for most of those days he was in Calais. This confusion may arise because on 3 June he was granted a 'passport' by the king to attend to the defences of Guînes. Before that date, he attended seven days of the session from 12 April to 3 June.

At the 1529 Parliament the opening session was dominated by a speech by the Chancellor, Sir Thomas More, who spelled out the charges against Cardinal Wolsey, after which Parliament adjourned for three days before business began in earnest. It is therefore necessary to outline the background to Wolsey's fall, a saga that has been much discussed and debated by others.[89] The principal concern at court from 1527 onwards for several years was the king's 'Great Matter', the fact that marriage to Anne Boleyn required the annulment of his marriage to Catherine. Anne refused to be Henry's mistress, unlike her sister Mary, and her insistence on marriage eventually led to Wolsey's downfall.

The episode can be summarised as follows. In 1527, Wolsey believed that he could persuade the pope to annul the marriage at a court held in England under his chairmanship. The pope was not convinced by Wolsey's arguments, but agreed eventually that the case could be tried in England under cardinals Wolsey and Campeggio. Wolsey accepted this response but did not understand that the pope was under pressure from the Holy Roman Emperor to not agree to the separation of his aunt, Queen Catherine, from Henry VIII. Campeggio arrived in London in October 1528. After nearly a year he adjourned the fruitless negotiations and proceedings and returned to Rome. These proceedings never restarted, so Wolsey had failed the king. This, together with his inept handling of foreign relations with France and the Holy Roman Empire, led to Wolsey's downfall in the autumn of 1529.

Sandys does not appear to have been a key player in the machinations at court to remove Wolsey from his role as the king's senior advisor and friend, but he did join the wolf pack of senior courtiers determined to ensure Wolsey's downfall. On 1 December 1529, Henry was presented with a document alleging that Wolsey had committed forty-four offences, for which Sandys was one of seventeen signatories. The others included the dukes of Norfolk and Suffolk, the Marquis of Exeter, the earls of Shrewsbury, Oxford, Northumberland, Lord Darcy and Sir Thomas More. Wolsey was accused of usurping the king's authority, placing the pope's authority above that of the king, taking money from the Church to which he was not entitled, subverting the course of justice, and breathing on the king when he was diseased.[90] These arguments eventually persuaded Henry that Wolsey should be removed from his administrative and advisory roles.

Sandys may have had concerns about signing the document, because he would be helping to disgrace the man who had supported and sponsored him at court. On the other hand, he may not have seen Wolsey as his advocate but as his 'puppet master'. A Spanish chronicler claimed that Sandys hated Wolsey, and had complained to the king that Wolsey had taken some of his revenue.[91] Yet, if Sandys had not signed he would have lost favour with many powerful colleagues in the Privy Council, such as the Duke of Norfolk, as well as Anne Boleyn and everyone who saw a chance of removing Wolsey from office. There was also the possibility that Sandys would gain from Wolsey's estate if he fell from grace. In the event, Wolsey retained his position as Archbishop of York, but much of his property was sequestrated by the Crown. Sandys subsequently (in June 1530) asked Wolsey for the office of Keeper of Farnham Castle, which Wolsey, as Bishop of Winchester and through Thomas Cromwell, granted to him. This may be surprising, as Wolsey must have known that Sandys had signed the articles against him, but perhaps he regarded Sandys as having influence with the king.[92] Wolsey was also told to live in Cawood Castle, Yorkshire, where he eventually arrived in September 1530, but he was not there long before being arrested by the Earl of Northumberland and returned to London. He did not reach London, as he died of dysentery at Leicester on 29 November.[93]

In July 1530, a few months before Wolsey's death, Sandys had signed a letter with the other lords asking the pope to consent to the divorce of the king and Catherine,[94] but it achieved nothing. Yet, his position at court seems to have been enhanced by Wolsey's demise. The Duke of Norfolk, a leader in engineering Wolsey's downfall, took over his administrative duties and led a powerful group of nobles, including the earls of Wilshire and Sussex,[95] the new Bishop of Winchester, Lord Darcy, and Lord Sandys.[96] Indeed, the early 1530s saw the zenith of Sandys' influence and power, as demonstrated by the size of the gifts he received from the king. As a senior courtier he received a substantial New Year's gift and was expected to offer a gift to the king in return. The king's gifts were usually elaborate gilt plate bowls or cups, and their weight was a measure of royal favour. The table below reveals that Sandys' gifts increased in weight after 1530 and exceeded those of the dukes of Norfolk and Suffolk in 1530. It also compares the weight of gilt plate given to Sandys with that given to Charles Brandon, Duke of Suffolk, and Thomas Howard, Duke of Norfolk.

Person	1528	1530	1532	1534
Archbishop of Canterbury	21		29	
Norfolk	31	37	37	37
Suffolk	29	36	84	86
Sandys	31	45	45	43

Note: the weights are in ounces.
References:
1528: TNA E101/420/4
1530: TNA E101/420/10
1532: TNA E101/420/15
1534: TNA E101/421/13

The lists provide more detail of the gifts. In 1532, Lord Sandys received a gilt cup and gilt cruse, both with covers, while Lady Sandys received a gilt goblet with cover weighing 34 ounces, the second highest for any lady. Sandys' gift to the king was a pair of candlesticks of silver and gilt, while his wife gave Henry a gilt cup with cover.

Another, and perhaps more important, indication of Sandys' relationship with the king at this time was the timing and context of a visit by Henry and Anne Boleyn to The Vyne in 1531. In April that year the first public statement of the king's case for the annulment of his marriage to Queen Catherine, 'the Gravissime Censurae', was issued. Despite this, she did not leave the court until July, when the court was at Windsor and she was instructed by Henry on 15 July to leave. On 22 July, Henry and Anne set off on a hunting trip, so that Henry would not be involved in Catherine's departure. She was still at Windsor on 25 July when she wrote to Henry that she understood that she was not to follow him but that it would have been some consolation if she could have 'bid him adieu'. Henry was angry that she had written and told the messenger that he had no need to 'bid her adieu' and that she should not ask to visit him or inquire after his health.[97] Catherine understood the finality of Henry's decision, and on 28 July left for her new home, the More, near Rickmansworth, which had been one of Wolsey's residences. Meanwhile, the hunting party travelled via the royal manor of Chertsey to Woolmer Forest, then on to Farnham Castle, arriving on 2 August. The following day they travelled the 14 miles to The Vyne, which would be their base for hunting in The Vyne, Beaurepaire and Basing Park lands, but by 10 August they arrived back at the royal residence at Easthampstead (Bracknell in Berkshire).[98] These details reveal that they stayed at only two non-royal residences during this difficult time, namely Farnham and The Vyne, the former being under Sandys' control and the latter his property.

The flurry of preparation at The Vyne is easy to imagine, not only because the king was visiting at short notice and accompanied by Anne Boleyn, but also because The Vyne contained many of Queen Catherine's heraldic symbols, some of which are visible today in the Oak Gallery and chapel. Tapestries and hangings were probably used to hide them.

At the same time, one must wonder whether Sandys had concerns about Queen Catherine's fate and the rise of Anne Boleyn. If so, no evidence is apparent, and he seems to have accepted the king's action and carried out his wishes to the best of his ability. No doubt he hoped to benefit from his loyalty, and it certainly gave him the best chance of survival. Like many others, he may not have been sufficiently astute to recognise the consequences for England of Henry's lust for Anne. Henry had gradually become convinced that the Church and clergy in England would not agree to his divorce while their loyalty lay with the pope, and his solution was to separate the English Church from Rome. In April 1532, he increased the pressure on the clergy by sending the Duke of Norfolk, Marquis of Exeter, Earl of Oxford and Lord Sandys to an ecclesiastical convocation at Canterbury, with a directive that resulted in agreement that the king would be head of the Church in England.[99]

The Duke of Norfolk's inner circle did not hold power for long, firstly because they were a loose alliance and relatively inexperienced in managing matters of State, but secondly because of the rise of Thomas Cromwell and his supporters. Cromwell had been close to Wolsey, acting as legal adviser and counsellor, and had closed some of the smaller monasteries to enrich Wolsey (and no doubt himself), which enabled him to establish Cardinal College at Oxford. Wolsey's downfall was a severe blow to Cromwell's career, but with support from Anne Boleyn and others of the Protestant persuasion he soon recovered and joined the king's council as junior member in January 1531. The stage was set for Cromwell to apply his energy, legal skill, ability and ruthlessness to realise the king's wishes, and the balance of power gradually shifted from the conservative nobles to the Protestant faction led by Cromwell, and then to Cromwell alone.

When Archbishop Warham died in August 1532 Henry appointed Thomas Cranmer in his place, but it was not until 23 May 1533 that Cranmer annulled the marriage between Henry and Catherine. On 1 September, Henry made Anne Boleyn the Marchioness of Pembroke, and Sandys attended the ceremony as a witness.[100]

Further Involvement in Calais and France

On 25 September 1532, Sandys was appointed Receiver General of the Earldom and Lordship of Guînes, further increasing his status and wealth.[101]

Henry had renewed the Anglo-French alliance against the emperor in the summer of 1532, and by August he had agreed with Francis I to meet in France in October. It was supposed to be a meeting 'without pomp or display' but inevitably became a great show of wealth and splendour on both sides, as might be expected. Preparation began in August, and on 20 August a ship sailed from England to France laden with tapestries and decorations.[102] Henry, accompanied by Anne, left England on 10 October and reached Calais the following day. Francis made his way to Boulogne and on 15 October sent the great lords of France to Calais to greet Henry. This was apparently unexpected, so Henry hurriedly dispatched the Duke of Norfolk, Marquis of Exeter, earls of Oxford, Darby and Rutland, Lord Sandys and Lord Fitzwater to meet the French party and escort them to him. On 21 October, Henry rode out of Calais with 140 lords and knights, including Sandys, and four bishops to meet Francis and his entourage at Sandingfield, 8 miles outside of Calais. Elis Gruffudd, the Welsh chronicler, wrote that the English were dressed in velvet and silk with their gold chains of office on their shoulders, and all were mounted on the most good-looking geldings a man could find anywhere in the world. The servants were also splendidly attired. He then described how the two kings met, embraced each other, and began their discussions. While they were talking a Frenchman released a small kite that had been blinded and sent hawks to pursue it to distract the throng's attention from the kings' meeting. Afterwards, the kings and their retinues retired to Boulogne for entertainment. A few days later the French king and lords travelled to Calais where they were similarly entertained. Following Mass in the morning, and bear- and bull-baiting in the afternoon, there was a banquet and dancing when the English ladies, led by Anne Boleyn, danced with the French. Sandys was present at the Garter meeting at Calais on 27 October when three senior French nobles were admitted to the order. Feasting and exchanges of gifts continued until 29 October, when Francis departed for Paris.[103] Henry planned to return to England early in November but was delayed by storms in the Channel, so it was not until 14 November that the royal party landed in Dover.

Such was Sandys' level of involvement in the Calais Pale that his chaplain, Nicholas Halle, was rector of Balyngham church and another of his staff was rector of Pytham church.[104] In December 1532, he and the dukes of Norfolk and Suffolk were appointed to survey the lands in the Pale that had been drained. The marshes surrounding Calais town were historically important, as its defensive strength relied not only on the fortress and town walls but also on the marshes. In 1528, Sir Robert Wingfield, as Deputy of Calais, had the marshes drained, which may have benefitted travellers and farmers but weakened the town's defences.[105] It is surprising that this had not prompted early action, but perhaps someone directed the king's attention to the condition of the marshes during his recent visit – probably Sandys, who was unhappy about Wingfield interfering in Guînes' matters.

Sandys returned to England before Christmas 1532, but an intriguing letter from a John Bonholt in Calais, dated 8 February 1533, illustrates the breadth of his involvement there over time. It concerns 'Parnell, your woman', in relation to affairs at the court of the Emperor Charles V, and ends with: 'Parnell desires you to remember a gown that you promised her.' She is mentioned again in November 1533 in a letter to Sandys from Anthoine Du Val, who says, 'I understand some report has been made to you of Mrs Parnell who was to have brought to you some young boars that she found dead. I assure you that it is not the case but they were strangled by dogs, and I have eaten their liver.'[106] One wonders what lies behind this letter! Mrs Parnell does not appear again in extant correspondence but is mentioned twice in *The Lisle Letters*, edited by St Clare Byrne, who suggests she was one of the spies maintained by Sandys in the empire and France. Reference to Sandys' promise of a dress suggests that they knew each other well.[107]

The Lisle Letters are the correspondence of Arthur Plantagenet, Viscount Lisle, who was Deputy of Calais from March 1533 until his arrest in 1539 for alleged treason committed in Calais. William, Lord Sandys was Captain of Guînes during this period, and a member of the Council of Calais. In addition to their business relationship, Sandys was a friend of Lord Lisle and his wife, Honor, but the friendship did not prevent Sandys from writing to Cromwell about events in Calais, and he seems to have done little to help Lisle when he was accused of treason. Indeed, St Clare Byrne suggests that Sandys may have been active in Lisle's demise. Following Lisle's arrest, his collection of letters was confiscated by the State, and most are now held by The National Archives at Kew, with some at the British Library. A few were edited in the late nineteenth century among the *Letters and Papers of Henry VIII*, but St Clare Byrne chose to revisit all the manuscript letters to transcribe, edit, and arrange them for publication as *The Lisle Letters* in six volumes in 1981. Sandys wrote forty-seven letters to Lisle during the period and St Clare Byrne published thirty-three. She has also published the letters from Lisle to Sandys and from Sandys to Honour Lisle, all of which provide valuable insight into Sandys' life, personality and contemporary events.

In describing Sandys, she comments that 'there is nothing in his manner to suggest the raffish gadabout into which he has been transformed in Shakespeare's *King Henry VIII*. His letters are gentlemanly and somewhat precise in tone: they have a courteous gravity well suited to his official position in the royal household and to a man of taste and culture who was largely responsible for the building and decoration of the Vyne – among the finest Renaissance dwellings of the early sixteenth century.'[108]

To illustrate Sandys' writing style, one of his letters is transcribed below. It starts with a long greeting, before requesting Lord Lisle to send him some pewits and grant him a licence to ship wine from Calais, and concludes with a long closing section, all of which are characteristic features of private but formal correspondence at this time:

Lord Sandys to Lord Lisle, 28 April 1534 (*Lisle Letters*, 177, Vol. 2, 141)

1. **Greeting:** My very good lord, in your right benign wise I recommend me unto your good lordship, with as entire hearty thanks for your especial goodness and favour daily continued and augmented for my sake unto my friends and servants in those parts of your lordships being, as by their report I have perfect revelation, whereby your lordship bindeth me to do you pleasure as of which you be assured to my power during life.
2. **Request:** Pleaseth it your good lordship to continue in memory that of your mere gentle disposition I have been accustomed heretofore, as time hath served, to be participant of your lordship's pewits. And my lord, although I know well that that I have at any time recompensed your lordship for the same, yet because I am loth that your prementioned goodness in that behalf should towards me take discontinuance, that is the occasion of my now renewing your remembrance and, my lord, in like manner to pray your favour that such French wines as I have required my loving friend Mr Vice-Treasurer [Robert Fowler] to buy for me at Calais may through your lordship's licence be shipped and transported over to me.
3. **Conclusion:** And thus I beseech your lordship that this my writing may present my most benign recommendations unto my lady your bedfellow; and if there be any pleasure that I may do your lordship in these parts or elsewhere, upon such knowledge had I will as gladly accomplish the same to the best of my power, as knoweth the Holy Ghost, who preserve your good lordship in his continual protection. At the Vyne the xxvii th day of April.

All your own assured to his power
Wylliam Sandys.

Sandys wrote to Lisle again on 9 June to say that he had received his pewits.[109] He was obviously partial to food and wine from Calais because a letter from Lisle in September 1533 says that he had sent a hogshead of claret and one of white wine, and if Sandys wished he would send herring and wine this winter.[110]

Return to England and Developments at Court

Sandys returned home from Calais for Christmas 1532 and the New Year, including the royal celebrations. It was around Christmas that Anne Boleyn agreed to share Henry's bed and became pregnant, and they were secretly married on 25 January 1533. The court then began to focus on Anne's coronation as queen and the birth of a child.

Meanwhile, Thomas Cromwell rose in status and displaced the conservative clique led by the Duke of Norfolk, which included Sandys. A key post was that of secretary to the king, which Cromwell acquired in 1533, and by April he was Receiver General, Master of the King's Jewel House, Clerk of the Hanaper, Master of the Court of Wards and Chancellor of the Exchequer.[111] This power shift is reflected in a change of tone in letters from Sandys to Cromwell. In September 1532, Sandys had written rather curtly, asking for money relating to the expenditure of members of the King's Chamber and Guînes, and concluding with: 'I leave one of the grooms to attend on you.' In November, describing himself as 'William, Lord Sandys, K.G. Captain of the town and castle of Guînes', he made a grant to Cromwell and others. A year later, in October 1533, he wrote from The Vyne about his son, Reynolde Sandys, asking Cromwell to make his excuses to the king for not visiting him and being absent from Parliament. This letter starts with 'I beg you will' and ends 'I shall always be willing to requite you for your kindness'. Later, Sandys wrote again from The Vyne, saying, 'I thank you for your goodness to me and my unthrifty son, the priest, and I beg a favour for Thomas Bullock, etc.'[112]

Much of Sandys' time during the early part of 1533 was occupied by the marriage and coronation of Anne Boleyn. As Lord Chamberlain of the Household he was one of two officers in charge of arrangements for the coronation in May. He was responsible for all ceremonies in the royal palaces and must have been heavily involved, as he does not feature noticeably in other matters at this time. The other officer was the Lord Great Chamberlain John de Vere, 15th Earl of Oxford, who was responsible for overall arrangements. For the coronation itself, both men were assigned lodgings in St Thomas's Tower at the Tower of London, which had been refurbished between June 1532 and spring 1533 to provide new accommodation for the event.[113] The de Vere coat of arms is depicted in the oak panels of the Oak Gallery at The Vyne and one of the window panels in the antechapel.

During autumn 1532 and until early autumn 1533, Princess Mary Tudor spent most of her time away from court in Kent. Her prolonged absence may have been a deliberate plan by the king to remove her during his marriage to Anne Boleyn, the formal annulment of his marriage with Catherine, and preparations for the coronation. From 27 November 1532 to 5 May 1533, she lived at Knole and occasionally dined with the wives of senior courtiers, such as Lady Grey and the Marchioness of Dorset. The only male courtiers who dined with her at Knole were Lord Sandys and Sir William Fitzwilliam on Thursday 10 April, the timing of which is significant as it was only two days after Parliament formally decided that the marriage between Henry and Catherine was null.[114] She left Knole on 6 May and moved close by to Otford until 2 July. With Henry's marriage to Catherine annulled he was free to marry again, and nobody could appeal to the pope as it was decreed that the pope had no authority in England. On 9 April, the king had sent the Duke of Norfolk, the Marquis of Exeter and many others to inform Catherine of Parliament's decision and take her to Ampthill Castle in Bedfordshire.[115]

The likely purpose of the visit by Sandys and Fitzwilliam to Mary on 10 April was to inform her about Parliament's decision, as the implications for Mary were significant, including illegitimacy, but the finality and wider implications for her and her mother were of wider concern. It is worth noting that two of the principal messengers to Catherine and Mary – Norfolk and Sandys –

were among the religious conservatives at court. Was Henry testing them, or was seniority the main factor? Was Fitzwilliam sent to keep an eye on Sandys? Sandys and Fitzwilliam would later fall out, so it is possible that he was sent as a minder. As for Mary's reaction, she attended the coronation in May but then continued to visit locations away from court.

Evidence that Sandys favoured the 'old' religion is seen in his association with the Duke of Norfolk and the indulgence to celebrate Mass granted to him and a few others by Pope Clement VII in August 1533, although the king had been excommunicated and the country placed under Apostolic Interdict, which banned participation in the rites of the Catholic Church.[116] Other indications of conservative persuasion include his connection with Eustace Chapuys, Ambassador of the Holy Roman Emperor and a strong Roman Catholic; building the Chapel of the Trinity in the Chapel of the Holy Ghost at Basingstoke; working with Richard Fox to establish the voluntary Guild of the Fraternity of the Holy Ghost at Basingstoke;[117] and commissioning the Chapel at The Vyne dedicated to the Virgin Mary. His letters often conclude with 'beseeching the Holy Ghost to preserve you'.

After his visit to Princess Mary at Knole, Sandys returned to London to finalise preparations for the coronation. The event started on 29 May and finished on Sunday 1 June. On the first day, Anne travelled in a richly decorated barge from Greenwich to the Tower of London with many senior nobles. Her boat was accompanied by about fifty large barges filled with lords and ladies, the mayor of London and other senior worthies. Guns were fired throughout the journey and one boat carried a 'great Dragon continually moving and casting wildfire, and around the boat were terrible monsters and wild men casting fire and making hideous noises'. Others carried musicians, and all were richly decorated. Arrival at the Tower was marked by a great gun salute. Anne and some of her entourage were welcomed by Sandys and the officers-at-arms who escorted her to the king – who kissed her in public. The couple retired into the fortress for the night.

That night, the king created eighteen Knights of the Bath. On the Saturday, Anne was escorted to Whitehall Palace in a great procession that included nobles and their ladies, no doubt including Sandys, senior clergy, foreign ambassadors, the mayor of London, servants and soldiers, all in their finery. Anne was carried on a litter of white cloth of gold, wearing a coat of fine white cloth and a mantle edged with ermine, and with her hair loose under a coif encircled with precious stones. Above her was a canopy carried by knights, and the route was lined with tableaux and fountains discharging red and white wine. Just before St Paul's Church, the Master Bakers of London presented her with a purse containing a thousand marks (£666). At Whitehall she changed her garments and went in her barge to Westminster, where she stayed with the king. The next day, Sunday, the coronation took place in Westminster Abbey. That evening, the new queen held a dinner in Westminster Palace attended by the nobility and senior clergy. The king, some ambassadors and his immediate staff watched from a room prepared for the occasion in St Stephen's Church.

Sandys was in the procession from the Tower to Westminster, next to the Lord Privy Seal, the Lord Admiral of England and the Great Chamberlain, and it is a fair assumption that he was present at the dinner, attending on the king.[118]

Despite all the pomp, free shows and wine the people of London were not enthusiastic, according to Eustace Chapuys, the imperial ambassador. In a letter to Charles V dated 16 June, two weeks after the coronation, he refers to 'Her [Anne Boleyn] coronation, which was a cold, meagre, and uncomfortable thing, to the great dissatisfaction, not only of the common people but also of the rest. And it seems that the indignation of everybody about this affair has increased by a half since the coronation.'[119] The Venetian ambassador was more restrained, reporting that the procession was conducted 'with the utmost order and tranquillity, the houses were crowded with persons of every condition', thus implying that people were interested in the spectacle but hardly rapturous in their reception of the new queen, unlike the previous coronation, which was a celebration enjoyed by all and sundry.

At the end of July Sandys and others, including Thomas Boleyn, Earl of Wiltshire, were granted a share of the lands formerly held by Lord Berners, sometime Deputy of Calais. For Sandys this may have been a reward for his work on the coronation.[120] On 23 August, he was involved in discussions with Eustace Chapuys about trade relations between England and the Flemish,[121] but this was relatively unimportant in court circles compared with the imminent royal birth, which happened on Sunday 9 September at three o'clock in the afternoon. As the child was female, the planned celebrations were simplified, but baby Elizabeth's christening was an elaborate occasion attended by the extended Boleyn family and many Howards, because Anne was granddaughter to the old Duke of Norfolk and his second wife Elizabeth, and niece to Thomas Howard, Duke of Norfolk.

Of deeper significance to Mary was that baby Elizabeth was declared the first of the king's legitimate children, thus confirming Mary as illegitimate in her father's eyes.

Activities Interrupted by Illness

After the royal christening in September 1533 Sandys went to Calais for a few weeks, which was unusually late in the year for that journey and the only visit that year.[122] He had pressing business concerning his brother Richard, who had been appointed bailiff of the island of Colne in the Calais Pale by royal warrant in May,[123] but the former mayor of Calais had refused to accept his authority. Sandys wrote to Lisle, asking him to make clear to the people in the Pale that they should accept Richard in his new role,[124] and it seems that the matter was settled as it is not mentioned again. He also took the opportunity to stock up with claret and white wine through Lisle, who offered to send herring and more wine in the winter 'for your own mouth', as Sandys evidently enjoyed herring.[125]

This Calais visit may have been curtailed for health reasons because Sandys spent most, if not all, of the rest of the year at The Vyne and unwell. During that time he wrote to Cromwell about his son Reynolde, a priest who apparently got into debt ('my unthrifty son'), and later thanked him for what he had done to assist. He also made a case to Cromwell to relieve a certain Thomas Bullock of a fine that 'he cannot bear'.[126] Both episodes reveal Sandys' care for family and friends alongside his lofty duties. It is unlikely that he and his wife were present at the king's New Year celebrations for 1534 but his gift from Henry was generous. Sandys' absence from court was noticed, and his return was mentioned by Sir Thomas Palmer who wrote to Lisle that 'my lord Chamberlain this day came to Court'.[127]

Some doubt has been expressed about whether Sandys' sickness was genuine. Chaloner Chute's work on the history of The Vyne says that Sandys 'retired from Court in 1534 on the plea of sicknesses', but there is clear evidence that he did not retire from court or Parliament. The records of the House of Lords for the 1534 session show that he attended all the January days, but none in February apart from the 26th, and none for the first half of March. After 14 March he attended all session days until the 28th, and the session finished on 30 March.[128] Evidence suggests he was fit in January, ill through February and half of March, then recovered, but fell sick again at the end of March and by April was seriously ill, as seen in extracts from letters to Lord Lisle in the spring of 1534:

Sir Thomas Palmer to Lisle, 28 March 1534
I hear say that my Lord Chamberlain is sore sick of ague and lies at Polles at his house. And as I hear say the reversion of Guînes to my Lord Leonard...

John Husee to Lisle, 1 April
... and my Lord Sandys is very sick. Men doubteth his recovery. Mr Rockewood thinketh, if your lordship might change the room for Guînes. In case my Chamberlain die...

John Husee to Lisle, 4 April
This ascertaining your Lordship that my Lord Chamberlain is ridden in a horse litter and is something amended.

Rokewood to Lisle, 6 April
Also my Lord Chamberlain hath been and is sore sick – and if anything should come to my Lord Chamberlain other than well, I would your lordship had the castle of Guînes.

Husee to Lisle, 8 May
Also if my Lord Chamberlain decease I doubt not there is such ways found that your lordship desire.

Lord Leonard Grey to Cromwell, 26 July
Has lately heard that the Lord Chamberlain is sore sick.[129]

These letters to Lisle and Cromwell remove any doubt that Sandys was seriously ill, resulting in speculation about who should replace him as Captain of Guînes.[130] One also reveals that he had a house close to St Paul's Cathedral, the location of which may be mentioned in John Stow's description of Queen Hythe Ward in his *Survey of London* (1598). Stow writes: 'Next is called Boss Lane ... then is one great messuage, sometime belonging to the abbots of Chertsey in Surrey and was their inn, wherein they were lodged when they repaired to the city. It is now called Sandie House by what reason I have not heard. I think the Lord Sands have been lodged there.' Thomas Pennant and Walter Thornbury are more specific, stating that Sandys' house was the former home of the abbots of Chertsey, near Trigg Steps, close to Baynard's Castle.[131] By today, the approximate site of the house is beneath the northern end of the Millennium Bridge.

Despite his illness, Sandys was able to write to Lisle at the end of April 1534 to ask for his wines to be shipped.[132] Yet, some may have seen him as a spent force, as the delivery was delayed and did not reach England until November,[133] when Sandys wrote to Cromwell asking for a licence to disembark twenty tuns[134] of wine for his house.[135] He probably continued at court, as he usually made a point of excusing himself if he could not, and he was certainly involved in court matters in October. He also took an interest in a dispute over a vacant post in Calais, and Cromwell told someone not to inform Sandys of recent developments because he already knew.[136] Yet, this was the first year since 1516 that he is not recorded as visiting Calais, although his presence was needed because problems between staff working at Guînes had been reported to the king but not to Sandys. Sandys claimed that Cromwell knew what had happened and reminded him that Sandys was Deputy of Guînes and a member of the king's council.[137]

His spirits must have been further dampened when the Crown sequestrated his income as Keeper of the Great Park and Manor of Stratfield Mortimer. Like other courtiers, including the Duke of Suffolk, he experienced the transfer of income to Anne Boleyn.[138]

Treasonable Thoughts?

Although Chute and others have assumed that Sandys effectively retired from court when he was ill, and he was certainly absent for much of 1534 and parts of 1535, he clearly returned in 1536 and had also been involved in developments in the previous year.

On 14 January 1535, the imperial ambassador, Eustace Chapuys, wrote to the emperor that he had received a communication from Sandys, whom he described as one of the country's most experienced soldiers. Sandys had apparently made two very direct statements: first, that he would support the emperor's troops if they invaded England; and second, that he was pretending to be ill to keep away from court.[139] Charles V received and replied to these letters. Support for an imperial army would also come from Lord Darcy, Sandys' brother-in law, the Earl of Northumberland, and others including both Lords Dacre, Lord Hussey, Lord Bray, the Marquis of Exeter, the Earl of Rutland[140] and Sir Geoffrey Pole.[141] Chapuys claimed that he gathered such information through medical people whom he cultivated because they gained access to people without raising suspicion, and he certainly had a medical contact with Catherine of Aragon.

There is no doubt that Chapuys believed the reports he received and included in dispatches to the emperor. Although he might emphasise negative aspects of events in England to attract his master's attention and provoke martial reaction, blatant untruths would have endangered his own career. In fact, war was unlikely at that time, as the imperial army was fully occupied fighting Turkish armies in Europe (Austria) and North Africa (Tunis).

For Sandys and the others, the risks were enormous. Any whiff of treason could result in execution and confiscation of estates by the Crown, depriving the families of their support. Given that many people were aware, it is a miracle that Cromwell did not discover that there were traitors in his backyard, especially as his spy network extended into Europe.

What could have driven Sandys, a loyal courtier and sometime friend of the king, to contemplate treason in late 1534/early 1535? The authors of English chronicles and contemporary correspondence are guarded for obvious reasons. It was probably an accumulation of events and concerns similar to those that Chapuys reported to the imperial court, which were:

1. The Act of Succession

In March 1534, Parliament passed the Act of Succession, which made Henry and Anne's unborn child successor to the throne instead of Mary, daughter of Catherine of Aragon, who was declared illegitimate as she was born out of wedlock, thus implying that Catherine had not been married to Henry. Every subject was required to swear an oath to recognise the Act and that Henry VIII was Supreme Head of the Church in England. Failure to do so was treason. Stephen Gardiner, Bishop of Winchester, reported to Cromwell that on 4 May 1534 he administered the oath to William, Lord Sandys and others in the Great Hall of Winchester Castle.[142]

2. Increasingly harsh treatment of Catherine, the ex-queen, and her daughter Mary

This is well described by others, such as Giles Tremlett in his biography of Catherine of Aragon.[143] After being dismissed from Windsor in 1531 Catherine was sent to the More in Berkshire, a royal residence previously owned by Wolsey that was quite large and comfortable, and she had a full brigade of staff. In April 1533, she was told that she was no longer queen and that neither she nor her staff should refer to her as such. She and Mary were given titles such as Prince Arthur's Dowager or Lady Catherine Dowager, and the Lady Mary (Princess Mary).[144] She was subsequently moved to a succession of other houses, each worse than the last, and her staff was reduced and replaced by unsympathetic people. By December 1533 she was at Kimbolton in Cambridgeshire when the king ordered the Duke of Suffolk, Charles Brandon, to move her to Somersham House in the Fens, described by Chapuys as 'surrounded with deep water and marshes, which is, she is informed, the most unhealthy and pestilential house in England'.[145] Catherine refused, saying that it would require force, and locked herself in her room.

Brandon also failed to persuade her to swear the Oath of Succession. While trying to do so, a crowd of sympathisers gathered outside the house threatening action, so he departed. Catherine had effectively imprisoned herself, remaining in her chamber except for visits to a nearby gallery to hear Mass and refusing to take food except what was prepared by a few trusted friends in her room. Henry began to spread the word that she suffered from dropsy, which was not true but led to concern that she would be poisoned.[146]

Mary fared little better and was not allowed to see her mother. Henry humiliated her by sending her to Hatfield House as lady's maid to the new Princess Elizabeth, where she was assigned a poor room and one chamber maid. Mary was not to be called 'princess', but could be described as Elizabeth's sister; however, what hurt most was her father's refusal to acknowledge her. When he visited Hatfield to see the new child he ordered that Mary should not be allowed into the room where he was. He sent Cromwell and others to coerce her to renounce her title, but she refused. When she asked to be allowed to kiss the king's hand he refused, and when he departed she watched from a terrace at the top of the house, knelt and put her hands together pointing towards him. Henry saw but ignored her, and then ordered that she and those around her should be guarded to ensure that no letters from the emperor or his court were received without his knowledge.[147]

3. Changes in power at court and the rise of Cromwell and the Boleyn family

It is unlikely that Sandys was particularly concerned about Cromwell's spectacular rise above him if it did not jeopardise his relationship with the king. Sandys was a competent administrator but not a strategist, nor was he a diplomat, so his relative rank with Cromwell was not an issue. But Cromwell's goals and means of achieving them were problematic. Similarly, while the Boleyn family did not pose a direct threat to Sandys, Anne was different. In some ways she was like Cromwell in intelligence, competence and ruthlessness, and there are several accounts of her pushing Henry to be more aggressive towards Catherine, Mary, and other courtiers who might be wavering, and of the changes she wanted to see in the Church and line of succession.

4. Major changes in long-established religious practices and buildings

Sandys was raised in the Christian tradition that evolved over more than a thousand years, becoming increasingly complex in theology and practice and further removed from what was described in the New Testament. By the late fifteenth and early sixteenth centuries in Western Europe the earlier, simpler message was being overshadowed by the cult of saints and the Virgin Mary, as fostered by literature such as the twelfth-century *Golden Legend*. Images of saints proliferated, often brightly coloured, and were deeply venerated.

Saints' days filled the Church Calendar and pilgrimages to their shrines and relics were essential to the practice of the Christian faith, especially for easing the transition of souls through Purgatory between death and Hell. Purgatory was a foretaste of the horrors of Hell, which, as described by Duffy, included boiling the usurious in molten gold, feeding the gluttonous with toads and serpents, and tormenting the sexually promiscuous in the loins.[148] It was obviously desirable to pass quickly through Purgatory and generally believed that this could be achieved through prayers, pilgrimages, the intercession of saints, and living a good life. Prayers could also be offered on behalf of the deceased, which led to the practice of paying priests to say Masses in chantry chapels. Sandys had two such chapels, one being the Chapel of the Holy Ghost in Basingstoke and the other at The Vyne.

5. The dissolution of the monasteries

Wolsey had begun the attack on the monasteries, which many considered justified because their reputation for corruption. The early 1530s witnessed a change of pace and scope, as Cromwell and Henry saw the monasteries as a reservoir of money for exploitation.

The combined effects of these five main issues created a climate of fear and distrust across the country and opposition from different levels of society. The Bishop of Rochester, John Fisher, and Sir Thomas More were imprisoned in spring 1534. They and others refused to swear the Oath of Succession, which implied that they refused to accept the break with Rome and that Catherine's marriage to Henry was against God's laws. Others were unhappy about changes and restrictions in religious practices and feared that following the new order would jeopardise their souls. Some, particularly monks and friars, were prepared to display their opposition and pay the price, but there was general horror at the execution of four Charterhouse monks, another monk and the vicar of Isleworth on 4 May 1535. Following their trial before the Lords at Westminster in April, they were killed in a barbaric manner, being 'ripped up in each other's presence, their arms torn off and their hearts rubbed upon their faces and mouths'.[149] A fuller account records:

> First, the 'said' four monks and one of the secular priests (because the young man was pardoned) were drawn from the Tower of London to the place of execution (about a French league distant) and without respect for their Order hanged with great ropes. While they were still alive the hangman cut out their hearts and bowels and burned them. Then they were beheaded and quartered, and the parts placed in public places on long spears. And it is believed that one saw the other's execution fully carried out before he died – a pitiful and strange spectacle, for it is long since persons have been known to die with greater constancy. No change was noticed in their colour or tone of speech, and while the execution was going on they preached and exhorted the bystanders with the greatest boldness to do well and obey the king in everything that was not against the honour of God and the Church.[150]

Like Sandys, some senior courtiers who were unhappy subscribed to the Oath of Succession,[151] but others followed different paths: Sir John Gage, Vice Chamberlain of the Household, left his post and became a Carthusian monk;[152] and Sir Brian Tuke simply left and stayed away.[153]

It may have been the treatment of Catherine and Mary, combined with the attack on religious beliefs and practices, that lay at the core of Sandys' and Darcy's concerns rather than the dissolution of the monasteries. The move towards Protestantism was certainly Darcy's biggest problem, but for Sandys it was both. Expressing views considered to be 'too Protestant' was also dangerous: Hugh Latimer, Bishop of Worcester, was branded a heretic for that reason, and Sandys found it necessary to apologise to Cromwell in April 1535 for his steward, Richard Clotton, who had attended a sermon preached by Latimer.[154]

Sometime in spring 1535 Sandys must have decided to acquiesce to Cromwell's wishes, as he saw no real prospect of help from the emperor. In mid-March he told Cromwell that he was available for Calais duties, thus demonstrating that he was back in action, but his offer does not seem to have been taken up.[155] He missed the April chapter meeting of the Garter knights at Greenwich but was nominated to attend the Grand Dinner on 9 May at Windsor,[156] and although there is no record of that meeting, it is fair to assume that he took the hint and was present. He was certainly fit until late June, but by the 25th, when he was at a hunting lodge in Woolmer Forest, he had the sweating sickness although he then managed to return to The Vyne.[157]

Throughout this time, Sandys must have hoped that Anne, the strongest opponent of Catherine and Mary, would fall out of favour with the king, and would have been aware through his contacts in the privy chamber that Henry's interest in younger ladies was rekindled in 1535. The Venetian ambassador to the English court reported on 3 June that 'the king is already tired to satiety of the new Queen',[158] and Eustace Chapuys had reported similar signs in February.[159] Elis Gruffudd, who was in Calais, wrote that he had heard courtiers say that 'there was much less love between them than had been previously'.[160] The troubles were clearly not over; if anything, they were worse. Fisher was beheaded in late June 1535, followed by More on 6 July, and many others were executed that year.[161] Maltreatment of Catherine and Mary continued, and Anne was increasingly strident in her demands, as if she was in charge rather than Henry or Cromwell. Her unpopularity increased.

Summer 1535 brought further consequences for Sandys' long absences from court and perceived loss of influence – and possible disaffection. Cromwell wanted his own man for a benefice to which Sandys had already appointed a relative of Lady Sandys. Sandys wrote to Cromwell that 'I marvel not a little you should ask me to do what is contrary to law, right and conscience. I have done nothing but what was proper',[162] indicating that he was prepared to stand up to him. In September Cromwell established a commission, led by Sir William Fitzwilliam, to investigate the state of Calais and the Pale: 'Ye shall inquire and present if any person imagined or has spoken treason – if the Deputy, the

Mayor, Captain of Guînes [Sandys] etc. ... have done their duty.' This had clear implications for Sandys, Lisle and the others responsible for administering the colony, and the initial findings were not good. Fitzwilliam reports: 'We have found the town and marches far out of order it would grieve any Englishman to see ... the ordinances have not been executed etc.'

They had obviously found decay, extortion, and oppression – but not treason.[163] Cromwell also told Fitzwilliam it would be right to go through Sandys' accounts at Guînes at some future time,[164] and helped a certain Henry Palmer 'redress the wrongs done me by my Lord Chamberlain's office'.[165] Was Cromwell trying to discredit Sandys or test a case against him? Henry Palmer was the brother of Sir Thomas Palmer,[166] Knight Porter, member of the Council of Calais and colleague of William Sandys. He appears in the 1533 Calais muster roll as a Spear with only two men under his command,[167] and then became Baily of Guînes in 1537.[168] Whatever Sandys had done to upset Palmer is not known, but after his appointment as Baily he caused problems at Guînes in 1537 and 1538 and tried to discredit Sandys before Cromwell and Lisle.[169]

Sandys was probably relieved when he heard that the king, Anne and a relatively small retinue would visit The Vyne in October 1535 on their return from visiting the West Country. This 1535 royal progress has been viewed as a campaign by Cromwell and Anne to ensure that the reforms were being implemented at local level. Halts were arranged with reformist supporters, and all was going well for the campaign which culminated in the consecration of three reforming bishops at Winchester on 19 September. By early September the royal party had reached Wiltshire and was quartered at Sir John Seymour's house, Wolf Hall, near Marlborough.[170]

Sir John was Jane Seymour's father, and it has been suggested that it was during this visit that Henry began to consider Jane as a replacement for Anne Boleyn. Eric Ives, in his book on Anne Boleyn, rejects this idea because there is no reference to Jane's presence there and Anne and Henry were happily married,[171] but it is valid to question whether we should expect Jane's presence to be mentioned as she was only a lady-in-waiting, first to Queen Catherine, then transferred to Queen Anne in 1533.[172] Perhaps the royal marriage was indeed sound, but Henry seems to have been casting around and there was no sign of another child who might be male. Jane's name was known to Henry because she appears in the 1534 New Year Gift list. Another recipient was one of the Shelton sisters (Mary or Margaret), who were related to Anne Boleyn, and one became the king's mistress early in 1535.

The stay of six days at Wolf Hall was long for a royal visit. Cromwell left the party and returned to London, probably assuming that Henry would follow the planned route, but on 10 October Sir William Fitzwilliam wrote to Cromwell that the king had decided to stay in Hampshire to visit Sandys and Paulet. This is significant as both Sandys and Paulet were conservatives,[173] but a visit to Elvetham near Fleet in Hampshire, another of Sir John Seymour's houses, was also included,[174] suggesting great interest in an ageing Sir John!

The visit by the Henry and his party to The Vyne, arriving on Friday 15 October, was important to Sandys as it showed the court that he still enjoyed the king's favour, but it was also a setback for Cromwell and Anne. Both Lord and Lady Sandys recognised this affirmation of confidence by writing to Cromwell that the king had visited, although they must have been aware that Cromwell already knew, and they requested a favour for a friend.[175] Lady Margery, whose letters seldom appear in in the records, also wrote to Cromwell pleading for pardon for the Prior of Worcester who had been accused of treason, and her request was granted.[176]

When Fitzwilliam's final report on the Calais problems appeared in early October 1535, it stated that Calais was 'in good conformity',[177] which differed from the initial findings, suggesting that Fitzwilliam was advised against criticising Lisle and Sandys too strongly. Perhaps the royal visit to The Vyne had revised Cromwell's view of Sandys.

The visit was also significant for Queen Anne because her cousin, Sir Francis Bryan, who was at The Vyne at the time, wrote on 19 October that the king was merry,[178] a comment that would be unremarkable if it were not for the fact that the royal couple had probably realised during the stay that Anne might be pregnant. An article by Dr B. M. Collins in the *Winchester Cathedral Record Extra* includes a well-argued case that Anne became pregnant in late September 1535 during the royal stay at Winchester, based on two pieces of evidence.[179] The first is a generally reliable contemporary source that said when Anne miscarried on Saturday 29 January 1565 'she reckoned herself at that time but 15 weeks gone with child'.[180] Fifteen weeks before that date was Saturday 16 October, when the royal couple were at The Vyne. The second piece of evidence is a statement by Emeritus Professor R. Weller, and expert obstetric colleagues at the University of Southampton, that medieval women counted their pregnancy from the date they missed their menstruation, which in this case would have been about 16 October. The miscarried foetus on 29 January was reportedly identifiable as male, but such identification is only possible after about thirteen weeks, which is consistent with the dates suggested above. Assuming Anne's reference to fifteen weeks and the medical opinions are correct, Anne's last menstruation in 1535 would have been around 18 September, and the first missed period would have occurred during the weekend of 15–18 October when the royal couple were at The Vyne. This would indeed have been cause for celebration and the comment by Anne's cousin that the king was 'merry'.

Yet, as autumn passed Henry's interest in his wife waned. By mid-January 1536, it was reported that Anne caught Jane sitting on Henry's lap 'and complacently receiving his most endearing caresses'.[181] Another version quotes Anne telling Henry, 'I saw this harlot Jane sitting on your knees while my belly was doing its duty.'[182] If correct, these reports indicate that Henry's relationship with Jane had begun before then. It was also said that Henry hardly spoke to Anne for many weeks before the end of January.[183]

On 15 or 16 October 1535, when at The Vyne, Sir William Fitzwilliam, then Sir William Paulet, reported that Henry had again changed his mind and decided to alter his route home because of outbreaks of plague.[184] Henry left The Vyne on Tuesday 19 October and the court travelled the short distance to Basing House, home of Sir William Paulet, an early sign of the increasing importance of Paulet and Basing House. This would also remind Sandys that royalty had somewhere else to stay in North Hampshire. The year ended with Sandys again requesting to be excused from court over Christmas.[185]

The year 1535 had been relatively calm for Sandys, compared with what was to come. In late December or early January 1536, Cromwell sent his personal physician to see Sandys, perhaps to check whether he was really unwell, although it may have been genuine concern because Cromwell himself had been dangerously ill in April 1535.[186] Whatever the nature of the treatment, it seems to have worked quickly, and on 6 January he was able to write to Cromwell from The Vyne that he was fit again and thank him for sending his physician.[187] It is assumed that Sandys then returned to court.

The day after that letter was sent, news arrived of Catherine's death. For some, including the king, this was good news because it removed the threat of invasion by the emperor, and perhaps Mary would be more compliant and accept her second-class role. At the same time, Anne was pregnant again and there was a new mistress in the offing, so 1536 looked as if it would be a good year for the king – so good that he and Anne marked Catherine's death by wearing bright yellow silk.[188] However, Cromwell probably had mixed feelings: on the one hand he need not worry about pressure from the emperor or pope, but on the other hand Anne was likely to focus on driving Henry towards the reforms she wanted, which was not good for Cromwell. Others were not pleased, notably Mary, as she now lacked any shield against Anne and the Boleynites and her cause would be neglected. As for Sandys, he had no option but to continue with his duties, although things could have been worse because he still enjoyed the king's favour and Cromwell was aware of that.

On 4 February 1536, Sandys was present at the start of the final session of the Reformation Parliament, which would last until 14 April – Good Friday. It began with the procession led by the king from his palace at Westminster to Westminster Abbey, with participants dressed in their robes of office. One of this Parliament's more important Acts, 'The Suppression of Lesser Religious Houses', resulted in the dissolution of the smaller religious houses, which directly affected Sandys. Three years later, in 1539, the larger establishments would be subjected to the same treatment. From the time when Wolsey first dissolved some of the religious houses, apparently without repercussions, there was a general feeling that they were in decline in terms of the numbers of monks and nuns and their behaviour. Henry had contemplated action to close the smaller houses from 1533, but did not commence in earnest until 1535, when the programme of royal visitations was conducted, the visitors having been selected for their known prejudice and tasked with providing the evidence needed by Henry and Cromwell to effect closures. The introduction to the 1536 Act leaves no doubt about the problem it aimed to address: 'For as much as manifest sin, vicious, carnal and abominable living, is daily used and committed amongst the little and small abbeys, priories and religious houses of monks, canons, and nuns where the congregation of such religious persons is under the number of twelve persons, whereby the governors of such religious houses and their convent spoil, destroy, consume and utterly waste.' The Suppression Act further impacted on Sandys' life, because later in 1536 it was a factor in the Lincolnshire and Yorkshire rebellions known as the Pilgrimage of Grace, when he was summoned to serve in a royal army to counter them.[189]

In late January 1536, Anne had a miscarriage, which she attributed to the news on 23 January that Henry had suffered a serious accident on the jousting field. The accounts of what happened are mixed, but Henry either fell or was knocked off his horse, which then fell on top of him. Given that both horse and rider were in full armour, the physical impact was considerable, and it was said that Henry was unconscious for two hours.[190]

Following Anne's miscarriage, Sandys would have been more aware than others of the threat to her position from Jane Seymour and that Henry was seeking a way out of his marriage. Eustace Chapuys reported that the Marchioness of Exeter had heard in strict confidence from a principal courtier that Henry claimed to have been seduced by Anne through witchcraft and sorcery and therefore considered the marriage to be null.[191] That source may have been Sandys. He knew the Exeters, who had visited The Vyne, had no love for Anne and had the ear of the king, whom he wanted to please.

Indeed, Sandys was probably actively involved in Anne Boleyn's downfall and Henry's subsequent marriage to Jane Seymour, as he would have known what was going on in the king's privy chamber. A late sixteenth-century account of Anne's downfall by a supporter, Alexander Ales, responds to accusations by Cromwell's spies that she had danced with gentlemen of the king's privy chamber: 'It is no new thing that the King's Chamberlain's [men] should dance with the ladies in the bed chamber.'[192] Sandys was responsible for paying the grooms and pages of the King's Chamber and those working in the Wardrobe of Beds,[193] so the dancing sessions and bed linen would have been an excellent source of gossip and information for him and others, including the king.

While Anne's position was increasingly precarious following her miscarriage in January 1536, Jane's developed steadily. By the end of January rumours of another marriage were spreading, and two weeks later the emperor's ambassador, Eustace Chapuys, mentions Jane Seymour as Henry's potential spouse.[194] In late March, Jane received a letter and purse of gold sovereigns from Henry and, after kissing the letter, she returned both items to the king, asking the messenger to say that 'she would not take either because she was a well-born damsel who valued no treasure in this world as much as her honour, which she would not lose on any account, even if she were to die a thousand deaths. Also, if the king wished to give her money, he should reserve it for such time as God would be pleased to send her an advantageous marriage.' When Henry received this message, letter and purse he praised Jane for her modest and prudent answer and virtuous action and said that his love for her had 'marvellously increased'. In future he would not converse with her except in the presence of one of her relatives,[195] so it was convenient that her brother Edward joined the staff of the privy chamber in the same month.[196] The apartment given to him and his wife was connected by a private corridor to the king's apartment, so Henry could visit Jane there, and it is said that she was always accompanied by a chaperone during these royal visits.[197]

Establishing the details of what happened to Anne in later life is difficult, as most accounts are either strongly for or against her, and much of the evidence was destroyed. For example, George Wyatt, whose life of Anne Boleyn is called *The Life of the Most Virtuous and Christian Queen, Anne Boleigne*,[198] was grandson to Sir Thomas Wyatt, who was allegedly smitten by Anne and imprisoned in the Tower with her other alleged lovers but never charged. By contrast, the chronicle by a Spanish merchant in London in 1552 recounts: 'How Anne Boleyn committed adultery and how it was found out,' and says, 'Soon after the death of the sainted Queen Katerine.' It includes a story about Anne's alleged affair with Mark Smeaton, describing how she went to bed and loudly asked trusted ladies-in-waiting to 'bring her marmalade'. This was the signal to bring the naked Mark, who was secreted in Anne's sweetmeat cupboard, to her bed. It was said to have happened several times.[199]

There is little doubt that Anne had developed a reputation for flirtatious behaviour, which continued after the loss of her child in January, apparently not realising the risks, especially when Henry's relationship with her was cooling. Whatever the truth, the day after a meeting of the Garter knights at Greenwich on 23 April, when most of the knights were together, a commission was appointed to investigate the conduct of Anne and others and whether it was treasonable. It included the dukes of Norfolk and Suffolk, the earls of Oxford, Westmorland, Wiltshire and Sussex, Lord Sandys, Lord Audley, Sir Thomas Cromwell, Sir William Paulet and nine judges.[200] Cromwell obviously believed that he had sufficient rumours and accusations to make a case against Anne or anyone else, and simply needed more 'evidence'. When it was clear that Anne no longer enjoyed Henry's favour, courtiers responded eagerly to his change of heart by reporting indiscretions, probably embellished, to settle old scores or earn favour.

Anne Boleyn's downfall has been discussed and debated at length, so present purposes are served by outlining three key factors after she lost favour with the king:

1. Evidence given by courtiers

No records of the trial or evidence are extant as they were either lost or destroyed,[201] but notes and other references mention four accusers: namely Elizabeth, Countess of Worcester, Anne Cobham, Margery Horsman and Lady Rochford.[202] The substance of their accusations is not known, but one source states that Lady Worcester had an altercation with her brother who was upset about her behaviour with other courtiers, and that she retorted that it was not as bad as that of the queen, who had offended with Mark Smeaton and her brother. This conversation was overheard and reported to Cromwell.[203]

Lady Jane Parker, George Boleyn's sister, was reported to have said that 'the whore' (Anne Boleyn) told her the king had not the capacity to copulate with her and was incapable and impotent.[204]

2. Anne committed a more serious crime – a conspiracy to procure the king's death

On 29 April, she had a heated argument with Henry Noreys, the King's Groom of the Stool and Chief Gentleman of the Privy Chamber, which was overheard and reported to Cromwell. Anne was evidently seeking compliments from Noreys when she asked why he did not marry Madge Shelton. He did not give a straight answer but said he would wait a while. Anne responded that 'he was waiting for dead men's shoes, for if aught came to the King but good, he would look to have her'. This was serious as it considered the death of the king – a treasonable offence – and was enough to condemn Anne to death. She confessed to it without coercion when hysterical after arrest, in the presence of Sir William Kingston, Constable of the Tower and others.[205]

3. Mark Smeaton's confession of his liaison with the queen, made on 1 May

How it was obtained is a matter of speculation, but Smeaton was summoned to Cromwell's house, confronted with rumours that Cromwell had heard and questioned about his increased wealth, which enabled him to afford fine clothes and horses well above a junior musician's potential possessions. Smeaton eventually confessed that the queen had given him money for sexual services rendered. He was then detained in Cromwell's house, but his arrest was not immediately made public.[206]

On May Day 1536, Smeaton, Noreys and Lord Rochford, Anne's brother, were formally arrested and sent to the Tower. The following day Anne was summoned to appear before the Privy Council, including Sandys, for interrogation. She attempted to defend herself but to no avail, and was then arrested and taken to the Tower by the Duke of Norfolk, the Earl of Oxford, Sandys and guards.[207] On the same day Cromwell wrote to Archbishop Cranmer, one of Anne's supporters because of her efforts to establish the Protestant Church, telling him of the queen's arrest. The next day Cranmer was summoned to appear before the Star Chamber and questioned by the earls of Oxford and Sussex, Sandys, and Audley. He was told of the evidence against Anne, which saddened him, but was unable to provide further evidence either against her or in her favour. In advance of the Star Chamber session he drafted a letter to the king to express his sadness at the news, and that he hoped Anne would be found innocent, but after the Star Chamber session he added a postscript: 'Since writing, my lords Chancellor, Oxford, Sussex and my Lord Chamberlain of your Grace's house, sent for me to come to the Star Chamber, and there declared to me such things as you wished to make me privy to. For this I am much bounden to your Grace. They will report our conference. I am sorry such faults can be proved against the Queen as they report.'[208]

On the same day Anne, still in a hysterical state, mentioned indiscretions with two other men from the privy chamber, Sir Francis Weston and William Brereton, who were arrested shortly after. Two more followed but were quickly released. The men were further interrogated by Cromwell at the Tower. Indictments for treason and adultery were drawn up for Anne and four men, and her brother was charged with incest. On 10 and 11 May, the indictments were laid before grand juries from Middlesex (at Westminster) and Kent (at Deptford), where the offences were alleged to have occurred. There was no doubt that the jurors would agree to the charges, so the trial of the four commoners was prearranged for 12 May at Westminster before the commissioners nominated on 24 April, including Sandys. The Lord Chancellor, Lord Audley, presided, and all were found guilty and sentenced to death. Anne and her brother were tried before their peers on 15 May in the Great Hall at the Tower. This time the Duke of Norfolk presided, supported by the Duke of Suffolk, Marquis of Exeter, the earls of Arundel, Oxford, Northumberland, Westmorland, Derby, Worcester, Rutland, Sussex and Huntingdon, and lords Lawarr, Mountague, Morley, Dacre of the South, Cobham, Maltravers, Powes, Mounteagle, Clinton, Sandys, Windsor, Wentworth, Burgh and Mordaunt, and Lord Audley, the Chancellor, who was not a peer, was present, but only as advisor to the Duke of Norfolk. When the evidence had been presented and the defendants questioned, the peers left the room; on their return each declared a guilty verdict. Both Anne and her brother were sentenced to death.

On 17 May, Cranmer held a convocation at Lambeth. It was attended by most of the king's council and resulted in Cranmer declaring that the marriage between Henry and Anne was null and void,[209] on the grounds that she had made a contract with the Earl of Northumberland before she met the king.[210] On the same day the men were executed by beheading, and Anne on 19 May. Sandys was present at Anne's execution, as were the rest of the Privy Council.[211]

Sandys must have been troubled by the sequence of events during Anne's short time as queen and how it ended, against the background of the religious changes and 'new order'. Only three years earlier it had been his duty to welcome and escort her to the king on the eve of her coronation. While he was certainly not the driving force behind Anne's downfall, it is noteworthy that he made himself available at all stages, unlike most of the commissioners. This probably reflects his antagonism towards her and what she was doing to the Church, but may also show that he did not condone the actions of offenders from the privy chamber, which was part of his overall responsibilities. Whether the cases against Ann and the other individuals were flimsy or fabricated were of little consequence to the king or Sandys. 19 May was a good day for him.

On the day after Anne's execution the king married Jane Seymour in secret. According to Eustace Chapuys this took place at the king's lodgings, which Friedmann has interpreted as Hampton Court but Wriothesely reported as Chelsea.[212] Friedmann is probably wrong, because he says that the king had stayed at Hampton Court for at least two weeks before the marriage, but he had in fact moved to Westminster by 16 May.[213] Friedmann also dismisses Wriothesley's statement by demeaning his status, not recognising that he was attached to Chancellor Audley, and sometimes drafted the king's letters as, for example, on 6 May.[214] Where in Chelsea the marriage took place is not recorded, but at that time Sandys owned a large manor house there so this is a possible location, especially as a month later the king exchanged this Chelsea property with Sandys for Mottisfont Priory.

On Wednesday 7 June, there was a great pageant on the Thames to celebrate Henry's marriage less than a month before. A fleet of barges travelled from Greenwich to Whitehall with each lord in his own barge, then came the royal barge carrying Henry and his new bride, followed by a barge carrying the royal guard. As the royal barge passed, each ship fired its cannon. The greatest salute – 400 guns – was made at the Tower, which was decked with flags and banners.[215]

The next parliament began on 8 June 1536, but lasted only until 18 July. Its main purpose was to ratify the king's divorce and declare Princess Elizabeth illegitimate, which was accomplished in the Act of 1 July. Sandys was recorded as carrying the king's train in the opening procession, so he had probably done the same in the February ceremony.[216] After the opening ceremony few peers, bishops or abbots attended the sessions and, like Sandys, were represented by proxies. Neither of the two archbishops was present, just seven senior clergy. Of the fifty-one peers listed, only six attended on the day the Act of Succession was passed. Several private member's bills were also presented, following on from the Dissolution Act, including one for Mottisfont Priory, which had been dissolved on 30 May.[217] A Harry Huttoft wrote to Cromwell on 26 March asking for this desirable property,[218] but was unsuccessful because it was already planned that Sandys should receive it in exchange for his Chelsea manor and lands in Paddington, which the king wanted. The deed of exchange was dated 27 June, and the private Act received assent on 7 July.

Following this exchange, Henry arranged for work to be done on the Chelsea property, but it was not until the seventeenth century that major changes were made. There is no evidence that the king stayed there, but it became part of Queen Catherine Parr's dower in 1544, and Anne of Cleves later lived there.[219] It is not clear why Henry wanted these properties, but Chelsea seems to have been his main target as he also sequestrated land there belonging to Westminster Abbey, thus acquiring most of Chelsea, although he did not take Sir Thomas More's property, which had been given to Sir William Paulet after More's execution.[220] The river frontage would certainly provide easy access from many of Henry's other properties on the Thames.

Sandys had inherited the Chelsea and Paddington properties from Sir Reynold Bray, who purchased them in the late fifteenth century, as his wife Margery was Bray's niece.[221] At that time Paddington was a largely rural area outside London while Chelsea was more urban and had a manor house that fronted directly onto Cheyne Walk, which was probably built by Bray, not Henry VII or VIII as sometimes suggested. However, there is no record that

Sandys or any member of his family lived there. The exchange deal with the king whereby Sandys acquired Mottisfont Priory was unusual, because the Crown did not sell the priory and its lands to Sandys, unlike the arrangements with most other courtiers who paid the Crown for the confiscated properties. Although Mottisfont Priory had been home to only ten canons, its property was extensive, including manors and advowsons, mostly in Hampshire and a few in Wiltshire, and the combined value of Chelsea and Paddington was roughly equivalent to Mottisfont and its lands.[222] Sandys certainly did not suffer financially from the arrangement and seemed pleased with it. A few weeks after acquiring Mottisfont he travelled there, no doubt to make plans because he would soon remodel the priory into a fine two-courtyard house for his own use.[223] Indeed, at the time of his death in 1540 his house inventories reveal that he had started to move some of the better goods from the larger Vyne house to Mottisfont.[224]

One of the reasons for poor attendance by lords at the parliament that began on 8 June 1536 was the number of major events during the session. On 15 June, the king and his new queen attended Mass together at Westminster Abbey, processing in their finery from Whitehall to the abbey with 'all the lords, spiritual and temporal' in attendance, then returning to Whitehall after Mass.[225] Sandys does not appear to have played any special role at this event, but a great display on the Thames near Whitehall Palace on 29 June, to celebrate the marriage of Lord Thomas Howard, son of the Duke of Norfolk, to a Mrs Gamage, almost resulted in the death of Sandys' son John. This event went ahead despite the serious illness (and subsequent death on 23 July) of the Duke of Richmond, Henry's illegitimate son and potential heir to the throne, with Henry and Jane as spectators, no doubt surrounded by the usual entourage. Lord Thomas and Mrs Gamage were married in the Henry VII Chapel at Westminster, and the subsequent entertainment began with a mock sea battle, in which a large ship, which had been dressed to look like a galleon, was attacked by three smaller vessels decked out as galleys, all complete with guns and armoured men-at-war. Although the swords were made of wood and the pikes and arrows fitted with wool and leather tips, things did not go smoothly. After two hours, a man who fell between a galley and the galleon was drowned, then a gun on a galley exploded, ripping out the side of the ship and splitting it in two. John Sandys was in that boat and said to be 'in great danger to be lost'. Several others were injured and at least one was drowned by the weight of his armour. At this point the king stopped the proceedings, but the revelry continued with a jousting session.[226]

Sandys' family had little time to recover from this dramatic event, because a triple family wedding took place on 3 July at the house of the Earl of Rutland in Shoreditch, a family connection resulting from the marriage of Sandys' eldest son Thomas to Elizabeth, the Earl of Rutland's sister. It involved three children of the 4th Earl of Westmorland, who was Edith Sandys' son and hence Lord William's nephew, and illustrates the social network in which Sandys lived. The three couples were Ralph, Lord Neville, son and heir of the Earl of Westmorland and Lady Anne, eldest daughter of the Earl of Rutland; Lady Dorothy Neville, eldest daughter of the 4th Earl of Westmorland and John de Vere, Lord Bulbeck, son and heir of the Earl of Oxford; and Lady Margaret, the ten-year-old daughter of the Earl of Westmorland who married ten-year-old Henry, Lord Roos, son and heir of the Earl of Rutland. The marriages were attended by the dukes of Norfolk and Suffolk, the Marquis of Dorset, the earls of Derby and Surrey and many other lords. Although William Sandys and his wife Margery are not mentioned, it would be very surprising if they and their family were not present, especially as the Earl of Westmorland visited The Vyne six months later. The Mass was followed by a great dinner, after which the king arrived with eleven others in Turkish costume for a masque, followed by a dance and a forty-dish banquet.[227]

To return to the attendance at the House of Lords and the parliamentary session, it is interesting to note that on 29 June 1536, the day of the dramatic event on the Thames that ended in danger and injury, Sandys and several other lords who witnessed the event were registered as attending the House of Lords. This suggests that registration did not require a lengthy period of attendance.[228] Sandys made a couple more appearances before the king closed the parliamentary session, which finished on 18 July.

Problems in Calais and England

After Anne Boleyn's execution on 19 May 1536 there was no rest at court, and Sandys anticipated that he would have no time to visit Calais or Guînes that year. He therefore applied for, and was granted, a licence on 25 May 1536 to stay in England, which proved useful given the diverse events that followed. Interestingly, he was described as 'Keeper, Governor, Surveyor and Lieutenant of Guînes Castle in Picardy and the town and county of Guînes', leaving no doubt that he was officially in charge.[229]

When the parliamentary session closed on 18 July the court stayed in London for just over a week, then the royal couple visited Dover for three or four days. Lord Lisle, Deputy of Calais, asked to see the king and was permitted to do so. He and his wife travelled from Calais to meet the royal couple on 22 July, stayed with the court until the 29th and then returned to Calais.[230] Lisle wanted to obtain some lands confiscated from Anne Boleyn's alleged lovers, but this request was not granted, although he was given some monastic property. Subsequent events suggest that he also sought royal approval for changes in the management of Guînes Castle and the town, which was granted.

In late July or early August, Sandys went to Mottisfont Priory and remained there at least until 4 August, no doubt inspecting the property and planning its conversion into a dwelling fit for a lord.[231] However, in the first week of August he received disturbing news from Calais: Lord Lisle, the deputy, and other members of the Council of Calais had sacked Sandys' deputy, who was Sandys's son John, his Vice-Baily of Guînes, and tried to remove the Serjeant Royal, all apparently on the king's orders, which suggests that this had been raised by Lisle with the king at Dover.[232] Sandys wrote four letters to Cromwell during August, the last three in response to letters from Cromwell, which have not survived.[233] The first was from Mottisfont and the other three were from The Vyne, and they mostly relate to problems at Guînes, which Sandys had not visited for nearly three years. It is hardly surprising that he had lost some control there. It was also difficult to complain when apparently changes had been made on the king's orders, but Sandys was very unhappy that Cromwell had not mentioned this matter when they last met, when 'the King's favour and Cromwell's friendship had made him in heart much younger than before'.

After writing this letter, Sandys heard that Lisle and others had again been to Guînes and given instructions to remove a hundred loads of wood from the castle to make bricks for Calais, presumably for the new fortifications there. In response, he wrote to his son at the castle that he should not deliver the wood except on explicit orders from the king or Cromwell.[234] A letter to Cromwell concludes with a heartfelt message: 'They think to make me weary of the Castle which they shall not do as long as the King keeps him there,' and 'a Captain was never so vexed and rudely handled as he has been without cause.'[235]

Sandys did not doubt that he had enemies who were trying to reduce his power to advance their own causes, and that Lisle appeared to be one of them. Lisle and his friends were known to want the Captaincy of Guînes instead of the role of Deputy of Calais, as the former did not require full-time attendance in the Pale. His actions against the castle in August without talking to Sandys could hardly be considered friendly, but later letters suggest they had reached a better understanding, if not become friends, perhaps because Lisle recognised that Sandys had better access to the king and Cromwell. Cromwell's eventual reply to Sandys' letters reveals that he knew nothing about the wood issue, but he advised Sandys to comply with the request. However, by the time Sandys received the reply, Lisle had reflected on the matter and written to his deputy to release the wood. Sandys also asked Cromwell to persuade the king to reverse the staff changes at Guînes, and it seems that he did so, because Sandys' deputy at Guines Castle in February 1536 was John Sandys.[236] That had been John Cheyne until his death in 1534.

Cromwell clearly took an interest in Sandys' son, John, as he chided Sandys for neglecting John by not maintaining him as his status warranted. Sandys disagreed, claiming that he maintained John well for his status as a younger brother, 'considering he has many other sons, daughter and his brother's [Sir Richard] children', and that he kept John at court to serve the king and obtain his favour, which would help to pay his keep. Sandys thanks him for his kindness to John and trusts he will 'long endeavour to do him service'. This exchange suggests that John had been on Cromwell's staff.

Sandys also expected to see Cromwell during Henry's imminent visit to Easthampstead and invited him to visit 'the poor hermitage of the Vyne inhabited with an old man and an old woman your faithful friends in heart'.[237] These feelings, together with the appointment of Sandys' brother Richard to the personal staff of the Lady Elizabeth shortly after Anne Boleyn's death, support the idea that Sandys' colluded with Cromwell in the removal of Anne Boleyn.[238]

One event reported by John provides a glimpse into life at Guînes Castle. He and the Constable of the Castle had held court on Perot de Lator, tailor of Guînes, following an incident when he and others were drinking at the house of William Morgan. Perot and another man started to fight, Morgan pulled them apart and told the tailor to keep the peace in the king's name, to which Perot replied, 'A turd on the King's name.'[239] Perot's punishment is not recorded, but it was sufficiently serious for John to inform his father, who then informed Cromwell. Perot wold not get off lightly.

While Sandys was at The Vyne in August 1536, momentous events that would erupt in September were in gestation. Henry would soon be faced with the most serious rebellion of his reign, the Pilgrimage of Grace. At one stage, more than 30,000 well-organised rebels from the north of the country were likely to overwhelm Henry's fragmented forces, which, because of panic and indecision in London, were in no shape to stop the rebellion, which had many supporters in the south.

It is not clear when discontent turned to rebellion, but unrest had grown since Parliament passed the legislation making Henry Supreme Head of the Church in England and Wales in 1532. He forbade the bishops from making payments to the pope, took one-tenth of all clerical income, and began preparatory work that led to the dissolution of the religious houses in February 1536. Another change was the publication of the articles of faith, which were largely devised by the king. These were endorsed by a convocation of clergy in August and included only three sacraments, namely baptism, the Eucharist and penance, instead of the traditional seven. They also restricted the use of images and reduced the concept of Purgatory. Later, Cromwell reduced the number of ecclesiastical feast days.[240] Taken together, these changes represented a clear move towards Protestantism and upset many.

Preliminary work for the dissolution included visitations by commissioners who assessed the value of the religious houses and the behaviour of the monks and nuns. The behavioural reports were generally damning, implying that religious houses were places of debauchery and financial mismanagement or fraud. While there was an element of truth in the accusations, and a general feeling that reform was needed, the totality of the changes caused anger. Cromwell and his supporters were regarded as initiators of the reform, not the king, which was unjust, because it was Henry who wanted the power and money. Cromwell provided the means and tackled the task with ruthless efficiency.

The unhappiness was nationwide, but the areas of strongest opposition were in the north, where key factors included:

1) Yorkist feelings against the Tudor usurpers who lacked interest in the north. Henry VII had visited York in 1487, but his son never did. Wolsey, although Archbishop of York, had never visited until forced to do so prior to his death.

2) The relative poverty of the north compared to the south combined with deep anger at the changes in religious practice and beliefs.
3) The role of monasteries in relieving poverty was also greater in the north, so there was greater support for the religious houses.
4) The commissioners sent to the north by Cromwell also played their part. They had a reputation for extorting large sums of money from the clergy and exaggerating reports of bad behaviour by monks and nuns.

September 1536 saw rising discontent across Lincolnshire and Yorkshire, but the first open rebellion occurred in Louth, Lincolnshire, on 1 October. The vicar of Louth told his congregation that the church's treasures accumulated over centuries would be confiscated by king's commissioners the following day. After evening prayers, the men in the congregation resolved to guard the treasures and keep the king's men out. Next morning, when the commissioners' men arrived, they faced a hostile group of about a hundred men who barred their entry to the church. This act of defiance sparked the revolt, and the rest of the county quickly joined the uprising.[241] When news reached the king, he decided to lead an army to quell the rebellion. A muster was called at Ampthill in Bedfordshire, and Sandys and his retinue were despatched between 1 and 7 October to prepare the king's residence there.[242] Sandys was also to provide 400 men and the Duke of Norfolk's quota was 600, but Cromwell's was only a hundred.[243] Henry changed his mind and decided to send an army under Charles Brandon, Duke of Suffolk, to quell the Lincolnshire uprising. It included Lord William Sandys' brother, Sir Richard, and his retinue of twenty men.[244]

The rebels rapidly increased in number and by 7 October more than 10,000 marched on Lincoln. The gentry began to join, and a series of articles was drawn up and sent to the king, demanding the reversal of some recent changes. Henry replied in strong terms that there would be no changes and extreme punishments would be imposed if the rebels did not give up. At the same time the royal army, although relatively small with 3,000 men, was at Stamford Bridge, only 40 miles from Lincoln. The rebels discussed Henry's response on 10 October, and it seems that his strong words and his army's proximity caused the Lincolnshire rebellion to crumble, although there were further sporadic outbreaks. One of its legacies was that its banner, which included the symbols of Christ's five wounds, was adopted by the Yorkshire and other northern rebels in the Pilgrimage of Grace.

In the meantime, more serious problems erupted in Yorkshire and spread rapidly through Lancashire, Westmorland and Northumberland. By 16 October, 10,000 men had marched into York and taken control of the city, but they were well behaved, disciplined and had an agreed a leader, a lawyer called Robert Aske. The gentry and noblemen began to join the cause, including Thomas, Lord Darcy (on 17 October), who was William Sandys' brother-in-law before his sister Edith died. The northern earls of Northumberland, Derby and Westmorland did not join. Westmorland was Sandys' nephew and was captured by the rebels, held in his own castle and effectively neutralised. By

23 October, Aske had an effective army of 30,000 to 40,000 well-motivated and disciplined men just north of Doncaster.

By contrast, Henry and his London advisors were in chaos, issuing orders that were almost immediately contradicted. At first the Duke of Norfolk was told remain in Norfolk, then to report to Windsor, but on his way received instructions to go to Ampthill to muster, then to help Suffolk in Lincolnshire. His Norfolk-based troops were marching to Ampthill under his son, the Earl of Surrey, when Cromwell instructed him to stay where he was in Cambridge. So, the duke had to raise another army. Sandys and the Earl of Exeter were at Ampthill, but Exeter's troops from Gloucester were still on the march towards Ampthill. Following the duke's arrival there on 17 October, he and Sandys jointly wrote to Henry requesting arms and money. Together with the Earl of Essex they wrote again on the same day asking for instructions and did the same the following day.[245] Then, on 19 October, Henry instructed them to disband their armies at Ampthill.

In the meantime, the Earl of Shrewsbury had been sent north to quell the rebellion and was well on his way. On 19 October, Norfolk, Exeter and Sandys left Ampthill and were marching towards Cambridge when they received instructions to disband the army, but on 20 October that order was rescinded. Sandys, Paulet and Kingston were to proceed with 2,000 men to assist the peacekeeping in Lincolnshire, while Norfolk and Exeter went north to support Shrewsbury, who was heading towards the River Don in South Yorkshire with only 8,000 men, which was no match for the rebels. This caused a major problem because most of the men had left Ampthill to return home. Paulet and Kingston, but not Sandys, wrote to the Privy Council in London from Beaconsfield, presumably also going home, and said they would return to Ampthill and try to gather men for Lincoln.[246] Sandys must have already received further instructions from the king and Privy Council to return to London, as he was at the Privy Council on 26 October with the Lord Chancellor, the earls of Oxford and Sussex, Cromwell and others to examine Christopher Aske.[247] The reason for his recall is not clear, but the Privy Council may have needed his expertise on military matters, or perhaps feared he might switch sides as he was known to be a religious conservative. The fact that Darcy, his brother-in-law, had become a rebel, albeit reluctantly, may also have been relevant.

Norfolk and Exeter continued to march north, but by 23 October had only reached Newark. In order to gain time they proposed to the rebels that they should meet at Doncaster to discuss their demands and thus avoid bloodshed. This was agreed, and on 27 October a truce was called, during which two rebel leaders would take their grievances to London, where they arrived on 2 November. Meanwhile, Henry had written his reply to the rebels' petition, which would have inflamed the situation and led to civil war. Norfolk again counselled caution. It was proposed that a conference should be held between the rebels and Norfolk to clarify their demands, and the king's requirement for the ten ringleaders to be arrested should be dropped, allowing all the rebels to be pardoned. This was agreed, and the rebels drew up twenty-five articles that included the following requirements:

i) The religious reforms be reversed
ii) Princess Mary be made legitimate
iii) Lord Cromwell, the Lord Chancellor, and Sir Richard Rich be punished
iv) A parliament be held either at Nottingham or York
v) Certain tax changes be implemented.[248]

Terms for the meeting, which took place on 2–4 December, were agreed and the rebels pardoned, and because they thought they had won their case they disbanded. Westmorland was released. Aske was invited to London by the king via a gentleman of the privy chamber on 15 December, indicating that Aske would receive a reward. He went to London, spent Christmas with the king and court, and must have felt that a task had been well done. Henry went out of his way to convince Aske that he did not know the state of affairs in the north, but now that his eyes were opened all would go well. He would hold the next parliament at York and the queen would be crowned there. Aske apparently believed that Henry was sincere and that Cromwell, not Henry, was the source of the problems.[249] He did not know that behind this understanding façade Henry was furious and wanted revenge.

Henry's excuse to dispense punishment came in the New Year, when a small number of rebels rose again in Yorkshire because they were not prepared to agree to the compromises. This time the king struck hard and fast, sending Norfolk and the Earl of Sussex to arrest those involved as well as the leaders of the earlier rising, including Aske and Darcy. They were tried and executed. Sandys did not serve on the jury for his fellow peer, Thomas Darcy, as he was in Guînes at the time. Aske's execution was at York in front of the Duke of Norfolk on 7 July 1537, while Darcy was executed at Tower Hill on 30 June. Henry did not visit York until 1541, and then only because he thought he would meet James V, King of Scotland, there. Cromwell never went north again. The rebellion continued to be a main preoccupation for Henry and Cromwell during the first half of 1537, but not for Sandys.

Sandys probably spent New Year 1537 at The Vyne, as he wrote to Cromwell on 4 January expressing disappointment that his son John had not been received by the king when he was charged with giving his father's New Year's gift to Henry.[250] Also, Sandys' nephew, the Earl of Westmorland, visited his uncle at The Vyne in early January 1537.[251] The earl's capture and imprisonment by the rebels was probably a major topic of discussion, but the main purpose of his visit was to seek Sandys' assistance in persuading the king not to make Westmorland Lord of the Marches.

Late in 1536, events in Calais had again caused trouble for Sandys when Henry Palmer, Spear of Calais and later Baily of Guînes, tried to discredit him, but John Husee wrote from London to Lord Lisle on 14 January 1537 that Sandys 'is in good favour as ever he was'. Palmer remained a thorn in

Sandys' side throughout 1537 and 1538 but somehow, perhaps through his brother, Thomas Palmer, became part of Cromwell's network of men and was able to report directly to the great man. Henry Palmer was influential in the establishment of a commission to examine the granting of offices in the Pale, which included other members of the Council of Calais and was chaired by Lord Lisle, Deputy of Calais. Sandys was aggrieved by this commission, as he contended that offices granted by him had always been in the gift of the Captain of Guînes. In a letter to Cromwell on 4 January 1537, he 'begs Cromwell to order the matter and that he may enjoy his office at Guînes as other Captains before him' but received little comfort in return.[252] In another letter, dated 19 January, he offers his resignation if the king thinks he is unfit to grant those offices, but it was not accepted.[253] Whatever misconduct Sandys was accused of, the commission cleared him of wrongdoing, and Cromwell wrote to him in February that his status at Guînes was not under threat.

However, by 7 March Sandys felt it necessary to return to Cromwell about Calais issues because his son John had informed him that his hunting rights in Guînes Forest had been removed and demands made for a large quantity of wood from Guînes, and that if this order for wood was upheld Sandys would have to close his brewhouse there.[254] This was a serious matter for Sandys as his beerhouse at Guînes was reputed to create income of 'a clear £500 per year'.[255] It seems that his absence from the Pale during 1535 and 1536 made it easier for others to cause trouble for him, but when Henry Palmer expelled Sandys' servant from the post of Serjeant Royal at Guînes in 1538, Cromwell told Palmer not to meddle with that office.[256] Palmer was himself the focus of a commission in summer 1539, and Lisle was again in the chair, but Sandys, Sir John Wallop (English ambassador to France) as well as members of the Council of Calais were also involved. Serious charges against Palmer were brought by the Constable of Calais and the chief porter, including the release of a murderer, letting 'strangers (foreigners), murderers, and thieves live in the Pale and permitting them to steal tenants' crops and the King's firewood and intermarrying English subjects and charging to graze sheep'. The commission upheld the charges, which Palmer denied, and reported to Cromwell who replied to Lord Lisle that the commission and Palmer should reconcile their differences and he could not understand why the king should be 'troubled with such trivia. Union in such a town is the strongest fortress.'[257]

As St Clare Byrne comments, whatever the outcome of the Palmer episode it revealed the deplorable state of civil government in Calais and the Pale at this time,[258] and that Cromwell and the king had little concern for those living there. When such episodes were combined with lack of pay for the soldiers and workers and general corruption, it is not surprising that morale was low, and Sandys was no better than the others in authority. He and Palmer eventually reconciled their differences, but not until late summer 1539.[259]

The relationship between Lisle and Sandys was complex. Their correspondence is polite and sometimes suggests friendship, and Lisle readily meets Sandys' requests for provisions. But it was no secret that Lisle wanted Sandys' position as Captain of Guînes; it paid well and did not require full-time attendance in the Pale, thus enabling the post-holder to access the king and court. He did not actively campaign against Sandys, but did not help him either, and he sometimes supported Palmer against him.[260] Lisle was also aware of Sandys' closeness to the king, which made him cautious in their relations. For his part, Sandys was upset by any attempt to remove his power or income, despite his absence from the Pale for most of 1534, 1535, and 1536. He upset Lisle in 1534 by complaining to Cromwell about an incident in the Pale when Sandys' servants were denied access to the body of his deputy at Guînes, John Cheyne.[261]. As it transpired, Lisle had nothing to do with that incident,[262] but it revealed that Sandys was very ready to complain to Cromwell or the king about Lisle. It appears that there was little mutual loyalty, but this was characteristic of the Tudor court, where individuals fought for themselves to maintain or increase power and influence.

Returning to the divisive issues in England, despite the humiliation of the Pilgrimage of Grace in 1536, Cromwell did not waiver in his drive for religious reform towards Protestantism but not as far as Lutheranism. His views were not supported by the Duke of Norfolk, Sandys and many other senior courtiers. The king wanted reform but also to retain some traditional beliefs, such as transubstantiation, and this restrained Cromwell.

The general situation in England by late spring 1537 is eloquently summarised by Gairdner in his preface to *Letters & Papers of Henry VIII*, Vol. 12, Part 2:

> There was no longer any resistance to the King. Martial law had done its work in the North, and the country had been completely terrified into submission. Trees and gibbets along the highways bore pitiful burdens suspended in ropes or chains, and, however great the sympathy with the victims, it could not be safely expressed. Women, however, had ventured to sally forth at night to cut down their husbands' bodies and bury them decently where they could in consecrated ground, for rectors and vicars durst not connive at such defiance of authority. All other expression of feeling seems to have been most effectively supressed.

In May, Cromwell ordered that the wives, mothers and sisters of rebels must stop cutting down the bodies of their men. The corpses should be displayed as a warning to others.[263]

In addition to this domestic tension, there was increasing concern about the situation in Continental Europe. The Holy Roman Emperor was no longer England's friend after the treatment of his aunt Catherine, but his relationship with the French king had improved, so England was in danger of being isolated or worse.

Sandys did not leave The Vyne and return to court until after 19 January 1537, on which date he told Cromwell that he would be there shortly. In early March he went to his new house at Mottisfont and dealt with seditious behaviour by two priests, one of whom he imprisoned because when he was 'overcome with drink' in an alehouse he called others fools if they paid their duty to the king.[264]

On 26 March, he went to Guînes, where he found that that his kitchen in the castle had been demolished and not yet rebuilt. The fact that he wrote to Cromwell to complain about this is a reflection of his character in later years.[265] Given the national agenda and problems facing Cromwell at this time, such complaints must have been seen as whining by an old man, which would weaken any appeal by Sandys for more resources for Guines and the Pale, where he stayed until the end of September. During these six months Sandys wrote to Lisle about once a week, although they lived only 6 miles apart. The letters are largely focused on local matters, with occasional references to the French and imperial armies then at war, and little to suggest the religious turmoil that would later afflict the Pale. One highlight was the news that the queen was pregnant, which Sandys received via Lisle, and he replied that Guînes would celebrate the event with a *Te Deum* Mass, bonfires, and cannon fire.[266] Sandys returned to England at the end of September 1537 via the court, which was at Esher and Bagshot, and to The Vyne on 1 October.

At about that time Henry's daughter Mary may have visited The Vyne. A tantalising entry in her accounts indicates that some of her horses were stabled at Basingstoke in October 1537. Like Sandys, she was in Bagshot at the beginning of that month and perhaps accompanied him to Basingstoke and made a short visit to The Vyne. Any visit must have been brief, because Sandys and Mary would have been summoned to Hampton Court Palace to celebrate the birth of Jane Seymour's baby boy on 12 October and subsequent christening.

News of the event spread quickly and the *Te Deum* was sung at St Paul's in London. Guns were fired and bonfires lit, and by 15 October, the date of the christening, the royal chapel at Hampton Court had been decorated with rich tapestries and cloth of gold and a platform bearing a silver font erected for the ceremony. A procession was assembled in order of seniority, and on a signal from Lord Sandys to the Serjeant of Trumpets a fanfare called the assembly to order. It began walking from the prince's lodging to the chapel, with the lowest ranks at the front and rear and the highest near to the baby. Sandys was with the Lord Great Chamberlain and the queen's chamberlain, all carrying their white sticks of office. Immediately behind, and higher in status, was Lord Thomas Cromwell, Lord Privy Seal, then the Duke of Norfolk and the Archbishop of Canterbury. Under a canopy supported by six knights was the baptismal party, in the centre of which was the baby, carried by the Lady Marquise of Exeter. Following the baptismal party was Princess Mary, the baby prince's godmother, and her party. After the christening, torches were lit and the *Te Deum* sung, before wine, spices and wafers were served to the high-ranking attendees. Finally, the procession reformed and returned to the prince's lodging.[267]

Sandys returned home to The Vyne via Esher, and on 28 October received news that the queen had died on 24 October at Hampton Court. He did not go to London immediately as he had been close to a sick person at Esher and was told to remain at The Vyne for a while before returning to court.[268] The king appointed the Duke of Norfolk and Sir William Paulet, now Treasurer of the Household, to organise the funeral. By the time Sandys reached Hampton Court the body had been embalmed and the entrails buried in the chapel. On 12 November, the queen's body was carried by horse-drawn carriage to Windsor Castle in a procession, at the core of which were Sandys and the two other chamberlains. The Duke of Norfolk and Archbishop of Canterbury were immediately in front of the carriage, while nobility carried banners at the sides. Princess Mary, as chief mourner, and her supporters were to the rear. On arrival at St George's Chapel, the coffin was placed on a bier while high-ranking ladies of the court kept watch. The next day the queen was buried in the chapel and the guests retreated to the castle where they were 'sumptuously provided for'.[269] The king played no part in the funeral. After the queen's death he moved to Westminster and kept himself 'close and secret for a great while', and the court remained in mourning until 2 February, Candlemas Day.

After the funeral it is difficult to keep track of Sandys, but he continues to be active. In the middle of November his servants, presumably on his orders, are reported as having taken a cargo from Flanders to Calais of 500 pairs of almain rivets (light upper-body armour) and 100 bills.[270] Cromwell conducted his business from mid-October to the end of the year in a manor house called Nete at Westminster. Sandys was present at some of those meetings as he reminds Cromwell in February 1538.[271]

Sandys did not seek permission to be away or apologise for absence from court over Christmas and the New Year, so it is fair to assume that he was with the king at this difficult time, and he was certainly around because he ordered one of the king's tailors to get him a new set of clothes for the New Year.[272] At New Year, Henry issued a list of 'those to be had in the King's most benign remembrances', which was topped by seventeen members of his council, including Sandys, followed by lists of 'widows and orphans, children of those persons attainted' and one of especial servants.[273]

In the meantime, Cromwell did not cease his endeavours to implement the Reformation reforms that provide the background and context for Sandys' next activities.

Continuing Challenges in the Last Years

Sandys started the New Year at The Vyne in 1538, but his main interest lay in remodelling his new home at Mottisfont. He did find time to receive Thomas, son of his nephew the 4th Earl of Westmorland, in April.[274] To allow himself more time for the Mottisfont work he was anxious to renew his licence to absent himself from Guînes, which had applied since the previous September, so he wrote in February and June 1538 to Wriothesley, the king's secretary, urging him to obtain a new licence before the old one expired.[275] He stayed in Hampshire until October, mainly at Mottisfont, where he established a temporary home with a local priest in Lord Lisle's pay.[276] The priest reported to Lisle on 24 August that Sandys 'doth lie and keep his household in my house in Mottisfont ever since the beginning of May and I think will continue until Allhallow Tide for the most part to oversee his works there where he maketh a goodly place of the Priory and intendeth there to lie for the most part of his life'.[277]

Sandys' wish for long and peaceful time at Mottisfont would never be fulfilled, but this stay enabled him to perform some duties in Hampshire he had been neglected for many years. One task involved removing 'an idol' from somewhere in Basingstoke and sending it to Cromwell, presumably for destruction.[278] Its location was probably the Holy Ghost Chapel or St Michael's Church. Baigent and Millard favour St Michael's Church in their *History of Basingstoke*, but then contradict their argument by saying that the Chapel of the Holy Ghost contained images of more than ordinary devotion, citing a ballad allegedly drafted by one of Cromwell's men:

> To the good holy ghoste
> That painted poste
> abyding in Basingstoke etc.[279]

Sandys' confidence in the king's affection is reflected in the fact that he was able to take a long period of leave in 1538, and his confidence was shared by many others but not everybody at court. This was illustrated when Thomas Brooke, a member of Lord Lisle's retinue at Calais, bid for one of Sandys' posts at Guînes by writing to Cromwell in August asking for the position of Receiver of Guînes as he was poor; he also said that Sandys was old, implying that age impaired his effectiveness in the role. Brooke dispatched the letter, but someone must have expressed disapproval because he sent another letter the same day hoping that Cromwell did not take ill what he had said, but that he really wanted to advance the king's profit and would accept a position with one of the king's general surveyors.[280]

While Sandys supervised the construction of his new home, the situation in England and Calais deteriorated to the extent that it would effectively destroy any hope of a peaceful retirement. During 1538–39 there was growing conviction that King Francis I and Emperor Charles V would join forces to attack England. It was assumed that the invasion would start in Calais, so Sandys was needed there to provide military expertise and experience. The religious problems also presented themselves in the Pale, both papist and Protestant elements, which added to the challenges posed by the fragility of Henry VIII's reformed Church. Sandys would be involved in further religious turmoil. In his *History of Henry VIII*, first published in 1649, Lord Herbert of Cherbury says, 'As affairs then stood, the King was both in that danger of rebellion at home, and invasion from abroad.'[281]

Meanwhile, in England the king and Cromwell had instigated an investigation into the Pole family, which would lead to the execution of three nobles and be close to threatening Sandys. At that time the family was headed by Margaret Pole, Countess of Salisbury and daughter of George Plantagenet, 1st Duke of Clarence, whose claim to the throne was as strong as, or stronger than that of the Tudors. She and her husband Sir Richard Pole, who died in 1504, had five children, namely Henry, Arthur, Reginald, Geoffrey and Ursula. Initially, Henry VIII had a good relationship with the Poles, and in 1513 made Margaret, by then a widow, Countess of Salisbury. Her eldest son Henry became Lord Montagu and Reginald joined the church, eventually moving to mainland Europe to continue his studies, starting in Italy. When Cardinal Wolsey died the king wanted Reginald Pole to become Archbishop of York, but he declined. Tension started with Henry VIII's separation from Catherine of Aragon and the move towards divorce, because the Poles were strong supporters of Catherine and the Roman Church and it was evident to others that this was the case. By 1533, the Holy Roman Emperor's ambassador, Eustace Chapuys, wrote to his master suggesting that Reginald Pole should marry Princess Mary and, with his help, take over the English throne. In 1536, the pope made Reginald a cardinal and Archbishop of Canterbury and encouraged him to defy Henry, which he did and used his position to encourage the rebels in the Pilgrimage of Grace. The pope also used Reginald to encourage Francis I and Charles V to declare war on Henry, who responded by unsuccessfully attempting to have Reginald kidnapped and returned to England.

Matters came to a head for the Pole family in England in August 1538, when Margaret Pole threatened a surgeon at a hospital she had founded with dismissal for his 'new learning'. He retaliated by reporting that Sir Geoffrey Pole had been in treasonable contact with his brother Reginald, while Sir Geoffrey attempted to protest his innocence by taking the surgeon to see Cromwell. Nothing much happened at first, but further evidence of treason was gradually gathered, largely from Sir Geoffrey himself, and he ended up in the Tower. A deposition by George Crofts, Chancellor of Chichester Cathedral, stated, 'He could tell of a great confederacy between the Lord Marquis (of Exeter), the Lord Montague, the Lord Chamberlain, and Lord Delaware as he was a messenger between them.'[282] Sandys' defence in this matter must have been good, because it seems that no action was taken against him. On 1 December, Lord Delaware was called before the lords of the council, who included the Duke of Norfolk and Cromwell on that day, but insufficient evidence of treason was found for further action against him, so he was released pending royal pardon, which was granted.[283] However, others fared differently: Lord Montague (Sir Geoffrey Pole's brother) and the Marquis of Exeter were imprisoned and tried before Lord Thomas Audley and a panel of lords on 2 and 3 December. Sandys was a member of that panel and he, like the majority, found the accused guilty of treason. Sir Geoffrey Pole and several others who were tried on 4 December were also found guilty. On 9 December, the lords were beheaded but Crofts was hanged, drawn, and quartered. Sir Geoffrey was not executed but imprisoned in the Tower, where he tried unsuccessfully to commit suicide. He was a broken man for the rest of his life.[284] In May the following year Margaret Pole was attainted and committed to the Tower; she was executed two and a half years later. Sir Geoffrey's daughter, Maria, was also punished by being forced to marry William Cufaude, a neighbour of The Vyne in Sherborne St John, who was well beneath her status and effectively removed any claim her offspring might have to the throne. Sandys may well have facilitated the arrangement as he was a kinsman of the Poles.

Sandys' wife is said to have been a cousin of the Countess of Salisbury, but no evidence has been found to support that claim.[285] However, Lord Sandys' mother, Margaret Cheyne, was first cousin once removed to Sir Richard Pole, husband of Margaret Pole, Countess of Salisbury, through Edith Stourton and Margaret Beauchamp, the same ladies who connected Margaret Cheyne to Margaret Beaufort, Henry VII's mother.[286] It is claimed that the marriage took place in The Vyne chapel as early 1539, but that date is most unlikely.[287] It might have been a betrothal. Evidence from two primary sources indicate that Maria and William had five children but the eldest, Alexander, was not born until 1556 and that in 1584 none of the male children had reached puberty.[288]

It seems that Sandys survived these troubles unscathed, but it was not the first time he was mentioned in proceedings about treasonous behaviour that year. In August, Friar Dove of the White Friars in Calais was interrogated, and several questions concerned his communications with the Lord Chamberlain.[289] Again, nothing came of this, but Sandys must have had uncomfortable moments in 1538.

Following the execution of the Marquis of Exeter and Lord Montague, Sir Nicholas Carew, Master of Horse, was arrested for his expressed sympathy with the Catholic cause and liaison with the Marquis; he was tried and executed on 3 March 1539.[290] In the meantime, the pope and Cardinal Pole strove to unite the emperor and King Francis I against Henry, not necessarily in war but certainly with trade sanctions in mind. They made no progress, but a sighting of imperial troops near the Pale stirred Henry and Cromwell into placing England on a war footing while striving to maintain cordial relations with France and the empire.

From the end of January 1539, the governors and captains of castles and fortresses were instructed to take direct charge of their military establishments, which required Sandys to go to Guînes and Sir John Wallop to Calais Castle.[291] Sandys did not rush and was reported to be with 'his lady and all the company at the Vyne in good health' in late February.[292] Later that month, an edict was issued to fortify Guînes Castle and increase the garrison. Similar instructions were issued for Calais Castle and fortresses along the south and east coasts of England, and all actions required speed.[293] Yet Sandys did not arrive at Guines until 16 March, when he was greeted with a salvo of gunfire.[294]

Shortly afterwards his wife, Lady Margery, died at The Vyne, and was buried on 31 March and 1 April 1539 in the new tomb that Sandys had built for Margery and himself in the Holy Trinity side chapel at the Holy Ghost Chapel at Basingstoke.[295] The funeral of the wife of a Knight of the Garter was an important occasion. When the wife of Sir Thomas Cheyne KG died in 1562, a large banner, with her arms in damask and gold, and flags were made for the funeral. The Garter officers and heralds were present and the Dean of St Paul's delivered the sermon.[296] Some senior courtiers attended Margery's funeral, including the newly ennobled William Paulet, Lord St John, and the local churches tolled their bells in tribute,[297] but Margery's husband could not have been there: he was at Guînes on 1 and 6 April and present at the opening of the new session of the House of Lords on 28 April,[298] returning to Guînes shortly after, where he stayed until the end of September.[299]

Sandys and Wallop were soon embroiled in the religious turmoil in the Pale in the late 1530s. Much has been written about the situation there at that time and the relative roles played by Henry VIII, Cromwell and Cranmer. Some have argued that all three, under Henry's leadership, treated the Pale the same as the rest of England, while others believe that Cromwell and Cranmer were using the region to pilot the new Protestant religion.[300] What is clear is that some clergy were prepared to preach vehemently against the pope and the Roman Church, but difficulties arose over the extent of the reforms advocated by others. Henry was reasonably consistent in his demands, which required recognition of his role as Supreme Head of the Church, dissolution of the monasteries and dismantling the shrines. He did not want the form of religion advocated by Luther and his followers, especially the doctrine that consecrated bread and wine were not the blood and body of Christ. Some preachers went further than the 'King's way' into the area of the New Learning, and a significant proportion of the inhabitants were prepared to listen and follow them. So, this small English enclave contained followers of the pope, Luther and King Henry VIII.

It is evident that Lord Lisle and the Council of Calais were not competent to cope with this situation, and in fairness to Lisle and the others it was difficult to discern what the 'King's way' was. Recognition of this difficulty in 1539 resulted in a parliamentary committee drafting six key principles, which in June became the Act for Abolishing of Diversity of Opinions, in Certain Articles Concerning the Christian Religion, better known as the Act of the Six Articles. These were inclined to be conservative and would have been welcomed by Sandys and the Duke of Norfolk, but not by Cromwell and his supporters. They can be summarised as:

- i) The consecrated bread and wine are the body and blood of Christ
- ii) It is not necessary for communicants to receive both bread and wine together
- iii) Priests may not marry
- iv) Any man or woman who has taken vows of chastity may not marry
- v) Private Masses may continue
- vi) Aural confession is necessary

When Sandys and Wallop arrived in Calais in spring 1539, they began a crusade against the New Learning. Elis Gruffudd, the Welsh chronicler living in Calais at the time, was one of those who believed in the 'New Way'. He wrote that it did not pay anyone to mention Bible stories that were called the New Learning, and that Lord and Lady Lisle had told Sandys and Wallop that half the town were critics and Sacramentarians and eager to create disunity and conflict. He added that 'although such people despised the Bishop of Rome according to their speech, nevertheless such fiendish work as he had blessed and had promised and were carried out were emanating from their hearts'.[301] He went on to say that they wrote to Cromwell, who they called 'the father and maintainer of heresy for the whole kingdom', but also wrote secretly to Sir Antony Brown to present these matters directly to the king, as he was close to him. The king tasked Sandys, Lisle and Wallop with reporting on the situation in Calais, as he now believed that the disunity could cause the town to be lost. The townspeople also reported that they knew about the disunity and disbelief, but they were not believed. So, the vintners, constables and aldermen wrote their reports, which were sent secretly to Cromwell, who showed them to the king. Elis Gruffudd continued, 'And this letter was written by the Lords of Calais while Lord Lisle ventured to sleep without a care in his bed of an evening without wearing his armour, even though one faction or the other could rise up against the other within the town and destroy it.' It is difficult to assess what Elis Gruffudd knew about what was going on at elevated levels in Calais and England, but his writings reflect the bitter feelings and tensions in the enclave at the time.

At the same time as Sandys and Wallop were sent to Calais, the newly created Earl of Hertford, Edward Seymour, was sent as a special commissioner to review the state of the fortifications, but he also reported on the religious position. On 6 May, Cromwell wrote to Lord Lisle on behalf of the king, making it clear that Henry was displeased with Lisle and the Council of Calais in what we might call 'a polite Tudor dressing down'![302] Hertford had found Sacramentarians and religious dissension in the Pale, contradicting Lisle's reports that there was 'perfect unity', and Cromwell expected Lisle to 'advance the reformation of things'. In response, Lisle sent details to the king in June 'concerning the misbehaviour and disobedience of a great number of persons in Calais that youre Lordship had a reformation of them'.[303] This was acknowledged, and he was told to expect more of the miscreants to be summoned from Calais to London. The next day Lisle's agent in London, John Husee, wrote to him advising that he should 'at all times answer for yourself when anything shall be laid at your charge', and that 'people are saying that my Lord Chamberlain and Mr Wallop hath set you a work, and will leave you in the briars when you trust them most'. This was a clear warning that Lisle should not expect support from Sandys or Wallop.[304]

A letter from Sandys to Lisle on 2 July reveals how he was exercising his zeal and reflects his activities in those six months at Guînes. He began by saying that his chaplains had reported giving Lisle some 'unreformed books' and that he had agreed to take action. The chaplains had then gone to St Peter's Church, where they found a former friar and the chaplain of the church 'reforming' books, one of which contained an 'unreformed' leaf of Thomas Becket, so the leaf was removed. Sandys therefore advised Lisle to examine more of the books being altered by these two men to make sure they were properly 'reformed'.[305]

He also reported that the emperor's spies had been in the Pale and he was aware that munitions were being assembled in Gravelines, near the border of the Pale.

Lisle went to England in August until mid-September, while Sandys remained at Guînes, sending periodic reports to Lisle, including the health of his wife and family who were evidently still in Calais. In his last letter to Lisle before returning to England, Sandys delights in saying that he had no news except that 'little Henry Palmer' took a coat to one of his servants whom he and Lisle had imprisoned, and that the servant escaped immediately afterwards with the coat and money given by Palmer. Sandys concludes 'we perceive what a fellow the vice-bailly is, and what men he supporteth'. It seems that Henry Palmer still enjoyed protection from Cromwell, much to Sandys' distress.[306]

Sandys planned to return home in the third week of September, but he was delayed in Calais for a week by bad storms, during which he stayed with Lady Lisle.[307] He was back in London by 5 October, where he met Lisle and both briefed Cromwell on the situation in the Pale.[308] He also wrote to Lady Lisle to thank her for her kind hospitality, saying, 'I am all yours to do all the service or pleasure that consisteth in my power during my life.'[309] But his most important duty was to report to the king, so he went to court with an escort of eighty mounted men to announce his return in style. Henry was shown plans of work completed at the castles of Hammes and Guînes and declared his satisfaction.[310]

By the end of October 1539, Sandys had returned to Mottisfont, where he received a report from Lisle that he had dismissed five soldiers, presumably for expressing Lutheran sympathies, and that they were being sent to England for examination.[311] Sandys replied that he fully agreed with Lisle's action and had given Sir William Kingston and Sir Antony Browne the 'book of articles' containing the evidence against the men, which would ensure that they were able to examine the men if Sandys could not be present. The men were duly examined and found not guilty. Sandys wrote to Lisle that he was not able to attend the examination because he had other pressing business at the time, but that if he had been present the men would have been found guilty. It appears that Cromwell stepped in to support the men, but later told Lisle that he had not seen the 'book of articles' and if he had they would have been found guilty. Sandys then wrote to Lisle that he had shown Cromwell the book. Obviously, someone was not telling the truth. St Claire Byrne considers this incident as evidence of Sandys being two-faced, but Cromwell may have forgotten the event, as he had bigger problems trying to arrange Henry's next marriage.[312]

On 6 October 1539, after some abortive attempts to find a suitable partner, Henry signed the treaty that arranged his marriage to Anne of Cleves, daughter of the Duke of Saxony.[313] There was much to be done before she came to England.

While these arrangements were being finalised, Sandys was dealing with a whistle-blower from Guînes. Cromwell had received a report from one of his men in the Pale that the wife of a soldier at Guînes Castle had complained about Sandys' failure to pay the men's wages for a year. She claimed that Sandys received £1,000 a year from the Crown for 100 soldiers, but only paid out £300. He did pay his son, who was the deputy, and one or two others. She also said that Sandys' beerhouse made over £500 a year for him. Since Sandys had departed there were only six men on duty at the castle and the French could easily take it. The man who reported this to Cromwell asked that the source should not be revealed as 'they would be in great jeopardy'. Cromwell ignored the request and told Sandys, who wrote to defend his actions, denying the accusations and stating that there was a full complement, other than fifteen men who returned with him to England and would return to Guînes when needed. Cromwell does not seem to have pursued the matter further.

This is not the only time Sandys was accused of not paying wages. It also indicates that his men were frightened of him.[314] It is similar to previous incidents in that Sandys always respected Cromwell's position as the king's senior minister and, superficially at least, did what he was asked to do, while Cromwell never took action against Sandys, suggesting that he acknowledged his seniority and access to the king.

Sandys spent the latter part of October 1539 at Mottisfont, which he described as 'being in the country', followed by time at The Vyne in November. Throughout that November the court was increasingly engaged with the arrival of Anne of Cleves, who was expected that month, but its members, including Sandys, had to wait through most of December because she was delayed, first by administrative problems and then by bad weather in the Channel. She eventually landed at Deal on 27 December, before making her way towards London with a large escort.[315] Henry did not wish to wait until the official reception for his first meeting with his new bride, so he and eight others travelled to Rochester on 1 January 1540, where he welcomed Anne and they dined together. Two days later, accompanied by a vast retinue, he made his way to Blackheath, where the betrothed couple would meet formally. When both parties had assembled at opposite ends of the heath, the king's party moved towards her tent, led by his trumpeters. The procession comprised the gentlemen of the king's privy chamber, followed by barons, bishops, earls, ambassadors, Cromwell, the Lord Chancellor, and the Marquis of Dorset, carrying the king's Sword of State. After Dorset came the king with the Great Chamberlain of England, the Earl of Oxford, on his right, and Sandys on his left, again demonstrating that Sandys was highly favoured. The Master of the King's Horse followed, leading the King's Horse of Estate, and then came the Pages of Honour, King's Guard, and King's Spears.

On reaching Anne's encampment they stopped and lined up, with the king at the front in the centre. She emerged from her tent, mounted a horse, and rode to the king with her escort. They met, talked, and paraded with their entourage around the heath, before travelling to Greenwich where they were greeted by decorated barges from the city. They were married on 6 January, followed by days of celebrations until 4 February, when the court transferred to Westminster.[316]

A few days later, the king dispatched the Duke of Norfolk to see the French king with the purpose of spoiling the developing cordial relationship between the French and the Holy Roman Empire. Norfolk arrived in Abbeville on 15 February and met with the king, who declared his love for Henry and gave assurances that France was not about to declare war on England or retake Calais. As a side mission, Norfolk stopped in Calais to assess for himself and the king the state of the defences and religious dissension. He subsequently reported that there was considerable dissension and evidence that the French were preparing for war, so he recommended establishing a commission to conduct a more detailed assessment. Henry agreed and established the Commission on 9 March to investigate the situation in Calais. Led by the Earl of Sussex, Robert Radcliffe, who was supported by Lord St John, Viscount Lisle, and others, it was tasked with making 'an inquiry touching the state of religion and observance of the laws there', calling offenders before them and sentencing, but they also had power to imprison offenders, banish them, or recommend the death penalty to the king. They were also to take musters of the soldiers, examine the state of fortifications and report their findings to the king.[317] It is surprising that Lisle was involved, but the commission's report to the king is not signed by him because he was called to give evidence. Sandys thought that he should have been included, or at least present in Calais, and wrote to Lisle from The Vyne on 7 April saying, 'I would have been glad to be there at this time if it had pleased the King's Majesty.'[318] He concludes with: 'My hand standeth there in witness with yours and others, which my part I will not fail to abide to,' thus indicating his support for Lisle. Sandys also said he would be in London in four days' time, where he would give more evidence against Adam Damplip and Lord Chichester to a messenger to take to the commissioners as they had requested. The commission's first report to the king came after three weeks of gathering evidence and finding dissension in Calais, naming two priests in particular, Adam Damplip and Sir William Smythe, who had preached 'against the Blessed Sacrament of the Altar ... and denying the real presence of the blessed body and blood of our Saviour Christ'. Others were named as their followers. The commissioners supported the members of the Council of Calais, except for Sir George Carewe, Captain of the fortress of Rysebank, so Lisle and Sandys were vindicated in their actions against the heretics to date.[319] On 7 April, Lisle wrote to Cromwell with evidence that the French in the area were preparing for war.[320] Ten days later the king wrote to Lisle requiring him to return to England,[321] which he and his wife believed to indicate promotion. Elis Gruffudd wrote that 'her ladyship took great happiness because she hoped in her heart that he should become an Earl or Lord Chamberlain of England', and it is a fact that both the Earl of Essex and Earl of Oxford, and the Lord Chamberlain of England had died in March.[322]

Lisle's return to England in April 1540 followed seven years in Calais, almost without a break. He immediately took up his duties as a member of the House of Lords and participated in the Garter ceremonies on 23 April,[323] but on 19 May was summoned to appear before the Privy Council, including the king, arrested for treason and sent to the Tower. The next day his wife and daughters in Calais were placed under house arrest by the Earl of Sussex and all personal effects sequestrated. Her crime was that her daughter Mary, by an earlier marriage, was betrothed to a papist Frenchman.

Lisle's arrest is subject to much speculation, especially regarding Cromwell's role. The Calais commissioners found that Lisle was associated with the Protestant faction there, as he and his wife made modest payments (shillings) to some Protestant priests, but nothing more, so it is surprising that he was charged with supporting the papists in Calais. One of his chaplains, Gregory Botolf, allegedly colluded in a plot to hand over Calais to the pope. Much has been written about the possible roles and motives of Cromwell, the king and others in Lisle's arrest.[324] Evidence suggests that the king heard of a problem with Botolf and papists in Calais but was not convinced of Lisle's involvement in any plot. At worst, he could be accused of lax administration in the conduct of religion in Calais. He was duly imprisoned and remained in the Tower for two years, but sadly died on 1 March, the day after his release. His wife was then released from house arrest in Calais. It seems that none of Lisle's friends and colleagues, including Sandys, said a word in their defence. Lady Lisle, in particular, was apparently a friend of Sandys as he stayed with her in Calais in September 1539, when her husband was in England, and wrote to thank her: 'Thanking you for your manifold kindness and gentle entertainment at Calais; which remaining firmly in my memory, albeit I cannot condignly requite ne recompense, yet I am all yours to do all the service or pleasure that consisteth in my power during my life.'[325] The feeling seems genuine, regardless of the Tudor language style.

When Sandys left The Vyne in April 1540 he returned to the court in London. On 18 April, he played a full part in the ceremony where Thomas Cromwell was made Earl of Essex, presenting Cromwell with the sealed patent declaring his elevation.[326] On 23 April, he was at the royal palace at Westminster for the Garter chapter meeting,[327] but sometime in May was tasked with looking again at the fortifications at Guînes in response to work undertaken on the French side of the border at Ardres. On 21 May, the French ambassador reported that Sandys was at Guînes looking at designs of various fortresses in Italy.[328] Fortress design at that time had changed little since the Middle Ages, but change was needed with the advent of powerful cannon. Italian engineers had developed a new design to thwart attacks on their towns by the French: instead of high walls with circular or square towers, it had lower angled bastions in the shape of a star, with no blind spots or dead ground between them. The walls were thick and backed by earth or sand to absorb shock and shrapnel caused by cannon shot; they also provided robust platforms for heavy guns defending the fortress and the whole was surrounded by multiple ditches.[329] Whatever Sandys saw and thought, it was not implemented. Much work had already been done across the Pale and it was probably considered too late to make radical changes.[330] When the English lost Calais in 1557, the fortifications would be redesigned by the French on the new principles.

Sandys' visit to the Pale must have been short as he was back in England in early June, but only for a few days as he was ordered to return to Guînes. The perceived seriousness of the situation in Calais is indicated by a licence granted to him on 3 June, empowering him to demolish the church, other buildings and bridges and fill in ditches around Guînes if he considered such action necessary.[331] This time he took 300 bowmen and 100 cavalrymen to counter the perceived French threat, arriving in Calais on the 7 June.[332] He reported to the king on 17 June that the frontier between Ardres and the Pale was quiet, but the French had 1,000 workmen on the fortifications and 300 foot and 200 horse soldiers at Ardres. To reduce the risk of accidental confrontations, which could escalate into major events, he and his French opposite number issued proclamations forbidding ill treatment of nationals on the other side. In his usual direct manner, Sandys added that no Englishman should enter French territory 'on pain of death' without specific permission.[333]

During this work a serious epidemic spread among the men, but the French did not stop because, according to Elis Gruffudd who was in Calais at the time, they were afraid of Lord Sandys and his men. Inevitably, the English were similarly afflicted. Henry VIII ordered Sandys and his men back to England at the end of August,[334] which 'emboldened' the French to encroach upon English soil.[335] They built a land bridge over the river and marshes between Ardres and the Pale, which was perceived as a threat to Calais, so the new deputy, Lord Maltravers, and the council ordered the bridge to be demolished. The French rebuilt it and the English demolished it again. This was brought to the attention of the king, and on 15 October Henry and the French ambassador met at a Privy Council session where Henry made it clear that if the French continued to fill the trenches the English would respond with equal force.[336] The French eventually opened the ditch.[337]

This episode demonstrates Sandys' deterrent effect and that the French held him in awe and respect as a soldier. He was back in England early in September 1540, but much had happened at court since June that would affect him. Firstly, Thomas Cromwell was arrested a few days after Sandys had departed for Calais and executed on 28 July. Less important on a national scale, but relevant to Sandys, was the execution of his former son-in-law Thomas, Lord Hungerford, immediately after Cromwell and on the same scaffold. He was found guilty of liaising with a priest who had called the king a heretic, speculating on the date of the king's death, which was a treasonable offence, and, lastly, having the dubious distinction of being the first person to be found guilty of the new crime of buggery.[338] Hungerford had married Sandys' daughter Alice in 1527, and Sandys had advanced his career until Alice died in 1532, and their son Edward, his grandson. Hungerford's coat of arms appears on the carved panels in the Oak Gallery at The Vyne.

The king's marriage to Anne of Cleves was annulled on 9 July 1540,[339] and was closely followed by his marriage to the teenage Katherine Howard, niece of the Duke of Norfolk. The marriage annulment, together with Cromwell's execution and the elevation of the Duke of Norfolk's niece would have given Sandys and other conservatives another signal that Protestant views were not those of the king.

On 10 August, revised arrangements for the Privy Council were announced. There were nineteen members, one of whom was Sandys, and it was ordained that the business of the council would in future record the name of everyone in attendance and the decisions made. In practice, the council met most days and in different places, but many members did not attend.[340] On 15 and 16 October, only three members and the secretary were present at meeting at the More – one of Cardinal Wolsey's former residences.[341]

After returning from Calais in September 1540, Sandys did not attend Privy Council until 7 November at Windsor, but was present every day thereafter until 22 November.[342] The following day the king and his new queen, accompanied by only four members of the council, left Windsor and went to Woking, where they stayed until 13 December. Sandys was not one of those chosen.[343]

It was not long after his last attendance at Privy Council on 22 November that Sandys' long and active life ended. Various dates and locations have been suggested, but evidence indicates that he died on 5 December 1540 at The Vyne, probably in his apartments on the top two floors of the Tudor three-storey section above the current Dining Parlour. The sources include the State Papers, an account by Elis Gruffudd, Sandys' will, and a document in the Hampshire Record Office. Elis Gruffudd's account is the most interesting, stating that Sandys went home to The Vyne to die because he was disillusioned after the king removed his stick of office, thus demoting him from his role as Lord Chamberlain of the Household. In view of the king's movements on 23 November, the probable date of Sandys' demotion was the previous day. Elis Gruffudd gives no indication of the cause or confirmation of Sandys' demise, but the rest of his account agrees with the State Papers.

Lord Maltravers, Deputy of Calais, wrote to Henry VIII on 7 December:

> Yester night, after the gates were closed, arrived Thadde, your post, who called over to the keeper of the walls to advertise me that Lord Sandes was dead. I had a letter thrown over the walls to Thadd, willing him to write how and where he died, and whether Thadde 'bare any signification thereof to Guînes', concluding with an order not to bruit it abroad. He wrote back that he supposed Lord Sandes died at the Vyne, that the news came to court on Saturday morning last, and that he brought no signification to Guînes.[344]

Elis Gruffudd's version reads:

> And that night [7 December] the King's letters to Lord Maltravers arrived ordering him to send certain of the Calais soldiers to keep Guînes Castle at which place the Marshall of Calais, who was called Master Sandys [this must be John, Lord William's son], had been for two or three days, he also had not received true information concerning the death of Lord Sand[y]s and Chamberlain of the Court, who had apparently died of indignation because the King had taken his staff and presented it to another man, thus giving him permission to visit his palace in the 'Veinn', at which place he died in an unexpected way.[345]

Further evidence that Sandys died at The Vyne is contained in his will, dated 4 December 1540, which was declared verbally (nuncupative) in the presence of witnesses, including Sir Humphrey Foster of Aldermaston Court and Sir William Essex of Lainbourne, Berkshire, who were local to The Vyne and sons-in-law of Sandys.[346] Foster married Sandys' second daughter, Elizabeth, and William Essex's son Thomas married Margaret, Sandys' third daughter.[347] The source of the last piece of evidence is a document at the Hampshire Record Office written for the 3rd Baron Sandys in 1612. It includes a note that William, Lord Sandys died on 5 December, which is consistent with the date of the nuncupative will.[348]

The last mention of Sandys in the Register of the Garter Knights states that on 9 January 1541 his stall in St George's Chapel was vacant.[349] Neither the register nor other records in St George's Archives mention his 'laying up' ceremony, when his hatchments (sword, crest, helm) and banner would have been offered at the altar during requiem Mass in the Garter Chapel (the day after the feast), neither is there any indication that he was treated differently from other members.[350]

No official regret at Sandys' death seems to have been expressed in the English records, other than concerns about security at Guînes. By contrast, the French ambassador in England wrote that Lord Sandys was much esteemed in London and one of the few ancient captains left.[351]

William, Lord Sandys was buried with his wife and parents in the vault beneath the floor of the Chapel of the Holy Trinity, which was part of the Chapel of the Holy Ghost at Basingstoke. There is no record of his funeral, but it is reasonable to assume that it was similar to that of his former colleague, Sir John Wallop, a fellow Knight of the Garter and Sandys' successor in the post of Captain and Governor of Guînes.[352] In 1551, Henry Machyn, the diarist, said that Sir John was buried with his standard, banners of arms, armour, helmet, crest, shield of the Garter and nearly a hundred flags.[353] Sandys' post as Lord Chamberlain of the Household was not filled until May 1543, when Henry appointed William Paulet.[354] Sandys' son John, whom he had installed as his Deputy at Guînes, was replaced early in March 1541.[355]

6

Sandys' Works and Patronage

By the time Sandys was fifty he had status and wealth, but his main residence was a relatively modest manor house, The Vyne. Around 1520 he decided that it was time to demonstrate his wealth and provide for his earthly remains and soul, so early in the 1520s he commissioned two major projects: the rebuilding of his Vyne home and enlargement of the Holy Ghost Chapel at Basingstoke. In 1536, he would exchange his Chelsea and Paddington manors with the king for Mottisfont Abbey, Hampshire, together with its properties, and begin redevelopment work there. Sandys also had a house close to St Paul's Cathedral in London, which had been built for the abbots of Chertsey, but no detail is available.

When Sandys was building his new house and modifying the Holy Ghost Chapel, England was experiencing a transition in the style of arts and architecture from Gothic to Italian Renaissance.[1] He was exposed to this change though his proximity to the king and court, Richard Fox, Bishop of Winchester and Winchester Cathedral, Cardinal Wolsey and Hampton Court and York Place (Whitehall Palace), and Flanders and northern France. London at this time was experiencing the effects of the Italian Renaissance directly through Florentine sculptors, particularly Pietro Torrigiani, and their work included the tombs of Margaret Beaufort, Henry VII and his wife Elizabeth, the bust of Henry VII, the bronze medallion of Sir Thomas Lovell, the terracotta roundels in Hampton Court and Whitehall, the high altar for the Henry VII Chapel, Westminster, and the tomb of Cardinal Wolsey, which was appropriated by Henry VIII.[2] The Italian influence was also experienced indirectly through the acquisition of Flemish tapestries, painted glass and majolica tiles.[3] Furthermore, Italian merchants in London were designing their houses in the Italian style. Thomas Cromwell's house at Austin Friars had belonged to an Italian company and was decorated by them,[4] while some of Sandys' contemporaries, such as Charles Brandon, Duke of Suffolk, builder of Suffolk Place, London, used Renaissance terracotta mouldings, as did Sir Richard Weston at Sutton Place just outside Guildford.[5]

There is no record of who designed or carried out most of the work at The Vyne and the Chapel of the Holy Ghost. Sandys was not able to supervise these projects closely because he was away from Basingstoke for much of the 1520s, whether at court, his London home, or in France or Calais. In a letter to Wolsey on 26 March 1522, he remarks that he 'is here (The Vyne) in his little house, seeing to business which he has not looked on for three or four years, but is hourly at Wolsey's command'.[6] It would not be surprising if Sandys' wife, or their son Thomas, was actively involved in managing the construction because his wife was niece to Sir Reynold Bray, who had funded and provided an outline specification for work on the Bray Chantry Chapel at St George's Chapel Windsor and the completion of St George's Chapel,[7] and was also involved in the construction of Henry VII's Lady Chapel at Westminster Abbey.[8]

The Chapel of the Holy Ghost, Basingstoke

The Holy Ghost Chapel at Basingstoke was built before 1244 and remained largely untouched until William, Lord Sandys refurbished it and added a chantry chapel,[9] called the Chapel of the Holy Trinity, in the early 1520s.[10] It was intended to be the burial place for Lord Sandys, his wife, parents and descendants, and is sometimes referred to as the burial chapel in the accounts of the Holy Ghost Chapel.[11] The main chapel was also home to the Guild of the Holy Ghost, which was established after Henry VIII granted permission to Sandys and Richard Fox, Bishop of Winchester, to do so in 1524.

William Camden, in the 1695 edition of his *Britannia*, describes the chapel as 'a very neat chapel dedicated to the Holy Ghost, built by William, Lord Sandys, who there lies buried',[12] while an article written in 1911 describes it as 'a gem of architecture without and within' and states that 'the windows contained some of richest painted glass in the country'.[13] Little of the chapel survives today, apart from the south wall and parts of the square west tower and the hexagonal tower at the south-west corner. Excavation work in the early nineteenth century revealed the foundations of the north wall, which enabled the creation of the plan included in Wayment's work on the painted glass of William, Lord Sandys.[14]

The square tower to the west of the chapel served as the bell tower,[15] while the hexagonal tower had a three-storey staircase, perhaps with a room and fireplace on each level.[16] The exterior of both chapels was decorated with figures of the Virgin Mary, saints, and the arms of the Sandys family. The holy figures have now disappeared, but traces of the armorial carvings survive. It is not possible to distinguish the decoration of the Holy Ghost Chapel from that of the Holy Trinity Chapel from descriptions. The interior had a vaulted roof, described by Camden in *Britannia* (1695) as, 'Upon the roof of it the history of the prophets, apostles and disciples of Christ is very artificially described.'[17] Excavations on the north side of the chapel in 1817,[18] as part of clearing rubbish in the graveyard, revealed fragments of tiles, and it was concluded that the floor was covered with glazed tiles bearing 'variegated figures'.[19] The Flemish majolica tiles which survive in The Vyne's chapel and date from just before 1520 may have come from the same source.[20]

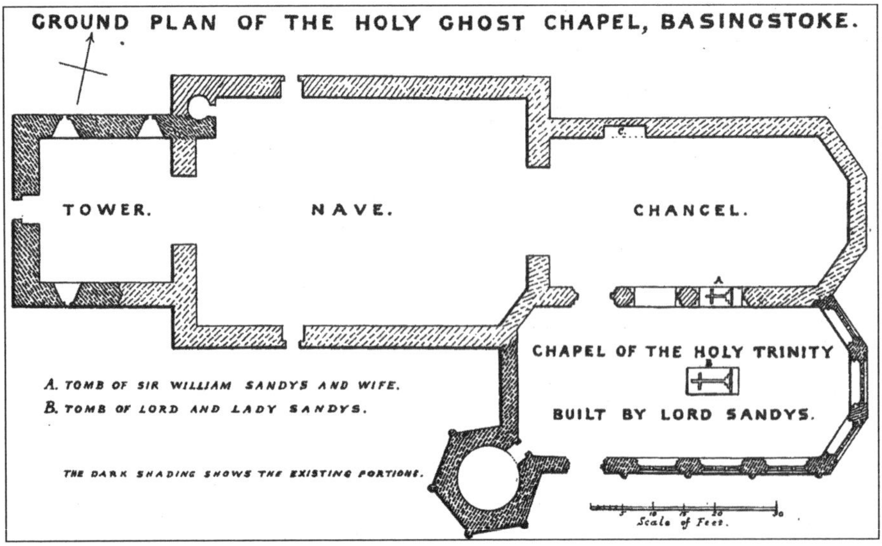

Ground plan of the Chapel of the Holy Ghost, Basingstoke showing the location of the tombs of William 1st Baron Sandys and Lady Sandys and the baron's parents. Copied from Baigent, Frances Joseph, and James Elwin Millard, 'A History of the ancient town and manor of Basingstoke in the county of Southampton with a brief account of the siege of Basing House, AD 1643-1645', Jacob, 1889.

Also found were fragments of fine white marble. One of the chapels contained an object worthy of devotion, which Thomas Cromwell instructed Sandys to remove and send to his men for destruction. Baigent and Millard say that it was located in St Michael's Church, Basingstoke,[21] but later provide evidence in the form of a ballad written in Thomas Cromwell's time that it was more likely to be in the Chapel of the Holy Ghost:

> To the good Holy Ghoste
> That Painted Post
> Abyding at Basingstoke
> Which doth as much good
> As a god made of wood
> And yet he beareth a great stroke.[22]

The Chapel of the Holy Trinity contained two tombs, both commissioned in 1536 and designed and made in Artois, which was then in Flanders. One was for William, 1st Baron Sandys, and his wife, and the other for his parents, Sir William and Lady Margaret. The tomb for Lord and Lady Sandys was a rectangular box about 8 feet long, 4 feet 6 inches wide, and 4 feet 3 inches high. It was made of Antoing stone, a dark grey limestone from the Doornik area of Belgium (then Flanders), which gives a shiny, almost black, surface when polished. Along each long side were three gilded armorial plaques, displaying the badges and arms of Sandys and Bray. The remains of one side were drawn by Elizabeth Chute in 1876, showing three plaques: the centre plaque bears the cross raguly arms of Sandys, flanked by two bearing the half-rose and half-star badges of the Cheyne family.[23] The top slab was embellished with a painted copper cross inscribed with the names of William and Margery Sandys. The gilded lozenges and painted copper cross would have contrasted strongly with the black stone. This tomb was placed in the centre of the Holy Trinity Chapel.[24] The tomb of William Lord Sandys' parents, Sir William Sandys and his wife Margaret Cheyne, was similar but smaller, and located beneath an arch in the wall between the north wall of the Holy Trinity Chapel and the south wall of the Holy Ghost Chapel. Damaged fragments of the sides of this tomb survive in the Chapel ruins. Beneath the floor of the Holy Trinity Chapel was a burial vault where members of the Sandys family were interred,[25] and distributed around the Chapel were heraldic symbols for the Sandys, Bray and Cheyne families.

Each chapel had an altar. One altar cloth, 9 feet long and 7 feet wide and made of purple velvet, was at Mottisfont in 1819. It was embroidered with gold and silver threads depicting Christ and the twelve Apostles, with Christ giving Judas a piece of bread. Other hangings from the chapels were also at Mottisfont at that time, but they are later in origin than the time of the 1st Lord Sandys.[26] There were also some rich red and blue velvet vestments, and white damask copes for a deacon and a sub-deacon.[27]

The high quality of the chapels' decoration by the 1st Baron is exemplified by the window glazing, some of which still exists. In 1522, Sandys commissioned Flemish glaziers to design and manufacture several painted glass windows for these chapels and possibly also for The Vyne chapel. The design reflects the change from traditional Gothic to the new Renaissance fashion, but the history of the glass after *c.* 1630–40 is complex and uncertain.[28]

During the English Civil War (1642–51) the chapels were extensively damaged, but fortunately the glass was removed and stored elsewhere, probably at Mottisfont Abbey. It was later dispersed from Mottisfont to various locations, mainly The Vyne chapel, All Hallows Church in Woolbeding, and St Michael's Church at Basingstoke. The glass in the Holy Ghost chapels (and now in The Vyne chapel) has been highly praised by experts since the seventeenth century. It was noted in the 1600s by Dr Peter Heylin, Fellow of Magdalene College, Oxford, in *Cyprianus Anglicus*, where he states that many images survived the Reformation, including those in the curious glass of Canterbury Cathedral, Fairford Church in Gloucester and the Holy Ghost Chapel, Basingstoke. He probably saw the glass between 1633, when he was made rector of Alresford Church in Hampshire, and 1638 when he had practically lost his sight. Westlake, in his seminal late nineteenth-century work, *A History of Design in Painted Glass,* stated that the glass is 'of very great importance and historical value'.[29] Wayment wrote in 1982 that the windows 'though much smaller in scale and extent than the glass in King's College Chapel, Cambridge they are no less distinguished in quality, and their state of preservation is almost as good'.[30] He later adds: 'In virtuosity and perspective the upper scenes at the Vyne excel Vellert's Massacre of the Innocents in King's College Chapel, Cambridge and are only equalled by his Last Supper in the same building.' In 2007, Steve Clare, who has worked on the glass at

Wells and Canterbury cathedrals and St George's Chapel, Windsor, wrote: 'The stained glass in the three windows at the east end of the chapel of the Vyne dating from about 1525 is in my opinion the most significant glass under the care of the National Trust and is undoubtedly amongst the most beautiful glass of this period in Europe. The glass is marked by the quality and palette of the glass and the superlative quality of the draughtsmanship and glass painting.'[31]

The Vyne

As already described in chapter 2, the property that William Sandys acquired was a based on a medieval moated manor house in a deer park, which had its own chantry chapel and support buildings close by. The house was sufficiently grand to accommodate a visit from the young Henry VIII and Catherine when they came to Hampshire on a hunting trip in 1510.[32] In around 1520 or earlier, Sandys decided to construct a more imposing country house as befitted a man of his wealth and status, and he effectively removed all traces of the medieval manor and its moat, leaving only parts of the cellars and possibly some foundations.[33] The rebuilding took several years, terminating with completion of the gallery wing in 1527.[34] Most of the work, including the chapel, was completed in 1526.

The configuration and extent of Lord Sandys' Tudor Vyne is not known in detail due to extensive demolition and rearrangement of the buildings in 1653 to 1654 after the sale of The Vyne by the 6th Baron Sandys to the wealthy London lawyer Chaloner Chute. He demolished around two-thirds of the house, destroying the buildings between the southern range of principal rooms and the river.[35] Later, during the eighteenth century, Anthony and John Chute, Chaloner's great-grandsons, progressively dammed that river to form the lake, which is still a feature of The Vyne.[36]

Despite the great changes over time, it has been possible to develop some understanding of what Lord Sandys built from archaeological studies and a variety of other evidence. The sources include internal archaeological studies of the residual Tudor parts of the house, external archaeological studies, the 1540 inventory of The Vyne compiled after William, Lord Sandys' death,[37] detail of the east (chapel) part of the house from a double portrait in 1641,[38] and comparison with other contemporary buildings, notably Hampton Court as rebuilt by Cardinal Wolsey, Sutton Place, and Compton Wynyates.

In general terms, the property would be expected to match the general contemporary principles spelled out by Andrew Borden in his *Advice on the design of a house.*[39]

> Make the Hall under such a fashion that the parlour be annexed to the end of the head of the hall and the buttery and pantry be at the lower end of the Hall, the cellar under the pantry, set somewhat abase; the kitchen somewhat abase from the buttery and pantry, coming with an entry by the wall of the buttery, the pastry house, and the larder house annexed to the kitchen. Then divide the lodgings by the circuit of the quadrangular court, and let the gatehouse be opposite or against

1. The Vyne north front. The chapel is on the left and the seventeenth century portico mid-way between the Tudor three-storey part and the seventeenth-century one. (Author's image, reproduced by kind permission of the National Trust)

2. Mottisfont south front. Mottisfont showing the largely eighteenth-century front. The courtyards of Sandy's house occupied the lawn depicted in the image. (Reproduced by kind permission of the National Trust, image 1185888)

3. Ruins of the Chapel of the Holy Ghost, Basingstoke. The image is of the remains of Sandys' Holy Trinity side chapel. William 1st Baron Sandys and his wife Margery's tomb and that of his parents were in the chapel. Only fragments of the tombs remain. (Author's image, courtesy of Basingstoke and Deane Council)

Left: **4. Sandys' Garter stall plate St George's Chapel, Windsor.** (Author's image, reproduced with the permission of the Dean and Canons of Windsor)

Below: **5. Procession of Garter Knights depicted in the Black Book of the Garter.** Sandys is in the top right-hand quarter with his back to the viewer. His cloak carries his arms. He is also one of the Knights gathered around Henry VIII. Because his relatively low rank as baron he is one of those furthest from the king. (Garter Procession SGC G., pp. 190–91, © Dean and Canons of Windsor)

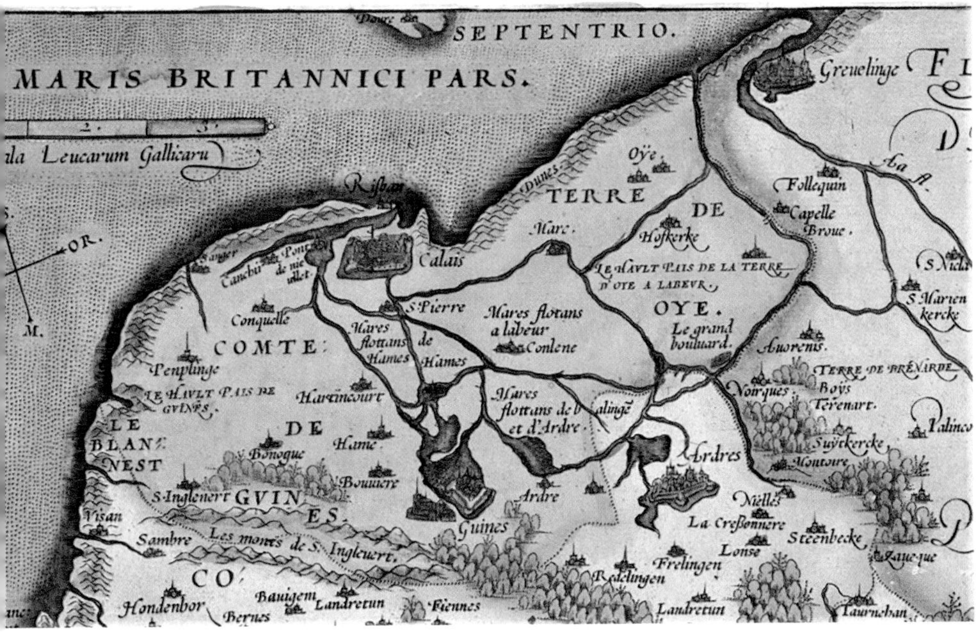

6. Detail of a map of Calais and Boulogne and of Vermandois 1571–84. The map depicts Calais, Guînes, Ardre and the water courses around the Calais Pale in the sixteenth century. (Detail of Atlas by Abraham Ortelius K PPN 369376781-024av-024br.jpg, courtesy of the Folger Shakespeare Library)

7. Detail of a plan of Calais about 1540 showing the town from the sea. (BL Cotton Augustus I ii 70, © British Library Board. All Rights Reserved / Bridgeman Images)

8. Henry VIII opening Parliament at Blackfriars, 15 April 1523. After being made baron in 1523, Sandys would have been sat on the cross bench in front of the king or on the right facing the viewer. After he was made the King's Chamberlain he probably sat closer to the king. (Royal Collection Trust / © Her Majesty Queen Elizabeth II, RCIN1047414)

9. The Field of the Cloth of Gold, 1520. Sandys was one of three commissioners tasked with providing the elaborate English facilities and liaison with the French. (Royal Collection Trust / © Her Majesty Queen Elizabeth II, RCIN406784)

Above right: **10. Margaret Tudor's head in the painted glass in the Vyne Chapel.** 'The glass (in the Vyne Chapel) is marked out by the quality and palette of the glass and the superlative quality of the draughtsmanship and glass painting' – Steve Clare, founder of Holy Well glass, stained glass conservator by Royal Appointment to Her Majesty the Queen, and National Adviser on stained glass to the National Trust. (Author's image, reproduced by kind permission of the National Trust)

Below right: **11. Detail of the Renaissance carved frieze in the Vyne Chapel.** The long, narrow frieze which fronts the canopy above the choir stall is in the Renaissance style. The carvings include many figures depicting flora, fauna, cherubs at play and human heads. The monkey and pomegranate shown may be an allusion to Catherine of Aragon. (Author's image, reproduced by kind permission of the National Trust)

12. Carved oak panel in the Oak Gallery of the Vyne with Henry VIII's coat of arms together with Sandys' arms and crest. This carving in the Renaissance manner is important because it carries Sandys' coat of arms and goat's head crest in the same panel as the king's arms. Henry would have been aware of it as it was in Oak Gallery when he visited the Vyne in 1531 and 1536. (Author's image, reproduced by kind permission of the National Trust except for Mottisfont)

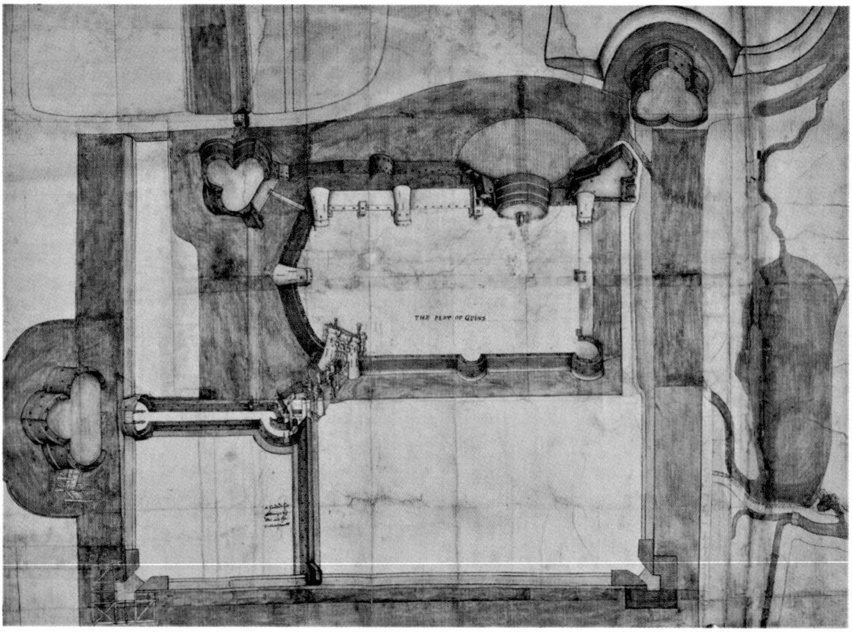

13. Plan of Guînes castle about 1545. In 1540 Sandys discussed modernisation of the defences of Guînes Castle with Italian military engineers. At that time they were at the masters of the design of defences which could withstand the impact of artillery. The refortification work started in early 1540. (BL Cotton Augustus I ii 52, © British Library Board. All Rights Reserved / Bridgeman Images)

14. Foot combat in 1513. Painting is of the Battle of Flodden in 1513. Sandys was not there as he was fighting in the king's forces in France but it gives a vivid picture of the experience that Sandys would have encountered in close combat. (Stephen Walsh, from *Flodden 1513*, pp. 70–71, © Osprey Publishing)

Above right: **15. Tudor man-at-arms of about 1524.** The knight is wearing a suit of heavy horse armour and carrying a war hammer. (BL Cotton Augustus III f. 26 © British Library Board. All Rights Reserved / Bridgeman Images)

Below right: **16. Sandys' armour depicted in fragments of the painted glass of St Michael's Church, Basingstoke.** There was an image in the painted glass in the chapel of the Holy Ghost, Basingstoke of Sandys praying before a statue of the Virgin Mary. That image was eventually put into a window of St Michael's Church, Basingstoke. The window was destroyed in a bombing raid of 1940. A few fragments of Sandys armour remain. They are sufficient to confirm it is the armour of Sandys, Knight of the Garter, and that it is high-quality heavy horse armour. (Author's reconstruction, photographs of the window by the author, courtesy of St Michael's Church, Basingstoke. The B&W image of the knight is taken from Westlake, N. H. G., *A History of Design in Painted Glass*, Vol. IV, 1894, p. 122)

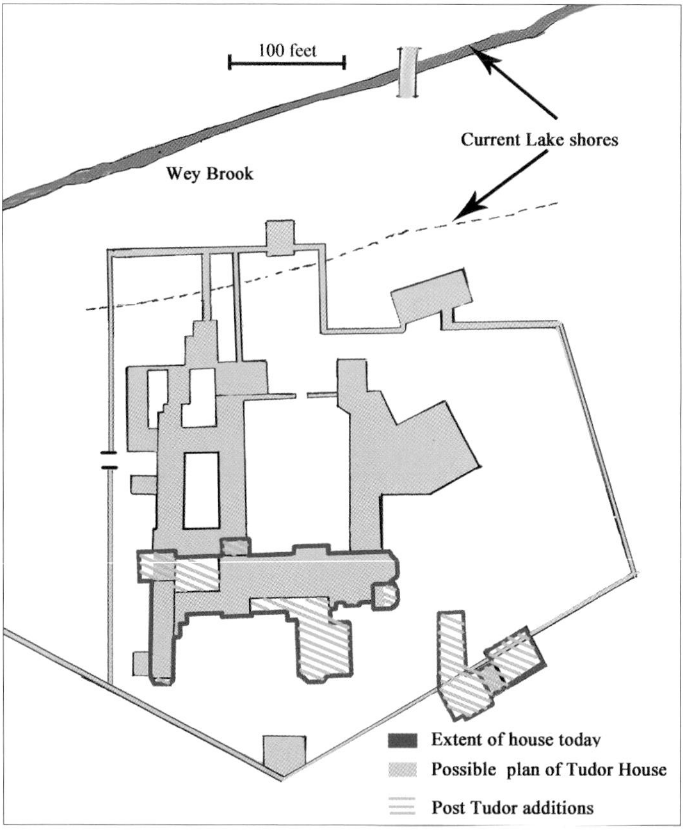

17. Conjectural plan of the Vyne palatial mansion about 1540. The plan has been constructed from archaeological studies, the Vyne 1540 inventory, a small detail showing a view of the house at the chapel end taken from a 1641 painting, and contemporary buildings such as Wolsey's Hampton Court Palace. (Author's image)

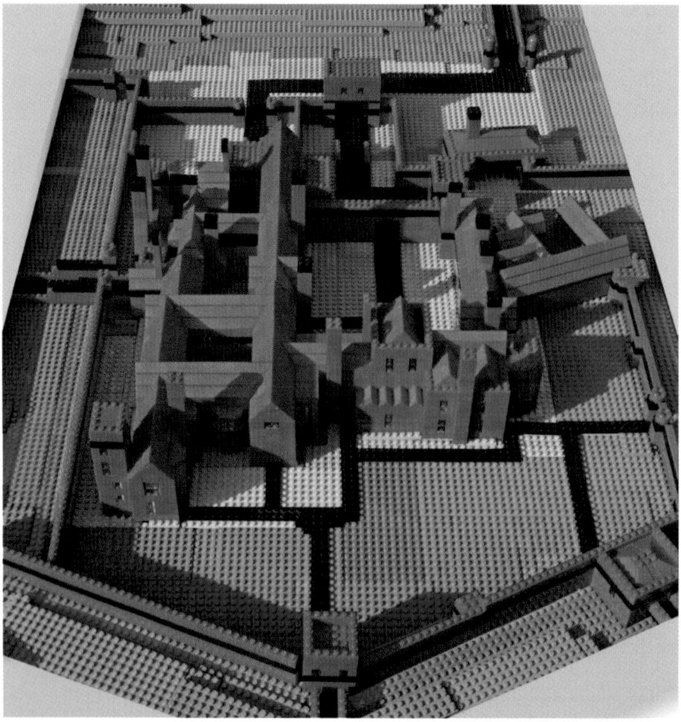

18. Outline model of the Tudor Vyne. The simple model based on the above above is rendered in LEGO to give an impression of the complexity and shape of the house and its courtyards. Those section with black brick are conjectural but evidence-based. (Author's image)

> the Hall door (not directly) but the Hall door standing a base, and gatehouse in the middle of the front entrance into the place: let the privy chamber be annexed to the chamber of state, with other chambers necessary for the building, so that many of the chambers may have a prospect into the chapel. If there be an outer court made, make it quadrangular, with houses of easement, (Let the common house of easement be over water or else elongated from the house) and but one stable for horses of pleasure, and see no filth nor dung be within the court, nor cast at the side, but see the dung to be carried far from the mansion. Also, the stables and slaughterhouse and a dairy (if any are kept) should be elongated the space of a quarter of a mile from the place. And also the bake house and brew house should be a distance from the place and from other buildings.
>
> When all the mansion is edified and built if there be a moat made about it, there should some fresh spring come to it; and divers times the moat ought to be scoured and kept clean from mud and weeds. And in no wise let not the filth of the kitchen descend into the moat.
>
> Furthermore, it is a commodious and a pleasant thing for a mansion to have an orchard of sundry fruits; but it is more commodious to have a fair garden replete with herbs of aromatic and redolent savours. In the garden may be a pool or two for fish, if the pools be clean kept. Also, a park replete with deer and conies is a necessary and pleasant thing to be annexed to a mansion. A dove house also is a necessary thing about a mansion place. And among other things, a pair of butts is a decent thing about a mansion; and other while, for a great man, necessary it is for to pass his time with bowls in an alley.

While there is no evidence that Sandys had a bowling alley or butts on site, his house did incorporate a suite of chambers, one fit for a king and another for a queen, an armoury and a schoolroom, presumably for his grandchildren.[40] A survey of The Vyne in 1651 says that the property occupied 17 acres, which contained outhouses, barns, stables, orchards, gardens, courts and watercourses. Surrounding the core manor house grounds were over 200 acres of meadows, orchards, fields, coppices and woods,[41] and despite what is said by some early histories of the Tudor Vyne,[42] it did have a deer park.[43]

Camden, in his *Britannia*, considered that The Vyne was 'a neat fair place'.[44] (OED says for 'neat', 'Of a thing or place characterised by an elegance of form or arrangement, with a freedom from unnecessary additions or embellishments.' It then cites for 1630: 'Hampton Court, the neatest pile of all the King's houses.') While Camden's statement adds little information about the house it appears that it impressed him. However, an indication of size is given by the number of people accommodated during the visit of the French ambassador, the Duc de Biron, in 1601, as he brought more than twenty members of the nobility and about 400 others, which required 140 beds to be installed.[45]

John Leland's *Itinerary of England and Wales* during 1535–43 states that the manor house created by Lord Sandys was a 'fair base court so at this time it is one of the principal houses in goodly building of all Hamptonshire'.[46] Examples of court dimensions (in feet) in other contemporary great houses at this time include 170 x 170 at Hampton Court, 80 x 80 at Sutton Place, 100 x 140 at Cowdray and 80 x 60 at Ingatestone, so it is reasonable to assume that Sandys's Vyne, given his status and wealth, had a base court around 100 x 100 feet.

The anonymous author of the article on The Vyne in *The Topographer* in 1789 states that 'there was a large rectangular court towards the water', but cites no reference.[47] Some clues about the extent of the Tudor property were gleaned during the 1840s by its then owner, William Wiggett Chute, who carried out extensive renovation work on Chaloner's house. Chute's refurbishment did much to save the property from dereliction, but he did not record in detail what was found during extensive work in the grounds adjacent to the house or in the lake. To make things worse from an archaeological perspective, he tried to remove underground structures and only stopped when that was too difficult. His notes on The Vyne, written towards the end of his life, recalled finding the foundations of 'very thick walls' when he lowered the ground on the south front. He removed most of these remains, but as they are very deep, traces of the walls are still visible in dry summers. When levelling the ground on the north front, he found the foundations of another thick wall, which he thought was part of the house, a few yards from the lake. Beyond that was another wall on the edge of the lake, probably that of the courtyard, extending some way beyond each extremity of the house. He also found a partly stuccoed recess in the north wall of The Vyne chapel, which he thought was part of the demolished wing of the Tudor house.[48] It was not until 1911 that progress was made, when Sir Charles Chute unearthed parts of the curtain wall to the south of the house and explored the culvert that runs along the south side of the lake.[49] The next revelation was made by a National Trust volunteer, Peter Cott, who in 1993 performed basic geophysical work on the north lawn, which indicated extensive remains.[50]

In 1995, Christopher Currie carried out archaeological excavations in the north lawn toward the lake and made observations in the partially drained lake, where he found large walls and the footings of a Tudor bridge on the north side. He also confirmed that there was an external brick tower at the south-eastern extremity of the Stone Gallery.[51] Later that year, he studied parch marks in the lawns that were evident in the dry summer of 1995. From this evidence he suggested that the Tudor house extended as far as the lake and into it. He also confirmed that there was a curtain wall on the south and north-east sides of the house and suggested that the outer gatehouse may have been at the north-east corner of the lawn where two curtain walls meet.[52] This work enabled Currie to suggest an outline plan of the Tudor house with four courtyards stretching from the extant Tudor range almost to the site of the eighteenth-century lake. Interestingly, his plan did not include features he discovered such as the curtain wall, the possible site of the outer gate, wide walls that go beyond the southern boundary of the later lake, and the location of the Tudor bridge he found on the north side of the lake. The bridge foundations indicate that the stream was on the north side of the lake.

In 1996–98, Wilson surveyed the interior of the present structure[53] and commissioned a geophysical survey of the lawns around the house.[54] Summary results of this work, co-authored with Howard, were published in 2003 in *The*

Vyne: A Tudor House Revealed.[55] Another study in 2002 focused on the area close to the brewhouse,[56] while a 2009 study to the south-west of the gallery wing suggested the line of a Tudor culvert/wall.[57]

Howard and Wilson's book provides a conjectural design of the Tudor house that should be revised for the following reasons:[58]

i) There is no suggestion for the location of the outer or any other gate. Gatehouses were essential features of houses in this period, one of which, the main gate, was usually opposite the Great Hall entrance on the opposite side of the base court. The Vyne inventory in 1540 mentions a gate, an outer gate and a possible portcullis gate. Currie suggested the far north-east corner as the possible sight of the outer gate.

ii) It largely ignores the findings of Currie's excavations near and under the lake, including the base and location of the Tudor bridge. It was found on the north side of the lake, well to the east of the bridge shown by Howard and Wilson.

iii) It effectively ignores the strong geophysical signals at right angles to the Brewhouse wall in the north lawn. These may come from Tudor buildings or the earlier manor house complex. They are clearly shown in Wilson's archaeological report but without comment.

iv) The 1540 inventory of The Vyne implies a first-floor loop of high-status apartments that are not drawn. The loop begins at the Great Chamber over the parlour and continues to the Portcullis Chamber, which includes the King's Chambers, the gallery, the Queen's Chambers, a small hall, and back to the Great Chamber over the parlour. Howard and Wilson suggest much of that loop was ground floor only.

v) It shows that the range that springs northwards from the chapel is single storey. Internal evidence in Lord Sandys' closet and the external scar at second-floor level indicate that this range should be full or almost full two-storey height.[59]

vi) There is no evidence of the 'large high-status buildings beside the lake' suggested by Wilson in 1998, which were 'perhaps similar to those standing to the South'.[60]

vii) The detail of the decorative moat around the brewhouse area should be changed in the light of the 2002 brewhouse study.[61]

viii) As the reconstruction was drawn before Marshall's work in 2009,[62] the west side curtain wall is depicted running north to south, parallel to the gallery wing. It is now thought to continue along the line of the curtain wall to the south-west of the house.

ix) There is no evidence of the ponds known to be around the house.

Consolidation of the results of the various archaeological studies produces a complex diagram that improves confidence in the model but falls far short of what is required for full understanding of the configuration and size of the Tudor residence.

In order to better understand the meaning of such plans, three scale models have been made using Lego bricks, one of which is shown in colour plate 18.

More recently, the National Trust commissioned further geophysical studies of the north lawn area and the pastureland on the north side of the lake, but these studies have unfortunately yielded little additional evidence, partly because of the dryness of the ground at the time.[63] The limitations of non-intrusive techniques, such as parch mark recording and surface geophysical measurements, inevitably make the configuration and size of William, Lord Sandys' home very speculative, because both techniques depend on the nature and moisture content of the ground and the depth of the features. If they are very deep they will not be revealed, and if they are shallow they will have been removed by post-Tudor groundwork. Real progress cannot be made without a comprehensive trenching programme.

However, these suggestions and indications do not readily correspond to one contemporary image of the Tudor Vyne. A map of the area around Beaurepaire House, dated 1613, includes a thumbnail image of The Vyne and Beaurepaire House.[64] It is easy to dismiss the depiction of The Vyne on the grounds that the author merely wished to show a grand mansion, but comparison of the thumbnail of Beaurepaire House with a later image indicates that they are reasonable representations of the structures, allowing for drawing conventions at the time. If that applies to the image of The Vyne, the suggested structure needs significant changes such as the inclusion of a large domed, circular or elliptical building, two towers to the south-east of the main range, and possibly a main entrance at the north-east corner of courtyard.

Whatever the detailed configuration of the Tudor Vyne was at that time, there is sufficient evidence to suggest that it differed from many contemporary homes such as Sutton Place, Compton Wynyates or Cowdray,[65] which were essentially quadrangular with ranges built around a central courtyard. Some features at The Vyne are common to Wolsey's Hampton Court Palace, with its multiple courtyards and the Long Gallery, which projected away from the main body of the house. It has been suggested that Wolsey's Long Gallery, built between 1515 and 1520 and estimated to have been around 200 feet long, was designed to facilitate views of the gardens as well as providing an exercise and meeting space.[66] Although The Vyne Gallery, which was 100 feet long, was much shorter than Wolsey's, it would probably have served the same roles,[67] as the eastern side overlooked a courtyard and the western side is likely to have faced a fish pond.[68]

There is little evidence of exterior decoration in Renaissance style at The Vyne, but clear evidence of high-quality decorative Gothic style, as in the chapel openwork vine-scroll bargeboards, the high-quality diaper brickwork and ornate central chimney stacks. As already noted, the exteriors of Sutton Place and Suffolk Place, which were constructed in the early 1520s by Sir Richard Weston and the Duke of Suffolk,[69] were clad in Renaissance-style decorated terracotta panels, as was the Long Gallery at Wolsey's Hampton Court.[70] The only evidence yet found of such terracotta work at The Vyne is a large fragment of a single tile. There were almost certainly more, but not enough to indicate

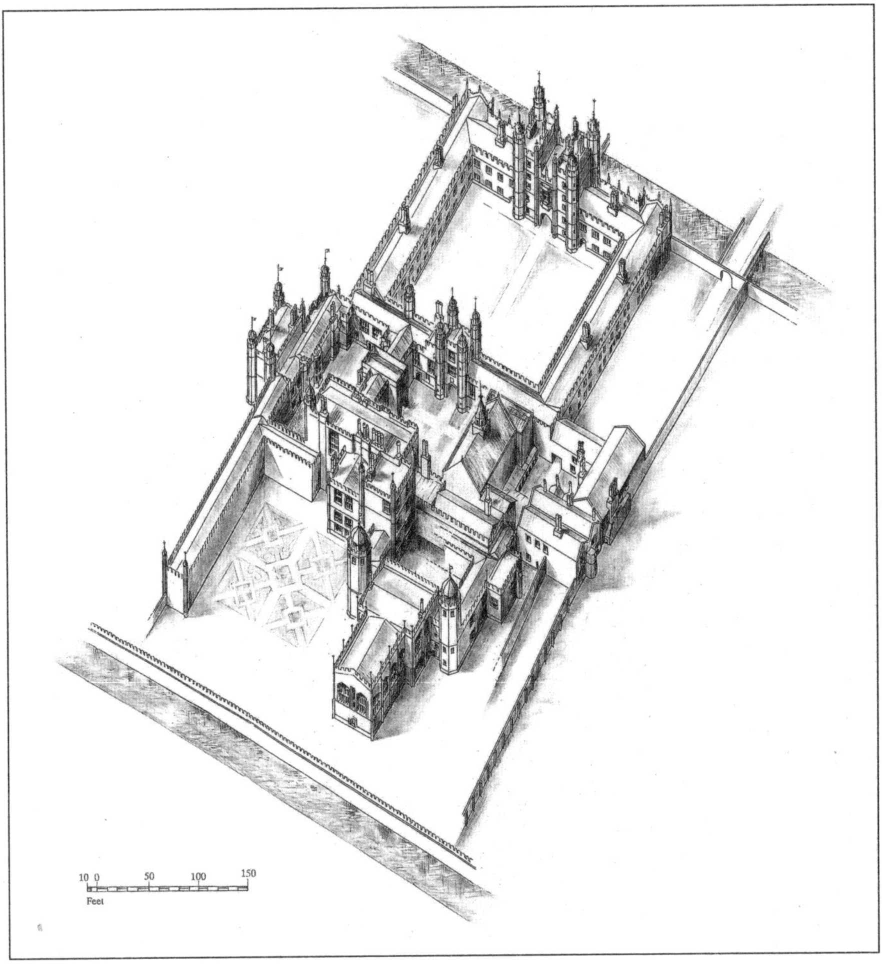

Hampton Court Palace was remodelled by Cardinal Wolsey during the period 1514–28, largely contemporary with the time that William, 1st Baron Sandys, was rebuilding and enlarging The Vyne. The Long Gallery is at the bottom left of the drawing, the base court is at top in the middle and the chapel at the bottom to the right of centre. (HRP HCP p.30, fig.26; Crown Copyright: Historic Royal Palaces; Drawing: Daphne Ford)

that a large part of The Vyne was externally decorated in that way. There may also have been terracotta roundels, similar to those in the Tudor gatehouse at Hampton Court or York Place, as there is a roundel of this kind in The Vyne's Stone Gallery, depicting the Emperor Probus, but it is generally accepted that this example came from another building, possibly York Place (Whitehall Palace) in London when it was demolished.[71]

The last section of the house to be completed was the Oak Gallery in around 1527, and dendrochronology applied to the timbers during the recent roof renewal dated them to 1526. This gallery is now 75 feet long internally and decorated with nearly 400 oak panels, arranged in tiers from floor to ceiling, but there were probably more panels in the part of the gallery that was demolished in 1653. Nearly all the panels are embellished with two heraldic devices, some of which are coats of arms while the other badges relate to the extended Sandys, Cheyne and Bray families or their high-status acquaintances. Other panels carry faces, grotesques, rebuses or war cries. A detailed catalogue was compiled in 1979.[72] The most significant single panel is above the west doorway and decorated in Renaissance style, with the coat of arms of Henry VIII in the centre held by two winged putti. To the left and below is a medallion bearing Sandys' coat of arms, while another medallion to the right displays a Sandys' winged goat crest. The fact that this panel was in the house during at least two royal visits (1531 and 1535) and the Oak Gallery is believed to be at the junction between the apartments of the king and queen reflects Sandys' confidence in his relationship with Henry VIII. Another prominent panel is circular, depicting St George on horseback conquering a dragon, and is the only gilded panel. Its presence ensures that visitors are aware that Lord Sandys was a Knight of the Garter. Also of interest is the fact that Pickvance, in his paper on the arrival of Renaissance influence on English furniture, shows a photograph of a lock plate on one of the doors to the Oak Gallery, bearing the initials 'W' and 'S', which are bound together by a knot. He dates the plate to the 1530s,[73] but that is not consistent with three other examples of the same symbol in The Vyne chapel frieze, which can be dated from Wilson's evidence that the chapel was complete *c.* 1526,[74] and with the recent dendrochronology results for the chapel.

The Vyne chapel probably offers the strongest 'Tudor' atmosphere in the whole property, which is not surprising as many features date back to the early sixteenth century. The author of the 1789 article in *The Topographer* was certainly impressed and says, 'The original chapel may be fairly represented as unique; and is more beautiful in its kind than anything I had ever the fortune of seeing.'[75]

The Tudor chapel complex was made up of what now is the chapel, the antechapel, the National Trust Vyne volunteers' room, and Lord and Lady Sandys' closets, positioned above and to the west and south of the main body of the chapel. The chapel was connected by doors at ground and first-floor level to the now destroyed north-east wing of the Tudor house, which was demolished in 1653–54. As the chapel was conceived before the Reformation, its design reflected Roman Catholic religious practice in which the priests, servers of the sanctuary, and occasionally a choir would be the only people in the space now deemed to be the chapel. Household retainers and visitors would attend Mass in the antechapel, not participating directly in the service until the moment when they were presented with the consecrated bread and wine by the priest. Most would only take the Sacrament once a year.[76] If Lord or Lady Sandys were in residence, they could hear Mass privately by using the closets, which overlooked the inner chapel and, as confirmed by the 1540 house inventory, contained altars. These closets were adjacent to their private chambers, so Sandys and his wife had easy and direct access to them. Each was decorated with rich tapestries bearing the Sandys coat of arms, and Lord Sandys' closet included a door leading to the now destroyed wing, which ran towards the river and was probably used to service the closets and religious personnel. A similar arrangement can be seen at the Royal Chapel, Hampton Court, where the closets of the king and queen are adjacent above and at the back of the chapel proper. The closets could also be used to view sung Mass in the chapel on feast days.

The main body of The Vyne chapel was illuminated by the three large extant windows in the apse and another in the south wall, where the entrance to the memorial chapel is now located.[77] The current glazing in the three apse windows is the Tudor Flemish glass of exceptional quality commissioned by William, Lord Sandys in 1522. There has been a lot of speculation about the history of the glass, but it is generally accepted that much came from the Chapel of the Holy Ghost in Basingstoke, as already mentioned. Regardless of its history, an expert on the early Renaissance in England, Dr Nicholas Riall, described it in 2007 by saying 'the glazing of which constitutes one of the glories of Renaissance England'.[78]

This raises a question about the nature of the original glazing in the four windows. One suggestion is that they depicted the donor or donors and their coats of arms and other heraldic devices. Sandys would have been familiar with such schemes, as seen today in Belgium, from his time in Calais. Armorial glazing relating to members of the extended Sandys family and the Tudor royal family, which is now in the antechapel, is of a similar vintage but also has an uncertain history. In the 1680s, it was in the possession of William Blunden, a wealthy Basingstoke merchant, with other panels now lost, and probably returned to The Vyne in the late seventeenth century. The record of the heraldic glass from The Vyne being in William Blunden's possession is found in the Herald's Visitation to Hampshire of 1686,[79] but the visitation was only concerned with heraldic matters, so Blunden may have had all or part of The Vyne chapel glass.

It is probable that the chapel, when first constructed, was more colourfully decorated throughout. This is supported by traces of wall paintings found behind the panelling in the apse, and of gold on some of the coats of arms on the underside of the choir stall canopies, while majolica tiles made by Guido Andries in Antwerp prior to 1520 decorate the chapel floor.[80] During the 1850s, William Wiggett Chute rearranged the tiles in his refurbishment of the chapel, but their earlier history is uncertain. It is likely that William, the 1st Lord Sandys, acquired them when he was Treasurer of Calais and The Vyne was being constructed in the 1520s, but where he put them is unknown. Sir Charles Chute found tiles of the same type close to the lake, and Wilson discovered others near the brewhouse. Many of the subjects depicted in the tiles are secular, but similar subjects were used on tiles made for religious establishments in Flanders, such as the abbeys of Herckenrode and St Bernard at Hemiksem, Antwerp. This may have prompted Sandys to acquire them for his chapels, which is supported by the presence in The Vyne chapel of a tile depicting the Sacred Heart.

The choir stalls in The Vyne chapel have been favourably compared with those in the Lady Chapel at Winchester Cathedral, both of which are thought to date from the 1520s, but difficulties arise when the evidence is examined. Part of the justification for dating the Winchester stalls to the 1520s is their similarity to those at The Vyne. In Charles Tracy's article on the Winchester stalls in 1995 he says, 'The Vyne Stalls are very similar in design to those in the Winchester Lady Chapel ... the style of the decoration is similar but the execution was by a different workshop. Stylistically, these stalls look as if they must have been made about the same time. The presence on the battlements of the chapel of the Sandys arms encircled by the Garter strongly suggests that the Vyne Chapel could not have been started before 1518.'[81] This statement has led some to assume that The Vyne stalls were made in the 1520s. For example, Wilson's report on the archaeology of The Vyne in 1998 states that the chapel construction occurred between 1524 and 1526, and then cites Tracy's article to attribute a date in the early 1520s to The Vyne stalls.[82] More recently, the stalls in the Winchester Lady Chapel have been dated to around 1501,[83] at the beginning of Richard Fox's episcopate as Bishop of Winchester, and Fox is known to have effected significant changes to the interior of the cathedral, including the Lady Chapel, Langton Chapel, the presbytery ceiling and cathedral glazing. Fox and William Sandys, the 1st Baron Sandys of The Vyne, knew each other well, as evidenced by Fox's commendation of Sandys to Cardinal Wolsey after the Southampton riots in 1517, their collaboration on the Chapel of the Holy Ghost at Basingstoke, and Sandys being named as one of Fox's executors in 1528.[84] It would therefore be surprising if Sandys did not take note of the work and design that Fox initiated, so the stylistic similarities between the Winchester and Vyne stalls suggest that the date of the latter should be reviewed.

One of the main differences between The Vyne and Winchester stalls is the presence of numerous carvings of pomegranates, paired with the Tudor Rose, in the main body of The Vyne stalls. Perhaps the best examples are the stall ends at the chapel entrance: the one on the south side contains Tudor roses, but that on the north side contains pomegranates. Some of the front panels of the stalls depict both symbols, and the coupling of the Tudor rose with the pomegranate is accepted as representing the coupling of the Tudor dynasty (the rose) with Catherine of Aragon (the pomegranate).[85] The same two symbols also appear together in the presbytery ceiling bosses at Winchester Cathedral, and it is thought that they relate to the visit of the young Henry, Prince of Wales, to the cathedral in 1506,[86] at which time he was betrothed to Catherine of Aragon. However, the use of the pomegranate was not usual in England until Catherine married Henry VIII in 1509, after which it served as a 'visual shorthand for the reigning queen'.[87]

The earliest date for The Vyne chapel stalls must therefore be around 1509/10, so they may have been made to celebrate the visit by the royal couple in July 1510. However, the plaques on the underside of the stall canopies in the chapel carry heraldic emblems, one of which is the Garter Cross, which suggests a date after 1518, but close inspection reveals that these plaques are pegged or screwed onto the main body of the canopy and could have been added any time after 1518. Also, some of the emblems, such as the Cheyne half-star and rose badge, are repeated in very different styles, which may indicate different dates of manufacture. Wilson suggested that evidence in the south wall indicates that the stalls were brought from elsewhere on completion of the Chapel in about 1526: namely, the fact that stone doorway behind the pews was partially sealed by the construction of the stalls. He concludes that 'it seemed more likely that the shell of the chapel had been constructed to await the arrival of the prefabricated fittings'.[88] Howard and Wilson have added a further perspective in *The Vyne: A Tudor House Revisited* by saying that although most of the woodwork is original, it shows signs of being moved in the nineteenth century.

Given the variety of evidence and opinions, it is worth suggesting that the main body of The Vyne chapel stalls were made in around 1510 for another chapel. An obvious location would be The Vyne chantry chapel, which was demolished when the shell of the extant chapel was completed.

Nevertheless, the Tudor carved frieze in The Vyne chapel, which lies along the front edge of the stall canopies, appears to be later. The carvings are not more than 3 inches high and the frieze was framed by wooden mouldings in the nineteenth century. These later mouldings obscure parts of the upper edge of the carvings, but they are generally in very good condition and do not seem to have been painted like those in the Oak Gallery.

Subjects depicted in the frieze include the coats of arms of the Sandys family, heads of individuals, musical instruments, animals, plants and putti tied together with vines, ropes and straps. The coats of arms are supported by putti in a manner similar to that in the Oak Gallery panel, which displays Henry VIII's coat of arms, together with Sandys' coat of arms and his winged goat badge. Celia Jennings, a recognised expert on early European woodwork, has commented on photographs of the frieze that 'the carvings are definitely Renaissance in flavour rather than medieval. The Vyne ones are good quality English or possibly done by Flemish craftsmen maybe in an English workshop. There seem to be at least two different styles, possibly three, but date wise they are very close.' She then goes on to say:

> The scenes of hunting, flora and fauna represent the pastoral idyll and prosperity of England during the reign of Henry VIII and Katherine. Musical instruments represent love. The male is usually shown with a pipe instrument with sexual connotations. The owl represents the wisdom of the male's choice of partner and the angle of the stick in the owl's beak is suggestive of sexual congress, as are the cherubs blowing horns. I would hazard a guess that in this context the female is represented by the drum. The cherub with bagpipes is sexual innuendo, the dog fidelity between the couple.[89]

Jennings suggests that the love represented is that between Henry VIII and Catherine, but it may refer to William, Lord Sandys and his wife, Margery, as their initials, joined by a love knot, are present in the frieze.

In the course of the recent project to renew the roof, dendrochronological analysis of the chapel roof timbers dated them to 1524. Allowing the normal period of a year for seasoning, the timber would have been used in about 1525, leading to completion of the chapel shell shortly after, a date that agrees well with that given by Wilson above.

If that is the case, the frieze was one of the elements that was made and installed around the same date as the completion of the chapel structure in around 1526. It is interesting that Riall's paper, cited above, states that apart from the glass the rest of the chapel is devoid of Renaissance ornament, because the frieze carvings contradict that assessment.

For this date, Wilson suggests that all the glass now in the windows must have been at the Holy Ghost Chapel, which was completed around 1524, but he does not mention possible locations for the woodwork or tiles. Another obvious original location for the glass, tiles and woodwork is the medieval Vyne Chapel, which was located close to the existing chapel.

The other furnishings in Sandys' Vyne palace are discussed in *The Vyne: A Tudor House Revealed* (pp.106–16) by Howard and Wilson, who highlight the wealth of tapestries mentioned in the 1540 inventory. Campbell subsequently published his definitive work *Henry VIII and the Art of Majesty* (2007) about Henry VIII's and Cardinal Wolsey's tapestries, providing deeper insight into their art and procurement.[90] The prices Campbell provides for the royal tapestries indicate that Lord Sandys' tapestries were not of the finest quality, but they were good. The king purchased some that were made with precious metal threads and cost up to £3 per ell,[91] while other tapestries in the royal collection ranged from nine pence to several shillings per ell, but most were at the higher end. Sandys' tapestries ranged in cost between 11*d* and 4*s* per ell, indicating that some were in the upper range of those made with wool and silk. He certainly commissioned new tapestries depicting Sandys' coat of arms, at least one of which was of sufficient quality to be taken into Henry VIII's collection.[92] Some of the sets Sandys procured depicted the same stories as those in the royal collection, so they may have ended up in that collection. It is also possible that some rooms in the Tudor Vyne were named after the tapestries displayed there, the most likely being the Rose Suite, perhaps named after a tapestry set depicting the *Romance of the Rose*.[93] Likewise, the Portcullis Suite may have been named after tapestries displaying the Beaufort Portcullis rather than an ordinary portcullis. We know that such tapestries existed because Campbell mentions that Margaret Beaufort owned examples.[94]

Other evidence reveals that Sandys decorated parts of The Vyne with high-quality tiles and wall paintings, traces of which were found in the Dining Parlour space during the 1996–98 refurbishment of the house. This area is considered to have been the ground-floor entrance to Sandys' personal quarters on the two floors directly above.[95]

In addition to wall decorations, Sandys also commissioned a substantial number of gilt items for tables and sideboards, and The Vyne inventory recorded nearly £1,000 worth of silver and gold plate. A pair of Sandys' gilt salts is easily identified in Henry VIII's inventory, because they were embellished with Lord Sandys' coat of arms.[96]

A piece of furniture now in St Mary's Church Hambleden, Buckinghamshire, probably came from the Tudor Vyne, namely an altar with an unusual frontal in the south transept, which has traditionally been associated with Cardinal Wolsey but it is more probably associated with William, 1st Baron Sandys of The Vyne. The frontal consists of a carved wooden panel around 5 feet 6 inches long by 2 feet 9 inches wide, which is divided into four sub-panels. When facing the frontal, the left-hand panel displays the royal coat of arms, below which is the coat of arms of Cardinal Wolsey surmounted by a cardinal's hat. The next panel carries the coat of arms of Richard Fox, Bishop of Winchester, above which are a Tudor rose, a castle of Castile, and then a lion's head. The arms indicate a date between 1515 and 1528 when William, Lord Sandys was active. The carvings on the next two sub-panels are largely covered by grotesque figures in the early sixteenth-century style, similar to those in the Wolsey Closet at Hampton Court Palace and the Epping Forest Museum.[97] The rear of the altar, which is now inaccessible, is faced with a similar panel which, together with the front of the altar, made up the front of a chest or screen. The complete double panel was in the church until 1959, when it was decided to cut it into two sections to make the front and back of the altar. An impression of what the double panel looked like is contained in an article published in 1903,[98] revealing that both front and rear panels are divided into four sub-panels, each decorated with grotesque creatures, while an article published in 2003 recorded the known history of the panels.[99]

The connection between The Vyne and the complete panel is made through Henry Sandys, eldest son and heir of Thomas, 2nd Baron Sandys, and grandson of William, the 1st Lord Sandys. Henry married Elizabeth, daughter of the second Baron Windsor, and lived in Hambleden where he and Elizabeth had three children. Their eldest son William became 3rd Baron Sandys because Henry died before his father in August 1551.[100] Elizabeth married again twice, and it has been suggested that the chest ended up in the church through her. William was about eighteen years old when he inherited the title in 1559, so Henry and Elizabeth probably married in about 1540, just before William, the first Baron, died. Henry is buried in the chancel of Hambleden Church.[101]

It is difficult to believe that either Cardinal Wolsey or Bishop Richard Fox would have had a piece of furniture displaying the other's coat of arms together with their own. On the other hand, William, Lord Sandys was a colleague of both, and a friend of Fox, and did display the coats of arms of both men in The Vyne's Oak Gallery. It is therefore likely that the chest or screen was commissioned by William, Lord Sandys before 1528 for The Vyne or the Chapel of the Holy Ghost, Basingstoke, and that it was given to Henry and Elizabeth by William or his son Thomas, the 2nd Baron.

Despite the many uncertainties in the configuration and extent of the Tudor Vyne buildings and the paucity of the internal Tudor decoration, sufficient has remained to enable Dr Simon Thurley, when director of English Heritage, to write in 2002 that 'the Vyne belongs to a small and treasured group of country houses built by the courtiers of Henry VIII, men who lived and worked in the king's inner circle and had the honour of entertaining the monarch at home – they have tremendous emotional and romantic power, not least when redolent of royal patronage and power as the Vyne certainly is'.[102]

Mottisfont

Mottisfont Priory was founded in around 1200 and grew through gifts of lands and churches in the surrounding parts of Hampshire, particularly during the thirteenth century. It was never home to large numbers of monks, and by the early sixteenth century there were only ten canons and twenty-nine other inmates, some of whom were probably lay brothers. A detailed history is given in Currie's survey of the Mottisfont estate.[103] The priory was dissolved in mid-1536, following the Suppression of Lesser Religious Houses Act, and Sandys exchanged his properties in Chelsea and Paddington for Mottisfont and its extensive lands by agreement with the king, as already noted.

Although the church and the prior's house were in good condition, the outhouses were ruinous. As soon as Sandys acquired the property he began to develop it into a large country mansion where he hoped to spend much of the rest of his life.[104] Little is known about the configuration of his mansion, but a map of the estate in 1724 shows a plan of the house with a double courtyard and entrance range, and that its size was around 150 feet square.[105] When the ground is parched, the double courtyard plan is still visible. Whether this reflects Sandys' actual conversion of the priory is not known, but it is a reasonable assumption as there is no evidence of major rebuilding after about 1540.

The inventory of Sandys' property and possessions undertaken at Mottisfont shortly after his death indicates that, like The Vyne, he was also decorating the walls at Mottisfont with good tapestries, but the full inventory details are not available because access is restricted and have not been published, except for a small fragment.[106] Evidence of William, Lord Sandys, the 1st Baron Sandys, at Mottisfont can be seen in a window panel that contains four excellent painted-glass coats of arms: two of the king, one of the Sandys' cross raguly and one of the cross raguly with the Bray arms as an inscutcheon.[107]

To summarise Sandys' work on his homes and chapels, it is obvious that he spent a large amount of money commissioning and buying luxury items, which is not unexpected, given his status and desire to remain in favour with the king. More broadly, the fine work on his homes and in his patronage of chapels show that he was in the vanguard of taste, but not leading. The design of his Vyne home was not novel compared with Hampton Court, and the exterior was not decorated in the latest Italian-inspired terracotta work like Sutton Place, Hampton Court or Suffolk Place. What was novel was the extent to which he used Flemish craftsmen. While the use of Flemish tapestries was not exceptional in great houses at the time, Sandys went further with his choice of Flemish craftsmen for high-quality glazing, family tombs and possibly majolica tiles. This is not surprising, because by 1520 he had been directly exposed to much of their work in Calais and the surrounding area. By contrast, any Italian influence was largely second-hand, coming through his Flemish contacts.

This plan shows Mottisfont after William, 1st Baron Sandys, had rebuilt it. The plan shows the courtyards and outbuildings. (Courtesy of the Hampshire Record Office: 13M63/420)

7

Descendants of William, the 1st Baron Sandys

After the death of William, 1st Baron Sandys, in December 1540, both the income and the political status of the family declined. The main factors were the Crown's demands to clear the debts accumulated by the 1st Baron, participation by the 3rd Baron in the Essex Rebellion in 1601 and supporting the king and the Royalist cause during the English Civil War in the 1640s.

Lord William, the 1st Baron, was succeeded by his eldest son Thomas as the 2nd Baron, after which the baronetcy continued through a further six barons, terminating in 1684. Not one of the seven who followed the 1st Baron was distinguished, although the 3rd Baron, William, achieved notoriety late in life by joining the Earl of Essex in the 1601 rebellion against Queen Elizabeth.

This chapter mentions the children of the 1st Baron and subsequent ones, with additional detail for the 3rd Baron because of his long life and the notoriety resulting from his role in the 1601 rebellion.

The Children of the 1st Baron Sandys

William had seven children with his wife Margery, daughter of John Bray, namely Thomas, his son and heir, Reynolde alias Reginald, John, Mary, Alice, Elizabeth and Margaret.

Reynolde, or Reginald, the second son, was a priest in 1533,[1] but according to a letter from Revd F. J. Baigent to C. W. Chute, 'Reynolde the priest was a Minorite friar who was presented with a living in Wiltshire and seems to have been a source of trouble to his father who speaks of him in a letter as his unthrifty son.'[2] This statement is confusing because Minorite friars belonged to the Order of St Francis and were pledged to poverty. If Reynolde had financial problems it is more likely that he was a parish priest in Wiltshire. His father asked Thomas Cromwell to intevene on Reynolde's behalf, but there is no more information about him.

John, the third and youngest son, joined the court and served Cardinal Wolsey. In January 1529, he was in St Germaine and Guînes in France,[3] and his father subsequently appointed him deputy in charge of Guînes Castle, a position he certainly held in 1536 and 1540,[4] but lost after his father's death in 1540.[5] His father also established him at court, where he was moderately successful, being one of the many esquires in the reception party for Anne of Cleves when she met Henry VIII in England on New Year's Day 1540.[6] He was also granted an annuity of 40 marks in May 1560 for service to Queen Elizabeth as a gentleman-at-arms, and previous service to Henry VIII, Edward VI and Queen Mary.[7] Sometime after 1541 he moved into a mansion in Sherborne St John, within The Vyne Park.[8]

Mary's first husband was Sir William Peckham, but after his death she married Sir John Palmer of Angering.[9]

Alice married Walter, Lord Hungerford of Heytbury, in 1527, but died by 1532. Walter then remarried twice, but after being accused of debauching with his daughter, buggering his servants, procuring a chaplain and two others, and discussing how long the king would live, he was beheaded immediately after Thomas Cromwell on 28 July 1540.[10] The heads of Cromwell and Hungerford were then displayed on Tower Bridge and their bodies buried at the Tower.[11] Walter's armorial badge is depicted in the Oak Gallery at The Vyne.[12]

Elizabeth married Sir Humphrey Foster of Aldermaston, which is close to The Vyne. He was present at William Sandys' deathbed in December 1540 and witnessed the nuncupative will.[13] The Foster coat of arms can be seen in the Oak Gallery and antechapel of The Vyne.

Margaret married Thomas Essex, son of Sir William Essex, and her father-in-law was also at William Sandys' deathbed and witnessed his nuncupative will.[14]

Thomas Sandys, the 2nd Baron

Thomas, the son and heir of Lord William Sandys, rarely features in contemporary documents before his father's death in 1540, but he was listed as an esquire at the reception of Anne of Cleves in 1540.[15] He married Elizabeth Manners, sister of Thomas Manners who became Lord Roos and then the Earl of Rutland.

It seems that neither the Crown nor others pressed Lord William to clear his substantial debts during his lifetime, and when he died they included £1,200 owed to the Crown, £100 to the estate of the late Cardinal Wolsey, £240 to the Abbott of Reading, and £106 to the Abbot of Glastonbury, amounting to over £1,500 in total.[16] Thomas was then pressed to clear his father's debts, and in 1548 received a certificate from the Court of Augmentations declaring that he had paid off his own debts and those of his father.[17] However, it seems that not all the debts had been cleared, because in 1550 Thomas entered into an agreement that relieved him of all his own and his father's debts in exchange for the transfer of lands.[18] Whatever the sequence of events, Thomas certainly sold many estates to clear the family debts (see Appendix 2).

Thomas lived at Mottisfont, probably from before his father's death, and was certainly there in September 1552 when Edward VI visited him during a royal progress, which suggests that Thomas was known in royal circles.[19] He does not appear to have held any position at court but attended the House of Lords.[20] After his death in late 1559 or early 1560, he was described as being 'of Mottisfont'.[21]

Thomas and his wife Elizabeth (Manners) had four sons, namely Henry, William, Walter and Humphrey, and six daughters, of whom Mary, Anne and Margery were unmarried in 1550.[22]

Henry was Thomas's son and heir but died in August 1551, several years before his father, and never took the title. He had married Elizabeth, daughter of Lord Windsor, and their son William would become the 3rd Baron. They also had another son, Thomas, and a daughter, Margery. Henry was buried with a pennon (a long, narrow flag bearing arms) and his surcoat, which bore his arms and four escutcheons (armorial badges),[23] at St Mary's Church at Hambleden in Buckinghamshire. His monument there does not state his date of birth or death, but is decorated with the Sandys' coat of arms and the winged goat crest together with the arms of Henry's mother Elizabeth (Manners). The church also contains two magnificent carved wooden panels, now part of an altar, which may have belonged to a bedhead or chest owned by William, Lord Sandys, decorated with the arms of Cardinal Thomas Wolsey and Bishop Richard Fox and their heraldic devices. Henry VIII's coat of arms and the Castile badge of Catherine of Aragon are also carved on these panels, and it has been suggested that they came to this church via The Vyne and Henry Sandys.[24]

Henry's brother Walter was at some time High Sheriff of Hampshire, certainly in 1592,[25] and Sheriff of Winchester. He was also knighted and lived at Mottisfont, probably from the time of his father's death until his own.[26] He died in 1609 and is buried in St Maurice's Church at Winchester.[27] Walter's son William occupied Mottisfont as a long-term tenant from at least 1619 to his death in 1628, and is buried in St Andrew's Church at Mottisfont.[28] A brass plate in the centre aisle of the church, bearing the Sandys of The Vyne coat of arms, commemorates his burial and refers to him as the 'Gilded Knight'.[29]

One of the younger sons of Thomas Sandys, the 2nd Baron, possibly Humphrey, was hanged on 18 June 1556. Machyn's diary states that Sandys and another 'robbed a cart with great riches' on Whitsunday and was hanged at St Thomas a Waterings, Southwark, London.[30]

William, the 3rd Baron

William was the son of Henry, son and heir of Thomas Sandys, and therefore grandson of the 2nd Baron and great-grandson of William, the 1st Baron. He was born around 1541, probably at Hambleden near Henley, the eldest son of Henry Sandys and Elizabeth Windsor, and lived a long life before he died in 1623.

William was a minor when he inherited the title of 3rd Baron from his grandfather, Thomas Sandys, in 1559,[31] and came of age sometime after March 1562 but before January 1563, as he first appeared in the House of Lords on 18 January 1563.[32] He had a brother Thomas, an uncle Walter (brother of his father Henry) and a cousin William, son of Walter. He married four times:

1) His first wife was Katherine Brydges (or Bridges), daughter of Lord Chandos and described as a beautiful lady. She was the mother of their only child Elizabeth, born between 1560 and 1570.[33] Katherine was alive in February 1578,[34] but a Lady Sandys, probably Katherine, was buried in the Chapel of the Holy Ghost at Basingstoke in 1580.[35] In 1585, her daughter Elizabeth married Sir Edwin Sandys of Eaton Bray, nephew of Archbishop Edwin Sandys, but Sir Edwin died in 1608.[36]
2) Sometime after 1580 William married Christiana or Christine Annesley, daughter of Sir Bryan Annesley.[37] She was pregnant in 1601 and tried to obtain her husband's release from prison after his arrest for his part in the Essex rebellion. She died sometime before 1605.
3) In 1605, William married Ursula, his third wife,[38] who gave birth in 1605 to their son and heir William who eventually became the 4th Baron, but she died before 1608.[39]
4) William's fourth wife was Anne Drewe, widow of William Drewe, whom he married at Hinton Ampner in 1608 and would survive him.[40]

William, the 3rd Baron, also had a mistress in the mid-1590s. She was Amy Grove, daughter of a shoemaker of Basingstoke, who bore him two children: a son called William who was born in 1594 and a daughter, Susanna, born late in 1596. William supported the family financially through two agreements made with Amy in December 1596 following the birth of Susanna. In the first, William gave Amy and her son William the mansion and associated land named the Chantry Land at The Vyne, while the second was a lease to Amy of more than 250 acres in Sherborn St John, including the Park Pruett estate with its Great and Little Lodges, for the duration of her life and that of William and Amy's daughter, Susanna Grove alias Sandys.[41] Amy and her family evidently thrived, as shown by her will made in 1640.[42]

William, 3rd Baron Sandys, had several homes. His main residence was The Vyne, described in his will as his 'chiefest manor', but when he was examined after the Essex rebellion he was described as being from Sherborne Cowdray. His London home in 1601 was at Charing Cross.[43] In October 1610, he was at Mottisfont.[44] Some confusion has also arisen between Lord William, the 3rd Baron, and his cousin Sir William Sandys, son of Sir Walter. During Lord William's later years, Sir William Sandys was living at Mottisfont, and this has led to statements that Lord Sandys was living at Mottisfont.[45]

Queen Elizabeth visited The Vyne twice during the 3rd Baron's time – in 1569 and 1601:

i) During the 1569 visit Elizabeth wrote to the Earl of Shrewsbury on 22 September to inform him that the Earl of Huntingdon would join him to take charge of Mary, Queen of Scots at Wingfield House, Derbyshire, as Shrewsbury, who was her custodian at that time, was sick. She also commanded that Mary's entourage be reduced to thirty persons and that access to her should be restricted.[46]

ii) The purpose of the 1601 visit to The Vyne was essentially to meet the French ambassador, the Duc de Biron, and his entourage of 400 who were quartered there. Sandys was not present because he was in custody for his part in the 1601 rebellion and the property and its contents had been sequestered by the Crown. The house was furnished with hangings (tapestries) and plate from the Tower and Hampton Court, and 140 beds and furniture provided by 'the willing and obedient people' of Hampshire. The queen was based in Basing House, but spent more time at The Vyne, where Sir Walter Raleigh also visited at this time.[47]

Mounting debts became a problem for the 3rd Baron. In 1598, he issued a declaration of indebtedness, which he attributed to several causes. The first was that he had been required to pay £2,000 to the Court of Wards for his marriage before he was twenty-one years old (before 1562). This indicates that he had been offered a wife by the court but preferred to marry someone of his own choosing. (It was not unknown for the court to offer someone who was not acceptable in order to receive payment. H. E. Bell refers to a case early in James I's reign when a male ward, aged fourteen, was offered a '28-year old harlot' as a spouse.[48]) The second was his modest income before his grandmother (presumably Lady Elizabeth Sandys) died, when much of the 1st Baron's estate was held by her through a marriage settlement by her husband Thomas, the 2nd Baron. The third was the cost of his visits to France with the earls of Lincoln and Derby and a four-and-a-half-year stay in France, including the cost of his horses, which amounted to £6,000. The fourth was the £3,000 dowry for his daughter Elizabeth on her marriage to Edwin Sandys, and fifth was the cost of lawsuits against his uncle Walter and Sir Brian Annesly, father of his second wife.

By 1598 the 3rd Baron owed £3,100, with an annual income of around £750.[49] After the rebellion in 1601 he was fined £10,000, later reduced to £5,000, but the fine was further reduced to £1,000 when he was pardoned by James I in 1603.[50]

Lord Sandys made several visits abroad for official and other reasons, including financial. In May 1572, he was part of the Earl of Lincoln's entourage when he went to France to confirm a treaty drawn up earlier that year. They went from Dover to Boulogne, then down to the Louvre in Paris where they met the French king.[51] Sometime in the 1580s Sandys was living in France, because on 12 March 1581 he wrote from Blois to the Earl of Leicester saying that he had stayed in France as he was impoverished.[52] In 1584, he accompanied the Earl of Derby, who had been appointed ambassador to the French court, to France, leaving Greenwich after seeing the queen on 20 January and not returning until 12 March. They went to the Louvre where they were presented to Henry III and exchanged letters between Queen Elizabeth and the king. The king was also presented with the Order of the Garter on behalf of the queen. Sandys took eight servants with him.[53]

Other service and duties included attending the House of Lords and occasionally serving on House Committees. He was a juror for the high-profile trials of Thomas Howard, Duke of Norfolk, in January 1572,[54] Mary, Queen of Scots in October 1586 at Fotheringay Castle, and Philip Howard, Earl of Arundel, in April 1589.[55]

Lord Sandys' involvement in the Earl of Essex's rebellion requires fuller explanation although the sources are limited.

Lord Burghley's death in 1598 created a void in Queen Elizabeth's court and an opportunity for senior courtiers to better themselves, either directly or through changes in positions and roles. The Earl of Essex was one who expected to benefit and did, being made Lord Lieutenant of Ireland in January 1559, but this involved significant risks because Ireland was in the throes of rebellion against the English. If Essex succeeded in subduing the rebellion he would be in favour, but if he failed he would face disgrace and worse.

Despite having the largest army ever sent by England to Ireland, Essex failed miserably and was dismissed from court. The queen also terminated his right to the import duty on sweet wines, which was a large part of his income, and he was placed under house arrest. Not surprisingly, Essex became disaffected and convinced that Sir Walter Raleigh, Sir Robert Cecil, and others wanted him dead. He was not alone in being aggrieved at this time, and by the end of 1600 he and a few others developed a plan to force the queen to see him and restore his privileges and position at court. It had several versions: one early idea was to use part of the army Essex had in Ireland, but a later idea involved taking the Tower of London and moving on to Whitehall Palace, as Essex believed that many in the city of London would follow his lead.[56]

Sandys denied that he was involved in hatching this plot, which was probably true, but he was a friend of Essex, so it is hard to believe that he knew nothing of his grievances and ambition. On the other hand, he must have understood the consequences of close association with a failed rebel, while also recognising that the success of such a venture could lead to financial rewards, for which Sandys had great need. In 1598, he was in debt for £3,100, a large sum at that time, and had been forced to mortgage several properties inherited from his grandfather, Lord Thomas Sandys.

The rebellion started early on Sunday 8 February, and Sandys was summoned from his house in Charing Cross to Essex House by the earl's servant. It was not a long journey because Essex House was on the Strand, close to Temple Bar. When he arrived, he found a small group of people, which grew with the arrival of the earls of Southampton and Rutland, Lords Cromwell and Mounteagle, and several knights, including Sir Christopher Blount. The queen heard about the meeting and quickly instructed four senior members of her Privy Council to order Essex to come to court and disband the rebels. The councillors arrived at around 10 a.m. and were confronted by a noisy cohort of men armed with rapiers, but they delivered the royal message, which was greeted with cries of 'kill them' and 'lock them up'.[57] One tried to negotiate privately with Essex, but he and the other three councillors were imprisoned in Essex House, a move that Essex later claimed was for their safety.[58] Essex, Sandys and about 150 men, armed only with rapiers, then moved along the Strand and Fleet Street to seek the support that they believed had been promised.[59] They went first to the Lord Mayor of London at his house in Seething Lane by the Tower, and then to Sherriff Smythe at his house in Gracechurch Street, but after lengthy discussions no men from the city joined the rebels. This was hardly surprising, as the queen and court already knew about Essex's move into the city and a royal proclamation had declared him a traitor, which caused the mayor, sheriffs and aldermen to abandon the sermon at St Paul's Cathedral and raise arms to defend the city. However, the city men did not apprehend the rebels, because although they may have had some sympathy with Essex and his men, they could not risk being deemed traitors. The hapless band remained in the city for more than four hours before deciding to make their way to Whitehall to see the queen. By the time they reached Ludgate, it was closed. The Bishop of London led its defence,[60] and when Essex cried 'Charge, Charge', his men responded and charged the gate, but to no avail.[61] Sir Christopher Blount, one of the authors of the original plot, was shot in the leg and his servant killed by the defenders.[62] Seeing that their situation was hopeless, the rebels ran down to the river and boarded boats at Queenhithe to take them back to Essex House,[63] where they barricaded themselves in and Essex set fire to a bag of papers about the earlier plot that would have incriminated his fellow plotters.

The battle commenced, and it was not long before the defenders were told that Essex House would be demolished by petards brought from the Tower. Essex responded by negotiating a truce, so that the ladies could leave before the bombardment began. He also declared that 'they would sooner fly to heaven' than surrender,[64] but they did eventually surrender after the Lord Admiral, who was in charge of the siege, promised to make Essex's grievances known to the queen. In the meantime, Queen Elizabeth was not happy and declared that 'she would not sleep till they were had out'. The siege was over between ten and eleven o'clock that night.[65]

Although Sandys was around sixty years of age and one of the oldest among the rebels, he fought hard and with spirit. Camden says 'and the Lord Sands, more aged than the rest cried that the stoutest counsailes are the safest; that it is more honourable for Noblemen to dye fighting than by the hand of the executioner'.[66] The lords Egerton (Lord Keeper), Buckhurst, Nottingham and Sir Robert Cecil gave evidence that 'no man showed himself more forward in the streets nor readier to fight and defend the house after their return against the Queen's force nor more earnest that they should not submit themselves than Lord Sandys; for when they all resolved to submit only Lord Sandys and Essex were resolved to end their lives with a sally'.[67] By 3 a.m. on 9 February, the earls of Essex, Rutland and Southampton and lords Sandys and Cromwell were in the Tower awaiting the inevitable retribution.[68]

The retribution started quickly. Late on 9 February Sandys' house in Charing Cross was sequestered and an inventory of goods began. Christine, Lady Sandys, who was pregnant, was there at the time and the doors were locked. The queen's men did not break into the house but entered the stables and removed horses.[69] On 13 February, the Privy Council instructed the Sheriff of Hampshire to go to Sandys' houses in that county (The Vyne and Mottisfont) and seize the house, land, goods and cattle, then make an inventory of all goods and cattle found.[70] On 16 February, Sandys ('of Sherborne Cowdray, Hampshire') was examined before Lord Chief Justice Popham and the Attorney General and claimed that he was summoned to Essex House, not thinking that this was the start of a rebellion. This raises the question of why he did not return home when the shouting and threats to the privy councillors began. By the following day (17 February) Lady Sandys, who had remained at the Charing Cross house and received provisions from 'Lord Sandys' house in country', i.e. The Vyne, had written to the Privy Council because the house and its contents had been sequestered by the queen, resulting in the cessation of goods being delivered to Charing Cross. The lords of the Privy Council decided that, as Lady Sandys was pregnant, she should receive provisions from her country household as she needed and instructed the Sheriff of Berkshire to allow this to happen.[71]

On 19 February, Essex's trial began.[72] Sandys gave evidence and said that he was not party to the original plot and only went to Essex's house on 8 February because of his friendship with Essex. Both Essex and Southampton were found guilty and sentenced as traitors. They were to be drawn through the streets of London on a hurdle, hanged, disembowelled and quartered, and their heads and quarters disposed of at Her Majesty's pleasure. The queen then reprieved Southampton's sentence, and commuted Essex's sentence to beheading.[73] He was executed on 25 February in a courtyard at the Tower. The axeman apparently took three strikes to separate the head, but claimed that Essex was senseless after the first blow.[74] Sir Christopher Blount was later tried and executed for committing high treason as one of the authors of the original plot.

By now, Sandys must have been increasingly anxious that he and the other senior rebels were being kept in the Tower. He appeared before the Privy Council early in March, where his petition concluded with: 'I am in remorse of conscience, tormented at my disloyalty, being blinded in my judgement by my affection, and drawn by fair pretences of danger unto the Earl of Essex, whose disloyal designs I never discerned until I was by him entangled in his rebellious action – to my confusion, unless by her Majesty's mercy be relieved.'[75] On 5 March, the Lord Steward was ordered to set up Sandys' trial, but when he was being taken to Westminster to be arraigned on 10 March a court messenger arrived with instructions to return him to the Tower.[76] Following a letter to the Privy Council from Lady Cromwell a few days later, claiming that her husband was getting 'corpulent and sickly',[77] it was agreed that Cromwell, Sandys and a few others should be allowed to take exercise at the Tower, providing that they did not communicate with each other.[78]

Throughout these troubling events, Lady Sandys did everything she could to prevent her husband being executed, and when that was achieved she sought a reduction in his fine. Shortly after 10 March, when a stay was placed on his arraignment, she wrote to the queen through Cecil, begging for mercy on her 'poor Lord' and offering everything they had in return for his life and honour, as he was 'dearer to her than her life'.[79] Over the next few weeks she wrote further letters to Cecil, begging him to petition the queen to show mercy to her husband as she was pregnant, sickly and near to her time, and that a doctor should see him as he was ill with stomach pains. She also offered to give Cecil her horses and said she 'would endure as much misery as it shall please the Queen to inflict on her' if Sandys was released.[80]

The epilogue to the Essex rebellion in terms of Sandys involvement is that he was eventually released from custody. His wife Christine, who had tried so hard to obtain his release, and their child died shortly afterwards. It seems that Sandys then moved 'to his lodgings in Charing Cross', London, from which he told Lord Cecil in May 1603 that he had paid off £1,000 of his debt but was in ill health, and that he would be absent from court but would return as soon as he could.[81] In November that year, following the accession of James I, Sandys' fine was reduced to £1,000, a sum he had already paid, and he was granted a royal pardon.[82] Two years later, in 1605, his third wife Ursula bore him a son, William,[83] who would become the 4th Baron. In the same year, 1605, Sandys wrote to the king saying that his infirmities prevented him from attending his majesty.[84] Ursula died, and in 1608 he married his fourth wife, Anne Drewe, who outlived him. In 1610 he wrote to Lord Salisbury asking to be excused duty in the House of Lords explaining he was ill and his eyes were bad.[85] He died in 1623 aged over eighty. He was buried in the Chapel of the Holy Ghost Basingstoke.[86]

William, the 4th Baron

William, son of the 3rd Baron and his wife Ursula, died without children in November 1629 and was buried in the Chapel of the Holy Ghost at Basingstoke.[87]

Elizabeth, the 5th Baroness

Given that William, the 4th Baron, died childless, the title passed to his half-sister Elizabeth, who married Sir Edwin Sandys of Eaton Bray[88] from a different Sandys family, and had three sons. The first two died young, leaving Henry Sandys as the senior male heir, but he died before his mother and never inherited the title. Her date of death is unknown, but it must have been between Henry's death in April 1644 and 1651, when her granddaughter Elizabeth made her will.

Henry Sandys

Henry, the son of Elizabeth, the 5th Baroness, married Jane, daughter of Sir William Sandys of Fladbury, Worcester.[89] Henry and Jane lived at The Vyne, as revealed by a mortgage indenture dated 1639 in the Hampshire Record Office, which refers to 'Henry Sandys of the Vyne',[90] and a painting of Henry and his mother Elizabeth in 1641, which shows the chapel end of The Vyne in the background.[91] That painting and others of later Sandys family members were in the custody of the Sandys of Graythwaite family in the Lake District.[92]

Henry was a Royalist who fought in Charles I's army with the rank of colonel, but he died in April 1644 from injuries received at Bramsdene in the Battle of Cheriton at Down, Hampshire.[93] He and Jane had four sons, namely William, Henry, Miles and Edwin, and six girls, Hester, Elizabeth, Margery, Mary, Jane and Margaret.[94] Miles died young and the three remaining sons inherited the title in turn, but none had children. This caused the barony to be placed in abeyance on the death of Edwin, the youngest son.[95]

William, the 6th Baron

William was the eldest son of Colonel Henry and his wife, and married Lady Mary Cecil, youngest daughter of the second Earl of Salisbury. His sister Elizabeth's will, dated 1651,[96] refers to him as the Lord Sandys, and the probate note in 1653 describes him as William, Lord Sandys, the natural and lawful brother of Elizabeth Sandys, so he must have gained the title *c.* 1650. In 1653, family debts caused him to sell The Vyne to a London lawyer, Chaloner Chute, and move the family to Mottisfont. In 1661, he was summoned to the House of Lords. He died childless in 1668 and is buried in the Holy Ghost Chapel at Basingstoke.[97]

Henry, the 7th Baron

Henry was also the son of Colonel Henry Sandys. Little is known about his life, but in 1679 he was a member of the Winchester Corporation, along with the Bishop of Winchester and seven other lords,[98] and it is reasonable to assume that his brothers fulfilled the same role when they were Baron Sandys. Henry died unmarried in 1682 and is buried in the Holy Ghost Chapel at Basingstoke. The title then passed to his brother Edwin.[99]

Edwin, the 8th – and last – Baron Sandys of The Vyne

Edwin was another son of Colonel Henry and lived at Mottisfont. He and his surviving sisters were granted the precedence they would have had if their father, Henry Sandys, had succeeded to the title of Lord Sandys of The Vyne.[100] He died unmarried on 3 June 1684 and is buried in the Holy Ghost Chapel at Basingstoke. His estates were divided among his six sisters, with Margaret, wife of Sir John Mill Bart., inheriting Mottisfont and its estate.[101]

8

Summary and Conclusions

The introduction to this work noted that William Sandys' extant biographies are no more than brief overviews in reference works such as the *Dictionary of National Biography*, the *History of Parliament*, and *The Vyne: A Tudor House Revealed* by Howard and Wilson. These are complemented by comments that usually focus on one aspect of his life in various works on early Tudor history, while more varied information and comment is scattered through the six volumes of St Clare Byrne's *The Lisle Letters*.

Visual images are also lacking, as no portraits or depictions of the faces of Lord Sandys or his wife have been identified to date, and his presence in the procession of the Knights of the Garter in the 1530s is a back view with two other knights, which merely indicates that he was of average build and height.

This study has presented a fuller and more coherent, but by no means complete, picture of Sandys, who was born into a period of significant turbulence that continued through most of his life. He witnessed the last years of the Wars of the Roses, the seizure of the throne by Richard, Duke of Gloucester, and then by Henry Tudor, and three major rebellions to dethrone Henry, which all failed. This was followed by Henry VIII's determination to raise the profile of the English Crown and court and regain power in Continental Europe, which resulted in wars with the French and Scots, while the last decade of Sandys' life saw England and Wales in a different kind of turmoil following the break with the Roman Catholic Church and Henry becoming head of the English Church. Confusion and terror prevailed as Henry pursued reforms that he and others regarded as necessary, including the closure of the long-established religious houses, dismantling of shrines, and destruction of objects regarded as idols. This was followed by rebellion and the execution of those who either adhered to the Church of Rome or indulged in the new Protestant beliefs.

Throughout these disturbances, Sandys generally managed to thrive and prosper. His entry at court was almost certainly facilitated by his connections with the Bray and Cheyne families through his wife and mother respectively, and less directly with the royal family through Margaret Beaufort, Henry VII's mother. He was knighted by Henry VII at the age of seventeen in 1487, and later made Knight of the Body, a role he continued to hold during Henry VIII's reign. He was even nominated for the Order of the Garter in 1499 at the age of twenty-nine, which was young for a commoner and indicates he had made his mark at court, but he was not elected on that occasion. Circumstantial evidence suggests that Sandys was attached to the court of Henry VII's wife, Queen Elizabeth, where the young Prince Henry was raised until his elder brother Prince Arthur died in 1501. While Queen Elizabeth was alive Sandys prospered, and when she died in 1503 he was a banner carrier at her funeral. A few months later, he was among the escort accompanying Princess Margaret to Edinburgh for her marriage to James IV of Scotland. Yet, for six years following the death of Queen Elizabeth there are few references to Sandys in the records, and he does not appear in any State activities until Henry VII's funeral in 1509. This apparent inactivity may have been the consequence of peace at that time and the court's low-key style during Henry VII's last years, but it also supports the notion that Sandys was more attached to the queen than the king.

Henry VIII retained Sandys as Knight of the Body, which gave him access to the king, but his precise duties are unclear. Less than a month after Henry's accession he was again nominated Knight of the Garter but not elected, yet within nine months of the coronation he was appointed Keeper of the Manor of Sherborne St John, Constable of Southampton Castle, and Keeper of the Freemantil Park. He was granted additional offices during 1510, but the highlight of that year for Sandys must have been the visit by Henry VIII and Queen Catherine to The Vyne for hunting, at which time Sandys' home was a relatively modest manor house. Progress continued, as he obviously demonstrated the administrative ability required to become Treasurer of War in the 1512 Anglo-Spanish campaign against the French. This was followed by his highly commended handling of the Southampton riots in 1517, as Constable of Southampton Castle, which led to his promotion to the lucrative post of Treasurer of Calais. A year later he was elected to the Order of the Garter.

Sandys' time at Calais was busy. In addition to his normal duties, he was one of three who organised the Field of the Cloth of Gold meeting between the kings of France and England, and shortly afterwards he was a key player in the war with the French. He was then elevated to the position of High Marshal of the Army in the 1523 campaign. Three years later he became the King's Chamberlain, often called 'Lord Chamberlain of the Household', which kept him in close touch with the king and senior courtiers. He was also Lieutenant of Guînes. Sandys retained these roles until his death in December 1540 and features regularly and frequently in contemporary records, yet he is rarely mentioned in published historical works. From 1526, he was present at virtually all great State occasions and frequently in the king's company.

Although his fortunes sometimes fluctuated, Sandys managed to maintain the support of the king and his high status almost to the end of his life, regardless of attempts to undermine him, particularly in his later years when he frequently excused himself from court for reasons of old age and bouts of sickness. Despite these afflictions he was remarkably active and made several cross-Channel journeys in his seventieth year.

His greatest strength was on the battlefield, where he was an excellent field commander, fighter and leader, and he remained on the front line into his mid-fifties. He also led from the front, as testified by Hall in his *Chronicles,* and was highly regarded by the French commanders and the ambassador of the Holy Roman Empire at the English court. Even in his last year the French considered Sandys a major deterrent, according to Elis Gruffudd, the eyewitness and chronicler who wrote, 'They [the French] greatly feared the Lord Chamberlain and his men.' He also had a ruthless streak and perhaps a strong temper, as no one doubted his intention when he threatened to hang priests for harbouring French soldiers in a church in 1522. Likewise, when he included 'On pain of death' in his proclamation to the inhabitants of Guînes in 1540, there was little doubt that he meant what he said. All the evidence therefore indicates that he was a military leader with ability, courage, ruthlessness, stamina and determination.

Sandys was also a loyal and trusted courtier for Henry VIII, but his loyalty to others is less clear. Cardinal Wolsey seemed to think well of him, as one of his few recorded disputes with the king was over Sandys' role in the 1523 expedition to France, when Wolsey argued strongly and repeatedly that Sandys should lead the expedition, but Henry did not agree. Yet, Sandys was among those who signed the articles against Wolsey in 1529, which led to his downfall. He survived Cromwell's regime, although they were at opposite ends of the religious spectrum, perhaps because of Sandys' strong relationship with the king. It is also possible that Sandys and Cromwell worked together to remove Anne Boleyn. Muriel St Claire Byrne suggests that Sandys was perhaps prepared to go along with Cromwell while Cromwell was in favour with the king. He was certainly sufficiently astute to survive and thrive, but he must have had some reputation for disloyalty because John Hussey wrote to Lord Lisle to warn him that Sandys, along with John Wallop, would 'leave him in the briars when you trust them most'. He was also quick to complain to Cromwell about a colleague, based on unchecked third-party information, if it suited him. Some writers have criticised Sandys for what they believe was his sycophantic behaviour towards the king, but without considering the environment of a court in which the king's favour was not only necessary for success but often for survival and any suspicion of loss of favour with the king would result in a human wolf pack seeking your positions and lands. Sandys' habit of writing directly to the king, particularly from Calais, may have upset Cromwell and others, but the fact that he continued to do so in his last years indicates that he felt his relationship with the king was direct and positive. At the same time, Henry appears to have trusted Sandys, while recognising his limitations in terms of innovation, diplomacy and thrift.

In terms of the religious changes known as the 'Reformation', Sandys clearly favoured the traditional beliefs and practices and was among those who held conservative, Roman Catholic views. This is supported by a range of evidence, which includes his association with the Duke of Norfolk; the indulgence granted to him by Pope Clement VII in late 1533; his close links with Eustace Chapuys, the ambassador of the Holy Roman Emperor and a keen supporter of the Catholic faith; building the Chapel of the Holy Trinity in the Chapel of the Holy Ghost at Basingstoke; and working with Bishop Richard Fox to establish the voluntary Guild of the Fraternity of Holy Ghost at Basingstoke. He also commissioned the chapel at The Vyne, dedicated to the Virgin Mary, and many of his letters conclude with 'beseeching the Holy Ghost to preserve you'. Yet, despite this personal conservatism, he signed the Oath of Allegiance to Henry VIII rather than suffer persecution or execution for his beliefs, and his activities in Calais in later years suggest zealous pursuit of those who had strayed from the king's religion in favour of the new Protestantism.

Although Sandys' income was significant, financial pressures caused personal difficulties as he chose to spend more than he received and was constantly in debt. He and his wife Margery managed to take much of the Bray inheritance away from the natural heir who was a minor at the time of Bray's death, but by 1528 Sandys was more than £6,000 in debt to the Crown, which was never repaid during his lifetime although the king reduced it by a half. In 1525, when Sandys knew he was to become the King's Chamberlain, he wrote to Wolsey hoping that he would not be deprived of the advantages derived from being Treasurer of Calais, considering his 'great poverty'. He had obviously made his position at Calais lucrative, although the formal payments were not large, and he was determined to receive his dues, but he caused hardship for his soldiers by not passing on their pay. He was also tardy in paying the postmen in the Pale in 1518 and had to be reminded by Wolsey to do so. Six months after Wolsey's deposition in December 1529 Sandys gained another sinecure, when the king made him Keeper of Farnham Castle. This involved asking Wolsey, who was now Bishop of Winchester, to countersign the patent to release the Farnham Castle role to Sandys, which he did.

It is not difficult to understand why Sandys felt poor. During the 1520s he constructed one of the grandest houses in England on a palatial scale and furnished it with the highest-quality woodcarvings and Brussels tapestries, some of which attracted the king's interest. Some of his silver gilt ware ended up in the royal collection. The windows of his residence were also of high quality, and when he remodelled the Chapel of the Holy Ghost in Basingstoke and added a chantry chapel to accommodate his burial vault this was also decorated with the finest Flemish glazing of the day. More construction costs arose from 1536 onwards for rebuilding and converting Mottisfont Priory as another residence.

Sandys also enjoyed good living, as indicated in 1539 to Lord Wriothesley: 'The good hospitality he keeps may not be well forthcoming in these parts [Guînes].' Several of his letters relate to the purchase of wine and food, and he apparently enjoyed hunting so much that he was caught hunting illegally in the king's park in 1504. This seems strange, as his own park at The Vyne was good enough for Henry VIII and two of his queens to hunt there during visits. Sandys also hunted in France with the French king.

He does not appear to have been involved in other field sports such as jousting, except as a marshal as at the Field of the Cloth of Gold. This is perhaps surprising, as the joust and tilt were the usual methods for honing battlefield skills and could also bring royal recognition and promotion at court.

The introduction to this study indicated that Sandys' relationships with others, particularly his family, would be included, but it has not been possible to shed much light on that subject, largely because little or no correspondence between Sandys and members of his family, including his wife Margery and elder sister Edith, Lady Neville, is extant. This lack of surviving family correspondence is not unusual, and it is possible that examples will be discovered in future. Letters relating to official business, especially associated with the Crown, are different, because they are records of ongoing issues and much more likely to survive. Most of Sandys' surviving letters are of a business nature and written in formal and ponderous language, reflecting the court style of the day, but the tone is polite, which may reflect personal attitude as well as the expected style at the time. A small number of his letters to Honor, Lady Lisle, wife of Lord Lisle, have also survived, because Lisle's correspondence was sequestered by the Crown on his arrest, and these show that Sandys could be less formal and capable of genuine affection.

There is little doubt that Sandys' wife Margery was literate, as she wrote to Cromwell and Wolsey seeking favours for others, but there is little or no evidence of her whereabouts for most of the time. She is not mentioned at court ceremonies but was certainly known there and exchanged gifts with the king at New Year. It is likely that husband and wife were separated for long periods, especially when he was on campaign, as in 1523, yet they produced several children. It is also interesting to note that the wooden frieze in The Vyne's chapel, which is decorated with carvings of armorial devices, mythical beasts and plants, includes a section where the initials of William and Margery Sandys are joined by a knot. Sandys was almost fifty when this frieze was created, suggesting that he shared a close and lasting affection with Margery. He also had reason to thank her for a large part of their fortune, as it was through Margery that a large proportion of Sir Reynold Bray's estates became theirs, without which The Vyne would have been more modest and less richly decorated. Sandys' sister Edith also wrote letters, but no correspondence with her brother has been discovered. It can be safely assumed that Sandys cared for his children, as he facilitated entry to court for two of his sons, although neither rose to a significant post. He was also prepared to write to Thomas Cromwell about his middle son, who was a priest in financial difficulties. With Margery's help, he no doubt arranged good marriages for the children and gave financial support.

Sandys' will does not indicate special attachments to, or affection for individuals, but that is not unusual in a formal, legal document that required careful construction and recording, especially when the testator was unwell. Margery had died the previous year, and Sandys' eldest son Thomas is barely mentioned, but that is not uncommon for the principal heir whose status was already recognised. His son John and his nephew John received modest annuities, as did his second grandson, William, but there is no mention of Henry, the first grandson. Outside the immediate family, two of Sandys' sons-in-law, Sir Humphrey Forster and Sir William Essex, were present when Sandys declared his will orally, and they received a bequest. Many of his servants and staff also received something, although there is no indication of his relationship with them – as is often the case in wills. On the other hand, there is evidence during his life that he was willing to help ex-soldiers by seeking jobs for them.

In conclusion, it is worth noting that while there is no evidence that Sandys was a significant innovator, policymaker or statesman, he was certainly a dedicated servant of his king who was trusted to lead on the battlefield, administer the king's household and, towards the end, enforce the king's religious reforms in the Calais Pale. His skills were clearly recognised and rewarded. Sandys valued the king's trust, which mattered to him in all aspects of his life, and he exploited it to maintain a good quality of life, sometimes to the detriment of others. He also defended his status, rights and perquisites with rigour. With hindsight, and to avoid inappropriate judgements, it is important to remember that Sandys' priorities and attitudes were not unusual during this period, and that the social challenges, uncertainties and political and religious turbulence were particularly difficult for everybody. But his service to the Crown both on and off the battlefield, loyalty to friends and family, commitment to personal religious views, and the taste and commitment he exhibited in developing his property, made him remarkable and worthy of much more attention than he has received to date.

APPENDIX 1

Chronology of William, Lord Sandys' Life

This appendix provides a summary of William, Lord Sandys' activities during his life, the corresponding location where known and the relevant references.

The following points should be noted to assist understanding:

- He is referred to as 'WS' whatever his status unless part of a quotation.
- Major national events that affected him are in given in bold.
- References to published works are noted in the same form as they appear in the footnotes, namely the surname of the author/editor, a slightly shortened title, and volume/page numbers as appropriate. This enables the full details to be easily identified in the Bibliography.
- Long publication titles are more heavily abbreviated, such as *L&P* for *Letters and Papers*, *Cal.P.R. or Cal.C.R.* for *Calendar of Patent* or *Close Rolls*, and *Cal.Inq.PM.* for *Calendar of Inquisitions Post Mortem*. These abbreviations are described at the beginning of the Bibliography.
- Not all the references in the Chronology are in the endnotes.

Year	Day, Month	Event	Location of WS 1470–1540	Reference
Before 1469	25 March	WS's father married Margaret Cheyne.		HRO 37M8513-FR1
c. 1470		WS was born.	Andover. Cholderton or Clatford	*Cal.Inq.PM. 12 Henry VII,* 1245, p.556; TNA 139/181/75
1478	11 December	WS's father signs an indenture concerning the estate for the marriage of his eldest son, John.		TNA C1/109/3

Year	Day, Month	Event	Location of WS 1470–1540	Reference
After 1478, perhaps 1485		WS becomes heir to his father's estate on the death of John, his elder brother.		TNA C1/1519-20
1483		WS's father attended the coronation of Richard III.	Andover. Cholderton or Clatford	Sutton and Hammond, *The Coronation of Richard III*, p.270
1484		WS's father was commissioned to arrest rebels in Hants. and Wilts., including John Cheyne.	Andover. Cholderton or Clatford	Horrocks, R. and Hammond, P. W., BL Harl.MS 433, 2nd Register
1487	16 June	WS was knighted at the Battle of Stoke and his coat of arms bears a labelled cross raguly.	Stoke	Leland, *De Rebus Brit. Collect.*, Vol. IV, pp.214–15; BL Cotton MS Claudius CIII f.60; Hay, *The Anglica Historia of PV*, pp.23–26
1488		WS was present at the Whitsuntide Feast	Windsor	Leland, *De Rebus Brit. Collect.*, Vol.IV, p.243
	20 May	The Vyne reverts to the Sandys family on the death of Bernard Brocas.		*Cal.Inq.PM. Henry VII*, Vol.II, 23 June, 395, p.168
	25 November	WS at the coronation of Queen Elizabeth, the wife of Henry VII.	Westminster	Leland, *De Rebus Brit.Collect.*, Vol.IV, p.232
1491	**28 June**	**Prince Henry was born.**		**Hamilton, *Wriothesley Chronicle*, p.2**
1492	April	WS's indenture for war was issued.		TNA E 101/72/3/1088
	After 6 September	WS went to Flanders.		Hay, *Anglica Historia of PV*, p.53
		WS in the party to meet the French ambassadors.		Gairdner et al., *L&P... Richard III and Henry VII*, Vol.2, pp.290–91
	After October	WS receives payment for war effort.		TNA E 101/36/285

Year	Day, Month	Event	Location of WS 1470–1540	Reference
1493	17 October	WS's father describes himself as 'the Elder' in his will and confirms the younger WS is a knight.		TNA Prob.11/11/22
1494	27 April 1494	WS married to Margery Bray before this date.		TNA CP25/1/207/36 No. 13
	31 October, 1 November	WS participates in the ceremony to create Prince Henry Duke of York and Knight of Bath.	Westminster London	Gairdner et al., *L&P… Richard III and Henry VII*, Vol.1, pp.388–404
	13 November	WS at celebratory feast for Prince Henry.	London	Gairdner et al., *L&P… Reigns of Richard III and Henry VII*, Vol.1, pp.388–404
1495	1 October	WS owed money to the Crown by obligation (later cancelled).		TNA E101/414/6
1496	26 October	WS's father died 26 October. *Inq. PM.* refers to his son William as 'aged 26 or more'.		*Cal.Inq.PM. Henry VII*, Vol.II, 1245, 1246, p.556–57; HRO 13M63-16 p.316
1497	16 June	WS fought at the Battle of Blackheath, described as 'Will' Sandes *miles*'.	Blackheath, London	Hay, *Anglica Historia of PV*, p.94; BL Stowe MS440, p.82
	June	WS was paid £21 *5s 3d* for wages and travel for fighting at the Battle of Blackheath.	London	TNA E 405/79/f.40r (trans. by Dr S. J. Davies)
	10 September	Edith Sandys, WS's sister and wife of Lord Ralph Neville, was widowed.		*Cal.Inq.PM. Henry VII*, Vol.II, p.331
1499	23 April	WS nominated as Knight of the Garter (KG) but was unsuccessful.		Anstis, *Register of the Most Noble Order of the Garter*, p.239
	15 July	WS made Sergeant-at-Law.		*Cal.C.R. Henry VII*, 15 July, 1157, p.343

Year	Day, Month	Event	Location of WS 1470–1540	Reference
	14 October	WS, Knight of the Body, was made Steward of Christchurch and Ringwood, Hants. and Constable of Christchurch Castle for life.		*Cal.Pat.R.Henry VII*, Vol.2, 14 Oct., p.187
c. 1500		Like his father, WS refused to pay a dower claim by Margaret Sandys (née Howard), wife of the late John Sandys.		TNA C1/109/3; C1/109/5; C1/1513/19–20; C1/186/88.
1500	25 June	Ralph Neville, 3rd Earl of Westmorland, died. WS's nephew became 4th Earl.		*Cal.Inq.PM. Henry VII*, Vol.II, p.253
1501	23 September	WS, Knight of the Body, became Ranger of Chute Forest, Wilts. and Hants.		*Cal.Pat.R. Henry VII*, 1501, September 23, p.265
	25 October	WS was one of the party to receive Princess Catherine of Aragon.		Gairdner et al., *L&P… Richard III and Henry VII*, Vol.1, pp.404–20; Leland, *De Rebus Brit. Collect.*, Vol.V, pp.352–56
	14 November	**Prince Arthur married Catherine.**		**Hamilton, *Wriothesley Chronicle*, p.4**
1502	**2 April**	**Prince Arthur died.**		**Leland, *De Rebus Brit. Collect.*, Vol.V, p.373**
	November	Servants of WS injured Nicholas Mathewe, yeoman of the Queen's Chamber. The queen paid the recompense.	Court	Nicolas, *Privy Purse Expenses of Elizabeth of York*, pp.70
1503		WS named in case before the Hants. bench for the conduct of men retained by him as steward of some royal manors.		Grummitt, *The Calais Garrison*, p.73

Year	Day, Month	Event	Location of WS 1470–1540	Reference
	2 February	WS was a banner holder at the funeral of Queen Elizabeth.	Westminster	TNA LC2.1 pt.1, p.59v; BL ADD. MS 45131, f.45
	27 June–13 August	WS and his sister Edith, Lady Neville, are listed among the persons accompanying Princess Margaret to Scotland.	To Scotland via Collyweston and York	BL HLR941, *Manuscripts of Duke of Rutland* Vol.1, p.118; Leland, *De Rebus Brit. Collect.*, Vol.IV, p.265
	5 August	**Reynold Bray died.**		**Condon, in *Profit, Piety and the Professions in Later Medieval England*, p.138**
1504	30 June	Grant to WS, Knight of the Body, of The Vyne.		*Cal.Pat.R. Henry VII*, Vol.2, p.354
		WS and his wife claim property from minors in the Bray family over the next few years.		Condon, in *Profit, Piety and the Professions in Later Medieval England*, p.157
1505	23 January	Grant taken from WS for John Lisle et al. (see 23 September 1501, above).		*Cal.Pat.R. Henry VII*, Vol.2, 1505 Jan.23, p.425
	6 February	Pardon to WS, Knight of the Body, for all trespasses in forests, etc.		*Cal.Pat.R. Henry VII*, Vol.2, 6 Feb. 1505, p.425
	21 October	WS was bound in an obligation to the queen.		TNA E36/214
1508	25 October	WS made Keeper of Stratfield Mortimer, Berks. and Easthampstede Park.		*Cal.Pat.R. Henry VII*, Vol.2, 1508, p.624
1509	**22 April**	**Henry VIII became king.**		**Mackie, *The Early Tudors*, p.231**
	11 May	WS at Henry VII's funeral.	Court	*L&P. Henry VIII* 1, 20, p13; TNA LC 2.1 pt.1, p.125
	18 May	WS nominated again for KG.		Anstis, *Reg. of the Most Noble Order of the Garter*, Vol.1, p.271

Year	Day, Month	Event	Location of WS 1470–1540	Reference
	NA	WS granted royal pardon for previous offences.		HRO 23M58/4
	24 June	**Henry VIII coronation.**		**Hamilton, *Wriothesley Chronicle*, p.7**
	27 Aug.	Recognisance to WS cancelled.		*L&P Henry VIII*, 1, 158 (77), p.58
	13 October	WS made keeper of the manor of Sherborne St John.		*L&P Henry VIII*, 1, 218, (26), p.110
1510	12 January	WS appointed Constable of Southampton Castle.		*L&P Henry VIII*, 1, 359 (9), p.163
	8 February	WS appointed keeper of Freemantil Park, Hants.		*L&P Henry VIII* 1, 381(32), p.172
	27 April	WS again nominated for KG.		Anstis, *Reg. of the Most Noble Order of the Garter*, Vol.1, p.274
	15 May	WS appointed parker of Freemantil Park, Hants.		*L&P Henry VIII*, 1, 519 (22), p.306
	25 July	Henry VIII and Queen Catherine visited The Vyne.	The Vyne	BL Add Man 214811; *L&P Henry VIII*, 1, 563.9, p.329; *L&P Henry VIII*, 2, 'King's Book of Payments', p.1447
	23 October	WS appointed steward and surveyor of the lordships of Ryngewood and Christchurch, constable of the castle, bailiff of the lordship of Christchurch, and keeper of the deer in the Bailiwick of Styrfield, Hants.		*L&P Henry VIII*, 1, 604, parag.43, p.346
	24 October	WS was granted the manors of Peryton, Somerset, and Westraddon, Devon.		*L&P Henry VIII*, 1, 604, 42, p.346

Year	Day, Month	Event	Location of WS 1470–1540	Reference
	9 November	WS made Sheriff of Hants.		*L&P Henry VIII*, 1, 632 parag.26, p.354
1511	15 March	Recognisance of 1,200 marks cancelled by Henry VIII.		*L&P Henry VIII*, 1,731, parag.52, p.339
	17 May	Recognisance of £1,250 cancelled by Henry VIII.		*L&P Henry VIII*, 1,784, parag.30, p.422
1512	8 April	WS appointed Constable of Southampton Castle.		*L&P Henry VIII*, 1, 1176, parag.10, p.549
	2 May	WS appointed to the expedition to Spain.		*L&P Henry VIII*, l, 1176, parag.i, 2, p.552
	10 May	WS appointed Treasurer of War.		*L&P Henry VIII*, 1, 1221, parag.6, p.563; parag.24, p.565
	8 July–20 October	WS at Fontrabia.	Spain	*L&P Henry VIII*, 1, 286, p.590; 1,1422, p.650; 1,1441, p.658; 1,1444, p.658; 1,1484, p.1676; 1,1496, p.690.
	September	WS visits the King of Aragon.	Spain	*L&P Henry VIII*, 1,1495, parag. iii, p.688; TNA E101/56/5
	1 November	WS's payments for war.		*L&P Henry VIII*, 1,1463, parag.9, p.671
	4 December	WS payments for war.		*L&P Henry VIII*, 1,1495, pp.687–90
	19 November	Reference to Ferdinand's answer to WS.		*L&P Henry VIII*, 1, 1484, p.677
	13–29 December	**John Stiles' account of war to the king.**		***L&P Henry VIII*, 1,1509, p.693–97**
1513	28 January	Sheriffs, including WS, to proclaim all men to be ready for French invasion.		*L&P Henry VIII*, 1602 parag.38, p.732
	29 January	Preparation for French invasion. WS and Sir John Lisle appointed 'Chief Captains of the power of the County' (Wilts.).		*L&P Henry VIII*, 1,1596, p.729

Year	Day, Month	Event	Location of WS 1470–1540	Reference
	12 February	Commissions to 'principal captains' for threatened counties include WS.		*L&P Henry VIII*, 1, 1662 (27), p.756
	11 March	WS appointed bailiff of Crokeham Manor and Fynchampstead.		*L&P Henry VIII*, 1,1732 parag.24, p.788
	13 May	WS and Sir Maurice Berkeley appointed to take charge of the 'Almains' (German soldiers).		*L&P Henry VIII*, 1, 1869 parag.5, p.851
	17 June	WS and Sir Maurice Berkeley landed at Calais with 700 'Almains'.	Calais	Nichols & Turpyn, *Chronicle of Calais*, p.11
	June	WS in charge of left wing of the Avountguarde of the King's Ward.	France	*L&P Henry VIII*, l, 2053, pp.925–27
	30 June	WS and the rest of King's Ward left Calais.		*L&P Henry VIII*, 1, 2053, p.927, parag.6
	16 August	The Battle of Spurs outside Thérouanne.		Nichols & Turpyn, *Chronicle of Calais*, p.14
	10 September	WS and 700 Englishmen defend a bridge to protect the king's retinue.	France	Hall, *Lives of the Kings, Henry VIII*, Vol.1, p.91
	November	WS paid off 'conduct money' with his men and army dismissed.		TNA E101/56/25; *L&P Henry VIII*, 1, 2480, p.1097
1514	18 April	WS and others appointed to survey the muster at Portsmouth.		*L&P Henry VIII*, 1, 2861, (33), p.1245
	23 April	WS again nominated for KG.		Anstis, *Reg. of the Most Noble Order of the Garter*, Vol.1, p.277
	19 May	WS and 100 men land at Calais.	Calais	Nichols & Turpyn, *Chronicle of Calais*, p.15

Year	Day, Month	Event	Location of WS 1470–1540	Reference
	2 October	WS in Princess Mary's escort party for her marriage to King Louis of France on 9 October.	Abbeville, France	Leland, *De Rebus Brit. Collect.*, Vol.II, p.701; *L&P Henry VIII*, 1, 3348, p.1408
1515	16 February	WS appointed to the Commission of the Peace in Hampshire.		*L&P Henry VIII*, 2, 170, p.58
	8 May	WS appointed to the Commission of the Peace in Berkshire.		*L&P Henry VIII*, 2, 430, p.124
	17 May	WS mustered at Canterbury under Lord Bergavenny.	Canterbury	*L&P Henry VIII*, 2, 471, p.134
	6 July	WS appointed to the Commission of the Peace in Berkshire.		*L&P Henry VIII*, 2,1247, p.327
	4 December	WS owes £100 to the king.		*L&P Henry VIII*, 2, 1364, p.370
1516	3 August –28 September	Inferred visit by Henry VIII, Queen Catherine and Queen Margaret of Scotland to WS at The Vyne.		Weir, *Henry VIII, King and Court*, pp.204–05; Wayment, *Archaeologia*, Vol.107, p.145
1517	1517–22	As treasurer, WS advanced £800 for the defences of Calais.	Calais	Colvin, *History of the King's Works*, Vol.III, p.343
	16, 17 March	WS was Seneschal of Andover (seneschal 1498–1517 and steward 1523–27).	Andover	HRO 37M85/18AH/10
	9,10 May	Salt marsh riots at Southampton.	Southampton	Merson, *Third Book of Remembrances of Southampton*, pp.21–22
	10 May	Fox wrote to Wolsey praising how WS handled the riots and glad Wolsey has good opinion of WS.	Southampton	*L&P Henry VIII*, Addendum 1, pt. 1, 185, p.20
	End May	WS to visit Calais.		*L&P Henry VIII*, 2, 3279, p.1050
	June 16	WS and others reply to Wolsey about the defences at Calais.	Calais	*L&P Henry VIII*, 2, 3371, p.1077

Year	Day, Month	Event	Location of WS 1470–1540	Reference
	11 July	WS writes to Wolsey from Calais.	Calais, and sometime before	*L&P Henry VIII*, Addendum 1, pt.1, 190, p.52
	28 July	WS appointed Treasurer of Calais from 6 October.		*L&P Henry VIII*, 2, 3527, p.1120
	28 July	Annuity of £56 granted to WS during 'pleasure' for services in Spain (1512), Guienne, Flanders (1492) and Picardy.		*L&P Henry VIII*, 2, 3528, p.1120
	August, September	Wolsey suggested to Henry VIII that WS would be suitable as Master of Horse or Master of Henchmen.		*L&P Henry VIII*, Addendum 1, pt.1, 196, p.53
	20 December	Henry VIII presented WS with a green velvet gown with sixteen gold buttons and a crimson jacket.	Court	Norris, H., *Tudor Fashion and Costume*, Dover,1997, p.166
1518		WS appointed with Sir Thomas Docwra and Sir Edward Poynings to investigate ruin and decay of the Calais fortifications.	Calais	Colvin, *History of Kings' Works*, Vol.III, p.344.
	24 April	WS successfully nominated for KG.		Anstis, *Reg. of the Most Noble Order of the Garter,* Vol.1, pp. 284–85
	1 May	WS and others to collect 26,315 gold crowns from the King of France for the return of Tournay to the French as agreed.		*L&P Henry VIII, 2*, 4148, p.1285; 4564, p.1398
	16 May	WS installed as Knight of Garter.	Windsor	Anstis, *Reg. of the Most Noble Order of the Garter,* Vol.1, p.285

Year	Day, Month	Event	Location of WS 1470–1540	Reference
	26 August	WS wrote to Wolsey confirming that the ships for transport of the 500 horses for the French ambassadors visit to England were ready.	Calais	*L&P Henry VIII*, 2, 4396, p.1353
	4 October	WS wrote to his sister Edith, now Lady Darcy, claiming poverty because of his costs in the king's wars, marriage of his children and money he loaned to his soldiers.	Calais	*L&P Henry VIII*, Addendum 1, pt.1, 224, p.61
	13 November	Complaint against WS at Basingstoke Court Leet for keeping too many sheep on common land, etc.		Baigent & Millard, *History of the Ancient Manor and Town of Basingstoke*, p.321
1519	22 January	WS informs Henry VIII that he has received some French hostages. He had no warning of when they would arrive.	Calais	*L&P Henry VIII*, 3, 37, p.10
	26 March	WS writes to Wolsey about shortage of craftsmen in Calais and demand for high wages.	Calais	*L&P Henry VIII*, Addendum 1, pt.1, 279, p.76
	January to June	WS receives warrants from Henry VIII and Wolsey.	Calais	TNA E 101/209/6
	27 April	Letters Patent to WS to receive 1 million gold crowns from the French.	Calais	*L&P Henry VIII*, 3,199, p.69
	24 May	WS attended the Garter Chapter meeting.	Windsor	Anstis, *Reg. of the Most Noble Order of the Garter*, Ed. App. ii, p.ii
	8 October	WS tells Wolsey that money has arrived in Boulogne.	Calais	*L&P Henry VIII*, 3, 464, p.165

Year	Day, Month	Event	Location of WS 1470–1540	Reference
	4 November	Letters Patent sent to WS for the lordship of Mark and Oye in Calais.	Calais?	*L&P Henry VIII*, 3, 493, p.172
	20 November	WS writes to Wolsey seeking pardon for a man.	Calais	*L&P Henry VIII*, 3, 517, p.178
	28 December	WS sends gift for Wolsey.	Calais	*L&P Henry VIII*, 3, 564, p.194
1520	Not given	WS mentioned as one of three commissioners to prepare for the Field of the Cloth of Gold events.		Caley, *Archaeologia*, Vol.21, 1827, pp.176–81
	16 March	WS and other two commissioners land at Calais to prepare for the Field of the Cloth of Gold.	Calais	Stow, *Annales of England to 1603*, p.853
	26 March	WS wrote to Wolsey about shortage of timber and worker demands.	Calais	*L&P Henry VIII*, Addendum 1, pt. 1, 279, p.76
	21 May	WS and others write to Wolsey about the great cost of the work and doubt that it will be finished in time for the arrival of the two kings.	Calais	*L&P Henry VIII*, 3, 826, p.287
	June	WS present at the Field of the Cloth of Gold.	Guînes	Jerdan, *Rutland Papers*. pp.31, 45
		WS made assistant marshal for jousts at Guînes.	Guînes	Nichols and Turpyn, *Chronicle of Calais*, p. 89
	10 July and before	WS and Edward Poynings appointed to 'view and appoint' ground for the meeting of Henry VIII and the emperor between Calais and Gravelines.	Calais	Jerdan, *Rutland Papers*, p.50–51

Year	Day, Month	Event	Location of WS 1470–1540	Reference
	16 July	WS and Sir Edward Guildford 'remaining at Calais'.	Calais	*L&P Henry VIII*, 3, 909, p.337
	6 October	WS reports to Wolsey that the French have halted the fortification of Ardres, but they will continue work on Calais.	Calais	*L&P Henry VIII*, 3, 1013, p.337
	6 October	WS writes to Henry VIII with the same message as he gave to Wolsey.	Calais	*L&P Henry VIII*, 3, Appendix 18, p.1573
1521	c.January	WS to give Henry Lacy possession of 'certain lands' and the last two years' profits in Calais.		*L&P Henry VIII*, Addendum 1, pt. 1, 331, p.99
	20 February	Lord Darcy regrets WS could not settle his differences with a cousin and asks him to send two tuns of good French wine to him via Hull.	Calais	*L&P Henry VIII*, 3, 1172, p.439
	10 March	WS arranged to deliver money to Lord Darcy.	Calais	*L&P Henry VIII*, 3, 1195, p.449
	Before Friday 17 May	WS and others led the Duke of Buckingham from the Temple to the Tower.	London	Stow, *Annales of England to 1603*. p.863; Hall, *Lives of the Kings, Henry VIII*, p.225
	*c.*15 July	WS made Commissioner of the Peace for Hants. and Wilts.		*L&P Henry VIII*, 3, 1451, p.594
	24 July	Henry VIII instructs Wolsey to give WS and Sir Thomas More details on Calais negotiations.		*L&P Henry VIII*, 3, 1437, pp.584–85; *State Papers Henry VIII*, Vol.1.1, p.20
	July–August	Wolsey tries to persuade Henry VIII that WS should lead the army in France.		*L&P Henry VIII*, 3, 1448, p.591; 1454, p.595;1459, p.597; *State Papers Henry VIII*, Vol.1.1, pp.24,26,30

Year	Day, Month	Event	Location of WS 1470–1540	Reference
	7 August	Wolsey again suggests to the king that WS should lead the army, but he refused.	Calais	*L&P Henry VIII*, 3, 1473, p.605; *State Papers Henry VIII*, Vol.I.1, pp.31–32, 35
	August	Wolsey argues with the king that WS should take charge of archers in Calais.	Calais	*L&P Henry VIII*, 3, 1474, p.605
	24 August	WS tells Wolsey that the French king is going to invade Navarre.	Calais	*L&P Henry VIII*, 3, 1504, p.618
1522	14 March	WS appointed as a Chamberlain of Receipt at the Exchequer in lieu of the Earl of Shrewsbury.		*L&P Henry VIII*, 3, 2145 parag.14.4, p.916
	March	WS brings Flemish glaziers from Calais to Basingstoke.	The Vyne	Koegler, *Öffentliche, Kunst-Sammlung*, pp.166–69, trans. by L. Eddie-Smith
	26 March	WS writes to Wolsey that he has 'not been seeing to business for three or four years' at his little house.	The Vyne	*L&P Henry VIII*, Addendum 1, pt. 1, 338, p.101
	26 March	WS receives the manor of Wyllesford, Wilts., and was made Keeper of Alishole and Woolmer Forest.		*L&P Henry VIII*, 3, 2145, parag.26, p.917
	27 April	Charles V wrote to WS, who was on his way to Calais, requesting him to release two of his men.	England	*L&P Henry VIII* 3, 2200, p.935
	2 May	WS writes to Wolsey from Calais seeking instructions on Charles V coming to Calais.	Calais	*L&P Henry VIII*, 3, 2222, p.945
	6 May	WS warns Wolsey from great musters by the French.	Calais	*L&P Henry VIII*, 3, 2229, p.949

Year	Day, Month	Event	Location of WS 1470–1540	Reference
	8 May	WS tells Wolsey that he cannot muster more than ten people as he is in Calais, and asks that his wife and brother do what they can to find more.	Calais	*L&P Henry VIII*, 3, 2238, p.951
	14 May	WS writes to Henry VIII from Calais that he needs money to pay a spy and for the garrison.	Calais	*L&P Henry VIII*, 3, 2256, p.958
	23, 25 May	**King Charles V was in Calais prior to visiting England.**		**Hall, *Lives of the Kings, Henry VIII*, Vol.1, pp.244–45**
	3 June	WS and Sir Maurice Berkeley write to Wolsey from Calais reporting an attack by 1,000 French.	Calais, Newnham Bridge	*L&P Henry VIII*, 3, 2301, p.975
	17 June	WS wrote to Wolsey from Calais reporting enemy attacks and an urgent need for more supplies.	Calais	*L&P Henry VIII*, 3, 2326, p.984
	20 June	The Council of Calais, including WS, wrote to Henry VIII about shortages in Calais.	Calais	*L&P Henry VIII*, 3, 2334, p.991
	20 June	The Council of Calais, including WS, wrote to Wolsey about the appointment of William Nanfan as clerk.	Calais	*L&P Henry VIII*, 3, 2335, p.991
	21 June	**The Earl of Surrey wrote to Henry VIII (from the Mary Rose) that he has embarked for France with 5,000 men but poor supplies.**	**Calais**	***L&P Henry VIII*, 3, 2337, p.991**
	22 June	WS writes to Henry VIII about Flanders troops helping in Calais and that the French are quiet.	Calais	*L&P Henry VIII*, 3, 2338, p.992

Year	Day, Month	Event	Location of WS 1470–1540	Reference
	27 June	WS reports to Henry VIII on the state of war.	Calais	*L&P Henry VIII* 3, 2352, p.995
	probably May/ June	WS received letters from a French spy and sent him to court at Richmond.	Calais	*L&P Henry VIII*, 3, 2446, p.1031
	3 July	WS writes to Wolsey from Calais about preparations for war with the French.	Calais	*L&P Henry VIII*, 3, 2364, p.1002
	4 July	WS informs Wolsey from Calais that the French were about to attack.	Calais, Newnham Bridge	*L&P Henry VIII*, 3, 2366, p.1003
	10 July	WS wrote to Wolsey requesting artillery.	Newnham Bridge	*L&P Henry VIII*, 3, 2378, p.1007
	10 July	WS's ownership of cargo taken from Spanish merchants is challenged.	Calais	*L&P Henry VIII*, 3, 2379, p.1007
	17 July	WS wrote to Wolsey about Calais finances and employment of a spy.	Newnham Bridge	*L&P Henry VIII*, 3, 2392, p.1011
	21 July	WS's recognisance to Henry VIII was cancelled.		*L&P Henry VIII*, 3, 2415 parag.21, p.1019
	25 July	WS and Sir Edward Guildford, Marshal, set fire to Whitsand (Wissant).	Calais	Hall, *Lives of the Kings, Henry VIII*, Vol.1, p.262
	12 August	French attack on village near Calais where Welsh soldiers are billeted.	Calais	Hall, *Lives of the Kings, Henry VIII*, Vol.1, p.266
	16 August	WS informs Wolsey that he arrived in Dover last night.	Dover to Calais	*L&P Henry VIII*, 3, 2443, p.1029
	19 August	WS and Lord Fitzwalter wrote to Henry VIII that supplies were short.	Calais	*L&P Henry VIII*, 3, 2451, p.1035

Year	Day, Month	Event	Location of WS 1470–1540	Reference
	22 August	Howard was in Calais. Army Front was led by Sir Edward Guildford, Middle by Lord Howard, and Rear by WS and Sir Richard Wingfield.		Hall, *Lives of the Kings, Henry VIII*, Vol.1, pp.266–67
	30 August	WS informs the king that he is with Thomas, Lord Howard, on expedition from Calais into Picardy.	Burthes	Nichols and Turpyn, *Chronicle of Calais*, p.32
	30 August	WS leads battle at Newnham Bridge: 'The last battle was led by two valiant knights of the Garter, Sir William Sandys and Sir Richard Wingfield.'	Calais	Hall, *Lives of the Kings, Henry VIII*, Vol.1, p.267
	1 September	The army marched to Guînes.		Hall, *Lives of the Kings, Henry VIII*, Vol.1, p.267
	2 September	The army met Burgundian allies at Guînes.		Hall, *Lives of the Kings, Henry* VIII, Vol.1, p.267
	10 September	WS describes to Henry VIII the campaign against the French around Calais.	Burthes	*L&P Henry VIII*, 3, 2530, p.1073
	12 September	WS describes the same campaign to Wolsey.	Fauxe	*L&P Henry VIII*, 3, 2541, p.1079
	22 September	WS tells Wolsey that he has taken the castle of Domperre.	Heydn	*L&P Henry VIII*, 3, 2560, p.1086
	After 16 October	WS, Sir Maurice Barkley and Sir William Fitzwilliam, with 3,000 men burned Marguison and many villages, also took many prisoners and returned to Calais with this 'great booty'.	Marguison	Hall, *Lives of the Kings, Henry VIII*, Vol.1, pp.270–71

Year	Day, Month	Event	Location of WS 1470–1540	Reference
	2 December	Sir Robert Wingfield wrote to Wolsey saying that he had asked WS to ask Lady Margaret, Duchess of Savoy, for 500 troops to prevent the French re-victualling Thérouanne.		*L&P Henry VIII*, 3, 2696, p.1136
	27 December	WS ordered to pay wages to some Calais troops who had not been paid for four years.		*L&P Henry VIII*, 3, 2727, p.1149
1522	(Calendared as December 1526)	WS submits accounts for fortification of Guînes.		*L&P Henry VIII*, 4, 2751, 1226
1523	17 January	WS, Treasurer of Calais, signs a treaty between Charles V and Henry VIII about the price of wool passing through the Staple.	Calais	*L&P Henry VIII*, 3, 2777, p.1171
	February	WS wrote to Henry VIII that a spy reported that 'the drum beats to arm the village' and requested more munitions.	Guînes	*L&P Henry VIII*, 3, 2858, p.1200
	5 March	WS received £100 for fortifying Guînes Castle.		*L&P Henry VIII*, 3, 2874, p.1211
	27/28 April	WS was made Lord Sandys.	Bridewell	BL ADD.MS 5504 f.105; *L&P Henry VIII*, 3, 2982, p.1260
	After 24 May	WS involved in a raid near Boulogne.	Calais	Hall, *Lives of the Kings, Henry VIII*, Vol.1, pp.290–91
	10 July	WS leads skirmish with the French and threatens to hang priests who shelter Frenchmen in their churches.	Calais	Hall, *Lives of the Kings, Henry VIII*, Vol.1, pp.291–93

Year	Day, Month	Event	Location of WS 1470–1540	Reference
	11 July	WS burns the castle of Hedyngham.	Calais	Hall, *Lives of the Kings, Henry VIII*, Vol.1, p.293
	19 July	WS, described as marshal and captain of the vanguard, leaves Calais.	Calais	Hall, *Lives of the Kings, Henry VIII*, Vol.1, p.297.
	20 August	Wolsey asks the king to send more troops with the Duke of Suffolk for the French expedition and mentions WS.		*L&P Henry VIII*, 2, 3256; *Cal.St.P. Henry VIII*, pt.1, p.123
	22 August	100 men land at Calais for WS.	Calais	Nichols and Turpyn, *Chronicle of Calais*, p.33
	24 August	The Duke of Suffolk lands in Calais.		Nichols and Turpyn, *Chronicle of Calais*, p.33
	30 August	Wolsey informs English ambassadors in Spain about the leaders of the forthcoming expedition, including WS.		*L&P Henry VIII*, 3, 3281, p.1360
	August	WS described as High Marshal of the Army (20*s* a day), second to the Duke of Suffolk (100*s* a day).		*L&P Henry VIII*, 3, 3288, p.1370
	8 September	Suffolk and his army camped outside Calais.	Calais	Hall, *Lives of the Kings, Henry VIII*, Vol.1, p.297
	10 September	Count De Buren, from the emperor's army, writes to WS.		*L&P Henry VIII*, 3, 3316, p.1381
	19 September	The army leaves Calais with WS as captain of the Vanguard.	Calais	Hall, *Lives of the Kings, Henry VIII*, Vol.1, 297
	19 September	100 men land at Calais for WS.	Calais	Nichols and Turpyn, *Chronicle of Calais*, p.33
	24 September	WS given charge of Guînes Castle.		*L&P Henry VIII*, 3, 3352 p.1394

Year	Day, Month	Event	Location of WS 1470–1540	Reference
	27, 28 September	WS attacks and takes Belle Castle.		Martin, 'Sir John Daunce's Accounts', p.295; *L&P Henry VIII*, 3, 3516, p.1463
	29 September	Army moves to Esquerdes alias Cordes between St Omers and Thérouanne.		Hall, *Lives of the Kings, Henry VIII*, Vol.1, p.298
	1 October	Tuke tells Surrey that WS has captured Belle Castle.		*L&P Henry VIII*, 3, 3380, p.1413
	October	Bishop of Winchester (Fox) writes to Wolsey about subsidies. WS is beyond sea in the king's wars.		*L&P Henry VIII*, 3, 3492 p.1451; Allen, *Letters of Richard Fox*, p.132
	After 17 October	WS, 'Marshall of the Army', with 3,000 men took Anker and Bone (Bon?) Castle.	Anker	Hall, *Lives of the Kings, Henry VIII*, Vol.1, p.306
	21 October	WS leads the crossing of the Somme.	Bray	Hall, *Lives of the Kings, Henry VIII*, Vol.1, p.308/9; *L&P Henry VIII*, 3, 3516, p.1463
	After 28 October	WS and others receive the town of Mondidier.	Mondidier	Hall, *Lives of the Kings, Henry VIII*, Vol.1, p.312
	30 October	WS's brother Richard is knighted by Suffolk. (*L&P Henry VIII*, 3516 gives date as 1 November)		Hall, *Lives of the Kings, Henry VIII*, Vol 1, p.312
	6 November	WS at Veane.		Hall, *Lives of the Kings, Henry VIII*, Vol.1, p.312
	8 November	WS leaves Suffolk's expedition to plead with Henry VIII.	France	Hall, *Lives of the Kings, Henry VIII*, Vol.1, p.313
	2 December	WS writes to Wolsey.	Calais	*L&P Henry VIII*, 3, 3590, p.1493

Year	Day, Month	Event	Location of WS 1470–1540	Reference
	7 December	Wolsey writes to Henry VIII with instructions for WS and Sir William Fitzwilliam to aid Lady Margaret of Austria.		*Cal.St.P.* Vol.I, pt.1, p.149; *L&P Henry VIII*, 3, 3613, p.1500
	14 December	Suffolk returns to Calais, then home.		Nichols and Turpyn, *Chronicle of Calais*, p.34
	December	WS owed the Crown more than £800.		*L&P Henry VIII*, 3, 3694, p.1528
1524	11 January	WS was 'beyond the seas'.	Calais?	TNA E 179/173/174
	15 January	Proposal to send WS to Lady Margaret of Austria.	Calais?	*L&P Henry VIII*, 4, 30, p.14
	23 February	WS appointed Keeper of Chute Forest, etc.		*L&P Henry VIII*, 4, 136, p.58
	11 March	Margery Sandys wrote to Wolsey about her son Reginald.	Margery was at The Vyne. WS was elsewhere.	*L&P Henry VIII*, 4, 154 p.62
	28 March	WS and Robert Fowler are paid expenses for Calais: £6,666 for the period 1/3/1524 to 1/7/1524.		*L&P Henry VIII*, 4, 214, p.85
	8 May	WS excused from being at the Garter feast.		Anstis, *Reg. of the Most Noble Order of the Garter*, pp.364–67
	13 May	WS's assessment for tax was £1,333 (March 1527 in Calendar).		*L&P Henry VIII*, 4, 297, p.1332, final parag.
	8 July	WS arrives at Calais.	Calais	*L&P Henry VIII*, 4, 484, p.204
	14 July	WS informs Wolsey that he arrived at Calais on 8 July.	Calais	*L&P Henry VIII*, 4, 493, p.207
	5 September	WS writes to Wolsey about Richard Pole, a spy.	Calais	*L&P Henry VIII*, 4, 631, p.279
	31 October	Fitzwilliam wrote from Calais to Wolsey that WS was not at Guînes.	England?	*L&P Henry VIII*, 4, 781, p.350

Year	Day, Month	Event	Location of WS 1470–1540	Reference
	2 November	Fitzwilliam refers to one of WS's spies.		*L&P Henry VIII*, 4, 794, p.357
	November	WS appointed Commissioner for the Peace in Hants.		*L&P Henry VIII*, 4, 895, parag.12, p.391
	16 November	Henry VIII issues Letters Patent to WS and Richard Fox for the Guild of the Holy Ghost.	England	Baigent, *History of Ancient Town and Manor of Basingstoke*, p.120
1525	1 January	Complaint to Wolsey that WS has paid a man for only two months' work out of twenty-two.	Probably Calais	*L&P Henry VIII*, 4, 985, p.431
	26 February	Lord Berners wrote to Wolsey from Calais that WS will look after Lord Beevers (Belvoir?) and report to Wolsey when he reaches Dover.	Calais, but about to go to London	*L&P Henry VIII*, 4, 1128, p.495
	April	WS made Commissioner of the Peace for Hants.		*L&P Henry VIII*, 4, 1298, parag. 'Commissions of Peace. *Hants.*', p.569
	April/May	WS's Garter stall in St George's Chapel was No. 12 on the prince's side.		Ashmole, *The Institution, Laws & Ceremonies of the Most Noble Order of the Garter*, p.381
	10–12 June	Visit by the Earl of Devon to The Vyne on his way to London to be created Marquis of Exeter.	The Vyne	*L&P Henry VIII*, 4, 1792. pp.794–95
	18 June	WS witnessed ceremony making Henry Fitzroy the Earl of Nottingham.	Bridewell	*L&P Henry VIII*, 4, 1431, p.639
	21 July	WS wrote to Wolsey that the French ambassador arrived yesterday.	Calais	*L&P Henry VIII*, 4, 1508, p.675
	1 August	Lord Berners wrote to Wolsey that WS had not paid someone.	Calais?	*L&P Henry VIII*, 4, 1535, p.691

Year	Day, Month	Event	Location of WS 1470–1540	Reference
	23 August	WS thanks Wolsey for the positions of Lord Chamberlain and Deputy of Guînes, but he is in 'great poverty' and needs money.	Calais	*L&P Henry VIII*, 4, 1580, p.712
	25 August	WS and the others commissioned for this work produced *Booke of Newe Ordenaunces* for the county of Guînes.	Calais	Nichols and Turpyn, *Chronicle of Calais*, p.130
	1 September	Fitzwilliam and WS write to Wolsey that they have discharged garrisons.	Calais	*L&P Henry VIII*, 4, 1612, p.723
	1 September	WS begs Wolsey to be allowed to return to England as peace has been proclaimed.	Calais	*L&P Henry VIII*, 4, 1613, p.723
	21 October	WS was present at the election of new Garter knights.	England (Windsor?)	Anstis, *Reg. of the Most Noble Order of the Garter*, p.382
	8 November	WS writes to Wolsey with further thanks for his promotion.	Calais	*L&P Henry VIII*, 4, 1752 and 1753, pp.778–79
	29 November	WS surrenders Treasurer of Calais position to Sir Richard Weston.		*L&P Henry VIII*, 4, App.58, p.3095
1526	January	The Eltham Ordnances are issued, ranking WS after the Lord Chamberlain.		*L&P Henry VIII*, 4, 1939, pp.860–73
	January.	As King's Chamberlain, WS will bear a white staff at court.		*L&P Henry VIII*, 4, Appendix 66, p.3096
	26 February	Letter patent issued 'for William, Lord Sandys' Office of King's Chamberlain in place of Charles, Earl of Worcester'.		*L&P Henry VIII*, 4, 1996, p.896
	12 April	The king writes to WS as Captain of Guînes.		*L&P Henry VIII*, 4, 2088, p.935

Year	Day, Month	Event	Location of WS 1470–1540	Reference
	April/May	WS's Garter stall was No.12 on the prince's side.		Ashmole, *The Institution, Laws and Ceremonies ... of the Garter*, p.322
	31 July,1 August	Henry VIII visited WS at The Vyne.	The Vyne	TNA E101/419/13 f.25
	6 August	WS asks Wolsey for more income from property in the Pale.	Arundel	*L&P Henry VIII*, 4, 2377, p.1061
	21 August	WS was asked to carry letters from Wolsey for the king.	Hampshire	*L&P Henry VIII*, 4, 2420, p.2420
	24 August	WS delivers package from Wolsey for the king and says he is in 'great need of money'.	Thruxton	*L&P Henry VIII*, 4, 2428, p.1086
	27 September	WS appoints Wingfield as Deputy of Calais and Fitzwilliam as governor of the castle on behalf of the king.	Ampthill	*L&P Henry VIII*, 4.2, 2518, p.1122
	29 September	WS receives annuity of £30 from Thomas, Lord Darcy.		*L&P Henry VIII*, 4, p.2527
	24 October	WS arrives at Calais.	Calais	*L&P Henry VIII*, 4, 2611, p.1159
	25 October	'William, Lord Sandys the King's Chamberlain and Captain of Guînes, Knight of the order of the Garter' gives the Calais keys to Sir Robert Wingfield.	Calais	HRO 31M/57/808
	6 November	WS tells Wolsey and Henry that he had arrived at Calais on 24 October.	Guînes	*L&P Henry VIII*, 4, 2611, p.1159; 2612, p.1160
	28 December or October? (date and place do not match in *L&P Henry VIII*, 4, 2611, 2740)	WS reports to Wolsey that Calais is 'marvellously sore decayed'.	Calais	*L&P Henry VIII* 4, 2730, p.1217
	End December	WS witnesses a grant to Wolsey.	London	*L&P Henry VIII*, 4, 2740, p.1222

Year	Day, Month	Event	Location of WS 1470–1540	Reference
1527	3 January	WS was present at the masking at Hampton Court.	Hampton Court	Hall, *Lives of the Kings, Henry VIII*, Vol.2, p.78; Cavendish, *Thomas Wolsey*, pp.54–56; Brown, *Cal.St.P... Venice*, Vol.IV, 1527–33, 4, pp.2–3
	2 March	WS tells Wolsey that he followed instructions to imprison gentlemen in Sanctuary.	London (WS also there on 1 March)	*L&P Henry VIII*, 4, 2936, p.1315
	1 April (1528 date in *L&P Henry VIII*, is incorrect)	WS in Guildford to oversee a muster.	Guildford	Nichols and Turpyn, *Chronicle of Calais*, pp.205–06
	April /May	WS's Garter stall was No. 12 on the prince's side.		Ashmole, *The Institution, Laws and Ceremonies... Noble Order of the Garter*, p.322
	16 June	Canonry and prebendary of the Chapel Royal granted to WS and others.		*L&P Henry VIII*, 4, 3213, 16, p.1463
	30 June (incorrect, probably 1526)	Letter to Lord Darcy from his son Arthur that the king is going to Hampshire to see the Lord Chamberlain.	The Vyne	*L&P Henry VIII*, Addendum 1, pt.1, 538, p.181
	3 July	Wolsey departs for France with a 'magnificent retinue', including WS.	London	Brown, *Cal.St.P... Venice*, Vol.IV, 129, p.69
	9 July	WS was granted the release of a property.		*L&P Henry VIII*, 4, 3324, p.1506
	11 July	Wolsey and party in Calais.	Calais	Brown, *Cal.St.P... Venice*, Vol.IV, 129–68, pp.69–91; *Cal.St.P.Henry VIII*, Vol.1, pp.237–39
	22 July	Wolsey leaves Calais with WS in his party.	Calais	Hall, *Lives of the Kings, Henry VIII*, Vol.2, p.98

Year	Day, Month	Event	Location of WS 1470–1540	Reference
	4 August?	Party in Amiens where WS, Bishop Tunstall and others were saluted by the French king's mother.	Amiens	*Cal.St.P.Henry VIII*, 1527, p.233
	4 August	Commission issued to WS and Bishop Tunstall.		Hall, *Lives of the Kings, Henry VIII*, Vol.2, p.100
	9 August	WS, the Bishop of London, Sir Henry Guildford, and Sir Thomas More saluted by the King of France.	Amiens	*L&P Henry VIII*, 4, 3337, p.1511; Hall, *Lives of the Kings, Henry VIII*, Vol.2, p.100
	21 August	Sir Antony Brown reported to Henry VIII that he and WS disliked the French king's way of hunting.	Amiens	*State Papers Henry VIII*, Vol.VI, Part 5, letter CLXIII, Aug.1527, p.598; *L&P Henry VIII*, 4, 3368, p.1525
	17 September	Wolsey returning home.	Compiegne	*Cal.St.P…Venice*, Vol.4, 168, p.91
	November	WS and other senior courtiers receive pensions from French king.	England?	*L&P Henry VIII*, 4, 3619, p.1626
	11 November	WS at a special Garter Chapter to install the King of France into the order (by surrogate).	Windsor	Anstis, *Register … Noble Order of the Garter*, App.V, p.xxxii
	24 November	John Cheyne, Deputy Captain of Guînes Castle, wrote to WS about a spy.	England?	Nichols and Turpyn, *Chronicle of Calais*, p.206
	9 December	WS writes to Sir Robert Wingfield about shortage of provisions in Calais and reporting him to Wolsey.	The Vyne	*L&P Henry VIII*, 4, 3651, p.1640
	14 December	Robert Wingfield wrote to WS rebutting his charges.	The Vyne?	*L&P Henry VIII*, 4, 3659, p.1642
1528	1 January	WS receives a generous gift from the king.		TNA E101/420/4

Year	Day, Month	Event	Location of WS 1470–1540	Reference
	March	The king proposes that the Duke of Suffolk and WS conduct an expedition to Flanders.	The Vyne	Hall, *Lives of the Kings, Henry VIII,* Vol.2, p.136
	7 March	Complaint against WS for keeping merchandise he thought was French but belonged to the emperor's subjects.		*L&P Henry VIII*, 4, 402, p.1786
	March	WS tells Sir Thomas Cheney about mutiny at Guînes and his illness.	The Vyne	*L&P Henry VIII, 4,* 4026, p.1786
	9 and 13 March	WS replies to Wolsey about the king's concerns over disquiet among the clothiers of Westbury. He will try to settle the matter peacefully.	The Vyne	*L&P Henry VIII*, 4, 4043 p.1796; 4058, p.4080
	16 March	More advises Wolsey to put WS on a state of readiness for war at Guînes with the Flemish.		*Cal.St.P.Henry VIII,* Vol.I, p.286; *L&P Henry VIII*, 4, 4080, p.1806
	18 March	WS speaks to Du Bellay about providing corn for Guînes. He will not go there until supplies arrive and mentions his illness.	London	*L&P Henry VIII,* 4, appendix 156, p.3142
	26 March	French ambassadors to England advise Francis I that WS is raising men and expected to move to France at Easter.	London	*L&P Henry VIII,* 4, appendix 158, p.3144
	1 April (Should be 1527?)	Henry VIII writes to Sir A. Fortescue to muster himself and ten soldiers to serve under WS.	Guildford	*L&P Henry VIII*, 4, 4127, p.1825

Year	Day, Month	Event	Location of WS 1470–1540	Reference
	23 April	WS is excused attendance at the Garter Feast in May and allocated stall 12 on the prince's side.		Anstis, *Reg. of the Most Noble Order of the Garter*, p.384, Ed. App.VI, p.xxxiv
	25 April	WS tells Wolsey that he is trying to muster men.	The Vyne	*L&P Henry* VIII, 4, 4199, p.18854
	12 May	WS released from all debts incurred as Treasurer of Calais.		*L&P Henry VIII*, 4, 4313, Grants in May, parag.12, p.1897
	16 May	WS signs indenture for more than £3,000 owed to the king.		HRO 23M58/5
	1 July	WS asks Wolsey for some offices held by the late Sir William Compton. He had not visited Wolsey or the king because of sweating sickness in his house.	The Vyne	*L&P Henry VIII*, 4. 4450, p.1951
	2 July	WS recommends a man to Wolsey for a position.	The Vyne	*L&P Henry VIII*, 4, 4454, p.1952
	10 September	WS and Fitzwilliam commend two men to Wolsey for work at Guînes.	Calais	*L&P Henry VIII*, 4, 4712, p.2044
	5 October	Bishop Richard Fox dies and bequeaths tapestry to WS.		Allen, *Letters of Richard Fox*, p.170
	30 October	Sir Richard Weston tells Wolsey that WS asked for payment of outstanding debts as Captain of Guînes and Treasurer of Calais.	Calais?	*L&P Henry VIII*, 4, 4887, 2116
	20 November	The Bishop of Bath wrote to Wolsey, mentioning WS 'to go over to France with a number of men'.	The Vyne or Court?	*L&P Henry VIII*, 4, 4955, p.2149

Year	Day, Month	Event	Location of WS 1470–1540	Reference
	29 November	WS and Sir Robert Wingfield to go to Calais as commissioners.	The Vyne or Court?	*L&P Henry VIII*, 4, 4985, p.2164
	November	John Cheyne writes to WS from Guînes about the build-up of the emperor's men and problems with guns, gunners and food.	The Vyne or Court?	*L&P Henry VIII*, 4, 4988, p.2166
1529	12 January	WS and others write to Henry VIII about strengthening Calais and Guînes fortifications.	Guînes	*L&P Henry VIII*, 4, 5167, p.2272
	13 January	WS and others write to Wolsey re fortifications	Guînes	*L&P Henry VIII*, 4, 5168, p.2272
	15 January	Margaret of Savoy wrote to Henry VIII about 'proceedings of Sir William Sandys' against merchants who are the emperor's subjects.		*L&P Henry VIII*, 4, 5173, p.2273
	18 January	John Sandys writes to Wolsey from St Germaine, after being at court on Christmas Eve.		*L&P Henry VIII*, 4, 5185, p.2280
	23 January	WS writes to unnamed person, mentioning his son John in France and that WS is bedridden and cannot walk.	Guînes	*L&P Henry VIII*, 4, 5197, p.2284
	26 January	WS tells Wolsey about a Spanish spy who murdered a man in Antwerp and took refuge in the Pale. Lady Margaret wanted the spy returned.	Calais	*L&P Henry VIII*, 4, 5214, p.2298

Year	Day, Month	Event	Location of WS 1470–1540	Reference
	26 January	John Sandys reported to WS from Guînes that Italians were helping the French with fortifications at Ardres and that all WS's retinue at Guînes are merry.	Calais?	*L&P Henry VIII*, 4, 5215, p.2298
	January	WS made Commissioner of the Peace for Hampshire.		*L&P Henry VIII*, 4, 5243, p.2310
	1 February	WS and others issue Ordinances for Guînes.	Guînes	*L&P Henry VIII*, 4, 5247, p.2314
	15 February	WS wrote to Wolsey wanting to be home for Easter, and fortifications at Guînes were much worse than seemed at first sight.	Calais	*L&P Henry VIII*, 4, 5296, p.2331
	4 April	WS and Wingfield (Deputy of Calais) write to Wolsey about expenses due for building works.	Calais	*L&P Henry VIII*, 4, 5420, p.2380
	6 April	WS tells Wolsey that money is short for himself and Calais fortifications.	Calais	*L&P Henry VIII*, 4, 5433, p.2390
	8 April	Verdict of a trial against the ordinances that WS issued and had caused properties to flood. The rivers need to be banked.	Guînes?	*L&P Henry VIII*, 4, 5439, p.2392
	11 April	WS writes to Henry VIII about a letter to the Captain of Boulogne.	Guînes	*L&P Henry VIII*, 4, 5453, p.2400
	11 April	Oudart du Bies (Captain of Boulogne) wrote to WS as '*mon bon voisin*' and '*parfaict amy*'.	Guînes	*L&P Henry VIII*, 4, 5454, p.2400

Year	Day, Month	Event	Location of WS 1470–1540	Reference
	13 April	J. Hackett writes to Wolsey about a letter from WS concerning wool exports through Calais.		*L&P Henry VIII*, 4, 5461, p.2404
	18 April	Letter from Wingfield to Tuke includes a letter from WS and Wingfield about lack of money for fortifications and the sea breaching walls at Bray.	Guînes	*L&P Henry VIII*, 4, 5466–67, p.2406
	25 April	Wingfield writes to Tuke with information gained by WS from a spy about potential war between the Emperor and France.	Guînes	*L&P Henry VIII*, 4, 5494, p.2427
	29 April	Letter from Wingfield and WS to Henry VIII about land decay since repairs to the sluice ceased.	Guînes	*L&P Henry VIII*, 4, 5504, p.2431
	22 May	Wingfield tells Tuke that Suffolk arrived and went to see the Captain of Boulogne (CoB) with WS. He and WS have visited the CoB and the truce has been published.	Guînes	*L&P Henry VIII*, 4, 5585, p.2471
	29 May	WS and Wingfield wrote to Henry VIII about flooding and other issues in Calais.	Calais	*L&P Henry VIII*, 4, 5603 p.2478
	3 June	Wingfield tells Wolsey that WS is still in Calais.	Calais	*L&P Henry VIII*, 4, 5632, p.2490
	27 June	WS writes to Wolsey that he was not receiving royalties from Guînes county and that the king had sequestered them.	Calais	*L&P Henry VIII*, 4, 5724, p.2534

Year	Day, Month	Event	Location of WS 1470–1540	Reference
	1 July	WS and Wingfield ask Wolsey to speed up payment for fortifications. One bill was £1,000.	Calais	*L&P Henry VIII*, 4, 5752, p.2563
	22 August	Funeral of WS's sister Edith in London.	Stepney, London?	Stapleton, *Plumpton Correspondence,* p.267–69, Letter CLXV
	30 August	WS has left Calais for England with accounts.	Calais to Dover	*L&P Henry VIII*, 4, 5892, p.2635
	25 October	WS was present when Thomas More took the oath as Chancellor.	East Greenwich	*L&P Henry VIII*, 4, 6026, p.2681
	3, 7 November	WS at the State opening of Parliament and supporting the king in procession.	Blackfriars	Lehmberg, *The Reformation Parliament 1529–36*, p.77
	17 November	WS sends a wild boar to the king at York Place.		*L&P Henry VIII*, 5, 1799, p.747, Payments Nov. 1529
	1 December	WS and seventeen other senior Lords subscribe to articles against Wolsey.	House of Lords?	*L&P Henry VIII*, 4, 6075, p.2712; Lord Herbert of Cherbury,*'Life and Reign of King Henry Eighth'*. p.302; TNA Cres 40
	1 December	WS sends a wild boar to the king at York Place.		*L&P Henry VIII*, 5, 1799, p.748, Payments Dec. 1529
	8 December	WS witnessed Thomas, Viscount Rochford made Earl of Wiltshire.	York Place, London	*L&P Henry VIII*, 4, 6085, p.2718
1530	1 January	Gifts to WS from the king and from WS to the king.		TNA E 101/420/10
	14 February	WS is in debt to the Crown.		*L&P Henry VIII*, 4, 6216, p.2790
	23 April	WS at the Garter Chapter.	Windsor	Anstis, *Reg. of the Most Noble Order of the Garter*, p.385, Ed. App.VII, p.xxxv

Year	Day, Month	Event	Location of WS 1470–1540	Reference
	9 May	WS at the Garter feast.	Windsor, in the king's closet	Anstis, *Reg. of the Most Noble Order of the Garter*, p.382, Ed. App.VII, p.xxxv
	1, 4 and 17 June	Wolsey, as Bishop of Winchester, grants WS, the King's Chamberlain, the office of keeper of the lordship of Farnham Castle with an annuity of 100 marks.	Windsor	*L&P Henry VIII*, 4, 6420, p.2888; 6435, p.2889; 6460, parag.2, p.2903
	13 July	WS signs a letter to the pope seeking support for the king's divorce.		*L&P Henry VIII*, 4, 6513, p.2929
	29 November	**Cardinal Wolsey died.**		**Mackie, *The Earlier Tudors, 1485–1558*, p.698**
	16 December	WS given a licence to export 500 quarters of malt to Guînes. (Presumably for his brewery there.)		*L&P Henry III*, 4, 6803, Parag.16, p.3077
1531		WS given licence to purvey livestock and grain to Guînes and Hammes for victualling.		Grummitt, *The Calais Garrison*, p.71
	5 March	WS made Commissioner of the Peace for Hants.		*L&P Henry VIII*, 5, 166, Parag.15, p.78
	19 April	'The Queen [Catherine] still follows the King'		*Cal.S.P. Venice*, Vol.4, 1531, 664, p.279
	6/7 May	WS and Lord Lisle install Earl of Northumberland as Garter Knight.	Greenwich	*L&P Henry VIII*, 5, 204, p.96; Anstis, *Reg. of the Most Noble Order of the Garter*, p.388; Ed.App.X, p.xxvi.
	1531, after 7 May	WS with the Earl of Northumberland, Lord Mountjoy and Sir William Fitzwilliam to commemorate death of the Marquis of Dorset.		Anstis, *Register of the Most Noble Order of the Garter*, footnote to p.386

Year	Day, Month	Event	Location of WS 1470–1540	Reference
	15 July	**Queen Catherine writes last letter from Windsor.**		***Cal.St.P... Venice*, Vol.4, 1531, 674, p.282**
	6 August	The visit by Henry VIII and Anne Boleyn to The Vyne in July.		*L&P Henry VIII*, 5, Privy Purse expenses, p.755 f.78b
	September or November	WS indebted to the estate of the late Abbot of Glastonbury.		*L&P Henry VIII*, Addendum 1, pt.1, 742, p.249
	10 November	The Venetian ambassador reports on the state of England and the court: 'The Chamberlain carries a white stick.'		*Cal.St.P...Venice*, Vol.4, 1531, 694 p.298
	December	WS given a licence to purchase malt and ship it from Dover to Guînes Castle		*L&P Henry* VIII, 5, 627, Parag.17, p.285
1532	1 January	Gifts from Henry VIII for Lord and Lady Sandys.		TNA E 101/421/15
	1 January	Gifts from WS (two silver gilt candle sticks) and Lady Sandys (gilt cup with cover) to Henry VIII.		TNA E 101/421/15
	28 January	WS conveyed the king's appreciation to the Secretary of Calais.	London?	*L&P Henry VIII*, 5, 758, p.361
	18 April	WS given licence to export three horses to Calais for the Castle of Guînes.	London?	*L&P Henry VIII*, 5, 978, parag.22, p.457
	24 April	WS at the Garter Chapter.	Greenwich	*L&P Henry VIII*, 5, 962, p.452; Anstis, *Reg. of the Most Noble Order of the Garter*, Vol.1, p.388
	April to May	WS, the Duke of Norfolk, Marquis of Exeter, Earl of Oxford, Thomas and George Boleyn attended a convocation.	Canterbury	Bernard, *The King's Reformation*, p.66

Year	Day, Month	Event	Location of WS 1470–1540	Reference
	7 May	WS and Lisle install the Earl of Northumberland as Garter Knight.		Anstis, *Reg. of the Most Noble Order of the Garter,* Vol.1, p.385
	September	WS selected to accompany the king to France.		*L&P Henry VIII, 5,* Appendix 33, p.773
	1 September	WS witnessed Anne Rochford (Anne Boleyn) made Marchioness of Pembroke.	Windsor	*L&P Henry VIII, 5,* 1370, Parag.2, p.585
	18 September	WS writes to Cromwell about payment for staff expenses in the King's Chamber and Wardrobe.	London	*L&P Henry VIII, 5,* 1323, p.587
	25 September	'WS de le Vyne, KG, Lord Sandys King's Chamberlain, to be receiver general of the Earldom and Lordship of Guînes.'		*L&P Henry VIII,* 5, 1370, Parag.22, p.587
	11 October	The king crossed the Channel to Calais.		*Cal.St.P... Venice,* Vol.4, 1532, 817, p.358; Nichols and Turpyn, *Chronicle of Calais.*Vol.1, p.41
	21 October	Henry and the French king in conference in Calais.		*Cal.St.P... Venice,* Vol.4, 1532, 823, p.364
	October	WS was in the king's entourage.	Calais	Elis Gruffudd, Chronicle, trans. D.Ifans, f.497r&v
	27 October	WS at the election of the King of France as Garter knight.	Gifors, France	Anstis, *Reg. of the Most Noble Order of the Garter,* Vol.1, pp.389–91
	10 November	Licence granted to WS to import four tuns of wine given by his friends.	Calais	*L&P Henry III,* 5, 1598, parag.22, p.669
	13 November	**Henry and Anne Boleyn leave Calais.**	**Calais**	**Nichols and Turpyn, *Chronicle of Calais,* p.43**

Year	Day, Month	Event	Location of WS 1470–1540	Reference
	26 November	WS grants various tenements by deed for the use of the king.	Calais	*L&P Henry VIII*, 5, 1580, p.662
	December	WS made Commissioner of the Peace in Hants. for 1533.		*L&P Henry VIII*, 5, 1694, parag.ii, p.705
	December?	Lord Chamberlain's chaplain named as rector of Balyngham Church, near Calais.		*L&P Henry VIII*, 5, 1703, p.711
	December	WS appointed a commissioner to survey lands, fortifications and drainage at Guînes.	England	*L&P Henry VIII*, 5, 1705, p.712
1533	1 January	Gifts from Henry VIII to Lord and Lady Sandys.		*L&P Henry VIII*, 6, 32, p.14
	8 February	John Bunholt of Calais writes to WS that he has seen his woman, Parnell, who asks WS to remember the gown he promised her.	England	*L&P Henry VIII*, 6, 138, p.58
	9 April	The dukes of Norfolk and Suffolk, Marquis of Exeter, Earl of Oxford, the Treasurer and Controller of the King's Household, take Katherine to Ampthill.	Ampthill Castle	Hamilton, *Wriothesley's Chronicle*, Vol.1, p.18
	10 April	WS dined with Princess Mary.	Knole	*L&P Henry VIII*, 6, 1540, parag.iii, p.621
	12 April	**Anne Boleyn was declared Queen of England at Greenwich.**		**Hamilton, *Wriothesley's Chronicle*, Vol.1, p.17**
	29 May	Anne Boleyn welcomed at the Tower by WS, the King's Chamberlain.		*L&P Henry VIII*, 6, 563, p.250; *Ibid.*,6, 601, p.276; Hall, *Lives of the Kings, Henry VIII*, Vol.2, p.231

Year	Day, Month	Event	Location of WS 1470–1540	Reference
	6 June	WS granted a licence to export victuals from England to Guînes.		*L&P Henry VIII*, 6, 737, parag.9, p.330
This relates to 1536: See St Clare Byrne, *Lisle Letters,* Vol.3, 735, and Hamilton, *Wriothesley's Chronicle*, Vol.1, p.49	30 June	John Sandys nearly killed on a boat on the Thames when a gun exploded.	London	*L&P Henry VIII*, 6, 728, p.323
	4 August	WS wrote to Lord Lisle about his brother's problems in Calais.	The Vyne	St Clare Byrne, *Lisle Letters*, Vol.1, 23, p.497
	20 August	Papal indulgence to WS that four masses may be said during his life.		*L&P Henry VIII*, 6, Appendix 6, parag.1, p.683
	23 August	WS dined with Chapuys at Windsor.	Windsor	*Cal.St.P.Henry VIII*, 1533, p.773; *L&P Henry III*, 6, 1018, p.434
	13 September	Lord Lisle offers WS herrings and wine.	Calais?	St Clare Byrne, *Lisle Letters*, Vol.1, 49, p.557.
	Before 24 September	WS presents invoice to the Council of Calais for his pay as Lieutenant of Guînes, spy costs, soldiers and muster roll for Calais.	Calais?	Nichols and Turpyn, *Chronicle of Calais*, p.139
	17 October	WS writes to Cromwell about his son, Reynold, a priest, and asks him to excuse his absence and not being able to visit.	The Vyne	*L&P Henry VIII*, 6, 1307, p.527
	2 November	WS thanks Cromwell for kindness to him and his unthrifty son.	The Vyne	*L&P Henry VIII*, 6, 1390, p.555
	22 December	WS asks Cromwell to excuse him from Parliament because of age and sickness.	The Vyne	*L&P Henry VIII*, 6, 1556, p.627

Year	Day, Month	Event	Location of WS 1470–1540	Reference
	23 December	Chapuys reported to Charles V that Catherine of Aragon was locked up.		*L&P Henry VIII*, 6, 1558, 628
1534	1 January	WS receives a generous gift from the king.		TNA E 101/421/13
	14 January	Cromwell's Remembrances include arranging a benefice for WS's son.		*L&P Henry VIII*, 7, 49, p.20
	January 17, 19, 21, 22, 24, 26–29	WS was at the House of Lords (HoL).	HoL/London	House of Lords' Journal online (HoLJ)
	29 January	Sir Thomas Palmer reports, 'My Lord Chamberlain came this day to Court.'	Court	St Clare Byrne, *Lisle Letters*, Vol.2, 121, p.41
	3–24 Feb.	WS not present at HoL.		HoLJ online
	26 Feb	HoL.	HoL, London	HoLJ online
	2–14 March	WS not at HoL.		HoLJ online
	March 16, 17, 19, 20, 21, 23, 24, 26–28, 30	HoL.	HoL, London	HoLJ online
	21 March	WS's income from Stratfield Mortimer was transferred to Anne Boleyn. Other courtiers were similarly affected including the Duke of Suffolk.		*L&P Henry VIII*, 7, 352, p.146
	28 March	Sir Thomas Palmer wrote to Lord Lisle that WS was sick at St Paul's, London: 'I hear say that my lord chamberlain is sore sick of an ague and lies at Polles at his house.'	WS's house at St Paul's	St Clare Byrne, *Lisle Letters*, Vol.2, 151, p.89
	1 April	John Husee wrote to Lord Lisle: '...and my lord Sandys is very sick. Men doubteth his recovery'.		St Clare Byrne, *Lisle Letters*, Vol.2, 152, p.91

Year	Day, Month	Event	Location of WS 1470–1540	Reference
	4 April	John Husee tells Lord Lisle that WS was taken to The Vyne in horse litter.	The Vyne	St Clare Byrne, *Lisle Letters*, Vol.2, 155a,p.100
	6 April	John Husee writes to Lisle that WS 'is yet sore sick'.		St Clare Byrne, *Lisle Letters*, Vol.2, 156, p.101
	17 April	Thomas More was imprisoned.		*L&P Henry VIII*, 7, 502, p.202
	28 April	WS asks Lisle for some pewits and a licence to import wine.	The Vyne	St Clare Byrne, *Lisle Letters*, Vol.2, 177, p.141
	5 May	WS and others take the Oath of Succession.	Winchester	*L&P Henry VIII*, 7, 610, p.240
	8 May	John Husee writes to Lord Lisle: 'If my Lord Chamberlain Decease…'		St Clare Byrne, *Lisle Letters*, Vol.2, 185, p.149
	1 June	Sandys was having difficulty obtaining a licence to import wines.		*L&P Henry VIII*, 7, 766, p.294
	9 June	WS thanks Lisle for the pewits.	The Vyne	TNA-SP3/7/69; *L&P Henry VIII*, 7, 816, p.310
	26 July	Lord Grey reports to Cromwell that 'my Lord Chamberlain is sore sick and like to die' and asks him to sign a bill that WS had not done.		*L&P Henry VIII*, 7, 1010, p.384
	19 September	John Husee tells Lord Lisle that WS had complained against Lisle.		St Clare Byrne, *Lisle Letters*, Vol.2, 259, p.254
	23 September	John Husee tells Lisle that he told Cromwell: 'My Lord Chamberlain had unjustly complained about Lisle.' WS had acted on information received from Calais.		St Clare Byrne, *Lisle Letters*, Vol.2, 260a, p.257

Year	Day, Month	Event	Location of WS 1470–1540	Reference
	2 October	John Husee writes to Lisle: 'And as for my Lord Chamberlain Mr Cromwell saith you shall not need pass thereon for he knoweth of the matter.'		St Clare Byrne, *Lisle Letters*, Vol.2, 264, p.268
	12 November	The king appoints Robert Seymour as Lieutenant of Newnham Bridge. 'He receives the custody of the houses, gardens which Will. Lord Sandys had.'		*L&P Henry VIII*, 7, 1424, p.537
	26 November	WS asks Cromwell for permission to disembark twenty tuns of wine for The Vyne.	The Vyne	*L&P Henry VIII*, 7, 1479, p.550
	2 December	WS writes to Cromwell with concern that his men at Guînes are being badly treated and complaints made about the state of Guînes Castle. He had done what he could with available funds and John Cheyne, his deputy at Guînes, is dead. (Did WS promote his son John to the deputy's position at this time?)	The Vyne	*L&P Henry VIII*, 7, 1504, p.562
1535	13 January	Chapuys tells the emperor that WS told him he was disgusted with the court and had faked illness to stay away. He says WS is 'one of the best men of war in the Kingdom'.	The Vyne	*Cal.St P...Spain*, Vol.5. 1, 127, p.375; *L&P Henry VIII*, 8, 48, p.14
	22 January	WS reports to Cromwell that his brother caught a man killing deer in Queens Park, Mortimer.	The Vyne	*L&P Henry VIII*, 8, 86, p.28

Year	Day, Month	Event	Location of WS 1470–1540	Reference
	28 January	Chapuys reports to the emperor that Lord Darcy and WS were ready for rebellion, and WS is 'The best Captain in England'.		*L&P Henry VIII*, 8, 121, p.38
	26 February	The emperor writes to Chapuys, mentioning the affection Darcy and WS showed to Queen Catherine and the princess.		*L&P Henry VIII*, 8, 272, p.108
	1 March	WS signed a contract for tombs for him and Margery and for his parents.		Baigent & Millard, *History of ... Basingstoke*, p.693
	4 March	Chapuys wrote to the emperor denying rumours that WS was ready to take the castle of Gravelines.		*L&P Henry VIII*, 8, 327, p.129 *Cal St.P.. Spanish* Vol.5.1, 38, p.411
	6 March	WS reports to Cromwell the problems victuallers had in obtaining cattle.	The Vyne	*L&P Henry VIII*, 8, 350, p.140
	14 March	WS tells Cromwell he will sort out problems at Guînes Castle if needed.	The Vyne	*L&P Henry VIII*, 8, 389, p.154
	11 April	WS apologises to Cromwell that his servant, Richard Clotton, attended a sermon by Hugh Latimer.	The Vyne	*L&P Henry VIII*, Addendum 1, pt.1, 981, p.343
	23 April	WS absent from Garter Chapter but expected to attend the next feast. His Garter stall was No.13 on the king's side.	Greenwich	*L&P Henry VIII*, 8, 587, p.221; Bodleian Library, Ashmolean MS 1113, f.37a
	9 May	WS present at the Garter Feast and described as 'of the King's bed chamber'.	Windsor	*L&P Henry VIII*, 8, 694, p.260; Anstis, *Reg. of the Most Noble Order of the Garter*, Vol.1, pp.395–97

Year	Day, Month	Event	Location of WS 1470–1540	Reference
	25 June	WS writes to Cromwell about his failure to exercise his legal right to appoint his wife's kinsman to a benefice: 'I marvel not a little you should ask me to do what is contrary to the law, right and conscience.' He also says he cannot 'wait upon the King' as there is sickness in his house.	Woolmer forest	*L&P Henry VIII*, 8, 924. p.363
	1 July	Thomas More was executed.		Hamilton, *Wriothesley's Chronicle*, Vol.1, p.29
	13 July	WS tells Cromwell that he is at The Vyne and sick with great sweat.	The Vyne	*L&P Henry VIII*, 8, 1034, p.408
	August	Sir William Fitzwilliam reported to Cromwell that Calais is 'farre out of ordre'.		Nichols and Turpyn, *Chronicle of Calais*, pp.130–33
	2 September	Sir William Fitzwilliam agreed with Cromwell that 'it will be right to go through the accounts of my Lord Chamberlain'.		*L&P Henry VIII*, 9, 255, p.86
	6 September	'Since the death of Cardinal Fisher and Sir Thomas More no less than 27 more have died on the scaffold.'		*Cal St.P... Spain*, Vol 5.2, 202, 'Spain: September 1535, 1–30', in De Gayangos, *Cal. St.P... Spain, Vol.5, Pt.1, 1534–1535*, pp.535–44.
	23 September	Henry Palmer thanks Cromwell for 'redress of wrongs done me by my lord Chamberlain's office'.		*L&P Henry VIII*, 9, 416, p.136
	29 September	WS was granted £4 11*s* 3*d* for accommodation in Windsor Castle		*L&P Henry VIII*, 9, 476, p.155

Year	Day, Month	Event	Location of WS 1470–1540	Reference
	2 October	Sir Richard Greville complains to Cromwell about failure to gain a post in Calais that he says he was promised by WS with the Duke of Norfolk and the Treasurer.		*L&P Henry VIII*, 9, 525, p.172
	9 October	A letter to Cromwell suggests he is going to visit WS.		*L&P Henry VIII*, 9, 570, p.190
	15–19 October	Henry and Anne Boleyn visit WS and The Vyne.	The Vyne	*L&P Henry VIII*, 9, 663, p.224
	19 October	Sir Francis Brian wrote to Cromwell that the king was merry at The Vyne.	The Vyne	*L&P Henry VIII*, 9, 639, p.215
	21 October	Lady Margery Sandys writes to Cromwell pleading for the Prior of Worcester: 'He will give you in ready money as much as any man.'	The Vyne	*L&P Henry VIII*, 9, 656, p.220
	22 October	WS tells Cromwell the king came to The Vyne.	The Vyne	*L&P Henry VIII*, 9, 663, p.224
	22 November	WS sought favour from Cromwell for a widow and excused himself from court at Christmas as he was unwell.	The Vyne	*L&P Henry VIII*, 9, 870, p.293
	27 November	John Husee wrote to Lord Lisle that Cromwell will write to him 'concerning WS and his officers'.		*L&P Henry VIII*, Addendum1, pt.1, 1140, p.390
1536	6 January	WS thanks Cromwell for Mr. Augustine's services (a physician). He 'has done a great cure on me'.	The Vyne	*L&P Henry VIII*, 10, 32, p.12

Year	Day, Month	Event	Location of WS 1470–1540	Reference
	23 January	Henry VIII has a serious fall from his horse.		Friedmann, *Anne Boleyn, Vol 1, p.lxxxii; L&P Henry VIII,* 10, 282 p.104, dated 10 Feb.
	29 January	**Funeral of Catherine of Aragon and Anne Boleyn's miscarriage.**		**Friedmann, *Anne Boleyn, Vol 1, p.lxxxii; L&P Henry VIII*, 10, 284, p.104**
	4 February	WS present at the opening of Parliament, then attended intermittently. The session included an Act re the dissolution of lesser monasteries, pilgrimages and the worship of relics.	Westminster	BL Harl.158. f.137 now 148, 'Order of Proceeding from Palace at Westminster to Cathedral Church'; *L&P Henry VIII*, 10, 244, p.87
	7 March (dated 1537 but 1536 from internal evidence)	WS's son John is deputy at Guînes Castle.	John at Guînes, WS at The Vyne	*L&P Henry VIII*, 12, 589, p.270
	22–24 April	WS attended Garter Chapter, starting with vespers on 22 April and ending with a Mass for dead knights on 24 April.		*L&P Henry VIII,* 10, 715, p.301; Anstis, *Reg. of the Most Noble Order of the Garter,* Vol.1, pp.398–400
	24 April	The king commissions Lord Audley, Duke of Norfolk, Sir William Paulet, WS and others to enquire into treason by Anne Boleyn.		Friedmann, *Anne Boleyn,* Pt.2, p.243; TNA, *Baga de Secretis*, pouch VIII, memb.10 &14.
	2 May	The Privy Council interrogates Anne Boleyn.	Tower of London	Friedmann, *Anne Boleyn,* Vol.2, p.252
	2 May	WS and the Duke of Norfolk, with Anne Boleyn's chamberlain and four women, take her ('the concubine') from Greenwich to the Tower.	London	*L&P Henry VIII*, 10, 782 p.330; Friedmann, *Anne Boleyn*, Vol.2, p.253

Year	Day, Month	Event	Location of WS 1470–1540	Reference
	3 May	WS, Lord Chancellor Audley, the earls of Oxford and Sussex tell Cranmer about Anne Boleyn's activities.	Star Chamber	*L&P Henry VIII*, 10, 792, p.334; Friedmann, *Anne Boleyn*, Vol.2, p.257
	6 May	Anne Boleyn pleads innocence to the king.	London	*L&P Henry VIII*, 10, 808, p.341
	12 May	The Duke of Norfolk, WS and others are appointed as a special commission to try Weston, Norris, etc.	Westminster	*L&P Henry VIII*, 10, 849, p.351
	13 May	The dukes of Norfolk and Suffolk, WS and twenty-four other peers are summoned to the trial of Anne Boleyn. WS is described as among those who joined the conspiracy against her.	London	Friedmann, *Anne Boleyn*, Vol.2, pp.274–75
	15 May	**At Anne Boleyn's trial WS voted 'guilty'.**	**Great Hall Westminster**	***L&P Henry VIII*, 10, 876, p.361; Friedmann, *Anne Boleyn*, Vol.2, p.275**
	17 May	Cranmer declared the king's marriage to Anne Boleyn null and void.	Lambeth Palace	Friedmann, *Anne Boleyn*, Vol.2, p.290; *L&P Henry VIII*, 10, 896, p.373
	22 May	Dissolution of Mottisfont Priory.		See 'Houses of Austin canons: Priory of Mottisfont', *in Doubleday and Page, History of the County of Hampshire, Vol.2*, pp.172–75.
	25 May	WS receives licence to remain in England.		*L&P Henry VIII*, 10, 1015, parag.23, p.418
	5 June (year date corrected in *L&P* errata 1537.)	WS writes to Lady Lisle asking her to hasten the wine delivery to him.	Guînes	St Clare Byrne, *Lisle Letters*, Vol.3, 715, p.403; *L&P Henry VIII*, 10, 1064, p.439

Year	Day, Month	Event	Location of WS 1470–1540	Reference
	8 June	WS in the procession for the opening of Parliament, bearing the king's train.	London	Hamilton, *Wriothesley's Chronicle*, p.45
	27 June	WS exchanges his Chelsea and Paddington property with the king for Mottisfont Priory/ estates		HRO 13M63/107; *L&P Henry VIII*, 11, 202, (29) July 1536
	29 June	WS's son John nearly killed by accident when a gun exploded.		St Clare Byrne, *Lisle Letters*, Vol.3, 735, p.440; Hamilton, *Wriothesley's Chronicle*, Vol.1, p.49
	29 June and 4, 14, July	WS at the House of Lords.	London, House of Lords (HoL)	*House of Lords Journal*, Vol.1: '4 July 1536', pp.92–93
	18 July	WS at the House of Lords	HoL	*L&P Henry VIII*, 11, 104, p.48
	7 August	WS complains to Cromwell that the Deputy of Calais has discharged his son and others from posts at Guînes:'reports have been spread by his enemies and… he has been used'.	The Vyne	*L&P Henry VIII*, 11, 241, p.105
	12 August	WS tells Cromwell that he has been rudely handled 'they think to make him weary of the castle'.	The Vyne	*L&P Henry VIII*, 11, 288, p.123
	16 August	WS asks Cromwell to remedy 'what is done against him in those parts beyond the sea'. He plans to meet Henry VIII at Esthamsteade or Reading, and invites Cromwell to The Vyne, 'his poor Hermitage' (Hamytage).	The Vyne	*L&P Henry VIII*, 11, 313, p.130

Year	Day, Month	Event	Location of WS 1470–1540	Reference
	21 August	WS writes to Cromwell about timber at Guînes and replies to a comment that he should be a good father to his son John Sandys.	Vyne	*L&P Henry VIII*, 11, 341, p.138
	Soon after 1 October	WS heading towards Ampthill to prepare lodgings for the king and his retinue prior to the muster there.	Ampthill	*L&P Henry VIII*, 11, 643, p.254
	October	During the Pilgrimage of Grace (the Northern Rebellion) WS was supporting the king with 400 men.		Hamilton, *Wriothesley's Chronicle*, pp.56–57; *State Papers Henry VIII*, I, pp.506, 508, 646; *L&P Henry VIII*, 11, 580, p.232
	17 October	The Duke of Norfolk and WS write to the king about shortages of men and money.	Ampthill	*L&P Henry VIII*, 11, 754, p.290
	17 October	WS, the Duke of Norfolk and Marquis of Exeter all signed a letter to the king seeking instructions.	Ampthill	*L&P Henry VIII*, 11, 755, p.291
	18 October	WS, the Duke of Norfolk and Marquis of Exeter signed another letter to the king seeking instructions and money for troops.	Ampthill	*L&P Henry VIII*, 11, 776, p.298
	20 October	Instructions sent from the Privy Council to Norfolk and Exeter that WS should go to Lincoln, with Paulet and Kingston and 2,000 men, to keep peace in Lincolnshire.		*L&P Henry VIII*, 11, 799/800, p.309
	20 October	Paulet writes to the Privy Council that most of the army was discharged. WS not with him.		*L&P Henry VIII*, 11, 803, p.311

Year	Day, Month	Event	Location of WS 1470–1540	Reference
	26 October	WS was one of the members of the king's council to examine the rebel leader, Christopher Aske, leader of Pilgrimage of Grace.	London	*L&P Henry* VIII 11, 879, p.350
	November	The king refers to WS as 'our Chamberlain' in a letter to the rebels refuting their charges.		*L&P Henry VIII*, 11, 957, p.384
	27 November	Husee writes to Lisle: 'The Lord Privy Seal promised to write to you concerning the Lord Chamberlain and his officers'.		St Clare Byrne, *Lisle Letters*, Vol.3, 786, p.525
1537	4 January	WS complains to Cromwell that people are trying to take his job as Captain of Guînes, and he is amazed that an inquiry should consider his affairs.	The Vyne	*L&P Henry VIII*, 12.1, 17, p.12
	14 January	Husee writes to Lisle, referring to him taking WS's post and reports that WS 'is in good favour as ever he was'.		St Clare Byrne, *Lisle Letters*, Vol.4, 915, p.240
	19 January	WS writes to Cromwell about the offices in Calais. The Earl of Westmorland, WS's nephew, visited his poor uncle.	The Vyne	*L&P Henry VIII*, 12.1, 151, p.68
	22 January	Husee wrote to Lisle about a benefice WS might receive, not Lisle.	London	*L&P Henry VIII*, 12.1,195, p.83
	17 February	Husee tells Lady Lisle that 'WS not here' (in London).		St Clare Byrne, *Lisle Letters*, Vol.4, 867, p.119
	18 February	Husee tells Lisle that he was trying to facilitate Lisle taking WS's job.		St Clare Byrne, *Lisle Letters*, Vol.4, 929, p.266

Year	Day, Month	Event	Location of WS 1470–1540	Reference
	1 March	WS expected in Calais.	The Vyne	*L&P Henry VIII*, Addendum 1, Pt.1, 1200, p.407
	7 March	WS wrote to Cromwell about offices in Guînes and describes John Sandys as deputy of Guînes Castle.	The Vyne	*L&P Henry VIII*, 12.1, 589, p.270
	11 March	WS tells Cromwell about seditious behaviour by a local person he has jailed, and that he will attend the king on Monday.	Mottisfont	*L&P Henry VIII*, 12.1, 627, p.281
	26 March	WS wrote to Cromwell from Calais that he wants a kitchen in the castle of Guînes.	Calais	*L&P Henry VIII*, 12.1, 750, p.329
	9 April	WS tells Lisle that he has no news.	Guînes	*L&P Henry VIII*, 12.1, 885, p.396
	16 April	WS seeks a favour from Lisle for a gunner.	Guînes	*L&P Henry VIII*, 12.1, 954, p.434
	18 April	WS tells Lisle that he needs more gunners and has heard that the French are marching there.	Guînes	*L&P Henry VIII*, 12.1, 971, p.439
	23 April	WS wrote to Lisle with news on the French.	Guînes	*L&P Henry VIII*, 12.1, 1016. p.459
	25 April	WS asks Lisle to help an old man whose daughter was married against his will.	Guînes	*L&P Henry VIII*, 12.1, 1041. p.477
	30 April	Lisle is asked to persuade WS to change his mind on prohibiting strangers and cattle in the Pale.	Guînes	*L&P Henry VIII*, 12.1, 1075, p.488
	4 May	WS tells Lisle he has sequestered some corn but will supply Lisle with corn as needed.	Guînes	St Clare Byrne, *Lisle Letters*, Vol.4, 950, p.295
	5 May	WS tells Cromwell that the guns are useless.	Guînes	*L&P Henry VIII*, 12.1, 1140, p.526

Year	Day, Month	Event	Location of WS 1470–1540	Reference
	11 May	WS wrote to Lisle that he has heard from Cromwell that the surveyor of fortifications at Calais and Guînes will be paid. He has closed the gates of Guînes as the French are on the move.	Guînes	*L&P Henry VIII*, 12.1, 1179, p.542
	17 May	WS informs Lisle about a payment dispute.	Guînes	*L&P Henry VIII*, 12.1, 1230, p.566
	24 May	WS asks Lisle for any weapons he can spare.	Guînes	St Clare Byrne, *Lisle Letters*, Vol.4, 958, p.310
	25 May	WS asks Lisle to help a man.	Guînes	St Clare Byrne, *Lisle Letters*, Vol. 4, 958a, p.310
	1 June	WS wrote to Lisle about celebrating Queen Jane Seymour's pregnancy.	Guînes	St Clare Byrne, *Lisle letters* Vol.4, 961, p.315
	5 June (re-dated from 1536 in *L&P* Errata 1537)	WS was at Guînes and asked Lady Lisle to hasten delivery of wine to him.	Guînes	St Clare Byrne, *Lisle Letters,* Vol.3, 715, p.403
	14 June	WS welcomed news from Cromwell that the king is pleased with fortification plans for Guînes and Calais.	Guînes	*L&P Henry VIII*, 12.2, 93, p.32
	18 June	WS tells Cromwell about incursions into the Pale by the emperor's Burgundian troops.	Guînes	*L&P Henry VIII*, 12.2, 113, p.40
	24 June	WS reports to Lisle that the imperial army has taken Montreuil and is close to the Pale.	Guînes	St Clare Byrne, *Lisle Letters,* Vol.4, 972, p.330
	29 June	WS tells Lisle that the imperial army is besieging Theroune.	Guînes	St Clare Byrne, *Lisle Letters,* Vol. 4, 972a, p.330

Year	Day, Month	Event	Location of WS 1470–1540	Reference
	29 July	WS wrote to Lisle about safeguarding the parish priest of Guînes to await the king's pleasure.	Guînes	*L&P Henry VIII*, Addendum 1, pt.1, 1238, p.424
	6 August	WS asks Lisle about giving a position to an old servant of the king.	Guînes	St Clare Byrne, *Lisle Letters*, Vol. 4, 997, p.371
	6 August	WS informs Cromwell about the election of a new mayor of Calais. He is content with the outcome.		*L&P Henry VIII*, 12.2, 463, p.187
	7 August	WS accepts Lisle's apology for opening a letter from Cromwell and asks him not to repeat the mistake.	Guînes	St Clare Byrne, *Lisle Letters*, Vol.4, 999, p.374
	23 August	WS tells Lisle he will see him soon in Calais. Both are commissioners on a case.	Guînes	*L&P Henry VIII*, 12.2, 573, p.215
	7 September	Sir Thomas Palmer reported that the king had asked when WS would return home.		*L&P Henry VIII*, 12.2, 661, p.240
	16 September	WS tells Lisle that sickness is at Guînes.	Guînes	*L&P Henry VIII*, 12.2, 710, p.255
	28 September	WS writes to Cromwell that he is in London and will be at court tomorrow.	London	*L&P Henry VIII*, 12.2, 773, p.275
	1 October	WS informs Cromwell about implementing arrangements for tenants and strangers at Calais.	Bagshot	*L&P Henry VIII*, 12.2, 801, p.283
	2/3 October	WS tells Lisle that he has briefed the king who is pleased that Lisle is doing well; the king has given WS time to go home, and Cromwell will sort out a wrong affecting people in Calais.	Bagshot to The Vyne	St Clare Byrne, *Lisle Letters*, Vol.4, 1021, p.413

Year	Day, Month	Event	Location of WS 1470–1540	Reference
	October	A possible visit by Princess Mary to Basingstoke and Bagshot.		*L&P Henry VIII*, 12.2, 1147, parag.ii, p.402
	12 October	**Jane Seymour wrote to the Privy Council that she has a boy child.**	**The Vyne**	***L&P Henry VIII*, 12.2, 889, p.310**
	15 October	WS attends the christening of Edward V and is ranked 15 in precedence.	Hampton Court	Leland, *De Rebus Collectanea*, Vol. II, p.673–77; Law, *History of Hampton Court Palace*, p.187
	18 October	WS seeks a favour from Cromwell for a former member of the Calais retinue.	Esher	*L&P Henry VIII*, 12.2, 941, p.329
	24 October	**Jane Seymour died.**		***L&P Henry VIII*, 12.2. 972, p.339**
	28 October	WS tells Cromwell he has received news of the queen's interment and asks when he will be needed at court. He has not been there because he was in contact with a sick person at Esher.	The Vyne	*L&P Henry VIII*, 12. 2, 994, p.346
	1 November	The Earl of Surrey and Lord Chamberlain are summoned to attend the queen's funeral.	The Vyne	*L&P Henry VIII*, 12.2, 1012, p.355
	1 November	WS was granted a manor which had belonged to Robert Aske, the rebel.		*L&P Henry VIII*, 12.2, parag.1, 1150, p.404
	12 November	WS present at Jane Seymour's funeral.	Hampton Court to Windsor	*L&P Henry VIII*, 12.2, 1060, p.372
	17 November	WS writes to Lisle about the queen's interment.	London	St Clare Byrne *Lisle Letters*, Vol. 4, 1035, p.451
	21 December	WS paid tithe as Lord of Clewer.		*L&P Henry VIII*, 12.2, 1241, p.435

Year	Day, Month	Event	Location of WS 1470–1540	Reference
1538	1 January	WS listed in the King's Remembrance as a member of the 'Council'.		*L&P Henry VIII*, 13.1, 1, p.1
	20 January	WS informs Cromwell that he is at home with royal licence.	The Vyne	*L&P Henry VIII*, 13.1, 111, p.38
	9 February	WS writes to Cromwell in favour of an honest man hurt by Christopher Aston: 'Many honest persons stand in great dread of him.'	The Vyne	*L&P Henry VIII*, 13.1, 245, p.85
	16 March	WS not at court.		*L&P Henry VIII*, 13.1, 514, p.193
	16 April	Earl of Westmorland's son Thomas was with WS, his uncle.	The Vyne?	*L&P Henry VIII*, 13.1, 790, p. 295
	23 April	WS probably attended the Garter ceremony.	Windsor?	*L&P Henry VIII*, 13.1, 828, p.305
	6 June	WS tells Wriothesley he has jailed an 'indiscreet priest' and asks what he should do with him.	Mottisfont	*L&P Henry VIII*, 13.1, 1141, p.427; TNA SP7/3/f42
	21 June	WS wrote to Cromwell seeking leave from court and about priests.	The Vyne	*L&P Henry VIII*, 13.1, 1229, p.455; TNA SP 7/3/f 45
	25 July	WS wrote to Cromwell thanking the king for enforcing his right to execute justice. He will not be at court because infection is in his house.	The Vyne	*L&P Henry VIII*, 13.1, 1459, p.539
	22 August	Henry Palmer, Baily of Guînes, expels a servant appointed by WS.	?Mottisfont	*L&P Henry VIII*, 13.2, 161, p.64
	24 August	A priest informs Lady Lisle that WS is overseeing Mottisfont refurbishment and expects to be there until the end of October.	Mottisfont	*L&P Henry VIII*, 13.2, 176, p.60; St Clare Byrne, *Lisle Letters*, Vol. 5, 1209, p.204

Year	Day, Month	Event	Location of WS 1470–1540	Reference
	End August	The Prior of Calais is interrogated about his contacts with WS.		*L&P Henry VIII*, 13.2, 248, p.97
	1 September	WS tells Cromwell that he will remove an image from Basingstoke at the king's command.	Mottisfont	*L&P Henry VIII*, 13.2, 259, p.102
	29 September	WS features in Windsor Castle accounts (covers periods 1535–37) for rents and allowances.		*L&P Henry VIII*, 13.2, 453 paras. Charges, i, Outgoings,3, Repairs 5, pp.171–73, Repairs 5p. 174
	12/13 November	A courtier was examined and WS accused of being in confederacy with the Marquis of Exeter, Lord Montacute and others. The accusation was dismissed.		*L&P Henry VIII*, 13.2, 829, para..II, p.336
	12/18 November	Henry Palmer wrote to Cromwell about a sergeant's post and says he is no longer involved with the matter.		*L&P Henry VIII*, 13.2, 863, p.360
	3 December	WS was a member of the panel to try Lord Montague & the Marquis of Exeter for treasonable activities. They were found guilty.	Westminster	*L&P Henry VIII*, 13.2, 979, p.417
1539		The Lord Chamberlain of the Household is described as the King's Chamberlain in the House of Lords Precedence Act, 1539.		*The House of Lords Precedence Act 1539, clauses IV, V, X.*
	7 January	John Husee tells Lord Lisle that Sir John Wallop and WS are coming to Calais.		St Clare Byrne, *Lisle Letters* Vol. 5, 1323, p.371

Year	Day, Month	Event	Location of WS 1470–1540	Reference
	21 February	Report states 'my Lord, my Lady and all at the Vyne are in good health'.	The Vyne	*L&P Henry VIII,* 14.1, 331, p.129
	16 March	WS arrives in France.	Calais	*L&P Henry VIII,* 14.1, 568, p.221
	19 March	Sandys was reported to have arrived at Guînes and been received with 'salvos of gunfire'.	Calais	*Cal.St.P…Spain,* 1539, Vol.6.1, 48 p.135
	31 March /1 April	Margery Sandys dies and is buried from The Vyne.	The Vyne	Williams, *Hampshire Churchwarden's Accounts*, p.29; *L&P Henry VIII,* 14.1, 634, p.246; 662, p.331–32
	6 April	WS advised Lord Lisle on victualling the Pale.	Guînes	St Clare Byrne, *Lisle Letters,*Vol. 5, 1374, p.426
	13 April	WS thanks Wriothesley for his good company during his visit and asks him to ask Cromwell about his revenues from Hanningfield hospital.	Guînes	*L&P Henry VIII,* 14.1, 759, p.365
	28 April	WS listed as present at the House of Lords but seems to have been at Guînes (see below).	London	*House of Lords Journal,* 28 April 1539, p.104
	29 April	WS writes to Lisle about the transportation of wine and beer.	Guînes	St Clare Byrne, *Lisle Letters*, Vol. 5, 1397, p.454
	12 May	WS wrote to Lisle to pass on some letters.	Guînes	St Clare Byrne, *Lisle Letters,* Vol. 5, 1410, p.474
	21 May	WS wrote again to Lisle: 'I trust your patience and good zeal towards Christ's true faith and the observing of the King's injunctions and proclamations shall be acceptable to God.'	Guînes	St Clare Byrne, *Lisle Letters,* Vol. 5, 1424, p.487

Year	Day, Month	Event	Location of WS 1470–1540	Reference
	22 May	WS tells Lisle that the king has entered debate about the Sacrament.	Guînes	St Clare Byrne, *Lisle Letters,* Vol. 5, 1426, p.491
	31 May	WS's Garter stall is No. 12 on the king's side	Guînes	Bodleian Library Ashmolean MS 1113, f.125b
	22 June	Lisle is warned that WS and Wallop 'will leave your lordship in the briars when you trust them most'.		St Clare Byrne *Lisle Letters,* Vol. 5, 1457, p.541
	2 July	WS informs Lisle that his chaplains have found people with 'unreformed books'.	Guînes	St Clare Byrne, *Lisle Letters,* Vol. 5, 1469, p.564
	3 July	WS tells Lisle that he will be with him tomorrow for dinner.	Guînes	St Clare Byrne, *Lisle Letters,* Vol. 5, 1471, 568
	6 July	WS informs Lisle and the Council that he has overridden them on the future of a person.	Guînes	St Clare Byrne, *Lisle Letters,* Vol.5,1474, p.571
	9 July	WS writes to Lisle, trying to ensure that he imprisons Henry Palmer.	Guînes	St Clare Byrne, *Lisle Letters,* Vol. 5, 1484, p.591
	21 July	WS, Lisle and a council member hear complaints about a breakdown of law and order. 'For lack of justice everything is out of course and good order', and Henry Palmer is blamed for everything.	Guînes	*L&P Henry VIII,* 14.1, 1296, p.567
	25 July	WS writes to Lisle about the future use of grain stocks and supplies.	Guînes	St Clare Byrne, *Lisle Letters,* Vol. 5, 1496, p.596
	c. 26 July	WS, Lord Lisle and the Calais Council write to Cromwell that Henry Palmer refused to take action on various crimes, including murders.	Guînes	St Clare Byrne, *Lisle Letters,* Vol. 5, 1493a, p.591

Year	Day, Month	Event	Location of WS 1470–1540	Reference
	12 August	WS informs Lisle about provocative action by the French at Ardres.	Guînes	*L&P Henry VIII*, 14.2, 40, p.11
	18 August	WS writes to Lisle about payment for a tradesman.	Guînes	*L&P Henry VIII*, 14.2, 61, p.18
	End of August	Sir Thomas Palmer wrote to Lisle that he and Mr Wallop have made WS and Harry Palmer friends.		St Clare Byrne, *Lisle Letters*, Vol. 5, 1532, p.641
	13 September	Lord Lisle was in Dover.		*L&P Henry VIII*, 14.2, 158, p.47
	15 September	WS informs Lisle that 'little Palmer sent money to his servant, Pickering whom you and I put into jail. Pickering being comforted broke jail. We may perceive what a fellow Palmer is and the men he supports'.	Guînes	St Clare Byrne, *Lisle Letters*, Vol. 5, 1540, p.648.
	22 September	Henry Palmer wrote to Cromwell that WS and Wallop had ordered men from every parish to write in a book of complaints against him. Cromwell should not take notice of the book.		*L&P Henry VIII*, 14.2, 208, p.61
	26 September	WS and others dined with Lady Lisle.	Guînes	*L&P Henry VIII*, 14.2, 226, p.69
	27 September	Husee writes to Lady Lisle that the king welcomed her husband and entertained him 'lovingly'.	Guînes	*L&P Henry VIII*, 14.2, 228, p.69
	27 September	WS and others are delayed by bad weather when returning home from Calais. WS stayed with Lady Lisle.	Guînes	*L&P Henry VIII*, 14.2, 230, p.70

Year	Day, Month	Event	Location of WS 1470–1540	Reference
	5 October	WS thanks Lady Lisle for her hospitality.	London or Windsor	*L&P Henry VIII*, 14.2, 283, p.95
	5 October	Richard Cromwell writes to Lord Cromwell that WS arrived at court with eighty men on horseback and showed the king plans of Hammes and Guînes, which pleased him.	Windsor	*L&P Henry VIII*, 14.2, 290, p.110
	26 October	WS tells Lisle that he is pleased that he thinks he will not be in Calais much longer and the king thinks highly of him.	Mottisfont	*L&P Henry VIII*, 14.2, p.396
		Henry Lacy reports to Cromwell that WS has not paid soldiers at Guînes, and sometimes there were only six people at the castle.		St Clare Byrne, *Lisle Letters*, Vol. 5, pp.692–93
	11 November	WS wrote to Cromwell defending his position on non-payment of soldiers.	The Vyne	*L&P Henry VIII*, 14.2, 499, p.177
	22 November	WS writes to Lisle and others, agreeing with Lisle against Cromwell about the correctness of the dismissal of men.	The Vyne	St Clare Byrne, *Lisle Letters*, Vol. 5, 1604, p.711; *L&P Henry VIII*, 14.2, 568, p.198
1540	3 January	WS was in the king's welcome party for Anne of Cleves.	London	Hall, *Lives of Kings, Henry VIII*, Vol.2, p.298
	31 January.	The Lord Chamberlain signs a bill for preparations for Queen Anne of Cleves.	London	Nicolas, *Privy Purse Expenses, Henry VIII*, p.28
	Before 31 March	The Duke of Norfolk and WS were the deputy's most powerful supporters against heresies in Calais.		St Clare Byrne, *Lisle Letters*, Vol. 6, p.58, parag.i

Year	Day, Month	Event	Location of WS 1470–1540	Reference
	5 April	Commissioners write to Henry VIII supporting WS, Lisle and Wallop.		St Clare Byrne, *Lisle Letters*, Vol. 6, pp.62–63
	7 April	WS writes to Lisle about a commission into religious 'problems' in Calais. The commission has cleared WS but the king prevents him from being in Calais.	The Vyne	*L&P Henry VIII*, 15, 471, p.195; St Clare Byrne, *Lisle Letters*, Vol. 6, 1664, p.70
	10 April	WS was in London.		*L&P Henry III*, 15, 471, p.195
	18 April	WS presents Cromwell with his letter patent for the title of Earl of Essex at a ceremony.	Westminster Palace	*L&P Henry VIII*, 15, 541, p.242 BL Harl.MS 6074, f.57 B
	23 April	WS at Westminster for an Order of the Garter ceremony.	Westminster palace	*L&P Henry VIII*, 15, 560, parags.1,3, p.251; Anstis, *Reg. of the Most Noble Order of the Garter*, Vol.1, p.413–15
	End April	WS's salary as Treasurer of Calais is noted as £1,526 (inc. soldiers' pay); as Lieutenant of Guînes, £1,085 (inc. pay for spies and 999 soldiers); and he still receives an annuity as Treasurer of Wars.		*L&P Henry VIII*, 15, 608 parag.1, 3, p.272; parag.3, p.273, parag.4. iii, p.274; 609, p.276
	5 May	WS surrenders position as Keeper of Freemantil in favour of Sir Humphrey Foster (his son-in-law).		*L&P Henry VIII*, 15, 733, parags.6, 30, p.342
	17 May	WS was at the Garter Feast.	Windsor	Anstis, *Reg. of the Most Noble Order of the Garter*, Vol.1, Ed.App., p.xlvi
	19 May	Lisle is arrested in London.		*L&P Henry VIII*, 15, 697, p.320

Year	Day, Month	Event	Location of WS 1470–1540	Reference
	21 May	Letter from Marillac to Montmorency mentions WS: 'The Lord Sandys having taken 'des Amys' of various fortresses in Italy has gone to fortify Guînes.'	England (see 6 June)	*L&P Henry VIII*, 15, 697, p.326
	24 May	WS donated £3 6*s* 8*d* for prayers for the souls of deceased Knights of Garter, and his stall position at St George's Chapel was joint No. 12.	England	*L&P Henry VIII*, 15, 707, p.329
	3 June	WS received a passport to go to Guînes, and a licence to pull down the church, buildings and trees at his discretion in aid of fortification.	England	*L&P Henry VIII*, 15, 744, p.353; 831, parags.10,11, p.403
	6 June	WS tells Cromwell that he intends to sail to Calais next day.	Dover	*L&P Henry VIII*, 15, 754, p.359
	7 June	WS arrives at Calais (see above)	Calais	*L&P Henry VIII*, 15, 754, p.359
	10 June	**Thomas Cromwell committed to the Tower for treason.**		***L&P Henry VIII*, 15, 766, p.363**
	12 June	WS issues proclamation at Guînes, forbidding Englishmen entering French territory on pain of death.	Guînes	*L&P Henry VIII*, 15, 777, p.366
	15 June	The French send WS a red deer, but he thinks the bearer is a French spy.	Guînes	*L&P Henry VIII*, 15, 781, p.368
	17 June	WS reports to the king about refurbishment of fortifications and the general situation.	Guînes	*L&P Henry VIII*, 15, 795, p.374

Year	Day, Month	Event	Location of WS 1470–1540	Reference
	18 June	WS was appointed Commissioner of the Peace for Hants.		*L&P Henry VIII*, 15, 831, parag.47, p.407
	28 July (Marillac gives 29 July)	**Thomas Cromwell was executed.**		**Hamilton, *Wriothesley's Chronicle*, Vol 1, p.120; *L&P Henry VIII*, 15, 926, p.458**
	28 July	Walter Lord Hungerford, sometime brother-in-law of WS, was executed.		Hamilton, *Wriothesley's Chronicle*, Vol.1 p.120; *L&P Henry VIII,* 15, 26. p.458
	1 August	WS and other Lords are commissioned by the king to take and receive recognisances.		*L&P Henry VIII*, 15, 1027, parag.7, p.504.
	10 August	WS at the Privy Council.	London	Nicolas, *Proceedings & Ordinances of the Privy Council.* Vol. VII, p.4
	23 August	The Privy Council decides in favour of Thomas Combes in his complaint against WS.	Calais	*L&P Henry VIII*, 15, 997, p.497
	28 August	WS signs a letter as a member of the Council of Calais concerning a Common way in Calais.	Calais	*L&P Henry VIII,* 15, 1014, p.500
	30/31 August	WS absent from the Privy Council which instructed him to discharge the 106 men he took to Guînes.	Guînes	*L&P Henry VIII,* 15, 1018, p.502; 1021, p.504
	August	The king orders WS to return to England because of fever in the Pale: 'They [the French] greatly feared the Lord Chamberlain and his men.'	Guînes	Elis Gruffudd, Chronicle, ff.564v–565r

Year	Day, Month	Event	Location of WS 1470–1540	Reference
	7–22, November	WS at the Privy Council.	Windsor	*L&P Henry VIII,* 16, 243, p.106; 252, p.109; 260, p.111; 114, p.112; 266, p.112; 268, p.114; 272, p.116; 277, p.199; 280, p.120; 283, 284, p.120; 286, 121
	23 November to 7 December	Henry VIII and the queen left Windsor for Woking, with few others. Lords of the Privy Council were told to go home.	WS to The Vyne?	Nicolas, *Proceedings and Ordinances of the Privy Council,* Vol.VII, p.89
	3/4 December	WS makes his nuncupative will.	The Vyne	TNA Prob.11/29/107
	4/5 December	Death of WS. He requests burial in the Chapel of the Holy Ghost.	The Vyne	TNA Prob.11/29/107
	5 December.	Death of WS.	The Vyne	HRO 13M63/15. p.316
	7 December	Lord Maltravers informs the king from Calais that he received the message that WS had died.		*L&P Henry VIII,* 16, 317, p.149
	7 December	Henry VIII tells the Deputy of Calais that WS has died.		*L&P Henry VIII,* 16, 315, p.149
	7 December	Elis Gruffudd reports WS's death at The Vyne after being made to hand over his staff of office.		Elis Gruffudd, *Chronicle*, f.567v, trans. by D.Ifans
	10 December	The French ambassador in England wrote that WS was much esteemed in London and one of the few ancient captains left.		*L&P Henry VIII,* 16, 321, p.151
1541	9 January	WS's stall in the Garter Chapter was 'vacant'.		Anstis, *Reg. of Most Noble Order of the Garter,* Vol.1, pp.239,421

APPENDIX 2

Sandys' Manors and Lands *c.* 1490–1612

One measure of the Lord Sandys' substantial wealth is his property holdings. The table below is an attempt to list the manors and lands held by the family. In addition to more than 100 properties, they also had rents and advowsons that generated further income. This list was compiled from the references shown in the second table. It is difficult to construct a definitive list because of variations in names and spelling, and boundary changes between the counties and properties. Nevertheless, this list shows that the family received income from many properties, which lay in several counties in England – from Northamptonshire to Sussex. Hampshire is presented first because of the dominant number of properties; thereafter, the counties are listed in alphabetical order.

These holdings were largely acquired by William, Lord Sandys, the 1st Baron, in three tranches:

1) His father's legacy in 1496.
2) The legacy from the estate of Sir Reynold Bray, who died in 1503. He was uncle to Sandys' wife, Margery Bray, and much of his extensive holdings eventually came to Margery and her husband after the settlement of a contested will.
3) The exchange with Henry VIII of Sandys' property in Chelsea and Paddington for the dissolved priory of Mottisfont and its estates in Hampshire and Wiltshire.

Following Sandys' death in 1540 the estate was much reduced, firstly by his son, the 2nd Baron, Thomas, settling his father's debts, then by the 3rd Baron in settling his debts, especially his fine for participation in the 1601 Essex rebellion.

Manors and Lands	County	Date Sold	References (see table attached for details)
Alton	Hampshire	Pre-1612	G
Ayliffes in Andover			A, E
Andover			D, F, G, I, J
Appleshaw		Pre-1612	A, C, E, F, G
Barnardsbury		Pre-1612	G
Babridge, alias Bay Bridge		Pre-1612	A, D, E, F, G, H, I
Bentley			E, F, G, H, I, J
Byddesdeane			E
Bramley		Pre-1612	A, D, G
Broke next Cantterton			E
Broke next Compton			E
Broughton			C, E, F, G, H, I, J
Catherington, alias Catheryngton		Pre-1612	A, D, E, F, G, H, J
Chadbury			E
Chalton and Hillend			F, J
Cherleton by Andover			D, G
Cowick			G
Drayton			E
Durley			C, E, F, G, H, I, J
East Cholderton, alias Choldwarton, Chalverton			A, D, E, F, G, H, I, J
Eastdeane cum Huddstreet			C, E, F, H, I, J
Eldon alias Elden			J
Elinge		Pre-1612	G, H, I
Ellisfield			A, D, E, F, G, H, I, J
Empshot			D
Enham Knights or Enham militis			A, D, E, F, I, J
Faccombe			A, D, F, G, H, I, J
Flood		Pre-1612	B, D, G, J
Fyfefield		Pre-1612	A, D, E, G
Hattesford			E
Havant		Pre-1612	G, J
Kimpton			E
Kingeston			D
King's Enham, alias Enham Regis			A, F, G, H

Manors and Lands	County	Date Sold	References (see table attached for details)
King's Somborne or Sambourne Regis			E, F, G, H, I, J
Lockerly			E
Longstock			A, D, E, F, G, H, I, J
Longstock Harrington			E, F, G, H, I, J
Longstock cum Millstreete			C, E
Lords Land		Pre-1612	D, G
Mottisfont			C, D, E, F, G, H, I, J
Mottisfont Bentley			C
Mottisfont cum Ford			C
Netherden or Neterelden			C, E, F
Nether Wallop			C
Newton			E
North Ashley			A, D, E, G, I
Oakley			A
Olden			I
Park Pruet			G, I
Preston Candover		Pre-1612	A, D, E, F, G
Portsmouth		Pre-1612	G
Redenham			A, D, E, H, J
Romsey			E
Snoddington			A, E, G
Sandes Manor in Andover			A
Sherborne Cowdray, The Vyne		1653	A, D, F, G, H, I, J
Sherborn St John		1653	E, F, G, H, I
Southampton			D, E, G
Stockbridge			C, E, I, J
Sombourne			C, I
Someborne Parva			D, I, J
Somebourne Regis			F, H, I
Tymberbury, alias Timbury, Timsbury			C, E, J
Upclatford			C, D, E, F, G, H
Up Sombourne			C
Upton		Pre-1612	G, E, G
Winchester, alias Winton			D, E, G
Woodcote			E

Sandys' Manors and Lands c. *1490–1612*

Manors and Lands	County	Date Sold	References (see table attached for details)
Bray	Berkshire		D, G, J
Buntingbury (Winkfield)		1546	B, D, G
Burkfield alias Burghfield?			D, G
Buckhurst		Pre-1612	G
Brocas (in Clewer)		1546	B, D, G
Clewer		1546	B, D, G
Choldrington	Berkshire/Wiltshire	Pre-1612	E
Charleton iuxta Hungerford		Pre-1612	G
Colmansmore			E
Cookham		Pre-1612	G
Crutchfield in Bray		1577	B, D
Dedworth Maunsell		1546	B
Fossebury			E
Foxley		1639	B, D, G, I, J
Haywards (in Sonning)		1609	B
Hinton Pipard	Formerly in Wiltshire	1606	B, D, E, G
Hopgrass (in Hungerford)		1606	B
Hurst		Pre-1512	D, G
Madenham			D
Merton with Burbage & Woolton			E, F, H, I
Remenham (Remischen in 1st Baron Sandys' will)		Pre-1612	B, D, G, H
Sandhurst			D
Sonning			D, G
Vialls			E
White Waltham in Sonning and Hurste		Pre-1612	D, E, G
Willesford			E, G, I, J
Winkell			D
Great Rissington	Gloucestershire	1571	B, D, G
Queen Hoo	Hertfordshire	1536	B
Chelsea	Middlesex	1536	B, G
Paddington		1536	B
Barnsbury		1540	B
Steane	Northamptonshire	1551	B, D, G
Hinton		1551	B, D, G

Manors and Lands	County	Date Sold	References (see table attached for details)
Wells	Somerset		D
Wandesworth	Surrey		H
Berkham	Sussex		D
Broadwater		1605	B, D, E, G
Chermanbury alias Shermanbury			A, D, G, I
Crawley		Pre-1612	G
Dorington			E
Fletching		Pre-1612	G
Jevington		Pre-1612	D, E, G
Kingston Bowsey			A, D, G, I, J
Knill			E
Lampham (Laumpham in 1st Baron Sandys' will)		Pre-1612	D, E, G
Leybrooke			E, G
North Tisted		Pre-1612	H
Shermanbury alias Chermanbury			A, D, G, I, J
Terringe		Pre-1612	E
Worthing			E
Illmington	Warwickshire	1550	B, D
Burbridge alias Burbage	Wiltshire		C, J
Barwick St James			H, I, J
Marton alias Merton	Hampshire/ Wiltshire		C, I, J
Stratton St Margaret			D, E, F, G, I, J
Willeford alias Willesford			D, E, H, I
Wolton alias Wootton			C, H, J
	Unplaced		
Bentfield			G
Cumeton			G
Fletching		Pre-1612	G
George lands			G
Mounthyde			G
Periton		Pre-1612	G

REF.	Details
A	*Cal.Inq.PM*, Henry VII, Vol.11, 1497, 1245, 1246
B	The Bray inheritance 1503; Condon, M., in *Profit, Piety and the Professions in Later Medieval England*, pp.160–62, 1990
C	Mottisfont Grant 1536: HRO 13M63/107
D	William Sandys' Will 1540: TNA Prob 11/29/107
E	*Cal.Pat.Rolls*, 2 Elizabeth, 22 July 1560, p.329
F	Rental of Sandys' Manors 1586–1611: HRO 13M63/162
G	Summary of Sandys' Deeds 1612: HRO 13M63/15,
H	Pleading against 3rd Lord Sandys 1596: TNA C2/Eliz/A3/16
I	Declaration of Lord Sandys' Lands, 1598: TNA SP12/269 79/80
J	An Account of Sandys Lands 1684: HRO 23M58/35

APPENDIX 3

Transcription of William Sandys' Will, December 1540

Taken from the copy in the Probate Registers of the Prerogative Court of Canterbury at TNA (TNA Prob.11/29/107).

William Sandys' will is a very important document in terms of understanding his family connections, property and attitudes. Although it is difficult to extract precise details of properties and bequests because of variations in names and spelling, and subsequent boundary changes between counties and properties, both the will and the lists compiled from it indicate the family's main properties and sources of income.

The introductory explanations and careful checking of the transcript of Sandys' will, as recorded in the Probate Register, have been undertaken by Dr Susan J. Davies, who is skilled in reading, understanding and editing manuscript records, including testamentary and probate records.

The Format of this Will in the Probate Register

This is a 'nuncupative' will, which is a will made by oral declaration when the testator was not expected to live long and in a weak physical (or highly infectious) state, and unable to sign a written will. Such wills were not uncommon in medieval and early modern times and were accepted by the courts as long as there were sufficient witnesses to the oral declaration who could testify to the accuracy of the written form, which was produced as soon as possible after the oral declaration – often on the same or following day. The procedure to seek probate usually took longer, as time was allowed for the discovery of any other will made by the deceased.

This copy, from the Probate Registers of the Prerogative Court of Canterbury, is in three sections, and rather unusual because the section containing the details that are usually at the beginning of a will is actually the second section in the register copy, with a marginal note describing it as '*Testamentum eiusdem*' (the will of the same). Starting with 'In the name of God Amen', the testator commits his soul to God and his body for burial at Basingstoke, makes financial bequests to two churches and for his 'forgotten tithes', declares that he is of sound mind, and makes personal gifts to individuals. The executors and witnesses are also named in this section, but are usually found at the end of a will.

The first section in the register copy is a detailed list of William Sandys' wishes for the disposition of his property and bequests for his staff, and starts with the heading 'This is the last will of me William Sandes...', alongside a marginal note describing it as '*Ultima voluntat' domini Willelmi Sand*' (the last wishes of lord Willam Sandes). It ends with the statement that William Sandys has applied his seal. This section raises the question whether it may have been written a little earlier – but we shall never know.

The third section is the usual probate note, which would be added to the original documents when the process was complete. It reveals that the will was presented for probate in May 1542, more than twelve months after William Sandys died, and this was done by a procurator (proxy), who was a notary public, on behalf of the executors named in the will. Notaries public (now called public notaries) were lawyers who functioned in most legal courts in Europe, but in England and Wales were largely confined to the ecclesiastical courts.

Medieval and early modern wills are rarely easy to understand, especially when the testator held substantial property and had many family links as well as public roles. One reason is that wills were the business of the ecclesiastical courts until 1858, but the tenure of land was a matter for the secular courts and various rules of descent. It was also common practice for families with significant landholdings to arrange transfers in advance of the death of the main landholder, so the will does not indicate which individuals have benefited in this way. Sandys' will shows clear commitment to ensure that his wishes were carried out and that all beneficiaries received their benefits. It was also carefully planned and suggests genuine care for his family and staff.[1]

Editorial Notes

The original spelling and use of capitals (with a few exceptions) is retained in this transcript, but a single capital F has been used instead of a double lower-case 'ff', which was the old way of representing a capital 'F'. Standard abbreviation methods used at the time have been extended, and minimal modern punctuation has been used where breaks are obvious to assist the reader. Line numbers have aso been inserted.

It is important to note that copies of documents included in probate registers often contain small errors in spelling – especially where the original documents may have been difficult to read or rapidly written. Personal and property names are particularly affected (and vary within the copy), and are therefore difficult to relate to known names, as is the case in this copy of William Sandys' will.

Transcript

Page 1

(A) **Marginal note: Ultima voluntat' domini Willelmi Sand'** ***(the last wishes/ will of Lord William Sandys).*** [The first line is written in large flourished capital letters.]

1. THIS YS THE LAST WILL OF ME WILLIAM SANDES, KNIGHT, LORDE
2. Sandes, Chamberleyn to our sovereign Lord Henry the Eight, king of England and Fraunce,
3. defensour of the faith, lorde of Ireland and in erthe supreme hedd of the Churche of England made and
4. by me declared the thirde daye of December the xxxij [32] yere of our sayd soveraigne lordes reigne as to the
5. disposicion of as moche of all my londes, tenementes, medows, pastures, woodes, underwooddes, rents, reversions and
6. services, and all other hereditamentes set, lying and being within the realme of Englonde as shall extend and
7. amounte unto the yerely value of two partes of the same. In three partes to be devided in certaintie and by
8. speciall devisies as it may be knowen in severaltie according to the statute lately therof made in the seyd
9. xxxij[ti] [32nd] yere of the reign of our sayd soveraigne lorde, that ys to saye, whereas I myselfe stond and am
10. lawfully ceased [seised] of estatute of inherytaunce of and in the late priory of Mottesfounte and of landes
11. tenementes and hereditamentes lately belonging and apperteyninge unto the said late priory within the counties
12. of Southampton and Wiltes', and of and in the manors of Willefford and Stretton Sancte Margarete
13. within the said countie of Wiltes, and in the manours of Steyn and Hynton within the countie of
14. Northampton, and of and in the Manours of Ilmyngdon within the county of Warr', and of and in the
15. manor of Jevington within the countie of Sussex, amounting in the hole to the clere yerely value and rent
16. over and above all charges and reprisez of CClxxij li. iiij s. [£272.4s.], whiche ys the thirde parte and a greate deale more
17. of all and every of my sayd manours, landes, tenementes and hereditamentes sett, lying, and being within the Realme of
18. Englonde or els where being devyded in three partes without any diminucion, dower, frawde, coven, charge
19. or abbrigement of any of the said iij[de] parte or of the full profietes thereof. My full mynde and last will

20. ys that this my last will shall not extend to or touch any parte or parcell thereof, but that it shall hole
21. remayn and abide unbequethed and unwilled according to the tenour of the sayd late estatute made in

Page 2

1. the said xxxij[ti] [32nd] yere of our sayd soveraigne lordes reign. Item where as I am seased in my demeane as a fefee of
2. and in the manours, landes, tenementes and hereditamentes called Brodwater, Kingeston Bouncye Bourne, Laumpham,
3. Berkham Shermanbury, with their appurtenaunces set, lying and being in the county of Sussex, and of and in
4. the manours landes tenementes and hereditamentes called Long stocke, Upclatford, Enham Militis, Andover, Choldwarton,
5. cum membris Preston Candover, Ellefeld, Babrige Caterington. The manors of Floode, Faccombe, North Assheldey,
6. Civitas Winton Bramley. The manor of Vine, otherwise called Sherborne Cowdre, Empshote and Kingeston
7. with their appurtenaunces sett, lying and being within the said Countie of Southampton, and of and in the manours,
8. landes, tenementes and hereditamentes called Cluer Buntyngbury. Brockes Winckull, Madenham and Cockham,
9. Estging lordes, Londe Hinton piperd Remicham Bray, Sonning, and Hurst Burkfeild and White Waltham Foxley
10. Sandhurst with their appurtenaunces sett, lying and being in the countie of Berkes'. And of and in the manours
11. landes and tenementes and hereditmentes callyd Ryssingdon Magna within the countie of Glouc' and of and in
12. the manours, tenementes and hereditamentes called Well', within the said county of Somers'. My full mind ys and
13. by thies presentes I the sayd William Sandes, Knight, lorde Sandes, will and ordeyn that my sone John Sandes shall
14. have and enyoie as moche of all and every thes our foresayd manours, landes, tenementes and other hereditamentes last
15. recited other then the said manours, landes, tenementes and hereditamentes abovesaid reserved and forprised out of
16. this my last will at his ellecion, as shall amount unto the yerely value of Fiftye poundes yerely unto such
17. tyme as my sone and heire apparaunt Thomas Sandes his heirs or assigns by his sufficient deid
18. in the lawe shall have graunted unto my said sone John Sandes one annuytie or yerely rent of Fiftye
19. poundes goyng out of my sayd manour of Cluer with thappurtenaunces, to have and perceyve the same to him

20. and his assignes for terme of his lyfe, with sufficient clause of distresse to be conteyned in the sayd
21. deid as shalbe devysed by the lernyd counsell of the sayd John Sandes. Item yt is my full mind and by
22. thies presentes I the said William Sandes, knight, lorde Sandes, will and ordeyn that Sir Humfrey Foster,
23. knight, and dame Elizabeth his wyfe and the longer lyver of them shall have and enyoie asmoche
24. of all and every thes aforesayd manours, landes, tenementes and other hereditamentes last recyted other than
25. the said manours, landes tenementes and hereditamentes above reserved and forprised out of this my last wyll
26. and the manours, landes, tenementes and hereditamentes that my sayd sonne John Sandes shall take the
27. eleccion of or shalbe charged unto hym by my sayd eldest sone Thomas as is aforesaid at their
28. eleccion and at theleccion of the longest lyver of them as shall amounte unto the yerely value of
29. xiij li. vj s. viij d. [£13.6.8.] untill such tyme as my said sonne as heire apparaunte Thomas Sandes as is aforseid,
30. his heires or assignes by his sufficient deid in the lawe shall have graunted unto the sayd Sir Humfrey
31. and Elizabeth his wyfe one annuitie or yerely rent of xiij li. vj s. viij d. [£13.6.8.] going out of my sayd manour
32. of Upclatford with appurtenaunces, to have and perceyve the same to them and their assignes for terme of
33. their lyves and the longest lyver of them with sufficient clause of distres to be contayned in the sayd
34. deid as shall be devised by the lernyd counsell of the sayd Sir Humphrey Foster and Dame Elizabeth or the
35. longest lyved of them. Item it is also my full mynde and by thies presentes I the sayd William Sandes, Knight,
36. lord Sandes, will and ordayn that William Sandes now one of the sonnes of my said sonne and heir
37. apparaunte Thomas Sandes shall at his full age of xxj [21] yeres have and enyoie asmoche of all and
38. every thes aforesaid manours, landes and tenementes and hereditamentes last recited, other than the said manours,
39. tenementes and hereditaments abovesaid reserved and forprised out of this my last wyll, and the sayd manours,
40. landes, tenementes and hereditamentes that my sayd son John Sandes and the manours, lands,
41. tenementes and hereditamentes that the said Sir Humfrey Foster, knight, and my lady his wyfe shall
42. take thelleccion of or shalbe charged unto them by my sayd eldyst sonne Thomas as aforesayd

43. at his elleccion as shall amount unto the yerely value of Twenty pounds, unto such tyme as my
44. sayd sonne and heir apparaunte Thomas Sandes his heirs and assigns by his sufficient dead
45. in the Lawe shall have graunted unto the sayd William Sandes one annuytie or yerely rent of
46. xx li. by the yere going out of my sayd manour of Kingeston Boune with thappurtenaunces to have and
47. perceyve the same to hym or his assignes for terme of his lyfe with sufficient clause of distres to be
48. conteyned in the sayd dead as shalbe devysed by the lernyd counsell of the sayd William Sandes. Item
49. my full mind ys and by thies presentes I the said William Sandes knight lord Sandes will and ordeyn
50. that John Sandes, called the son of Sir Richard Sandes, knyght, deceased, have and perceyve during his
51. lyfe one annuytie or yerely rent of Tenne pounds out of my said manour of Brodwater and that
52. Richard Gifford, secunde sonne of Sir William Gifford Knight, have and perceyve during his life one
53. annuytie or yerely rent of Tenne pounds out of my said manour of Brodwater. And also that
54. Humfrey Barkeley, called the son of Sir Morrys Barkley, knyght, deceased, late lord Barkeley,
55. have and perceyve during his lyfe one annuytie or yerely rent of vj li. xiij s. iiij d. [£6.13.4.] out of the sayd manour
56. of Brodwater. And that in lyke maner my servaunt Richard Clutton have and perceyve during his lyfe one
57. annuytie or yerely rent of Twenty pounds out of the said manour of Brodwater. And that my servaunte
58. Peter Swyft have and perceyve during his lyfe one annuytie or yerely rent of liij s. iiij d. [53s. 4d.] out of
59. my sayd landes, tenementes and hereditamentes called Sandhurst. And that my servaunte John Bourne shall have
60. and perceyve during his lyfe one annuytie or yerely rent of lxvi s. viij d. [66s. 8d.] out of my sayd manour of
61. Brabrige. Item I will that my servauntes William Cokeson, John Cely, Roger Bradfeld, John Lynerlond,
62. Frauncis Millett, Christofer Haner, William Gunter, and every of them during their lyves and the

Page 3

1. lives of every of theym shall severallie have and perceyve one annuytie or yerely rent of liij s. iiii d. [53s. 4d.] out of
2. my said manours, landes, tenementes, hereditamentes called Enham Militis et Andover. And also I will that

3. my servauntes Thomas Harrys, Richard Dier, John Corbuk, James Morton, Henry Barwicke, William
4. Grace, William Villet, George Arkyns, Thristrame Asheley, Thomas Breis, Edward Musgrave
5. Peter Hilling, John Colly, Alice Hart and Richard Berd, and every of them severally have and
6. perceyve during their lyves and the lyves of every of theym one annuitie or yerely rent of xl s. [40s.] going out
7. of my said manour of Rumpham. And that my servauntes John Daniell, Nicholas Dudnall, Richard Fuller,
8. John Cooke, and every of them severally have and perceyve during their lyves and the lyves of every of them
9. one annuytie or yerely rent of xxvj s. viij d. [26s. 8d.] doing out of my said manour of Katerington and that my
10. servaunte William Underwood have and perceyve yerely out of my said manour of Vine otherwise called
11. Sherbourne Cowdre one annuytie or yerely rent of fyve poundes for term of his lyfe and that all and
12. every my said sevauntes named in this my present will shall severally distreyne in their aforesayd manours,
13. landes, tenementes, and hereditaments whereout the sayd annuyties be severally going for every one of
14. their sayd annuyties or yerely rents being behynd as often as the said annuytie or annuyties
15. and every of them shulde be behynd as often as the sayd annuytie or annuyties and every of them
16. shalbe behinde unpayde at the yearly feastes of Saynt Michell Tharchangel and the Annunciation of our
17. Lady, at whiche feastes I will yt shall be payable by even porcions. Also I will that my Executors
18. of all thies my manours, landes, tenementes and hereditamentes other then suche as I have forprised to be in
19. no parcell of this my wyll shall clerly take and perceyve of the yerely profyttes comyng and growing
20. of the same as shall remayn over and above all and every of the said annuyties and yerely rentes
21. yerely contented and payd towardes the payment of my dettes and contentation of my creditors unto
22. suche tyme as the sayd dettes be fully contented and payd and no longer. Provided alwayes that
23. yf my sayd servauntes and every of them cannot severally enyoie all and every theyr sayd annuyties in maner
24. and forme as I have declared by this my last wyll, that then they and every of them severally shall

25. have and enyoie all and every these aforesaid manours, landes, tenementes and hereditamentes wherout their
26. sayd annuytie ?er severally going, unto suche tyme as my said sonne and heire apparaunt shall have
27. assured them and every of them there sayd annuyties for terme of all and every of their lyves by his
28. owne graunte or grauntes in lyke maner and forme by hym to them and every of them to be graunted
29. as ys conteyned within this my last will. In witness wherof I have sett my seale the daye and yere above wrytten

(B) **Marginal note: Testamentum eiusdem [will of the same]**

1. IN THE NAME OF GOD AMEN. The Saturdaye next after the feast of Seynt Andrew the
   [NB feast of St Andrew is 30 November – In 1540, it was a Tuesday so the following Saturday was 4 Dec]
2. Appostell, viz the … [blank] day of December in the year of our Lord a thousand fyve hundred and fourtie
3. and of the Reigne of our Soveraigne lorde Henry VIII by the Grace of God King of Englande and
4. of Fraunce, Lord of Ireland, and in yerthe immediatly under God of the Churche of England
5. Supreme hedd xxxij[ti] [32nd]. Sir William Sandes Knyght of the noble order of the Garter/lorde Sandes
6. and Chambleyn to our soveraigne lorde, being of good mynde and memory made his testament
7. nuncupative [oral] in maner and forme folowing. First he gave and bequethd his soule to Almightie
8. God and his body to be buryed in the Chapell of tholy gost in Basingstok, to the whiche chapell
9. he gave and bequeath xl s. [40*s*]. Item he gave and bequethed to the parishe church of Shirbourne Saint
10. John *pro decemis oblitis* [for forgotten tithes] xl s. [40*s*] Item he gave and bequethed to his eldyst sonne Thomas his best
11. gowne of velvit. Item to Sir Humfrey Foster, knight, his next best gown. Item to Sir William Essex,
12. knight. his thirde best gown. Item to Walter Chalcott a gown and a cote of damaske. Item to
13. Smyth the kinges servant a cote of velvet. Item to Barkley his servant a cote of velvet. Item to
14. Marmaduk his servant a cote of clothe garded with velvet. The resydue of all and singular his goodes
15. and cattalles wheresoever they were he gave and bequethed holy unto Thomas his sone and heire

16. apparaunt and Elizabeth his wyf whome he ordenyd and constituted Executors of his sayd
17. Testament nuncupative, and required and charged them to see his dettes contentyd and payd and his
18. sayd Testament nuncupative performyd and fulfilled. Then and there being present Sir Humfre Foster,
19. Sir William Essex, knightes, Walter Chalcott, Richard Gyfford and others.

(C) **Probate Note** (in Latin, as usual until 1733. Some standard elements are heavily abbreviated, as was usual practice.)

1. PROBATUM fuit testamentum unacum ultima voluntate predict' coram domino apud London' decimo die mensis Maij anno
2. domini millesimo quingentesimo quadragesimo secundo [10 May 1542]. Juramento Roberti Alen Notarii Publici procurator Executorum
3. in ?huiusmodi testamento nominatorum. Ac approbatum ac insinuatum. Commissaque fuit administracio omnium et singulorum
4. bonorum, jurium, et creditorum dicti defuncti prefatis executoribus. De bene [et fideliter administrando....] etc. Ac de pleno et fideli Inventario etc.
5. conficiend'. Necnon de plano et vero compoto redd'. Ad Sancta dei Evangelia in persona dicti procuratoris jurato.

English Translation of Key Points

This will, together with the last wishes aforesaid, was proved at London before the [presiding] lord on 10 May Anno Domini 1542 by the oath of Robert Alen, Notary Public, procurator of the executors named in the will. The administration of all and singular the goods, rights, and credits of the said deceased was committed to the said executors and sworn on the Holy Gospels by the procurator. The will should be administered well and faithfully etc., and a full and faithful Inventory together with a clear and true account were required.

Note

1. *Perceyve* is an old English word for 'hold' (see OED shorter version).
2. HRO 13M63/15 states that William Sandys died on 5 December 1540.

People in Sandys' Will

Relatives and Friends	**Description**	**Benefit**	**Notes**
John Sandys	Son	£50 per year	Annuity from Clewer Manor
Thomas Sandys	Son and heir apparent	Residue, and Sandys' best gown of velvet	Heir to residue of estate. Named executor in Sandys' will dated 4 December 1540
Elizabeth	Wife of Thomas Sandys		Executrix named in will
Sir Humfrey Foster, knight		£13 6*s* 8*d* residue plus next best gown	Witness to will, beneficiary in an annuity from Upclatford Manor
Dame Elizabeth, wife of Sir Humfrey		£13 6*s* 8*d*	Sandys' daughter. Annuity from Upclatford Manor
William Sandys	Son of Thomas Sandys and a minor	£20 per year	Annuity from Kingeston Borne Manor
John Sandys	Said to be son of Sir Richard Sandys, knight	£10 per year	RS was WS' younger brother. Annuity from Broadwater Manor
Richard Gifford	Second son of Sir William Gifford, knight	£10 per year	Witness to will, beneficiary in annuity from Broadwater Manor
Humfrey Barkeley	Said to be son of Sir Morris Barkeley, knight, late Lord Barkeley	£6 13*s* 4*d* per year	Annuity from Broadwater Manor
Sir William Essex	Knight	Third best gown	Witness to will and beneficiary. His son, Thomas, married Margaret, daughter of Lord William Sandys.[2]
Walter Chalcott	?	A gown and coat of damask	Witness to will and beneficiary
Staff			
Richard Clutton or Clotton	Steward to Lord Sandys	£20 per year	Mentioned in Lisle Letters.[3] Granted annuity from Broadwater Manor. Wrote to Cromwell in April 1535 apologising for the upset caused by Clotton going to a sermon by Hugh Latimer.[4]

Relatives and Friends	Description	Benefit	Notes
Peter Swift	Servant, was paid for a captain and 106 soldiers at Guînes for a month in 1540.[5]	54*s* 4*d* per year	Annuity from Sandhurst Manor
John Bourne	Servant	66*s* 8*d* per year	Annuity from Brabridge Manor
William Cokeson	Servant	53*s* per year	Annuity from Enham Militis (Enham Knights) of Andover
John Cely	Servant	53*s* per year	Annuity from Enham Militis of Andover
Roger Bradfield	Servant	53*s* per year	Annuity from Enham Militis of Andover
John Lynerlond	Servant	53*s* per year	Annuity from Enham Militis of Andover
Francis Millett	Servant	53*s* per year	Annuity from Enham Militis of Andover
Christopher Haner	Servant	53*s* per year	Annuity from Enham Militis of Andover
William Gunter	Servant	53*s* per year	Annuity from Enham Militis of Andover
Thomas Harrys	Servant	40*s* per year	Annuity from Manor of Repenham
Richard Dier	Servant	40*s* per year	Annuity from Remenham
John Corbuk	Servant	40*s* per year	Annuity from Remenham Manor
James Morton	Servant	40*s* per year	Annuity from Remenham Manor
Henry Barwick	Servant	40*s* per year	Annuity from Remenham Manor
William Grace	Servant	40*s* per year	Annuity from Remenham Manor
William Villet	Servant	40*s* per year	Annuity from Remenham Manor
George Arkyns	Servant	40*s* per year	Annuity from Remenham Manor
Thristrame Asheley,	Servant	40*s* per year	Annuity from Remenham Manor
Thomas Breis	Servant	40*s* per year	Annuity from Remenham Manor
Edward Musgrave	Servant	40*s* per year	Annuity from Remenhan Manor

Relatives and Friends	Description	Benefit	Notes
Peter Hilling	Servant	40*s* per year	Annuity from Remenham Manor
John Colly	Servant	40*s* per year	Annuity from Remenham Manor
Alice Hart	Servant	40*s* per year	Annuity from Remenham Manor
Richard Berd	Servant	40*s* per year	Annuity from Remenham Manor
John Daniell	Servant	26*s* 8*d* per year	Annuity from Catherington Manor
Nicholas Dudnall	Servant	26*s* 8*d* per year	Annuity from Catherington Manor
Richard Fuller	Servant	26*s* 8*d* per year	Annuity from Catherington Manor
John Cooke	Servant	26*s* 8*d* per year	Annuity from Catherington Manor
William Underwood	Servant	£5 per year	Annuity from Vyne Manor
Smyth	The King's servant	A velvet coat	Mentioned in will
Barkely	Smyth's servant	A velvet coat	Mentioned in will
Marmaduk	Smyth's servant	A cloth coat garded with velvet	Mentioned in will

Endnotes

Introduction

1. Harrison, *Annals of an Old Manor House*, 1893
2. Brewer, *L&P Henry VIII*, 1864
3. St Clare Byrne, *The Lisle Letters*, 1981, 1983
4. National Library of Wales (NLW) MS 5276D & 3054D
5. Ives, *The Life and Death of Anne Boleyn*, 2004, p.155
6. Weir, *Henry VIII - King and Court*, 2002, p.133
7. Gunn, *Charles Brandon: Henry's VIII's Closest Friend*, 2015, p.90
8. Guy, *Tudor England*, 2013, p.126
9. Wilson, *In the Lion's Court*, 2002, pp.217, 295
10. Lipscomb, *A Visitor's Companion to Tudor England*, 2012, p.7
11. St Clare Byrne, *The Lisle Letters*, 1981, Vol.3, p.406
12. *Cal.Pat.R.* 1377–88. p.263
13. BL Harl. MS.2169, f.37b, p.50; *Cal.Pat.R.* 1374-1377, p.222,
14. Brewer, ed., *L&P Henry VIII*, 3.1, 1130
15. Barker, *Agincourt: the King, the Campaign, the Battle*, 2005, p.3

1. William, Lord Sandys: His Ancestors and the Medieval Vyne, Hampshire

1. Peter de Coudray, The Charter of Confirmation lease mounted on the Vyne Ante Chapel wall
2. *HRO 72M85/4/5/6*
3. Mitchell-Fox and Page, ed., *The Hampshire Tax List of 1327*, 2014
4. *HRO 13M63/16* pp.295-6
5. Barber, ed., *Life and Campaigns of the Black Prince,.... including Chandos Herald's Life of the Black Prince*, 1997, p.114
6. *Ibid.*, p.129
7. *Ibid.*, p.80
8. *Ibid.*, p.129; *Cal.Pat.R. 1374-1377*, pp.222, 295
9. Cited by Jones, *Knight: the Warrior and World of Chivalry*, 2011, p.129
10. Hewitt, *The Black Princes Expedition of 1355-1357*, 2004, pp.46-49

11. Froissart, *Chronicles of England, France and Spain*, 1857, p.168
12. Hewitt, *Cheshire under the Three Edwards*, 1967, p.68
13. Duffus Hardy, *Syllabus of documents known as 'Rymer's Foedera'*, Vol.1, 1066-1377, 1869, p.1011
14. *Cal.Inq.PM.10* Ric. II, 6 May 1387, 398/399 pp.144-145
15. Mortimer, *The Time Traveller's Guide to Medieval England*, 2009, p.37; *Cal. Pat.R.* 361-62, Dec.28 p.274
16. *Cal.Close R.*, Edw. 1374-1377, 43; *Cal.Close R.*, Edw. 1374-1377, 269; Roskell, Clark & Rawcliffe eds., *The History of Parliament: The House of Commons, 1386-1421*, at historyofparliamentonline.org
17. *Cal.Pat.R.1374-1377*, pp.222, 228, 295
18. TNA E 403/459
19. TNA E101/511/2 translated by Dr. S. Davies
20. TNA E101/511/20
21. HRO 31 M57/48; *Cal.Close R.*20 Ric. II (1397) p.95
22. *Cal.Pat.R.*1374-77, p.263
23. *Cal.Close R.*1374-1377, 1376, p.347
24. Roskell, Clark & Rawcliffe eds., *History of Parliament: The House of Commons, 1386-1421*, at: historyofparliamentonline.org
25. Green, 'Household and Retinue of Edward the Black Prince', 1998, Appendix 2
26. Emerson, *The Black Prince*, 1976, p.82
27. Living, *Records of Romsey Abbey*, 1908, pp.166/67
28. *Cal.Pat.R. 1377-1381*, 17 Sept.1377, p.22
29. *Cal.Pat.R.* 1377-1381, p.42
30. Saul, *Richard II*, 1997, p.33; Froissart, *Chronicles of England, France and Spain*, 1857, p.225
31. BL Stowe MS 440 p.20, 11 old pagination
32. Saul, *Richard II*, 1997, p.34; TNA E364/16 as translated by Dr. S. Davies; BL Stowe MS 440 p.11 old, 17 new; Roskell, Clark & Rawcliffe eds., *History of Parliament: The House of Commons, 1386-1421*, at historyofparliamentonline.org
33. *Cal.Fine R.*, Rich.II, 1377-1383, p.144
34. Himsworth, *Winchester College Muniments*, Vol. II, 1983, 2207, p.47
35. TNA E101/32/27 translated by Dr. C.Lloyd Morgan; *Cal.Pat.R.*, 1377-91, p.385
36. TNA E101/38/27
37. Morgan, *War and Society in Cheshire*, 1987, p.170
38. BL Stowe MS 440, p.14 old 20 new; TNA E101/38/27
39. Roskell, Clark & Rawcliffe eds., *History of Parliament: The House of Commons, 1386-1421*, at historyofparliamentonline.org
40. Saul, *Richard II*, 1997, p.33; *Cal.Pat.R.*1381-85, p.69
41. Stapleton, ed., *Conflict in the Community in Southern England*, 1992, p.xv
42. *Ibid.*, p.9
43. Green, 'Household and Retinue of Edward the Black Prince', 1998, Appendix 2, p.180; Roskell, Clark & Rawcliffe eds., *History of Parliament: The House of Commons, 1386-1421*, at historyofparliamentonline.org
44. *Shorter Oxford English Dictionary*, 1933
45. *Cal.Pat.R.* 1382, pp.327, 425; Mortimer, *The Time Traveller's Guide to Medieval England*, 2009 p.217

46. *Cal.Pat.R.*, 1386, pp.177, 258
47. *Cal.Pat.R*, 1390, p.201
48. HRO 31 M57/42, translated by Dr. S. Davies
49. James, *The Black Death in Hampshire*, Hampshire Papers No. 18, 1999, p.9
50. Harrison, *Annals of an Old Manor House*, 1893, p.23
51. *Cal.Inq.PM.* Ed. III, 1349, p.187
52. Fairbrother, *Faccombe Netherton*, 1990, Figures 3.11, 3.12, 3.13, pp.74, 76, 77
53. HRO 31M57/43 translated by Dr. S. Davies
54. Wilson, *The Vyne Archaeological Project 1996-1998*, 1998, Vol.I, Project Summary, p.25
55. Toulmin Smith ed., *Itinerary of John Leland*, Vol. II, p.8
56. Wilson, *The Vyne Archaeological Project 1996-1998*, 1998, Vol.II, The External Archaeology, p.49
57. TNA E301/51
58. *Cal.Pat.R.*, 1387, p.323
59. *Cal.Close R.*1392-96, p.116
60. *Cal.Close R.*1385-89, p.639
61. Roskell, Clark & Rawcliffe eds., *History of Parliament: The House of Commons, 1386-1421*, at historyofparliamentonline.org
62. *Cal.Fine R.* 3 July 1395, p.179
63. Roskell, Clark & Rawcliffe eds., *History of Parliament: The House of Commons, 1386-1421*, at historyofparliamentonline.org
64. *Cal.Inq.PM.* Henry V, Vols.1-5, 1413-1418, p.328
65. Roskell, Clark & Rawcliffe eds., *History of Parliament: The House of Commons, 1386-1421*, 1993
66. *Ibid.*, historyofparliamentonline.org, TNA C139 26/4 8 translated by Dr. S. Davies
67. *Cal.Inq.PM.* Henry V, Vol.7-14, 1404-13, p.402
68. Search 'Walter Sandes' at research.reading.ac.uk
69. *Ibid.*, 'Walter Sandes'
70. Roskell, Clark & Rawcliffe eds., *History of Parliament: The House of Commons, 1376-1435*, at historyofparliamentonline.org (Accessed March 2018); TNA E101/43/32, m.1
71. TNA E101/69/5/435; BL Stowe 440, 29 April 1415, p.23
72. TNA E101/69/5/435
73. TNA E101/44/30, roll 1
74. Curry, *Battle of Agincourt*, 2009; Mortimer. *Henry V's Year of Glory*, 2010; Barker, *Agincourt*, 2005
75. BL Stowe 440, 8 February 1416, p.28; TNA E101/70/2/609
76. Search 'Walter Sandes' at research.reading.ac.uk
77. *Cal.Pat.R.* 6 April 1422, p.443
78. *Cal.Pat.R.* 20 June 1421 323
79. Roskell, Clark & Rawcliffe eds., *History of Parliament: The House of Commons*, at historyofparliamentonline.org
80. *Ibid.* (Accessed March 2018)
81. *Cal.Pat.R.* 1 May 1434, p.354
82. Green, 'Household and Retinue of Edward the Black Prince', 1998, Appendix 1. p.20; Burrows, *The Family of Brocas of Beaurepaire and Roche Court*, 1886, p.146

83. HRO 13M63/15 p.263-6
84. HRO 13M63/15 p.268
85. *Cal.Inq.PM.* 23 June 4 Henry VII, 395, p.168
86. *Cal.Close R.*1435, 26 October, p.8
87. Roskell, Clark & Rawcliffe eds., *History of Parliament: The House of Commons*, at historyofparliamentonline.org (Accessed March 2018)
88. Nicolas, *Testamenta Vetusta*, 1826, p.249
89. Himsworth, *Winchester College Muniments*, Vol II, 1983, 2473, p.64
90. TNA C139/26/48
91. Toulmin Smith ed., *Itinerary of John Leland*, 1964, Vol. II, p.7
92. *VCH Hampshire*, Vol.4, pp.359-365
93. *Cal.Fine R.* Henry VI, Vol.17, 1437-1445, p.197; TNA C139/107/35
94. Himsworth, *Winchester College Muniments*, Vol.II, 1984, 2486, p.65
95. *Cal.Fine R.* Henry VI, Vol.17 1437-1445, p.300; *Cal.Pat.R.*1443, pp.214, 278; TNA C139/26/48
96. TNA C139/181/75
97. TNA C1513-10 and 20
98. HRO 37M85/13 FR1
99. Spaul, *Andover: A Historical Portrait*, 1977, p.24; HRO 37M8513-FR1n; HRO 37M85/18 AH/10
100. Williams ed., *Early Churchwardens Accounts of Hampshire*, 1913, p.9
101. St George & Squibb, *Visitation of Hampshire and the Isle of Wight 1686*, 1991, p.226
102. HRO 46M74/P293
103. Private Communication, Portcullis Pursuivant at the College of Arms, to John Jenkins, 27/01/2017
104. HRO 31M57 63/15 p.316
105. HRO 31M57/652 p.57
106. Madden and Bulkeley, *Collectanea Topographica et Genealogica*, 1834, Vol.1, pp.313, 314
107. Cokayne, *The Complete Peerage*, Vol.VII, 1896, p.252
108. TNA Prob.11/11
109. Crawford, ed. *Household Books of John Howard, Duke of Norfolk*, 1982, App. p.xliii
110. TNA C1/109/3, C1109/5, C1513/19 and 20, C1186/88
111. Madden and Bulkeley, *Collectanea Topographica et Genealogica*, 1834, Vol.1, pp.22, 299
112. *Cal.Inq.PM.* H.VII, Vol. II 1499, p.331; Brewer, ed., *L&P Henry VIII*, Vol.1, p.151
113. Stapleton, *Plumpton Correspondence*, 1839, p.269
114. Gill, *Richard III and Buckingham's Rebellion*, 1999, p.61, 63
115. Sutton & Hammond, *Richard III: Road to Bosworth Field*, 1985, pp.141-164
116. *Cal.Inq.PM.* Henry VII, Vol. II, pp.186.281
117. Walter, M., Salisbury Cathedral Visitor Services, private communication, 2004
118. Hearne ed., *Joannis Lelandi Antiquarii de Rebus Britannicis Collectanea*, 1774, Vol. IV, pp.191, 205
119. Jones & Underwood, *The King's Mother: Lady Margaret Beaufort*, 1993, p.101, and Gen. Tables 1 and 2

120. Roskell, Clark & Rawcliffe eds., *The History of Parliament: The House of Commons 1509-1558*, at historyofparliamentonline.org (Accessed March 2018)
121. Sutton & Hammond, *The Coronation of Richard III: The Extant Documents*, 1984, p.270
122. BL Harl M. 2nd Register, 32, f.121S
123. Horrox & Hammond., *BL Harleian MS 433, 1. Register of grants for the reigns of Edward V and Richard III*, 1980, 1st Register, 188, f.167, 2nd Register, 32, f.121
124. TNA Prob.11/11
125. *Cal.Inq.PM.*12 Henry VII, 1246, p.556

2. The Young William Sandys

1. *Cal.Inq.PM. 12 Henry VII*, 1245, p.556; TNA C139/181/75
2. Strutt et al., *The Sports and Pastimes of the People of England*, 1833, p.144
3. *Ibid.*, p.118
4. Watts, Karen, Senior Curator of Armour, The Royal Armouries, Leeds. Private communication Nov. 2004
5. Mortimer, *The Time Traveller's Guide*, 2009, p.66
6. Woodward and Wilson, *The Vyne: a Tudor House Revealed*, 1999, p.150
7. Leland, *De Rebus Britannicis Collectanea*, 1774, IV, p.204
8. Hall, *Hall's Chronicle containing the History of England.... end of the Reign of Henry Eighth*, 1809, p.434
9. Leland, *De Rebus Britannicis Collectanea*, 1774, IV, pp.214-215; BL Cotton Claudius CIII f.60; Hay, *The Anglica Historia of Polydore Vergil 1485-1537*, 1950, pp.23-26
10. Sandys, *The History of the Sandys Families*, Private, 1930, BL 9907b.27, Supplementary notes, p.209
11. BL Cotton Claudius MS CIII, fig 60; Metcalfe, *A book of Knights Banneret, Knights of the Bath and Knights Bachelor....*, 1885, p.15
12. Woodcock and Robson, *The Oxford Guide to Heraldry*, 1990, 2nd ed. 2001, p.203
13. Portcullis Pursuivant, The College of Arms, private communication, January 2017
14. Guillim, A Display of Heraldry, London 1724, p.427
15. BL Add Ms 5504 f.111
16. *Ibid.*
17. Leland, *De Rebus Britannicis Collectanea*, 1774, IV, pp.216-232
18. Condon, 'From Caitiff and Villain to Pater Patriae: Reynold Bray and the Profits of Office', 1990, p.139
19. Westminster Abbey Muniments 16030
20. Wilson, *The Royal Household and the King's Affinity*, 1986, p.173
21. See Condon, 'From Caitiff and Villain to Pater Patriae: Reynold Bray and the Profits of Office', 1990, pp.137-159; Richardson, *Tudor Chamber Administration 1485-1547*, 1952, Appendix
22. Hay, *The Anglica Historia of Polydore Vergil 1485-1537*, 1950, pp.133; Hall, *Hall's Chronicles.... end of the reign of Henry VIII*, 1809, p.497

23. Nicolas, *The Privy Purse Expenses of Elizabeth of York*, 1972, p.18
24. Leland, *De Rebus Britannicis Collectanea*, 1774, IV, p.243

3. Knight of the Body for Henry VII

1. TNA E35/214
2. Nicolas, *The Privy Purse Expenses of Elizabeth of York*, 1972, p.70
3. BL Add MSS 45131, f.45
4. Chrimes, *Henry VII*, 1999, p.28; Hay, *The Anglica Historia of Polydore Vergil 1485-1537*, 1950 pp.57-59
5. An abbreviation for *coustillier*, a servant of a man-at-arms armed with a *coutille* – a type of sword. See: Samman, 'Henry VIII's Court in the 1510s and 1520s', unpublished thesis 1989, p.134
6. Emery, *Greater Medieval houses of England and Wales 1300-1500*, Vol.3, 2006, p.278
7. TNA E101/72/3/1088 for Sandys, 1080 for Risley
8. Gairdner, *L.& P Illustrative of the Reigns of Richard III and Henry VII*, Vol.1 1861, pp.290-291
9. TNA E36/285
10. Hall, *Hall's Chronicle Containing the History of England during the Reign of Henry IV ... end of the reign of Henry VIII*, 1809, p.458
11. Gairdner, *L.&P Illustrative of the Reigns of Richard III and Henry VII*, Vol.1 1861, pp.388-404 (see pp.391, 404 for Sandys)
12. TNA CP25/1/207/36 number 13
13. *Cal.Inq.PM.* Henry VII, Vol II, 1245, p.556; 1246, p.557
14. TNA E405/75 f.40r (translated by Dr S. Davies)
15. TNA E405/75 f.40r (translated by Dr S. Davies)
16. Toulmin Smith, *Itinerary of John Leland in or about 1535-1543*, 1964, Vol.2, p.8
17. Nicolas, *Testamenta Vetusta*, 1826, Vol.1, p.446
18. Condon, 'From Caitiff and Villain to Pater Patriae: Reynold Bray and the Profits of Office', 1990, p.157
19. TNA E101/414/16 f.87
20. Arthurson, *The Perkin Warbeck Conspiracy*, 1997, p.165
21. Bentley, *Excerpta Historica: or, Illustrations of English History*, 1831 (and 2013), pp.113-115; Condon, 'From Caitiff and Villain to Pater Patriae; Reynold Bray and the Profits of Office', 1990, pp.160-162
22. Toulmin Smith, *The Itinerary of John Leland in or about 1535-1543*, 1964, Vol.2, p.8
23. Bentley, *Excerpta Historica: or, Illustrations of English History*, 1831 (and 2013), p.117
24. *Cal.Pat.R.* Henry VII, p.187
25. *Cal.Close R.* Henry VII, 15 July, p.1157
26. *Cal.Inq.PM.* Henry VII, Vol.II, p.281
27. Anstis, *Register of the Most Noble Order of the Garter*, 1724, p.239
28. *Cal.Pat.R.* Henry VII, 1494-1509, Vol.2, 14 Oct., p.187
29. Gairdner, *L.&P. Illustrative of the Reigns of Richard III and Henry VII*, Vol.1, 1861, pp.404-420; Leland, *De Rebus Britannicis Collectanea*, 1774, Vol.IV, 1774, p.258 (reprint 1970)

30. Leland, *De Rebus Britannicis Collectanea*, 1774, Vol.IV, p.258-264 (reprint 1970)
31. Nicolas, *The Privy Purse Expenses of Elizabeth of York*, 1972, p.70
32. *Cal.Inq.PM.* Henry VII, Vol.2, p.331
33. TNA LC2, the funeral of Queen Elizabeth 1 Feb.1503, p.54; BL ADD.MS. 45131, f.45
34. Leland, *De Rebus Britannicis Collectanea*, 1774, Vol.IV, p.265-300 (reprint 1970); Duke of Rutland's papers at the BL, HLR941, Vol.1, p.118
35. *Cal.Pat.R.* Henry VII, Vol.2 1494-1509, 20 May 1504, p.370
36. *Cal.Pat.R.* Henry VII 1494-150, p.658
37. *Cal.Pat.R.* Henry VII 1494-150, p.665
38. *Cal.Pat.R.* Henry VII, Vol.2, p.624
39. *Cal.Pat.R.* Henry VII, Vol.2, p.354
40. *Cal.Pat.R.* Henry VII, Vol 2, p.425
41. *Cal.Pat.R.* Henry VII, Vol.2, 1494-1509, 1501, p.265
42. Gachard, *Collection des Voyages des Souverains des Pay-Bas*, tome premier, 1876, pp.422-424, translated by Dr. C Lloyd Morgan
43. BL Add.MS. 214811; L&P Henry VIII, Vol.1, 563, para 9, p.329; L&P Henry VIII, Vol.2, King's Book of Payments, July 1510, p.1447
44. TNA LC2.1 p.125, 11 May 1503, the funeral of Henry VII

4. High Marshal of the Army

1. *L&P Henry VIII*, 3, 3288 p.1370
2. Leland, *De Rebus Britannicis Collectanea*, 1774, Vols. I-V, pp.214-215; BL Cotton Claudius C III, f.60; Hay, *The Anglica Historia of Polydore Vergil 1485-1537*, 1950, book XXVI, pp.232-26
3. Starkey, *Henry: Virtuous Prince*, 2008, pp.118-133
4. Mumby, *The Youth of Henry VIII*, 1913, pp.2-9
5. Brown, *Cal. State Papers Relating to English Affairs in the Archives of Venice*, Vol.1 1202-1509, (1864), pp.332-347. *British History Online*, pp.332-347 [accessed 19 April 2018]1509, 8 May, 942
6. Mumby, *The Youth of Henry VIII*, 1913, p.123
7. Mackie. *The Earlier Tudors, 1485-1558*, 1975, p.273
8. *L&P Henry VIII*, 1, 1176, paragraph 2, ii, p.554; 1221, paragraph 24, p.567
9. *L&P Henry VIII*, 1, 1495, paragraph 5, p.687
10. Davies, *An ill Journey for the Englishmen*, 2006, p.51
11. Hall, *Lives of the Kings, Henry VIII*, Vol.1, p.42
12. *L&P Henry VIII*, 1, 1286, p.590; 1422, p.650; 1444, p.651; 1495, p.687; 1496, p.690; 1509, p.693
13. Gruffudd, NLW MS3054D, ff.376-377 translated by Dafydd Ifans
14. *L&P HenryVIII*, 1, 1495, paragraph 3, p.688; TNA E101/65/5
15. *L&P Henry VIII*, 1, 1484, p.677
16. TNA E101/56/5
17. *L&P Henry VIII*, 1, 1495p.687
18. *L&P Henry VIII*, 1, 1495, paragraph 5, p. 689
19. *L&P Henry VIII*, 1, 1596, p.729; 1602 p.732
20. Hay, *Anglica Historia of Polydore Vergil 1485-1537*, 1950, p.209
21. TNA E101/ 56/25

22. *L&P Henry VIII*, 1, 2053, paragraph 3, p.926
23. Hall, *The Lives of Kings, Henry VIII*, 1904, Vol.1, pp.84, 85
24. Lodge, *Illustrations of British History*, Vol 2, 1791, f.83, no.1
25. *L&P Henry VIII*, 1, 2053, paragraph 6, p.927
26. Nichols & Turpyn, *The chronicle of Calais*, 1846, p.11
27. Hall, *The Lives of the Kings, Henry VIII*, Vol.1, pp.68-70
28. *Ibid.*, p.62
29. Trevelyan, 'Account of Henry the Eight's Expedition into France', 1836, pp.475-8
30. Gravett, *Tudor Knight*, 2006, colour plate B, after p.32
31. *Ibid.*, colour plate A
32. Hall, *The Lives of the Kings, Henry VIII*, Vol.1, p.86
33. Details of Henry VIII's 1513 campaign are abstracted from *L&P Henry VIII*, 1, 2391, pp.1057-1062, Oct. 1513; Herbert, *The life and reign of King Henry VIII*, 1682, pp.36-41; Moland, *Histoire du bon Chevalier Le Gentil Seigneur De Bayart*, 1882, pp.365-377, translated by C. Lloyd-Morgan; Hall, *Lives of the Kings, Henry VIII*, Vol.1, p.84; The 1513 campaign of Henry VIII and Maximilian I in France from the chronicle of Elis Gruffudd, ff.383v-394v, D. Ifans and J. Jenkins, March 2013, NLW ex 2815
34. *L&P Henry VIII*, 1, 3457, 'Henry VIII: November 1514, 11-20', in Brewer, *Letters and Papers, Foreign and Domestic, Henry VIII, Volume 1, 1509-1514*, pp.1444-1450. *British History* (accessed 3 November 2018)
35. See Cornish, *Henry VIII's Army*, 1987, p.5, '*The Battle of the Spurs*' (print by Hans Burgkmair)
36. *L&P Henry VIII*, 1, 2391, p.1060
37. Hall, *The Lives of the Kings, Henry VIII*, Vol.1, p.91
38. Herbert, *The life and reign of King Henry VIII*, 1682, p.41
39. *L&P Henry VIII*, 1, 2377, p.1054
40. Tremlett, *Catherine of Aragon*, 2011, p.193
41. Mackie. *The Earlier Tudors 1485-1558*, 1985 p.282
42. TNA E101/56/25
43. Mackie, *The Early Tudors 1485-1558*, 1985, p.283
44. BL ADD MS 45132 f.6
45. De Monstrelet, *The Chronicles of Enguerrand de Monstrelet*, 1840, Vol.2, p.514
46. Merson, ed., *The Third Book of Remembrances of Southampton 1514-1602*, 1952-79, Vol.1, pp.952-1979
47. Allen, ed., *Letters of Richard Fox*, 1929, p.97; *L&P Henry VIII*, Add. Pt.1, 185, p.20
48. *L&P Henry VIII*, 2, 3528, p.1120
49. *L&P Henry VIII*, Add. Pt.1, 185, p.20; 196, p.53
50. *L&P Henry VIII*, Add. Pt.1, 190 p.52
51. *L&P Henry VIII*, 2, 3528, p.1120
52. Jones, 'A Welsh Chronicler in Tudor England', *WHR*, 1960, p.13
53. Nichols & Turpyn, *The chronicle of Calais*, 1846, p.16
54. Dillon, 'Calais and the Pale', 1893, pp.289-388; Sandeman, *Calais under English Rule*, 1908; Grummitt, *The Calais Garrison*, 2008; St Claire Byrne, *The Lisle Letters*, 1989; Colvin, *History of the King's Works*, Vol.III, 1975
55. Grummitt, *The Calais Garrison*, 2008, p.7

56. BL Cotton Augustus I, ii, 57
57. St Claire Byrne, *The Lisle Letters*, Vol.1, p.439
58. Colvin, *History of the King's Works*, Vol.III, Pt.1, plates 30, 31
59. TNA E315/371
60. Nichols & Turpyn, *The Chronicle of Calais*, 1846, p.103
61. HRO 13M63/15, pp.110, 118
62. TNA E101/209/6
63. Nichols & Turpyn, *The Chronicle of Calais*, 1846, p.152
64. *Ibid.*, p.5
65. TNA E315/371
66. Nichols & Turpyn, *The Chronicle of Calais*, 1846, p.60
67. British Library MSS Cotton Augustus I, supplement 7
68. TNA E 315/371; Dillon, 'Calais and the Pale', 1893, p.322
69. Colvin, *History of the King's Works*, Vol. III, p.325; *L&P Henry VIII*, 5, 1705 p.712
70. Cruickshank, *Army Royal: an Account of Henry VIII's Invasion of France 1513*, 1969, p.109
71. Grummitt, *The Calais Garrison*, 2008, p.71n
72. Anstis, *Register of the Most Noble Order of the Garter*, 1724, Vol.1, pp.284, 285
73. Ashmole, *Institution Laws and Ceremonies of the most noble Order of the Garter*, 1672, p.226
74. Ashmole, *Ibid*,. p.335
75. Ashmole, *Ibid.*, pp.205, 220
76. Ashmole. *Ibid.*, Statute 38, Appendix (no page numbers given)
77. Anstis, *Register of the Most Noble Order of the Garter*, 2 Vols, 1724, Editor's Appendix. Paragraph II, p.xix
78. loc.cit. p.xxv
79. loc.cit. pp. 386, 397
80. Anstis, *Register of the Most Noble Order of the Garter*, 1724, Vol.1, Editor's Appendix, Paragraph V, p.xxxii
81. Anstis, *Ibid.*, Vol.1, p.285
82. Ashmole, *Order of the Garter* pp.322-324; Bodleian Library, Ashmolean MS.1113, f.37a, f.125b
83. Curtis, *St George's Chapel, Windsor Castle*, 2008, p.9
84. Jenkins & Simpson, *The Painted Glass of William, Lord Sandys*, private, BL shelf mark, General Reference Collection, YK2009. a.26680
85. *L&P Henry VIII*, Add. Pt.1, 338, p.101
86. Baigent & Millard, *History of the ancient town and manor of Basingstoke*, 1889, p.322
87. *L&P Henry VIII*, 2, 4396, p.1353
88. *L&P Henry VIII*, 2, 4148, p.1285; 4564, p.1398
89. *L&P Henry VIII*, 3, 199, p.69; 464, p.165
90. Allen, ed., *Letters of Richard Fox*, 1929, p.93
91. *L&P Henry VIII*, 2, 3279, p.1050
92. *L&P Henry VIII*, 2, 3371, p1077
93. Colvin, *History of the King's Works*, Vol. III, pp.343, 344
94. *L&P Henry VIII*, 4, 3254, p.1478
95. Nichols & Turpyn, *The Chronicle of Calais*, 1846, p.110
96. *L&P Henry VIII*, 3, 564, p.564

97. *L&P Henry VIII*, 3, 493, p.172
98. TNA E101/203/27; Grummitt, *The Calais Garrison*, 2008, p.8
99. *L&P Henry VIII*, Add.1, 224, p.61
100. *L&P Henry VIII*, 3, 1031, p.379
101. *L&P Henry VIII*, 3, 1261, p.478
102. *L&P Henry VIII*, 3, 517, p.178; 594, p.202
103. *L&P HenryVIII*, 3, 587, p.201
104. Caley, 'Interview between Henry the Eighth of England and Francis the First of France', 1827, pp.176-181
105. *Ibid.*, pp.176-181
106. Jerdan, 'The Field of the Cloth of Gold', *Rutland Papers*, 1842, pp.28-49
107. Anglo, 'The Hampton Court Painting of the Field of the Cloth of Gold considered as an Historical Document', 1966, p.287
108. Hall, *The Lives of Kings, Henry VIII*, Vol.1, 1904, p.192
109. (Figure-castle)
110. Caley, 'Interview between Henry the Eighth of England and Francis the First of France', 1827, pp.176-181
111. *L&P Henry VII*, Vol.3, 704, p.238
112. Stowe, *Annales of England to 1603*, pp.853
113. *L&P Henry VIII*, Add, Pt.1, 279, p.76
114. Nichols & Turpyn, *The Chronicle of Calais*, 1846, p.81
115. *L&P Henry VIII*, 3, 1704, p.238; Nichols & Turpyn, *The chronicle of Calais*, 1846, p.89
116. *Ibid.*, p.49
117. *L&P Henry VIII*, 3 Add., 18, p.1573; *L&P Henry VIII*, 3, 1013, p.372
118. *L&P Henry VIII*, 3, 1195, p.449; 1200, p.451
119. *State Papers Henry VIII*, Vol.1, p.20; *L&P Henry VIII*, 3, 1437, pp.584-5
120. Stowe, *Annales to 1603*, pp.853; Hall, *The Lives of Kings, Henry VIII*, Vol.1, 1904, p.225
121. *L&P Henry VIII*, 3, 1440, p.585
122. *L&P Henry VIII*, 1448, p.591; 1454, p.595; 1459, p.597
123. *L&P Henry VIII*, 3, 1462
124. *L&P Henry VIII*, 3, 1473, p.605; *L&P Henry VIII*, 1474, p.604
125. *L&P Henry VIII*, 11, 957, p.384
126. See 'All is True', Act 1, scene 4, p.422, in Wells & Taylor, *The Complete Oxford Shakespeare*, Vol.1. 1987
127. Manning, *The Household of Sir Thomas More*, 1906, p.81
128. *L&P Henry VIII*, 3, 1443, p.587
129. *L&P Henry VIII*, 3, 1458, p.597; Nichols & Turpyn, *The Chronicle of Calais*, 1846, pp.30-31
130. *Ibid.*, pp.96-97
131. *State Papers Henry VIII*, Vol.1, Pt.1, p.93
132. Koegler, 'Einiges über David Joris als Künstler', 1928-30, pp.166-169, translated by L. Eddie Smith
133. *L&P Henry VIII*, 3, 2238, p.951
134. See for example, St Clare Byrne, *The Lisle Letters*, 1981, Vol.3, 715, p.4403
135. *Ibid.*, 1981, Vol.4, 1034, p.450
136. *L&P Henry VIII*, Add. Pt.1, 338, p.101
137. *L&P Henry VIII*, 3, 2200, p.935

138. *L&P Henry VIII*, 3, 2229, p.949
139. Jerdan, *Rutland Papers*, 1842, pp.60-70
140. *L&P Henry VIII*, 3, 2238, p.951
141. *L&P Henry VIII*, 3, 2301, p.975
142. Hall, *The Lives of Kings, Henry VIII*, Vol.1. 1904, p.257; *L&P Henry VIII*, 3, 2338, p.992
143. *L&P Henry VIII*, 3, 2334, p.991; 2352. p.995
144. *L&P Henry VIII*, 3, 2337, p.997
145. *L&P Henry VIII*, 3, 2364, p.1003
146. *L&P Henry VIII*, 3, 2366, p.1003
147. Hall, *The Lives of Kings, Henry VIII*, Vol.1, 1904, p.266
148. Holinshed, *Chronicles of England, Scotland and Ireland*, Vol IV, 1808, p.680; Hall, *Lives of Kings, Henry VIII*, Vol.1, 1904, p.267
149. *L&P Henry VIII*, 3, 2530, p.1073; 2541, p.1079; 2560, p.1086
150. *L&P Henry VIII*, 3, 2696, p.1136
151. *L&P Henry VIII*, 3, 2858, p.1200
152. *L&P Henry VIII*, 3, 2982, p.1260; BL ADD MSS 5504
153. Hall, *The Lives of Kings, Henry VIII*, Vol.1, 1904, p.291
154. *Ibid.*, 1904, pp.290-293
155. Hall, *The Lives of Kings, Henry VIII*, Vol.1, 1904, pp.290-293; Martin, 'Sir John Daunce's Accounts of Money received from the Treasurer of the King's Chamber temp. Henry VIII', 1883, pp.318-320; for Elis Gruffudd's account translated by Davies see note 154 below
156. Gunn, *The Duke of Suffolk's March on Paris in 1523*, 1986, pp.596-634
157. Hall, *The Lives of Kings, Henry VIII*, Vol.1, 1904, p.297
158. *L&P Henry VIII*, 3, 2696, p.1136; Davies, *An ill journey for the Englishmen*, 2006, p.56
159. *L&P Henry VIII*, 4, 1526, App.87, Account of 12 August 1523 (dated 1522, content indicates 1523) p.3108
160. Davies, *An ill journey for the Englishmen*, 2006, p.7
161. Gunn, *The Duke of Suffolk's March on Paris in 1523*, 1986, p.603
162. *L&P Henry VIII*, 3, 3316, p.1381
163. *L&P Henry VIII*, 3, 3324, p.1384
164. Hall, *The Lives of Kings, Henry VIII*, Vol.1, 1904, p.298
165. *L&P Henry VIII*, 3, 3516, p.1463
166. Gunn, *The Duke of Suffolk's March on Paris in 1523*, 1986, p.615
167. Hall, *The Lives of Kings, Henry VIII*, Vol.1, 1904, p.306
168. *L&P Henry VIII*, 3, 3315, p.1380
169. Hall, *The Lives of Kings, Henry VIII*, Vol.1, 1904, p.306
170. *Ibid.*, pp.306-7; *L&P Henry VIII*, 3, 3516, p.1463
171. Hall, *The Lives of Kings, Henry VIII*, Vol.1, 1904, p.307; Davies, *An ill journey for the Englishmen*, 2006, pp.8-9
172. Hall, *The Lives of Kings, Henry VIII*, Vol.1. 1904, p.308
173. *L&P Henry VIII*, 3, 2, 3516, p.1463; Hall, *The Lives of Kings, Henry VIII*, Vol.1, 1904, pp.308-10
174. Davies, *An ill journey for the Englishmen*, 2006, p.9
175. *Ibid.*, p.10
176. Hall, *The Lives of Kings, Henry VIII*, Vol.1, 1904, pp.308-10
177. *L&P Henry VIII*, 3, 3516, 1463

178. Davies, *An ill journey for the Englishmen*, 2006, p.11
179. Lestocquoy, *Histoire de la Picardie*, 1962, p.66. Translated by Dr C. Lloyd-Morgan
180. *L&P Henry VIII*, 3, 3316, 1381
181. Hall, *The Lives of Kings, Henry VIII*, Vol.1, 1904, p.313
182. *L&P Henry VIII*, 3, Appendix 1526, 87 p.3109
183. Elis Gruffudd Chronicle, NLW 3054 D, Vol.2. f.445v. Translated by Dafydd Ifans
184. Davies, *An ill journey for the Englishmen*, 2006, pp.13-15
185. Hall, *The Lives of Kings, Henry VIII*, Vol.1, 1904, p.316
186. Hoyle, 'The Clifford Letters.' 1992, p.92
187. *L&P Henry VIII*, 3, 3590, p.1493
188. Hall, *The Lives of Kings, Henry VIII*, Vol.2, 1904, p.136
189. *L&P Henry VIII*, 4, 3088, p.1386; 4026, p.1786; App.156, p.3142
190. Fletcher and MacCulloch, *Tudor Rebellions*, 2004, Ch.4; Moorhouse, *The Pilgrimage of Grace*, 2002
191. Bergenroth, *Calendar of Letters... State Papers re England and Spain*, Vol.6, Pt.1. 48, 19 March 1539
192. *L&P Henry VIII*, 15, 697, p.326
193. Howard, 'Craftsmen and Courtiers: Italian Military Expertise at the Court of Henty VIII' in *The Anglo- Florentine Renaissance*, Ed. Sicca and Waldman, 2012, pp.276-277; Beverley, 'Sir Giovanni Portinari', 2004
194. BL Cotton MS. Augustus I, supplement 22
195. Colvin, *History of the King's Works*, Vol. IV, 1975, p.388; Lestocquoy. *Histoire de la Picardie*, 1962, p.66
196. BL Cotton MS. Augustus I, ii, 52; Tomkinson, 'The Henrician Bastions of Guînes Castle', 1998, pp.122-141
197. Nichols & Turpyn, *The Chronicle of Calais*, 1846, p.1910
198. *State Papers Henry VIII*, Vol.1, Pt.1, pp.24, 26, 30, 31, 32, 35
199. *L&P Henry VIII*, 8, 48, p.14
200. *L&P Henry VIII*, 8, 121, p.38
201. NLW MS 5276D & 3054D
202. *L&P Henry VIII*, Vol.16, 321, p.151

5. The King's Chamberlain

1. *L&P Henry VIII*, 4, 1996, p.896
2. SeeThe House of Lords Precedence Act 1539, clauses IV, V, X at legislation.gov.uk
3. *L&P Henry VIII*, 4, 1580, p.712
4. *L&P Henry VIII*, 11, 957, p.384
5. Baigent & Millard, *History of the ancient town and manor of Basingstoke*, 1889, p.118
6. *L&P Henry VIII*, 4, 984-985, paragraph 12, p.431
7. *L&P Henry VIII*, 4, 1128, p.495
8. *L&P Henry VIII*, 4, 1792, pp.794, 795
9. *L&P Henry VIII*, 4, 1431, p.639
10. *L&P Henry VIII*, 4, 1508, p.675
11. Nichols & Turpyn, *Chronicle of Calais*, 1846, p.130

12. *L&P Henry VIII*, 4, 1580, p.712
13. *L&P Henry VIII*, 4, 1613, p.7230
14. *L&P Henry VIII*, 4, 1580, p.712
15. *L&P Henry VIII*, 4, paragraph ii, 2377, p.1601
16. *L&P Henry VIII*, 4, ii, 2428, p.1086
17. *L&P Henry VIII*, 4, 4450, p.1951
18. *L&P Henry VIII*, 4, 488, p.2116
19. TNA E179/69/27
20. The English holdings are outlined in Annex 1
21. *L&P Henry VIII*, 3, 493, p.172
22. *L&P Henry VIII*, 4, 3619, p.1626
23. *L&P Henry VIII*, 4, 3619, p.1626
24. *L&P Henry VIII*, 4, 2428, p.1086
25. HRO 23M58/5
26. To put that sum in context, the Bank of England's online Inflation Calculator estimates a rise of 865 between 1520 and 2017
27. HRO 23M58/5
28. TNA 314/39/106; TNA SC11/63; *L&P Henry VIII*, Add.1, 742, p.249
29. St Clare Byrne, *Lisle Letters*, Vol.5, p.692
30. *L&P Henry VIII*, Add.1, 331, p.99
31. *L&P HenryVIII*, Add. Pt.1, 224, p.61
32. *L&P Henry VIII*, 3, 1172, p.438
33. *L&P Henry VIII*, 4, 1996, p.896
34. *L&P Henry VIII*, 4, App, 65, p.3096
35. *L&P Henry VIII*, 4, 154, p.62
36. TNA E36/231
37. *L&P Henry VIII*, 2, 4362, pp.1344-1345
38. House of Lords Precedence Act 1539, clause X. See online at legislation.gov.uk
39. Tanner, *Tudor Constitutional Documents 1485-1603*, 1922, p.249 et seq.
40. Loades, *The Tudor Court*, 1992, p.213
41. TNA E101/419/120, 188
42. *L&P Henry VIII*, 2, p.1447 (7-10 July); *L&P Henry VIII*, 1563, paragraph 9. p.329; BL Add MSS 214811
43. *L&P Henry VIII*, 4, 2377, p.1061
44. *L&P Henry VIII*, Add.538, p.181
45. *L&P Henry VIII*, 12, 589, paragraph 2, p.270
46. Nichols & Turpyn, *Chronicle of Calais*, 1846, p.139
47. *L&P Henry VIII*, 4, 2518, p.1122
48. HRO 31M 57/808
49. *L&P Henry VIII*, 4, 2611-12, p.1159
50. St Clare Byrne, *The Lisle Letters*, Vol.5, p.692-693
51. *L&P Henry VIII*, 4, 2740, p.1222
52. *L&P Henry VIII*, Add.1, 539, p.181
53. *L&P Henry VIII*, 2, 3337, p.1511
54. *State Papers Henry VIII*, Vol.1. p.293
55. Hall, *Lives of Kings, Henry VIII*, 1904, Vol.1, p.102
56. *State Papers Henry VIII*, Vol.VI Part 5, letter CLXIII, Aug.1527, p.598; *L&P Henry VIII*, 4, 3368, p.1525
57. Mackie, *The Earlier Tudors 1485-1558*, 1985, p.318

58. *Ibid.*, p.319
59. *L&P Henry VIII*, 4, 2936, p.1315
60. Cavendish, *Thomas Wolsey, late Cardinal*, 1962, pp.54-56
61. Hall, *Lives of Kings, Henry VIII*, 1904, Vol.2, p.78
62. Brown, *Cal. State Papers, Venice*, Vol.4, 4, pp. 2-3
63. See 'All is True', Act 1, scene 4, p.422, in Wells & Taylor, *The Complete Oxford Shakespeare*, Vol.1. 1987
64. Ives, *Life and Death of Anne Boleyn*, 2004, p.90
65. Brown, Calendar of State Papers, Venice Vol.4, 514 p.231
66. Samman, 'Henry VIII's Court in the 1510s and 1520s', 1989, p.378
67. Brown, *Calendar of State Papers, Venice*, 1527-33, 190, 205, 208, 210, 235; Hall, *Lives of Kings, Henry VIII*, 1904, Vol.2 p.110
68. Hall, *Lives of Kings, Henry VIII*, 1904, Vol.2, p.106-110
69. *L&P Henry VIII*, 4, 3619, p.1626
70. *L&P Henry VIII*, 4, 3651, p.1640
71. *L&P Henry VIII*, 4, 3659, p.1642
72. Nichols & Turpyn, *Chronicle of Calais*, 1846, p.206
73. Allen, *Letters of Richard Fox*, 1929, p.170
74. *L&P Henry VIII*, 4, 3088, p.1386; 4026, p.1786
75. Brown, *Cal. State Papers Venice*, Vol. IV, 1527-1533, 320 p.160
76. *L&P Henry VIII*, 4, 5752, p.2563
77. *L&P Henry VIII*, 4, 5197, p.2284
78. *L&P Henry VIII*, 4, 5197, p.2284; 5198, p.2284
79. Elis Gruffudd Chronicle, f.488a. translated by Dafydd Ifans
80. Brown, *Cal. State Papers, Venice*, Vol. IV, 1527-1533, 504, p.229; 506, p.229
81. Kirby, *The Plumpton Letters and Papers*, 1996, CLXV, p.269
82. Lehmberg, *The Reformation Parliament 1529-36*, 1970, p.77
83. Bodleian Library ASH MS Roll 45
84. Lloyd & Thurley, *Henry VIII: Images of a Tudor King*, 1990, p.19
85. 'The Opening of Parliament in 1523', Wriothesely Garter Book, Royal Library Windsor, RCIN 1047414
86. *L&P Henry VIII*, 15, 831, paragraph 10, 11, p.403
87. Lehmberg, *The Reformation Parliament 1529-36*, 1970, p.78 and references therein
88. See the House of Lords Journal at British History Online
89. See, for example, Ives, *The Life and Death of Anne Boleyn*, 2004, or Mackie, *The Earlier Tudors*, 1975
90. Herbert, *The life and reign of King Henry the Eighth*, 1682, p.302
91. Hume, *Chronicle of King Henry VIII of England, written in Spanish*, 1889, pp.27-28
92. *L&P Henry VIII*, 4, 6420, p.2889, 6435, p.2889
93. Herbert, *The life and reign of King Henry the Eighth*, 1682, p.341; Ives, 'The Fall of Wolsey', 1991
94. *L&P Henry VIII*, 4, 6513, p.2929; Herbert, *The life and reign of King Henry the Eighth*, 1682, p.340
95. *L&P Henry VIII*, 4, 6026, 2681, 6075, p.2712
96. Wilson, *In the Lion's Court*, 2002, p.295; Guy, *Tudor England*, 2013, p.126
97. *L&P Henry VIII*, Vol.5, 361, p.167

98. Nicolas, *Privy Purse Expenses of King Henry VIII*, 1827, p.xv; *L&P Henry VIII*, Vol.5, p.755, f.78b, p.249
99. Bernard, *The King's Reformation*, 2005, pp.65-67
100. *L&P Henry VIII*, 5, 1370, paragraph 2, p.585
101. *L&P Henry VIII*, 5, 1370, paragraph 22, p.587
102. Brown, *Calendar of State Papers, Venice*, Vol.4, 1527-33, 796, p.348; 797, p.349
103. *L&P Henry VIII*, 5, 1484, 1485; Elis Gruffudd Chronicle, f.97v & r; Hall, *The Lives of Kings, Henry VIII*, 1904, Vol.2, p.212
104. *L&P Henry VIII*, 5, 1703, paragraph iii, p.712
105. *L&P Henry VIII*, 5, 1705, p.712
106. *L&P Henry VIII*, 6, 1431, p.573. This was initially wrongly assigned but corrected in Vol.6 errata, 800
107. St Clare Byrne, *Lisle Letters*, 1981, Vol.1, 75; Vol.5, 1210
108. St Clare Byrne, *Lisle Letters*, 1981, Vol.I, pp.496-497
109. *L&P Henry VIII*, 7, 816, p.310
110. St Clare Byrne, *Lisle Letters*, 1981, Vol.1, 49, p.557
111. Hutchinson, *Thomas Cromwell*, 2007, p.53
112. *L&P Henry VIII*, 5, 1323, p.573; 1580, p.662; 6, 1307, p.527; 1390, p.550
113. Keay, *Elizabethan Tower of London*, 2001, p.31
114. *L&P Henry VIII*, 6, 1540, p.621
115. Brown, *Calendar of State Papers, Venice*, Vol. 4, 1527-1533, p.870; Hamilton, *A Chronicle of England 1485-1559, by Charles Wriothesley*, 1875-77, Vol.1, p.17
116. *L&P Henry VIII*, 6, p.683
117. Baigent & Millard, *History of Basingstoke*, 1889, p.118
118. Hall, *Lives of Kings, Henry VIII*, 1904, Vol.2, pp.229-242; Brown, *Calendar of State Papers, Venice*, Vol.4, 1527-1533, 912 p.149; *L&P Henry VIII*, 6, 561, 563, p.250; 601, p.276; 602, p.279
119. *L&P Henry VIII*, 6, 653, p.295
120. *L&P Henry VIII*, 6, 929, paragraph 49, p.404
121. *L&P Henry VIII*, 6, 1018, p.434
122. St Clare Byrne, *Lisle Letters*, 1981, Vol.1, letter 49, p.557
123. *L&P Henry VIII*, 6, 578, paragraph 12, p.258
124. St Clare Byrne, *Lisle Letters*, 1981, 23, 4 August 1533
125. *Ibid.*, 49, 13 September 1533
126. *L&P Henry VIII*, 6, 1307, p.527; 1390, p.555; 1556, p.627
127. St Clare Byrne, *Lisle Letters*, 1981, 121, 29 January
128. See House of Lords Journal at British History Online
129. *L&P Henry VIII*, 7, 1010, p.384
130. St Clare Byrne, *Lisle Letters*, 1981, 121, 151, 152, 155a, 156, 185
131. Stow, *A Survey of London 1598*, revised 1603, new ed. 2005, p.307; Pennant, *Some account of London*, 1791, p.342; Thornbury, *Old and New London*. 1878, Vol.1, p.285
132. St Clare Byrne, *Lisle Letters*, 1981, Vol.2, letter 177, p.141
133. *L&P Henry VIII*, 7, 766, p.294
134. A Tudor tun was 252 gallons, so 20 tuns were 5040 gallons. See Chapman. *How Heavy, How Much and How Long*, 1999, p.41
135. *L&P Henry VIII*, 7, 1479, p.550

136. St Clare Byrne, *Lisle Letters*, 1981, Vol.2, letter 264, p.268
137. *L&P Henry VIII*, 7, 1504, p.562
138. *L&P Henry VIII*, 7, 352, p.146
139. *L&P Henry VIII*, 8, 48, p.14
140. Lehmberg, *The Reformation Parliament 1529-36*, 1970, p.218
141. L&P Henry VIII, 7, 1368, p.520
142. Muller, *Letters of Stephen Gardiner*, 1933, reissue 2013, p.56; *L&P Henry VIII*, 7, 610, p.240
143. Tremlett, *Catherine of Aragon: Henry's Spanish Queen*, 2011, pp.351-416
144. St Clare Byrne, *Lisle Letters*, 1981, Vol.2, letter 141a, p.71; letter 245, p.235
145. *Ibid.*, p.386
146. 'Spain: January 1534, 1-20', in De Gayangos, *Calendar of State Papers, Spain*, Vol. 5 Part 1, 1534-1535, 1886, pp.1-15. See British History Online
147. *Ibid.*
148. Duffy, *The Stripping of the Altars*, 2005, pp.338-376
149. *L&P Henry VIII*, 8, 726, p.272; Gairdner, *History of the English Church in the 16th Century*, 1904, p.157
150. *L&P Henry VIII*, 8, 661, p.247
151. *L&P Henry VIII*, 7, 610, p.294
152. *L&P Henry VIII*, 7, 1534, Preface p.v
153. 'Spain: November 1535, 1-30', in De Gayangos, *Calendar of State Papers, Spain*, Vol.5 Part 1, 1534-1535, 1886, pp.562-574. See British History Online
154. *L&P Henry VIII*, Add.1, 981, p.343
155. *L&P Henry VIII*, 8, 389, p.154
156. *L&P Henry VIII*, 8, 587, p.221
157. *L&P Henry VIII*, 8, 924, p.363
158. Brown, *Calendar of State Papers, Venice*, Vol.5, 1534-54, 54, 3 June, pp.23-28. See British History Online
159. *L&P Henry VIII*, 8, 263, p.104
160. Elis Gruffudd Chronicle, NLW MS 3054iiD, f 510r, translated by Dafydd Ifans
161. Hamilton, *Chronicle of England 1485-1559*, by Charles Wriothesley, 1875-77, Vol.1, pp.28-29
162. *L&P Henry VIII*, 8, 924, p.363
163. *L&P Henry VIII*, 9, 192, p.60
164. *L&P Henry VIII*, 9, 255, p.86
165. *L&P Henry VIII*, 9, 416, p.136
166. St Clare Byrne, *Lisle Letters*, 1981, Vol.4, 986, p.356
167. Nichols & Turpyn, *Chronicle of Calais*, 1846, p.137
168. St Clare Byrne, *Lisle Letters*, 1981, Vol.4, no.1030, p.435
169. *Ibid.*, Vol.4, 1028a, p.433
170. See History of Parliament Online
171. Ives, *Life and Death of Anne Boleyn*, 2004, p.293
172. Loades, *Jane Seymour*, reprint 2014, p.26
173. Starkey, *Henry VIII: a European Court in England*, 1991, p.118
174. *L&P Henry VIII*, 9, 619, p.209
175. *L&P Henry VIII*, 9, 663, p.224
176. *L&P Henry VIII*, 9, 656, p.220

177. *L&P Henry VIII*, 9, 535, p.176
178. *L&P Henry VIII*, 9, 639, p.215
179. Collins, 'Winchester Cathedral Record Extra', November 2011
180. Hamilton, *Chronicle of England 1485-1559, by Charles Wriothesley*, 1875-77, Vol.1, p.33
181. Law, *The History of Hampton Court Palace*, Vol.1, 1903, p.177
182. Ives, *Life and Death of Anne Boleyn*, 2004, p.304
183. *L&P Henry VIII*, 10, 199, p.69
184. *L&P Henry VIII*, 9, 619, p.209; 620, p.210
185. *L&P Henry VIII*, 9, 870, p.293
186. *L&P Henry VIII*, 8, 501, p.193
187. *L&P Henry VIII*, 10, 32, p.12
188. *L&P Henry VIII*, 10, 141, p.54
189. Tanner, *Tudor Constitutional Documents 1485-1603*, 1922 (and 2013), p.58
190. *L&P Henry VIII*, 10, 282, p.102
191. *L&P Henry VIII*, 10, 199, p.69
192. Norton, *The Anne Boleyn Papers*, 2013, p.328
193. He wrote to Cromwell in September 1532 requesting payment for their wages, doublets, hose and bonnets, *L&P Henry VIII*, 5, 1323
194. Norton, *The Anne Boleyn Papers*, 2013, Chapuys letters 29/01/36 and 10/02/36
195. Norton, *The Anne Boleyn Papers*, 2013, p.288
196. *L&P Henry VIII*, 10, 495, p.200
197. Norton, *The Anne Boleyn Papers*, 2013, Chapuys' letter 1/04/36
198. Wyatt, 'Extracts from the Life of Anne Boleigne,' 1825, Vol.2, p.175
199. Norton, *The Anne Boleyn Papers*, 2013, p.299
200. Friedmann, *Anne Boleyn: a Chapter of English History*, 1884, Vol.2, p.243; This commission was not publicised and the relevant record is within TNA K8/9 'Baga de Segretis' ('The Secret Papers Bag' at TNA)
201. St Clare Byrne, *Lisle Letters*, 1981, Vol.3, p.376
202. *Ibid.*, Vol.4, letter 847; Ives, *Life and Death of Anne Boleyn*, 2004, p.332
203. *Ibid.*, p.334
204. Friedmann, *Anne Boleyn: a Chapter in English History*, 1884, footnote to p.280, Chapuys to Charles V, 19 May 1536, note 2 (in French), new translation by Dr C. Lloyd-Morgan 2015
205. *Ibid.*, Vol.2, p.252, and reference to a letter by Sir William Kingston
206. Norton, *Anne Boleyn Papers*, 2013, pp.302-303
207. Friedmann, *Anne Boleyn: A Chapter in English History*, 1884, Vol.2, p.253
208. *L&P Henry VIII*, 10, 792, p.333
209. *L&P Henry VIII*, 10, 896, p.373
210. Hamilton, *Chronicle of England 1485-1559 by Charles Wriothesley*, 1875-77, Vol.1, p.41(Wriothesley uses the word 'divorced)
211. Norton, *Anne Boleyn Papers*, 2013, pp.338-341, 351-354
212. *L&P Henry VIII*, 10, 908, p.376; Hamilton, *Chronicle of England 1485-1559 by Charles Wriothesley*, 1875-77, Vol.1, p.43
213. *L&P Henry VIII*, 10, 894, p.372
214. *L&P Henry VIII*, 10, 809, p.342
215. Hamilton, *Chronicle of England 1485-1559 by Charles Wriothesley*, 1875-77, Vol.1, p.44

216. *Ibid.*, p.45
217. House of Lords Journal 1536 at British History Online
218. *L&P Henry VIII*, 10, 557, p.217
219. *L&P Henry VIII*, 19, Part 1, 1036, p.644, paragraph 32
220. Scard, *Tudor Survivor: the Life and Times of William Paulet*, 2011, p.65
221. Condon, *From Caitiff and Villain to Pater Patriae*, 1990, p.137
222. See details in Section 10.2
223. Currie, *Archaeological and Historical Survey of Mottisfont Abbey Estate*, 1999, p.28
224. Howard & Wilson, *The Vyne: A Tudor House Revealed*, 2003, p.105
225. Hamilton, *Chronicle of England 1485-1559* by Charles Wriothesley, 1875-77, Vol.1, p.48
226. St Clare Byrne, *Lisle Letters*, 1981, Vol.3, 735, 30 June; Hamilton, *Chronicle of England 1485-1559* by Charles Wriothesley, 1875-77, Vol.1, p.48
227. *Ibid.*, Vol.1, p.50; St Clare Byrne, *Lisle Letters*, 1981, Vol.4, p.106
228. See House of Lords Journal for 29 July 1536 at British History Online
229. *L&P Henry VIII*, 10, Grants May, no.23
230. St Clare Byrne, *Lisle Letters*, 1981, Vol.3, p.462
231. *L&P Henry VIII*, 11, 241, p.105
232. *Ibid.*
233. *L&P Henry VIII*, 11, 241, p.105; 288, p.128; 313, p.130; 341, p.138
234. *L&P Henry VIII*, 11, 288, p.123
235. *Ibid.*
236. *L&P Henry VIII*, 12, 589, p.271
237. *L&P Henry VIII*, 11, 313, p.130
238. *L&P Henry VIII*, 10, 1187, p.494
239. *L&P Henry VIII*, 11, 589, p. 271
240. Hall, *Lives of Kings, Henry VIII*, 1904, Vol.2, p.269; Mackie, *The Earlier Tudors*, 1975, p.382
241. Fletcher & MacCulloch, *Tudor Rebellions*, 2004, Ch.4; Moorhouse, *The Pilgrimage of Grace*, 2002
242. *L&P Henry VIII*, 11, 643, p.254
243. *L&P Henry VIII*, 11, 580, p.232
244. *L&P Henry VIII*, Add.1, 1105, p.382; 11, 580, p.232
245. *L&P Henry VIII*, 11, 754, p.290; 755, p.291; 776, p.298
246. *L&P Henry VIII*, 11, 803, p.311
247. *L&P Henry VIII*, 11, 879, p.350
248. *L&P Henry VIII*, 11, 1246, p.508
249. *L&P Henry VIII*, 11, 1397, p.563
250. *L&P Henry VIII*, 12.1, 17, p.12
251. *L&P Henry VIII*, 12.1, 151, p.68
252. *L&P Henry VIII*, 12.1, 17, p.12
253. *L&P Henry VIII*, 12.1, 151, p.68
254. *L&P Henry VIII*, 12.1, 589, p.270
255. St Clare Byrne, *The Lisle Letters*, Vol.5, p.692,
256. *L&P Henry VIII*, 13.2, 863, p.360
257. *L&P Henry VIII*, 14.1, 1296, p.567; 1298, p.568
258. St Clare Byrne, *The Lisle Letters*, 1981, Vol.5, p.594
259. St Clare Byrne, *The Lisle Letters*, 1981, Vol.5, 1532, p.641

260. *L&P Henry VIII*, 13.1, 161, p.64
261. St Clare Byrne, *The Lisle Letters*, 1981, Vol.2, p.255
262. St Clare Byrne, *The Lisle Letters*, 1981, Vol.2, pp.254, 259
263. Borman, *Thomas Cromwell*, 2015, p.274
264. *L&P Henry VIII*, 12.1, 627, p.227
265. *L&P Henry VIII*, 12.1, 750, p.329
266. *L&P Henry VIII*, 12.2, 11, p.4
267. *L&P Henry VIII*, 12.2, 911, pp.318-320; Leland, *De Rebus Britannicis Collectanea*, 1774, Vol.2, pp.673-677
268. *L&P Henry VIII*, 12.2, 994, p.346
269. *L&P Henry VIII*, 12.2, 1060, p.372
270. St Claire Bryne, *Lisle Letters*, 1981, Vol. 4, 1034, p.450
271. *L&P Henry VIII*, 13.1, 111, p.38
272. *L&P Henry VIII*, 13.2, 1191 paragraph 2, p.499
273. *L&P Henry VIII*, 13.1, 1, p.1
274. *L&P Henry VIII*, 13.1, 790, p.295
275. *L&P Henry VIII*, 13.1, 298, p.102; 1141, p.427; 1230, p.455
276. A letter from Sandys dated April 1538 and sent from Guînes is included in St Clare Byrne, *Lisle Letters*, Vol.4, 1146, p.106, but is not included in *L&P Henry VIII*, 13.1. There are no other references to Sandys' presence in the Pale at the time, so the date in the *Lisle Letters* may not be correct
277. St Clare Byrne, *The Lisle Letters*, 1981, Vol.5, 1209
278. *L&P Henry VIII*, 13.2, 259
279. Baigent & Millard, *History of Basingstoke*, pp.34, 112, 113
280. *L&P Henry VIII*, 13.2, 122
281. Herbert, *Life and reign of Henry the Eighth*, 1682, p.511
282. *L&P Henry VIII*, 13.2, 232, p.829, p.336
283. *L&P Henry VIII*, 13.2, 968, p.409
284. *L&P Henry VIII*, 13.2, 986, p.421; 1056, p.451; Hamilton, *Chronicle of England 1485-1559* by Charles Wriothesley, 1875-77, Vol.1, p.91
285. *The Antiquary*, Vol.V January to June 1882, p.242
286. Jones and Underwood, *The King's Mother: Lady Margaret Beaufort*, 1993, p.101, Genealogical tables 1 & 2; Weir, *Britain's Royal Families, The Complete Genealogy*, 2008, p.105, 138-139, 148
287. Toogood, *History of Bramley, Hampshire*, 1993, p.14
288. The will of Constance Pole, 1570 as transcribed by Dr S. Davies, TNA Pro 1/152/361; Inq. P.ost M. for Simon Cufaude as transcribed by DR S. Davies, TNA C 142/222/14
289. *L&P Henry VIII*, 13.2, 248, p.97
290. *L&P Henry VIII*, 13.2, 122
291. *L&P Henry VIII*, 14.1, 144, p.53
292. *L&P Henry VIII*, 14.1, 331, p.129
293. *L&P Henry VIII*, 14.1, 331, p.129
294. *L&P Henry VIII*, 14.1, 568, p.221; Bergenroth, *Cal. State Papers, Spain*, Vol. 6.1, part I, 48, pp.134-5
295. St George, *Visitation of Hampshire and the Isle of Wight 1686*, 1991
296. Nichols, *Diary of Henry Machyn*, 1848, facsimile 2012, p.282-4
297. *L&P Henry VIII*, 14.1, 634, p.246; 662, pp.331-2; Williams, *Early Churchwardens Accounts*, 1913, p.29

298. St Clare Byrne, *Lisle Letters*, Vol.5, 1981, L.1371, p.422, L.1374, p.426; *L&P Henry VIII*, 14.1, 707, p348
299. House of Lords Journal April 1539 at British History Online
300. E.g. Bernard, *The King's Reformation*, 2005, pp.527-533, and St Clare Byrne. *Lisle Letters*, Vols.4, 5, 6
301. Elis Gruffudd Chronicle, f.528r, f.529r, 529v, translated by Dafydd Ifans 2016
302. St Clare Byrne, *The Lisle Letters*, 1981, Vol.5, letter 1403, p.462
303. *Ibid.*, Vol.5, 1456, p.540
304. *Ibid.*, Vol.5, 1457, p.541
305. *Ibid.*, Vol.5, 1469, p.564
306. St Clare Byrne, *The Lisle Letters*, 1981, Vol.5, L.1540, 648
307. *Ibid.*, 1540, p.648 1551.658
308. *Ibid.*, 1557, p.663
309. *Ibid.*, 1557, p.663
310. *L&P Henry VIII*, 14.2, 178, p.52
311. St Clare Byrne, *Lisle Letters*, Vol.5, 1981, p.692, 1568, p.676
312. *Ibid.*, p.692
313. *L&P Henry VIII*, 14.2, 286, pp.108-109
314. *L&P Henry VIII*, 14.2, 397, p.138; 499, p.178
315. *L&P Henry VIII*, 15, 14, p.4
316. Hall, *Lives of Kings, Henry VIII*, 1904, Vol.2, p.298; *L&P Henry VIII*, 15, 18, p.7; Hamilton, *Chronicle of England 1485-1559 by Charles Wriothesley*, 1875-77, Vol.1, p.111
317. *L&P Henry VIII*, 15, 316, p.128
318. St Clare Byrne, *Lisle Letters*, 1981, Vol.6, 1664, p.71
319. Report of the Commissioners for Calais, 5 April, as given in St Clare Byrne, *Lisle Letters*, 1981, Vol.6, p.63; *Ibid.*, Vol.6, p.64
320. *L&P Henry VIII*, 15, 472, p.196
321. St Clare Byrne, *Lisle Letters*, 1981, Vol.6, 1673, p.106
322. Elis Gruffudd Chronicle, f.548v, as transcribed by Dafydd Ifans
323. See House of Lords Journal, Vol.1, pp.130-131, for 17 April 1540, at British History Online [accessed 18 May 2018]; *L&P Henry VIII*, 15, 560, p.251
324. Bernard, 'Thomas Cromwell and Calais,' 2007; St Clare Byrne, *Lisle Letters*, 1981, Vol.6, pp.117-121
325. St Clare Byrne, *Lisle Letters*, 1981, L.1557, p.663
326. *L&P Henry VIII*, 15, 541, p.242
327. *L&P Henry VIII*, 15, 560, paragraph 1, 3, p.251
328. *L&P Henry VIII*, 15, 697, p.325
329. Kingra, *'The Trace Italienne and the Military Revolution during the Eighty Years' War'*, 1993, pp.431-46
330. Colvin, *History of the King's Works*, 1975, Vol.III, p.354
331. *L&P Henry VIII*, 15, 831, paragraph 11, p.403
332. Elis Gruffudd Chronicle, Vol.2, Part 2, f.553r, translated by Dafydd Ifans; *L&P Henry VIII*, 15, 795, p.374
333. *L&P Henry VIII*, 15, 795, 374
334. *L&P Henry VIII*, 15, 1018, p.502; 1021, p.504
335. Elis Gruffudd Chronicle, Vol.2, Part 2, f.564v, 565r, translated by Dafydd Ifans

336. Nicolas, *Proceedings and Ordinances of the Privy Council, 1834-7*, 15 Oct.1540, p.64
337. Elis Gruffudd Chronicle, Vol.2, Part 2, f.565r, translated by Dafydd Ifans
338. Herbert, *Life and Reign of Henry VIII*, p.524
339. *L&P Henry VIII*, 15, 861, p.430
340. Nicolas, *Proceedings and Ordinances of the Privy Council*, 1834-7, 10 August, p.2
341. *Ibid.*, 7 November, p.415, Oct.1540, p.64
342. *Ibid.*, 22 November, p.88
343. *Ibid.*, 23 November, p.89
344. *L&P Henry VIII*, 16, 317, p.149
345. Elis Gruffudd Chronicle, f.567v, as transcribed by Dafydd Ifans
346. TNA Prob/11/11/107
347. See History of Parliament Online
348. HRO 13M63/15 p.361
349. Anstis, *Register of the Order of Garter*, Vol.1, p.421 (footnote)
350. Mercier, K., Archivist, St George's Chapel Archives and and library, private communication
351. *L&P Henry VIII*, 16, 321, p.151
352. *L&P Henry VIII*, 16, p.689
353. Nichols, *The Diary of Henry Machyn*, 1848, reprinted 2012, p.8
354. Scard, *Tudor Survivor*, History, 2011, p.94
355. *L&P Henry VIII*, 16, 586, p.282

6. Sandys' Works and Patronage

1. See Gozzoli, *How to Recognize Gothic Art*, 1978, p.3; Conti, *How to Recognize Renaissance Art*, 1978, p.3
2. Sicca and Waldman ed., *The Anglo-Florentine Renaissance Art for the Early Tudors*, 2012
3. *Ibid.*, p.39
4. *Ibid.*, p.23
5. Anderson, Carr, Park and Holden, 'Architectural Terracotta from Westhorpe Hall', 2003, p.136; Harrison, *Annals of an Old Manor house: Sutton Place Guildford*, 1893, pp.128-131
6. *L&P Henry VIII*, *Add.* pt.1, 338, p.101
7. Ashmole, *Order of the Garter*. p.136
8. Tatton-Brown & Mortimer ed., *Westminster Abbey: The Lady Chapel of Henry VII*, 2003, p.84
9. Hare, *The Victoria County History: Basingstoke A Medieval Town, c.1000-c.1600*, 2017, p.83
10. Baigent & Millard, *History of the Town and Manor of Basingstoke*, 1889, p.118
11. HRO 46m74/PZ89
12. Camden, *Britannia*, 1695, facsimile 1971, p.124
13. Kelly, *Chapel of the Holy Ghost and St Michael's Church*, Basingstoke, 1911, pp.5-6
14. Wayment, 'Stained Glass of the Chapel of the Vyne and of the Holy Ghost, Basingstoke', 1982, p.141

15. TNA 117/11/2
16. Baigent & Millard, *History of the Town and Manor of Basingstoke*, 1889, p.111
17. Camden, *Britannia*, 1695, facsimile 1971, p.124. Note: the shorter OED (1947) defines 'artificially' as used in 1680 as 'skilful'
18. Chandler (pub.), *The History of the Holy Ghost Chapel*, 1819, p.70
19. *Ibid.*, p.72
20. Rackham, *Early Netherlands Majolica*, 1926, Ch.4 pp.53-73; Dumortier, *Ceramique de la Renaissance a Anvers*, 2002, Ch.10
21. Baigent & Millard, *History of the Town and Manor of Basingstoke*, 1889, p.33
22. *Ibid.*, p.113
23. Chute, *Drawings of the Vyne Gallery*, 1876; Siddons, *Heraldic Badges in England and Wales*, Vol.I, p.68
24. Baigent & Millard, *History of the town and manor of Basingstoke*, 1889, p.156; St George and Squibb, *The Herald's Visitation of Hampshire and the Isle of Wight*, 1686, 1991, pp.226, 227
25. Gomme, ed., *English Topography*, Vol.17, Part V (Hants.- Hunts. ed. F.A. Milne), London 1894; Anon. Art.I, 'The History and description of the Vine in Hampshire', May 1789, p.58
26. Chandler, *The History of the Holy Ghost Chapel*, 1819, p.12
27. TNA E117/11/28
28. Jenkins and Simpson, *The Painted Glass of William, Lord Sandys (1470–1540)*
29. Westlake, *A History of Design in Painted Glass*, 1881 onwards, Vol.4, p.52
30. Wayment, Hilary, 'The Stained Glass of the Chapel of the Vyne and the Chapel of the Holy Ghost, Basingstoke,' *Archaeologia*, Vol.107 (Society of Antiquaries of London, 1982), p.141
31. Clare, 'The Vyne Chapel, Stained Glass' 2007
32. BL Add Man 214811; *L&P Henry VIII*, 1, 563, 9, p.329; *L&P Henry VIII*, 2, King's Book of Payments, p.1447
33. Howard & Wilson, *The Vyne: A Tudor House Revealed*, 2003, p.80
34. Miles, 'The Further Tree-Ring Dating of the Vyne Sherborne St John, Hampshire 2017.' This report gives the dates of tree felling as 1526 and 1524/5, to which must be added a year for seasoning before use and fitting out time of about six months. (Private communication from George Roberts, National Trust Curator.)
35. Chute, *A History of the Vyne in Hampshire*, 1888, p.77
36. Rutherford, 'The Vyne Sherborne St John, Hants. Historic Landscape Appraisal of the Large Lake', 2017, pp.18-22
37. Howard & Wilson, *The Vyne: A Tudor House Revealed*, 2003, p.142
38. *Ibid.*, opposite p.80
39. Williams, *English Historical documents, Vol.5, 1485-1558*, 1967, pp.914-915
40. Howard & Wilson, *The Vyne: A Tudor House Revealed*, 2003, p.142
41. HRO 31 M57/585
42. Anon., Article 1, 'The History and description of the Vine in Hampshire', *The Topographer: containing a variety of original articles, illustrative of the local history and antiquities of England*, Vol. I (1789), Number II (May 1789), pp.51-63

43. HRO 101M99, Currie, 'The Vyne Estate, Sherborne St. John, Hampshire, An Archaeological and Historical Survey', Report to the National Trust, 1994, pp.32-33
44. Camden, *Britannia*, 1695, facsimile 1971, p.125
45. Stow, *Annales of England*, first edtion 1592, pp.1409-11
46. Toulmin-Smith ed., *The Itinerary of John Leland*, 1964, Vol.2, p.8
47. Anon. Art.I, 'The History and description of the Vine in Hampshire', May 1789, p.58
48. HRO 31M57/1072
49. HRO 31M57/1655 (Misc.88)
50. Currie, 'Trial Excavations at the Vyne, Sherborne St John, Hampshire', January 1995, p.4
51. *Ibid.*, p.11
52. HRO 46M 94; Currie, 'A Survey of the Parch Marks at the Vyne' August 1995, p.15
53. Wilson, *The Vyne Archaeological Project, 1996-98*, Vols.1-4
54. Stevens, Howman and Clark, 'A Resistivity Survey of Lawns surrounding the Vyne, Hants', April 1998
55. Howard & Wilson, *The Vyne: A Tudor House Revealed*, 2003, p.71
56. Martin and Knight, 'A description, interpretation and record of the Brewhouse at The Vyne Hampshire' Project Ref. 1409, 2002
57. Marshall, 'Report describing the results of an Archaeological watching brief over the trenches in the south and west parks and in the pleasure grounds at the Vyne Hampshire', 2009
58. Howard & Wilson, *The Vyne: A Tudor House Revealed*, 2003, p.70
59. Wilson, *The Vyne Archaeological Project, 1996-1998*, Vol.III, pt.II, p.342 and drawing
60. Wilson, *The Vyne Archaeological Project, 1996-1998*, Vol.I, p.30
61. See Note 45 above
62. See Marshall, Note 46 above
63. Marshall, personal communication
64. HRO/20M76/241
65. Harrison, *Annals of an Old Manor house: Sutton Place Guildford*, 1893, between pp.140-141; William Marquis of Northampton, *Compton Wynyates*, 1904, between pp.8-9; Roundell, *Cowdray, The History of a Great English House*, 1884, p.111
66. Thurley, *Hampton Court*, 2003, p.22
67. Howard & Wilson, *The Vyne: A Tudor House Revealed*, 2003, p.81. The Vyne Gallery Wing is now shorter at 75 feet. See Note 57 above, colour plate 3
68. HRO 31M57/589, 9 May 1753
69. Harrison, *Annals of an Old Manor house: Sutton Place Guildford*, 1893, pp.128-131
70. Thurley, *Hampton Court*, 2003, p.22
71. Howard & Wilson, *The Vyne: A Tudor House Revealed*, 2003, p.130
72. Harrison & Chandos, *Carvings, Oak Gallery, The Vyne*, 1979
73. Pickvance, 'The Slow Arrival of Renaissance influence on English Furniture' 2015, pp.126-127
74. Wilson, *The Vyne Archaeological Project, 1996-98*, Vol. III, pt.i, p.144

75. Anon. Art.I, 'The History and description of the Vine in Hampshire', May 1789, p.60
76. Duffy, *The Stripping of the Altars*, 2005, Ch.3, p.93
77. Wilson, *The Vyne Archaeological Project, 1996-98*, Vol.III, pt.i, p.114
78. Riall, 'The Early Tudor Renaissance in Hampshire', 2007
79. St.George & Squibb, *The Herald's Visitation of Hampshire and the Isle of Wight 1686*, 1991, pp.226-227
80. Rackham, *Early Netherlands Majolica*, 1926, Ch.4 p.53-73; Dumortier, *Ceramique de la Renaissance a Anvers*, 2002, Chap.10
81. Tracy, 'The Lady Chapel Stalls', 1993, pp.231-246
82. Wilson, *The Vyne Archaeological Project, 1996-98*, Vol. III, pt.i, p.144
83. Adams, 'The Wall Paintings in the Lady Chapel', Jan.2017
84. Allen, ed., *Letters of Richard Fox*, 1929, pp.170-171
85. Johnston, 'Catherine of Aragon's Pomegranate Revisited', 2005, pp.153-173
86. Crook, 'Witness from on High', 2015
87. Johnston, 'Catherine of Aragon's Pomegranate Revisited', 2005, pp.153-173
88. Wilson, *The Vyne Archaeological Project, 1996-98*, Vol. III, pt. i, p.144
89. Celia Jennings, private communication to the author
90. Campbell, *Henry VIII and the Art of Majesty*, 2007, pp.103-177
91. One Flemish Ell or Flemish Stick is equal to about 5 square feet
92. See for example Starkey, *The Inventory of King Henry VIII*, 1998, p.272, item 12014
93. Campbell; *Henry VIII and the Art of Majesty*, 2007, p.107
94. *Ibid.*, p.80
95. Howard & Wilson, *The Vyne: A Tudor House Revealed*, 2003, p.82
96. See e.g. Starkey, *The Inventory of King Henry VIII*, 1998, p.46, item 1344
97. Farley, 'Images for 'Waltham Abbey Panelled Room, Essex' [Data set]
98. Fox, 'A Curious piece of Furniture', 1903, p.547
99. Barksfield, 'The Wolsey Altar', 2003, pp.1-16
100. Nichols, *Diary of Henry Machyn*, 1848, pp.8 and 320
101. Woodcock & Flower eds., *Dictionary of British Arms*, Vol.IV, 2014, pp.360-361; The author also gratefully acknowledges the assistance of Lancaster Herald of the College of Arms in identifying the Windsor Arms
102. Thurley, in the Foreword to *The Vyne: A Tudor House Revealed*, 2003
103. HRO 101M99, Currie, 'Archaeological and Historical Survey of the Mottisfont Abbey Estate', 1999; Dale, 'Notes on Mottisfont Priory Hants', 1907, pp.339-341
104. Doubleday & Page, ed., *History of the County of Hampshire*, Vol.2, 1903, pp.172-175
105. HRO 13M63/420
106. Howard & Wilson, *The Vyne: A Tudor House Revealed*, 2003, pp.104-105
107. Jenkins & Simpson, *The Painted Glass of William, Lord Sandys (1470-1540)*, p.42, 43

7. Descendants of William, the 1st Baron Sandys

1. *L&P Henry VIII*, 6, 1307, p.527
2. HRO 31M57/652, p.87
3. *L&P Henry VIII*, 4, 5185, p.2280; 5215, p.2298

4. *L&P Henry VIII*, 12.1, 589 paragraph 2, p.271
5. *L&P Henry VIII*, 16, 586, p.282; 599, p.287
6. Nichols & Turpyn, *Chronicle of Calais*, 1846, p.179
7. *Cal.Pat.Rolls*, 25 May 1560, p.352
8. BL MS Harl. 607
9. Sandys, *History of the Sandys' Family*, 1930, Pedigree F
10. *Dictionary of National Biography*, 1885-1900, pp.259-260
11. Harrison, *The Tower of London Prisoner Book*, 2004, p.150
12. Author's personal observation
13. Will of Lord William Sandys, Dec.1540, TNA Prob.11/29/107
14. Sandys, *History of the Sandys' Family*, 1930, Pedigree F; Will of Lord William Sandys, Dec.1540, TNA Prob.11/29/107
15. *L&P Henry VIII*, 15, 14, p.6
16. TNA SC11/63
17. TNA E314/39/106
18. HRO 23M58/9
19. Jordan, ed., *Chronicle and Political Papers of Ed. VI*, 1966, p.142
20. E.g. 'House of Lords Journal Vol.1: 22 April 1559', in *Journal of the House of Lords: Vol.1, 1509-1577* (London 1767-1830), p.576. British History Online [accessed 21 August 2018]
21. TNA C42/126/143
22. HRO 23M58/9, 29M82/83
23. Nichols, *Diary of Henry Machyn*, 1848, facsimile 2012, pp.8, 320
24. HRO 23M/58/9; Fox. 'A Curious Piece of Furniture', 1903; See section 7 above
25. TNA SP46/38/38 f.240
26. July 1598, 16-31, in Roberts. *Cal.Cecil Papers in Hatfield House, 1899, Vol.8 1598*, pp.261-288. British History Online [accessed 24 Aug. 2018]
27. Sandys, *History of the Sandys' Family*, 1930, Pedigree F
28. Third Baron Sandys' will, TNA Prob.11/142/407`
29. Personal observation; translation from Latin by Dr. S. Davies
30. Nichols, ed., *Diary of Henry Machyn*, 1848, facsimile 2012, pp.108, 350; Harrington, ed., *Chronicle of England by Charles Wriothesley*, 1875-7, Vol.2, p.135
31. *Cal.Pat.Rolls*, 2 Eliz. Pt.5, 22 July 1560, p.329
32. *Cal.Pat.Rolls*, 4 Eliz. Pt. 5, p.313; Cokayne, *Complete Peerage*, 1896, Vol.VII, p.57
33. Chute, *History of the Vyne*, 1888, p.63; 3rd Baron Sandys' Will, TNA Prob.11/142/407
34. *Cal.Pat.Rolls*, Eliz.1575-78, 3486, p.508
35. HRO 46 M/74/ PZ89, Accounts of the Holy Ghost Chapel, p.42
36. Sandys, *History of the Sandys Family*, 1930, p.27
37. TNA C2/Eliz/A3/16
38. TNA Prob.11/142/407
39. *Ibid.*
40. *Ibid.*
41. HRO 31M57/518; HRO 31M/527
42. TNA Prob.11/198/239

43. TNA Prob.11/142/407; TNA E178/2979
44. *Cal. State Papers James I*, Vol.57, 1610, p.63
45. HRO W/F2/3 f.282b; TNA Prob.11/142/407
46. July-Dec. 1569, in Roberts. *Cal.Cecil Papers in Hatfield House, 1883, Vol.1, 1306-1571*, pp.414-459. British History Online [accessed 24 Aug.2018]; Chute. *History of the Vyne*, 1888, pp.57-59. Chute says the letter was written to the Earl of Huntingdon but it contained essentially the same message
47. Stow. *Annales of England to 1603*, pp.1409-1411
48. Bell. *Introduction to the Courts of Wards and Liveries*, 1953, reissued 2012, p.126
49. TNA SP12/269; *Cal. State Papers Dom. Elizabeth*, Vol.269, 51
50. *Cal. State Papers Dom.Elizabeth*, CCLXXI, p.88; *Cal.State Papers Dom.* James I, addenda Vol.XXV, p.424
51. Holinshed. *Chronicles of England, Scotland and Ireland*, 1808, Vol.4, p.266
52. *Cal. State Papers Dom.Elizabeth*, XXVII, p.40
53. Holinshed, *Chronicles of England, Scotland and Ireland*, 1808, Vol.4, pp.557-559
54. Salmon and Emlyn, *A Complete Collection of State Trials and Proceedings*, 1730, Vol.I, p.83
55. *Ibid.*, pp.135-156
56. Williams, *The Later Tudors, 1547-1603*, 1995, pp.372-376
57. Salmon and Emlyn, *A Complete Collection of State Trials and Proceedings*, 1730, Vol.I, p.192
58. *Ibid.*, p.192, 193
59. *Cal. State Papers Dom.Elizabeth*, 11 Feb 1601, p.550 paragraph 49
60. *Cal. State Papers Dom.Elizabeth*, 1600-1601, Vol.278, Feb.16, p.549, paragraph 49, 50
61. Salmon and Emlyn, *A Complete Collection of State Trials and Proceedings*, 1730, Vol.I, p.196
62. *Cal. State Papers Dom.Elizabeth*, 1600-1601, Vol. 278, Feb.16, p.575, paragraph75
63. Camden, *Historie of the Life and Reigne of Princesse Elizabeth*, 1630, Bk.4, p.177
64. *Cal. State Papers Dom.Elizabeth*, Feb.11, Vol.278, p.550, paragraph 49
65. *Cal. State Papers Dom.Elizabeth*, 1601, Vol.278, Feb.11, p.550, paragraph 49
66. *Camden, Historie of the Life and Reigne of Princesse Elizabeth*, 1630, Bk.4, p.178
67. *Cal.State Papers Dom.Elizabeth*, Feb.11 1601, Vol.1, 278, p.574, paragraph 49
68. *Cal. State Papers Dom.Elizabeth*, Feb.1601, Vol.281, p.89
69. TNA E178/2979
70. Dasent, *Acts of the Privy Council 1600-1601*, 1906, Vol.31, 13 February, p.149 (NB. There is some confusion in the official record - it says Sheriff of Berkshire for Sandys in paragraph 3, and in paragraph 8 goes on to say 'Sheriff of the county of (blank) to seaze upon the houses of the Earle of Southampton, the one called the Vine and the other (blank)'
71. *Ibid.*, 17 Feb. Vol.31, pp.166, 167. This time, only the Sheriff of Berks. is mentioned

72. Salmon and Emlyn, *A Complete Collection of State Trials and Proceedings*, 1730, Vol.1, p.190
73. *Ibid.*, p.201
74. *Ibid.*, p.201
75. Cecil Papers, *c.* 5 March 1601, Vol.11, 'Cecil Papers: March 1601, 1-10', in Roberts. *Cal.Cecil Papers in Hatfield House. 1906, Vol.11, 1601*, pp.100-119. See British History Online [accessed 7 Sept. 2018]
76. *Cal. State Papers Dom.Elizabeth*, Vol.279, p.90
77. Dasent, *Acts of the Privy Council 1600-1601*, 1906, Vol.31, p.222
78. *Ibid.*, p.222
79. Cecil Papers Misc. Vol.14, after March 10 p.114, 'Cecil Papers: Miscellaneous 1601', in Salisbury. *Cal.Cecil Papers in Hatfield House.* 1923, Vol.14, Addenda, pp.189-202. See British History Online [accessed 7 Sept. 2018]
80. Cecil Papers, 1601, Vol.11, 28 April, 'Cecil Papers: April 1601, 16-30', in Roberts. *Cal.Cecil Papers in Hatfield House.* 1906, Vol.11, 1601, pp.165-188. See British History Online [accessed 7 Sept. 2018]
81. Cecil Papers 1603, Vol.15, 14 May; *ibid.* 18 May, Cecil Papers: May 1603, 16-31', in Giuseppi, *Cal.Cecil Papers in Hatfield House. 1930, Vol.15, Addenda*, pp. 91-118. See British History Online [accessed 7 Sept. 2018]
82. HRO 29M82/36
83. Cokayne, *Complete Peerage*, 1896, Vol.VII, p.57
84. *Cal. State Papers, James I*, Vol.14, 1605, p.222
85. *Cal. State Papers, James I*, Vol.57, 1610, p.637
86. TNA prob/ 11/142/407
87. Cokayne, *Complete Peerage*, 1896, Vol.VII, p.56; HRO 46M74/pz.89; *Book of Accounts of the Wardens of the Fraternity of the Holy Ghost, 1557-1654*, 1882; Sandys, *History of the Sandys Family*, 1930, pedigree FHRO31M57/90 re. the Holy Ghost Chapel in Basingstoke, 1630, p.151
88. Sandys, *History of the Sandys Family*, 1930, pedigree F
89. *Ibid.*, pedigree F
90. HRO31M57/90
91. HRO 31M57/677
92. *Ibid.*
93. Godwin, *The Civil War in Hampshire*, 1904, p.186
94. TNA Prob 11/231/279
95. HRO 31M/677, Cokayne, *Complete Peerage*, 1896, Vol.VII, p.57
96. TNA Prob 11/231/279
97. HRO 31M/677; Cokayne, *Complete Peerage*, 1896, Vol.VII, p.57
98. Bailey, ed., *Transcripts from the Municipal Archives of Winchester*, 1856, p.171
99. HRO 31M/677; Cokayne, *Complete Peerage*, 1896, Vol.VII, p.57
100. *Cal. State Papers Dom.* Charles II, 10 July 1673, p.430
101. HRO 31M/677; Chandler, *The History of the Holy Ghost Chapel*, 1819, pp.80-81; Cokayne, *Complete Peerage*, 1896, Vol.VII, p.58

Appendix 3: Transcription of William Sandys' Will, December 1540

1. The most useful reference work on this subject is by Grannum and Taylor, *Wills and Probate Records*, TNA, 2nd ed. 2009
2. TNA C1/1348/104-107
3. St Clare Byrne, *Lisle Letters*, 1981, Vol 2.260a p.257
4. *L&P Henry VIII*, Appendix 1, 981, p.342
5. *L&P Henry VIII*, 380, f.133b, p.188

Bibliography

Abbreviations

Cal.Close R. – Calendar of Close Rolls
Cal.Fine R. – Calendar of Fine Rolls
Cal.Inq.PM. – Calendar of Inquisitions Post Mortem
Cal.Pat.R. – Calendar of Patent Rolls
Cal. State P. – Calendar of State Papers
HRO – Hampshire Record Office
L&P – Letters and Papers, e.g. *L&P Richard III and Henry VII* (see Gairdner, J., *Letters and Papers Illustrative of the Reigns of Richard III and Henry VII*, 2 vols, London 1861–63, below)
NLW – National Library of Wales
TNA – The National Archives (at Kew, Richmond)
VCH – Victoria County History
WAM – Westminster Abbey Muniments

Arrangement of Content

This bibliography and reference list is arranged alphabetically according to the surname/s of the author or editor, or very occasionally by the title if that is the key identifier. The references in the footnotes are slightly abbreviated, but always begin with the author's surname and include a shortened title of the work (if the full title is long) and the year of publication, thus allowing the full publication details to be easily found in the bibliography.

Major Record Series Publications

Many series of official records held by TNA and spanning several centuries have been published in 'calendar' form, which means that they have been carefully summarised in English to include all key details. By today these are available in various formats, ranging from original printed publications to digitised formats online or portable electronic media such as CD. Examples of relevant series used in this work include:

Calendar of Patent Rolls, Henry III – Elizabeth I, multivol., HMSO, 1901–78 (ongoing)
Calendar of Close Rolls, Henry III – Henry VII, multivol., HMSO 1902–63
Calendar of Fine Rolls, Edward I – Henry VII, multivol., HMSO 1911–63
Calendar of Inquisitions Post Mortem, Henry III – Richard II, 16 vols. HMSO 1904–74. (See also the work spanning Richard II–Richard III, by J. Caley and J. Bailey below)
Calendar of State Papers Domestic, Edward VI–William III and Anne, multivol., HMSO 1856–1925
Calendar of State Papers Foreign, Edward VI – Elizabeth I, multivol., HMSO 1861–1950
State Papers in the time of Henry VIII are largely included in Brewer, J. S. ed., *Letters & Papers, Foreign and Domestic, of the reign of Henry VIII 1509–30,* HMSO, Vols.1–4, 1864–76, as noted below under 'Brewer'. Some of Henry VIII's earlier State Papers were published by the State Papers Commission from 1830–52 onwards, such as, *State Papers during the Reign of Henry VIII*, Vols.1–10, London: State Papers Commission, 1830–52, as noted below under *'State Papers…'*.

Reports of Archaeological and Other Surveys

Some of these reports included in this bibliography were not published widely, such as National Trust reports and surveys relating to properties in their care. These may require contact with, or a visit to the relevant property, such as The Vyne, or an enquiry to the National Trust for guidance on how to access a report. This may also apply to surveys by archaeologists in university departments or reports listed online by the Archaeology Data Service, where an enquiry may identify an online source or copies held by a library or archives service.

Reference List and Bibliography

Adams, Julie, 'The Wall Paintings in the Lady Chapel', *Winchester Cathedral Record Extra* (January 2017).
Allen, Percy Stafford and Helen Mary, ed., *Letters of Richard Fox* (Oxford University Press, 1929).
Anderson, Sue, R. D. Carr, Julia Park, and Sue Holden, 'Architectural Terracotta from Westhorpe Hall,' *Archaeological Journal*, Vol.160 (2003), pp.125–59
Anglo, Sidney, 'The Hampton Court Painting of the Field of the Cloth of Gold Considered as an Historical Document', *The Antiquaries Journal* XLVI Part II (1966), pp.287–307.

Anon., Article 1, 'The History and description of the Vine in Hampshire', *The Topographer: containing a variety of original articles, illustrative of the local history and antiquities of England.*, Vol.1 (1789), No.2 (May 1789), pp.51–63.

Anstis, John, *The Register of the Most Noble Order of the Garter, from its Cover in Black Velvet, Usually Called the Black Book*, 2 Vols. (John Barber upon Lambeth Hill, 1724).

Arthuson, Ian, *The Perkin Warbeck Conspiracy 1491–1499* (Sutton, 1997).

Ashmole, Elias, *The Institution, Laws and Ceremonies of the Most Noble Order of the Garter* (London, 1672; facsimile published by Muller, 1971).

Ayton, Andrew, *Knights and Warhorses* (The Boydell Press, 1999)

Baigent, Frances Joseph, and James Elwin Millard, *A History of the Ancient Town and Manor of Basingstoke in the County of Southampton with a Brief Account of the Siege of Basing House, AD 1643–45* (1889, reproduction 2011).

Bailey, Charles, ed., *Transcripts from the Municipal Archives of Winchester* (Winchester, 1856).

Barber, Richard, ed., *The Life and Campaigns of the Black Prince from Contemporary Letters, Diaries and Chronicles, Including Chandos Herald's Life of the Black Prince* (Boydell Press, 1997).

Barker, Juliet, *Agincourt: the King, the Campaign, the Battle* (Abacus, 2005).

Barksfield, Joan, 'The Wolsey Altar, Hambledon Parish Church', *Journal of the Henley Archaeological & Historical Group*, Vol.18, Autumn (December 2003), pp.1–16.

Bell, H. E., *An Introduction to the History and Records of the Courts of Wards and Liveries* (Cambridge University Press, 1953; reissued 2012).

Bentley, Samuel (1785–1868), *Excerpta Historica: or, Illustrations of English History* (London, 1831; and HardPress Publishing, 2013).

Bergenroth, Gustave Adolph *et al.*, ed., *Calendar of letters, Despatches and State Papers Relating to the Negotiations Between England and Spain Preserved in the Archives of Simancas and Elsewhere*, 13 Vols (London: HMSO, 1862–1954).

Bernard, G. W., *The King's Reformation: Henry VIII and the Remaking of the English Church* (Yale University Press, 2005).

Bernard, G. W., 'Thomas Cromwell and Calais' (2007), *Southampton University Website*, 1–111.

Beverley, Tessa, 'Sir Giovanni Portinari', *Oxford Dictionary of National Biography* (2004, in print and online).

Borman, Tracy, *Thomas Cromwell: the Untold Story of Henry VIII's Most Faithful Servant* (Hodder & Stoughton, 2015).

Brears, Peter, ed., *The Book of Keruynge (Book of Carving) by Wynkyn de Worde 1503* (Southover Press, 2003).

Brewer, J. S., ed., *Letters & Papers, Foreign and Domestic, of the Reign of Henry VIII 1509–30*, HMSO, Vols.1–4 (1864–76; second expanded edition of vol.1 was published in 1920).

Brewer, J. S., J. Gairdner and R. H. Brodie, ed., *The Letters and Papers Foreign and Domestic of the Reign of Henry VIII, Vols. 1–15 and Addenda 1 parts 1&2* (Tanner Ritchie Publishing, Ontario Canada; On CD; A full reprint of all volumes was produced by the Kraus Reprint Co. in 1965).

Brown, Rawdon, ed. *Calendar of State Papers relating to English Affairs in the Archives Venice, Vol.IV, 1527–1533* (London, 1871).

Brown, Rawdon, ed., *Calendar of State Papers Relating to English Affairs in the Archives of Venice, Vols.1–7* (London, 1864–90).

Burrows, M., *The Family of Brocas of Beaurepaire and Roche Court* (Longmans Green, 1886).

Caley, J., 'Interview Between Henry the Eighth of England and Francis the First of France', *Archaeologia*, 21 (London, 1827), pp.176–81.

Caley, J. and J.Bailey, *Calendarium Inquisitionum Post Mortem sive Escaetarum (Richard II – Richard III)*, 4 vols. (London: Records Commission 1806–28).

Camden, William, *Britannia* (Edmund Gibson, 1695; facsimile by David & Charles reprints, 1971).

Camden, William, *The Historie of the Life and Reigne of the Most Renowned and Victorious Princesse Elizabeth, composed by way of Annals* (London: B. Fisher, 1630).

Campbell, Thomas P., *Henry VIII and the Art of Majesty* (Yale University Press, 2007).

Campbell, William, ed., *Chronicles and Memorials of Great Britain and Ireland during the Middle Ages: the Reign of Henry VII*, Vols.1–2 (London, 1877).

Cavendish, George, *Thomas Wolsey, late Cardinal, his Life and Death (written by George Cavendish his gentleman-usher)* (The Folio Society, 1962).

Chandler, Samuel (publisher), *The History of the Holy Ghost Chapel* (Basingstoke, 1819).

Chapman, Colin R., *How Heavy, How Much and How Long: Weights, Money and other Measures used by our Ancestors* (Dursley: Lochin Publishing, 1999).

Chrimes, Stanley Bertram, *Henry VII* (Yale University Press, 1999).

Chute, Chaloner William, *The History of the Vyne in Hampshire* (Winchester & London, 1888).

Chute, E.M. *et al.*, 'Drawings of the Vyne Gallery', Vyne Resource Room, 1876.

Clare, S., (Report, Holy Well Glass), 'The Vyne Chapel Stained Glass', Report to The National Trust, 2007.

Cokayne, George Edward, ed., *Complete peerage of England, Scotland, Ireland, Great Britain and the United Kingdom, extant, extinct, or dormant*, 8 vols. (London, 1887–98).

Collins, B. M., *Winchester Cathedral Record Extra* (November 2011).

Colvin, Howard Montagu, ed., *The History of the King's Works*, Vol.III (London: HMSO, 1975).

Condon, Margaret M., 'From Caitiff and Villain to Pater Patriae: Reynold Bray and the Profits of Office', in Michael Hicks ed., *Profit, Piety and Professions in later Mediaeval England* (Alan Sutton, 1990).

Conti, F., *How to Recognize Renaissance Art* (Mcdonald, 1978).
Cornish, Paul, *Henry VIII's Army* (Osprey, 1987).
Cornwall, Julian C. K., *Wealth and Society in early 16th century England* (London: Routledge, 1988).
Crawford, Anne, ed., *The Household Books of John Howard, Duke of Norfolk 1462–71, 1481–83* (Paul Watkins Publishing, 1982).
Crook, John, 'Witness from on High: New discoveries about Winchester Cathedral provide insights into the relationships between a prominent churchman and his Tudor kings', *History Today*, Vol.65, Issue 10 (October 2015, online 30 September 2015).
Cruickshank, C. G., *Army Royal: an Account of Henry VIII's Invasion of France 1513* (Clarendon, 1969).
Currie, Christopher K., 'A Survey of the Parch Marks at the Vyne' (National Trust, August 1995).
Currie, Christopher K., 'An archaeological and Historical Survey of the Mottisfont Abbey Estate, near Romsey' (1999; available at HRO 101M99).
Currie, Christopher K., 'The Vyne Estate, Sherborne St John, Hampshire, An Archaeological and Historical Survey' (Report to the National Trust, 1994).
Currie, C. K., 'Trial Excavations at the Vyne, Sherborne St John, Hampshire, SU 636568' (National Trust, January 1995).
Curry, Anne, *The Battle of Agincourt: sources and Interpretations* (Boydell Press, 2009)
Curtis, Eleanor, *St George's Chapel Windsor: A Portait* (D.Giles Ltd, 2008).
Dale, W., '[Notes on] Mottisfont Priory Hants.', *Proceedings of the Society of Antiquaries of London*, Second Series, Vol.XXI (1906–07), pp.339–41 (proceedings of 14 February 1907).
Dasent, John Roche, ed., *Acts of the Privy Council 1600–1601* (HMSO, 1906).
Davies, Jonathan, *An ill journey for the Englishmen: Elis Gruffydd and the 1523 French Campaign of the Duke of Suffolk*, transcribed by M.Bryn Davies, Pike and Shot Society (2006).
De Gayangos, Pascual, ed., *Calendar of State Papers, Spain, Vol.5 Part 1, 1534–1535* (London, 1886).
De Monstrelet, Enguerrand, *The Chronicles of Enguerrand de Monstrelet*, translated by Thomas Johnes, Vol.2 (London, 1840).
Dillon, Harold Arthur, 'Calais and the Pale', *Archaeologia*, Vol.53, Part 2 (1893), pp.289–388.
Doubleday, H. Arthur, and William Page, ed., *A History of the County of Hampshire*, VCH Hampshire, Vol.2 (London 1903; See British History Online).
Duffus Hardy, Thomas, *Syllabus of the documents in the collection known as 'Rymer's Foedera'*, Vol.1, 1066–1377 (Longmans Green, 1869).
Duffy, Eamon, *The Stripping of the Altars: Traditional religion in England 1400–1580*, 2nd revised ed. (Yale University Press, 2005).

Dumortier, Claire, *Céramique de la Renaissance à Anvers* (Amateur, 2002).
Elis Gruffudd, *Chronicle*, National Library of Wales, MS 5276D & 3054D.
Ellis, Sir Henry, ed., *Three Books of Polydore Vergil's English History comprising the Reigns of Henry VI, Edward IV, and Richard III* (Camden Society, 1844).
Emerson, Barbara, *The Black Prince* (Littlehampton Book Services Ltd, 1976).
Emery, Anthony, *Greater Medieval houses of England and Wales, 1300–1500, Vol.3: Southern England* (Cambridge University Press, 2006).
Fairbrother, J. R., *Faccombe Netherton* (British Museum Occasional Paper 74, 1990).
Farley, C., Images for 'Waltham Abbey Panelled Room, Essex' [Dataset].
Fox, John Charles, 'A Curious Piece of Church Furniture (Hambledon)', in *The Records of Buckinghamshire*, Vol.8 (Buckinghamshire Archaeological Society, 1903).
Fletcher, Anthony, and Diarmaid MacCulloch, *Tudor Rebellions* (Pearson Education, 2004).
Friedmann, Paul, *Anne Boleyn: a Chapter of English History 1527–1536* (Macmillan, 1884; also modern paperbacks 2009 and 2010).
Froissart, John, *Chronicles of England, France and Spain and the Adjoining Countries*, translated from French by Thomas Johnes (University of Michigan, no date).
Gachard, M., *Collection des Voyages des Souverains des Pay-Bas*, tome premier (Bruxelles, 1876).
Gairdner, James, *A History of the English Church in the Sixteenth Century from the Accession of Henry VIII to the death of Mary* (London: Macmillan, 1904).
Gairdner, James, *et al.*, ed., *Letters and Papers Illustrative of the Reigns of Richard III and Henry VII*, 2 vols (London, 1861–63).
Gairdner, James, *Letters and Papers, Foreign and Domestic of the reign of Henry VIII 1531–38*, Vols.5–13, HMSO, 1880–93.
Gairdner, James, and R. H. Brodie, *Letters and Papers, Foreign and Domestic of the reign of Henry VIII 1539–47*, Vols.14–21 (HMSO, 1894–1910; 2 vols. of Addenda published in 1929 and 1932).
Gairdner, James, ed., *Memorials of King Henry VII* (Longman, 1858).
Gairdner, James, ed., *The Paston Letters* (Sutton Publishing, 1986, microprint edition).
Gill, Louise, *Richard III and Buckingham's Rebellion* (Sutton Publishing, 1999).
Godwin, George Nelson, *The Civil War in Hampshire (1642–45) and the Story of Basing House* (Gilbert & Son, 1904).
Gomme, George Laurence, ed., *English Topography*, Vol.17, Part V (Hants.–Hunts. ed. F. A. Milne), London 1894, in *The Gentlemans Magazine Library* (a classified collection of the chief contents of the *Gentleman's Magazine* from 1731 to 1868), Hampshire pp.3–153, Basingstoke pp.37–42.
Gozzoli, M. C., *How to Recognize Gothic Art* (Mcdonald, 1978).

Grannum, Karen and Nigel Taylor, *Wills and Probate Records: a guide for family historians* (National Archives, 2nd edition, 2009).
Gravett, Christopher, *Tudor Knight* (Osprey Publishing, 2006).
Gravett, Christopher, *Knight* (Dorling Kindersley, 2007).
Green, D.S., 'The Household and Retinue of Edward the Black Prince' (unpublished doctoral thesis, University of Nottingham, 1998).
Grey-Egerton, Sir Philip de Malpas, ed., *A Commentary of the services and charges of William Lord Grey of Wilton KG by his son Arthur Lord Grey KG* (London: Camden Society, 1847).
Grummitt, David, *The Calais Garrison: War and Military service in England 1436–1558* (Boydell, 2008).
Guillim, John, *A Dislay of Heraldry* (London, 1724).
Guiseppi, M. S., ed., *Calendar of the Cecil Papers in Hatfield House: Addenda*, Vol.15 (London: HMSO, 1930).
Gunn, Steven, *Charles Brandon: Henry's VIII's Closest Friend* (Amberley Publishing, 2015).
Gunn, Steven J., 'The Duke of Suffolk's March on Paris in 1523', *The English Historical Review (EHR)*, Vol.101, 1986, pp.596–634.
Gunn, S. J. and P. G. Lindley, *Cardinal Wolsey, Church State and Art* (Cambridge University Press, 1991).
Guy, John, *Tudor England: A Very Short Introduction* (Oxford University Press, 2013).
Hall, Edward, *Hall's Chronicle Containing the History of England during the Reign of Henry IV and succeeding monarchs to the end of the reign of Henry VIII* (London: printed for J. Johnson et al., 1809).
Hall, Edward, *The Lives of Kings, Henry VIII*, 2 vols., with introduction by Charles Whibley (T. C. & E. C. Jack, London and Edinburgh, 1904).
Hamilton, William Douglas, ed., *A Chronicle of England During the Reign of the Tudors 1485–1559 by Charles Wriothesley, Windsor Herald*, 2 Vols. (Camden Society, 1875–77).
Hare, John, *The Victoria County History: Basingstoke A Medieval Town, c.1000–c.1600* (London: University of London, 2017).
Harrison, B. A., *The Tower of London Prisoner Book* (Leeds: Trustees of the Royal Armouries, 2004).
Harrison, Frederic, *Annals of an Old Manor House: Sutton Place Guildford* (London: Macmillan & Co., 1893).
Harrisson, W. R. D., and Viscount Chandos, *Carvings, Oak Gallery, The Vyne, Hampshire* (a pamphlet published in 1979).
Hay, Denys, trans. and ed., *The Anglica Historia of Polydore Vergil, A.D. 1485–1537* (Royal Historical Society, Camden Series Vol.74, 1950).
Hearne, Thomas, ed., *Joannis Lelandi Antiquarii de Rebus Britannicis Collectanea*, Vol.IV, (London, 1774).
Herbert, Edward, Right Honourable Baron of Cherbury, *The life and reign of King Henry the Eighth* (London, 1682).

Hewitt, Herbert James, *Cheshire under the Three Edwards* (Cheshire Community Council, 1967).

Hewitt, Herbert James, *The Black Prince's Expedition of 1355–1357* (Pen and Sword Military, 2004).

Hicks, Michael A., *Profit, Piety and Professions in later Mediaeval England* (Alan Sutton, 1990).

Himsworth, Sheila, *Winchester College Muniments* (Phillimore, Vol.I 1976, Vol.II 1983).

History of Parliament Online.

Holinshed, Raphael, *Chronicles of England, Scotland and Ireland*, 6 Vols. (J. Johnson, 1807–08).

Horrox, Rosemary and P. W. Hammond, *British Library Harleian Manuscript 433, 1. Register of grants for the reigns of Edward V and Richard III* (Richard III Society, 1980).

House of Lords Journal, at British History Online.

House of Lords Precedence Act 1539.

Howard, Maurice, and Edward Wilson, *The Vyne: A Tudor House Revealed* (London: National Trust, 2003).

Howard, Maurice, 'Craftsmen and Courtiers: Italian Military Expertise at the Court of Henty VIII' in Sicca and Waldman, eds, *The Anglo-Florentine Renaissance* (Yale University Press, 2012), pp.265–80.

Hoyle, Richard, ed.,'The letters of the Cliffords, Lords Clifford and the earls of Cumberland c.1500–1565', *The Camden Miscellany XXXI* (Camden Fourth Series, Vol.44) (RHS, 1992).

Hume, Martin Andrew Sharp, translation and introduction, *Chronicle of King Henry VIII of England: written in Spanish by an unknown hand* (London: George Bell & Son, 1889).

Hutchinson, Robert, *Thomas Cromwell: the Rise and Fall of Henry VIII's Most Notorious Minister* (Wiedenfeld, 2007).

Ives, Eric, *The Life and Death of Anne Boleyn* (Blackwell, 2004).

Ives, Eric, 'The Fall of Wolsey' in S. J. Gunn and P. G. Lindley, eds, *Cardinal Wolsey, Church State and Art* (Cambridge University Press, 1991).

James, Tom Beaumont, *The Black Death in Hampshire* (Hampshire Papers No.18, 1999)

Jenkins, J. M., and N. W. Simpson, *The Painted Glass of William, Lord Sandys (1470–1540)*, private, BL shelf mark YK.2009, a.26680.

Jerdan, William, *Rutland Papers. Original Documents Illustrative of the Courts and times of Henry VII and Henry VIII* (Camden Society, 1842).

Johnston, Hope, 'Catherine of Aragon's Pomegranate Revisited', *The Cambridge Bibliographical Society*, Vol.13, No.2 (2005), pp.153–73.

Jones, Michael K., and Malcolm G. Underwood, *The King's Mother: Lady Margaret Beaufort, Countess of Richmond and Derby* (Cambridge University Press, 1993)

Jones, Robert, *Knight: the Warrior and World of Chivalry* (Osprey, 2011).

Jones, Thomas, 'A Welsh Chronicler in Tudor England', *Welsh History Review*, Vol.1 (I), 1960, pp.1–17.

Jordan, W. K. ed., *The Chronicle and Political Papers of King Edward VI* (George Allen & Unwin, 1966).

Keay, Anna, *Elizabethan Tower of London* (London Topographical Society, 2001).

Kelly, Arthur, *Chapel of the Holy Ghost and St Michael's Church, Basingstoke* (1911).

Kingra, M.S., 'The trace italienne and the military revolution during the Eighty Years' War, 1567–1648', *Journal of Military History*, LVII (1993), pp.431–46.

Kirby, Joan, ed., *The Plumpton Letters and Papers* (Cambridge University Press for the Royal Historical Society, 1996).

Koegler, Hans, 'Einiges über David Joris als Künstler', *Öffentliche Kunstsammlung* (Basel, Jahrsberichte 1928–30), pp.157–201.

Larchey, Loredan, *Histoire du gentil seigneur de Bayard composée par le loyal Serviteur* (Hachette, 1882).

Law, Ernest, *The History of Hampton Court Palace, Vol. I: Tudor Times* (London: George Bell & Sons, 1903).

Lehmberg, Stanford E., *The Reformation Parliament 1529–36* (Cambridge University Press, 1970).

Leland, John, *De Rebus Britannicis Collectanea*, 1774, Vols.1–6 (Gregg Publishing reprint, Farnborough: Hants, 1970).

Lestocquoy, Jean, *Histoire de la Picardie* (Presses Universitaires de France, 1962).

Lipscomb, Suzannah, *A Visitor's Companion to Tudor England* (Ebury Press, 2012).

Living, Henry G. D., *Records of Romsey Abbey* (Winchester: Warren & Son, 1908).

Lloyd, Christopher, and John Thurley, *Henry VIII: Images of a Tudor King* (Phaidon Press Ltd, 1990).

Loades, David, *Jane Seymour: Henry VIII's favourite wife* (Amberley, 2013).

Loades, David, *The Tudor Court* (Headstart History Publishing, 1992).

Lodge, Edmund, *Illustrations of British History, Biography, and Manners: In the Reigns of Henry VIII, Edward VI, Mary, Elizabeth, and James I, Exhibited in a Series of Original Papers,* Vol. 2 (G. Nicol, 1791).

MacCulloch, Diarmaid, *Thomas Cromwell: a Life* (Allen Lane, 2018).

Mackie, John D., *The Earlier Tudors, 1485–1558* (Oxford: Oxford University Press, 1975, reprint 1985).

Madden, Frederic, and Bulkeley Bandinel, *Collectanea Topographica et Genealogica* (Nichols & Son, 1834).

Manning, Anne, *The Household of Sir Thomas More* (London, 1906).

Marshall, G., 'Report describing the results of an Archaeological watching brief over the trenches in the south and west parks and in the pleasure grounds at the Vyne Hampshire' (The National Trust, 2009).

Martin, Charles Trice, ed., 'Sir John Daunce's Accounts of Money received from the Treasurer of the King's Chamber temp Henry VIII', *Archaeologia*, Vol. LVII Issue 2 (1883), pp.295–336.

Martin, D. and S. Knight, 'A description, interpretation and record of the Brewhouse at The Vyne Hampshire', Project Ref. 1409 (2002).

Merson, A.L., ed., *The Third Book of Remembrances of Southampton 1514–1602*, 4 Vols. (University of Southampton, 1952–79).

Metcalfe, Walter C., *A Book of Knights Banneret, Knights of the Bath and Knights Bachelor made between the 4th Year of Henry VI and the Restoration of King Charles II* (Mitchell and Hughes, 1885).

Miles, D. H., 'The Further Tree-Ring dating of the Vyne Sherborne St John, Hampshire –2017, Oxford Dendrochronology Laboratory' (Report 2018/08).

Mitchell-Fox, P. and M. Page, ed., *The Hampshire Tax List of 1327* (Hampshire County Council, 2014).

Moland, M. Louis., *La très joyeuse, plaisante et récréative Histoire du bon Chevalier sans Peur et sans Reproche Le Gentil Seigneur De Bayart, composée par le loyal serviteur. Nouvelle Edition, avec une introduction et des notes par M.Louis Moland* (Garnier Freres, 1882).

Moorhouse, Geoffrey, *The Pilgrimage of Grace: the Rebellion that shook King Henry VIII's Throne* (Phoenix, 2002).

Morgan, P., *War and Society in Cheshire* (Manchester University Press, 1987).

Mortimer, Ian, *Henry V's Year of Glory* (Random House, 2010).

Mortimer, Ian, *The Perfect King: the Life of Edward III* (Vintage Publications, 2008).

Mortimer, Ian, *The Time Traveller's Guide to Medieval England* (Vintage Books, 2009).

Muller, James Ambrose, *Letters of Stephen Gardiner* (Cambridge, 1933; reissue 2013).

Mumby, F. A., *The Youth of Henry VIII: a narrative in contemporary letters* (London, 1913).

Nichols, John Gough, and Richard Turpyn, *The chronicle of Calais, in the reigns of Henry VII. and Henry VIII to the year 1540* (Camden Society, 1846; Scholar's Choice paperback 2015).

Nichols, John Gough, ed., *The Diary of Henry Machyn* (Camden Society, 1848; facsimile by Forgotten Books, 2012).

Nicolas, Nicholas Harris (Sir), *The Privy Purse Expenses of Elizabeth of York: Wardrobe Accounts of Edward the Fourth* (1830; facsimile edition by Frederick Muller Ltd, 1972).

Nicolas, Nicholas Harris (Sir), *The Privy Purse Expenses of King Henry VIII* (William Pickering, 1827).

Nicolas, Nicholas Harris (Sir), ed., *Proceedings and Ordinances of the Privy Council* (Records Commission, 1834–37).

Nicolas, Nicholas Harris (Sir), *Testamenta vetusta: being illustrations from wills, of manners, customs, &c. as well as of the descents and possessions of many distinguished families. From the reign of Henry the Second to the accession of Queen Elizabeth* (Nichols & Son, 1826).

Norton, Elizabeth, *The Anne Boleyn Papers* (Amberley, 2013).
Oxford Dictionary of National Biography (ODNB), 2004, 60 vols. and online (revised and extended version of original DNB 1885–1900).
Pennant, T., *Some Account of London* (London: John Archer, 1791).
Pickvance, Christopher, 'The Slow Arrival of Renaissance Influence on English Furniture: A study of the 1519 Silkstede, Shankin and the 1539 Garstang, Cirencester Chests', *Regional Furniture*, XXIX (2015).
Prestwich, Michael, *Knight , The Medieval Warrior's Manual* (Thames and Hudson, 2010)
Rackham, Bernard, *Early Netherlands Majolica with special reference to the Tiles* (London, 1926).
Riall, Nicholas, 'The Early Tudor Renaissance in Hampshire: Anthony Blunt and 'L'influence Francaise sur l'architecture et la sculpture dècorative en Angleterre pendant la première moitiè du XVI siècle' revisited', *Renaissance Studies*, Vol.21, No.2 (2007).
Richardson W. C., *Tudor. Chamber Administration 1485–1547* (Louisiana State University Press, 1952).
Roberts, R. A., ed., *Calendar of the Cecil Papers in Hatfield House: Vol.8, 1598* (London, 1899).
Roskell, J. S., L. Clark and C. Rawcliffe, eds, *The History of Parliament: The House of Commons, 1386–1421* (History of Parliament, 1993).
Roundell, Mrs Charles, *Cowdray, The History of a Great English House* (London, 1884).
Rutherford, S., 'The Vyne Sherborne St John, Hampshire, Historic Landscape Appraisal of the Large Lake' (April 2017).
Salisbury, E., ed., *Calendar of the Cecil Papers in Hatfield House: Addenda,* Vol.14 (HMSO, 1923).
Salmon, Thomas, and Sollom Emlyn, *A Complete Collection of State Trials and Proceedings for High Treason and other Crimes and Misdemeanours... from Richard II to George 1*, 6 vols (London, 2nd ed. 1730).
Samman, Neill, 'Henry VIII's Court in the 1510s and 1520s' (unpublished PhD thesis, Bangor University, 1989).
Sandeman, George Amelius Crawshay, *Calais under English Rule* (London and Oxford, 1908).
Sandys, E. S., *The History of the Sandys Family* (Private, 1930; BL shelf mark 9907b.27)
Saul, Nigel, *Richard II* (Yale University Press, 1997).
Scard, Margaret, *Tudor Survivor: The Life and Times of William Paulet* (History Press, 2011).
Sicca, C. M. and L. A. Waldman, eds., *The Anglo-Florentine Renaissance Art for the Early Tudors* (Yale, 2012).
Spaul, J. E. H., *Andover: An Historical Portrait* (Andover Local Archives Committee, 1977).
St Clare Byrne, Muriel, *The Lisle Letters* (University of Chicago Press, 1981, 1983).

St George, *The Visitation of Hampshire and the Isle of Wight 1686* (Harleian Society, 1991).

St George's Chapel, Windsor Castle (Scala Publishers Ltd, 2008).

Siddons, Michael Powell, *Heraldic Badges in England and Wales*, 4 vols, (Society of Antiquaries: London, 2009).

Singer, Samuel Weller, ed., *The Life of Cardinal Wolsey by George Cavendish his Gentleman Usher*, Vol.II (Chiswick, 1825),

Stapleton, B., ed., *Conflict in the Community in Southern England* (Alan Sutton, 1992).

Stapleton, Thomas, ed., *Plumpton Correspondence, a series of letters, written in the reigns of Edward IV, Richard III, Henry VII and Henry VIII, from Sir Edward Plumpton's book of letters* (Camden Society, 1839).

Starkey, David, *Henry: Virtuous Prince* (Harper Press, 2008).

Starkey, David, *Henry VIII: a European Court in England* (Collins & Brown, new ed. 1991).

Starkey, David, ed., *The Inventory of King Henry VIII, The Transcript* (Harvey Millar, 1998).

State Papers during the Reign of Henry VIII, Vol.1 (State Papers Commission, 1830).

Steel, Anthony, *The Receipt of the Exchequer 1377–1485* (Cambridge University Press, 2012).

Stevens, H., R. Howman, and K. Clark, 'A Resistivity Survey of the Lawns surrounding the Vyne, Nr. Basingstoke, Hants.' (University of Southampton, April 1998).

Stratford, Jenny, *Richard II and the English Royal Treasure* (Boydell Press, 2013).

Strutt, J., William Hone, John Haddon, Leon J. Whitsall and T. T. & J. Tegg, *The Sports and Pastimes of the People of England* (London, 1833).

Stow, John, *A Survey of London written in the year 1598* (John Windet, 1603).

Stow, John, *The Annales of England*, London: 1603. (Online at Archive.org, accessed in 2019).

Sutton, Anne F. and P. W. Hammond, *Richard III: the Road to Bosworth Field* (Constable, 1985).

Sutton, Anne F. and R. W. Hammond, *The Coronation of Richard III: The Extant Documents* (Palgrave Macmillan, 1984).

Tanner, Joseph Robson, *Tudor Constitutional Documents A.D. 1485–1603, with an Historical Commentary* (Cambridge University Press, 1922; also CUP, 2013).

Tatton-Brown, Tim, and Richard Mortimer, ed., *Westminster Abbey: The Lady Chapel of Henry VII* (Boydell, 2003).

The Antiquary: a magazine devoted to the study of the past, 51 Vols (E. Stock, 1880–1915).

Thomas, A. H. and I. D. Thornley, ed., *The Great Chronicle of London (by Robert Fabyan)* (Sutton Microprint Edition, 1983).

Thornbury, Walter, *Old and New London: a Narrative of its History, its People and its Places*, 6 Vols (Cassell, 1878).

Thurley, Simon, *Hampton Court: A Social and Architectural History* (Yale University Press, 2003).

Tomkinson, John, 'The Henrician Bastions of Guînes Castle', *FORT* (Fortress Study Group) Vol.26, (1998), pp.121–42.

Toogood, Revd R. C., *The History of Bramley, Hampshire* (Bramley Shell, 1993).

Toulmin Smith, L., ed., *The Itinerary of John Leland in or about the years 1535–1543* (London, 1964).

Tracy, Charles, 'The Lady Chapel Stalls' in John Crook, ed., *Winchester Cathedral: Nine Hundred Years 1093–1993* (Phillimore, 1993, pp.231–46).

Tremlett, Giles, *Catherine of Aragon: Henry's Spanish Queen* (Faber & Faber, 2011).

Trevelyan, W. C., ed., 'Account of Henry the Eight's Expedition into France AD 1513', *Archaeologia*, Vol.26 (1836), pp.475–78.

Victoria County History, Hampshire, Vol.4, pp.359–65.

Watts, Karen, *Royal Armouries* (private correspondence, 2004).

Wayment, Hilary, *Kings College Chapel Cambridge the Great Windows: Introduction and Guide* (King's College Cambridge, 1982).

Wayment, Hilary, 'The Stained Glass of the Chapel of the Vyne and the Chapel of the Holy Ghost, Basingstoke', *Archaeologia*, Vol.107 (Society of Antiquaries of London, 1982).

Weir, Alison, *Henry VIII: King and Court* (Random House, 2002).

Wells, Stanley and Gary Taylor, *The Complete Oxford Shakespeare*, 3 Vols. (Oxford University Press, 1987).

Westlake, Nathaniel Hubert J., *A History of Design in Painted Glass* (James Parker & Co. 4 vols., 1881–; also Andesite Press, 2015).

Weir, Alison, *Britain's Royal Families: The Complete Genealogy* (Vintage, 2008).

William Marquis of Northampton, *Compton Wynyates* (London, 1904).

Williams, C. H., ed., *English Historical Documents Vol.5, 1485–1558* (Eyre & Spottiswoode, 1967).

Williams, J. F., ed., *The Early Churchwardens Accounts of Hampshire* (Winchester and London, 1913).

Williams, Penry, *The Later Tudors, 1547–1603* (Clarendon Press, 1995).

Wilson, C. G., *The Royal Household and the King's Affinity* (Yale University Press, 1986).

Wilson, Derek, *In the Lion's Court* (Pimlico, 2002).

Wilson, E., *The Vyne Archaeological Project 1996–1998*, 5 Vols. (The National Trust, 1998).

Woodcock, Thomas and Sarah Flower, eds, *Dictionary of British Arms*, Vol.IV (Society of Antiquaries of London, 2014).

Woodcock, Thomas, and Martin Robson, *The Oxford Guide to Heraldry* (Oxford Paperbacks 1990; 2nd revised edition 2001).

Woodward, M. and E. Wilson, *The Vyne: a Tudor House Revealed* (National Trust, 1999).

Wyatt, George, 'Extracts from the Life of the Virtuous Christian and Renowned Queen Anne Boleigne' in Singer, S. W., ed., *The Life of Cardinal Wolsey by George Cavendish his Gentleman Usher*, Vol.II (Chiswick, 1825).

Acknowledgements

Dr Susan J. Davies of Aberystwyth University warrants special thanks for providing translations of Latin documents, considerable editorial assistance, informed constructive criticism and expert insightful comments. The author also thanks Dr Ceridwen Lloyd-Morgan and Dafydd Ifans, both former senior staff at the National Library of Wales, for providing translations of Anglo-Norman and Welsh documents. Many of the documents and texts in all languages presented considerable palaeographical challenges.

Emeritus Professor Prys Morgan of Swansea University is thanked for his route map to the late 1530s section of the Elis Gruffudd chronicle. The comments and insight provided by Celia Jennings, a recognised expert in early modern European woodcarving, on The Vyne chapel frieze are much appreciated.

Thanks also go to my fellow National Trust volunteers at The Vyne who encouraged me to pursue and complete this work. Several National Trust staff have also been helpful. Special thanks go to Karen Symonds, sometime House Manager of The Vyne, who did much to support my interest in the 1st Baron Sandys, and to Gary Marshall, former National Trust Archaeologist (London and South East Region), who has assisted me greatly in understanding the archaeological data gathered at The Vyne over the years.

I am grateful to the Hampshire Library Service, especially the Chineham Library staff, for their efficiency and helpfulness in acquiring books and articles for me to borrow, the staff at Hampshire Record Office and to the archivists at St George's Chapel archives, Windsor and Winchester College Archives for their assistance. Without the services and assistance of the staff of The National Archives, Kew, and the British Library, London, this work would be much poorer.

The late Mrs Nancy Rothwell is thanked for her contribution to the early stages of editing this work.

The biggest thanks must go to my wife Pamela, who tolerated, albeit reluctantly at times, the untidiness and domestic disruption that research projects of this kind inevitably involve. Her support throughout has been invaluable, especially with text editing and positive suggestions.

Notwithstanding the support and expertise generously shared with me, any mistake in facts or of their interpretation are mine alone.

Index